P9-DGU-271

CISTERCIAN STUDIES SERIES: NUMBER TWO-HUNDRED FOURTEEN

KURISUMALA

Francis Mahieu Acharya
A Pioneer of Christian Monasticism in India

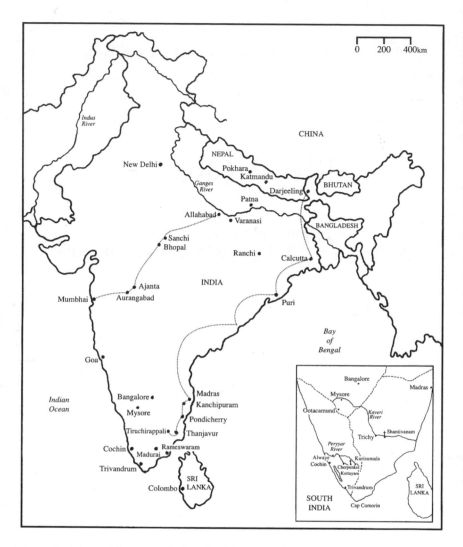

Figure 1. Map of India, with detail of South India and the location of Shanti-vanam and Kurisumala.

CISTERCIAN STUDIES SERIES: NUMBER TWO-HUNDRED FOURTEEN

KURISUMALA

Francis Mahieu Acharya
A Pioneer of Christian Monasticism in India

By Marthe Mahieu-De Praetere

Translated by Susan Van Winkle

CISTERCIAN PUBLICATIONS INC.

KALAMAZOO, MICHIGAN

Originally published as *Kurisumala. Francis Mahieu Acharya. Un pionnier du monachisme chétien en Inde*. Cahiers Scourmontois 3. Scourmont: Abbaye cistercienne Notre-Dame de Scourmont, 2001.

Maps drawn by Linda K. Judy.

The work of Cistercian Publications is made possible in part
by support from Western Michigan University
to the Institute of Cistercian Studies.

Library of Congress Cataloging-in-Publication Data

Mahieu-De Praetere, Marthe.
   [Kurisumala. English]
   Kurisumala : Francis Mahieu Acharya, a pioneer of Christian
monasticism in India / by Marthe Mahieu-De Praetere ; translated by
Susan Van Winkle.
     p.   cm. — (Cistercian studies series ; no. 214)
   Includes bibliographical references and index.
   ISBN 978-0-87907-614-6
   1. Acharya, Francis. 2. Catholic Church—India—Clergy—Biography.
3. Cistercians—India—Biography. 4. Monasticism and religious
orders—India—History. I. Title.

BX4705.A2334M34   2008
271'.12502—dc22
[B]   2007050188

TABLE OF CONTENTS

Foreword   ix

Preface   xi

FIRST PART
CHILDHOOD AND YOUTH (1912–1935)

A Family During the War   3
Roots   5
The Beautiful Lady from Evreux   7
Return to Belgium   9
College Years   10
The Priest's Troop   13
Jean's Stubbornness Manifests Itself for the First Time   14
A Career All Mapped Out   16
London   19
In the 'Second Lancers'   22
The Accident   24
The Decision   25
The Trip to the Orient   28
You Shall Leave Your Father and Your Mother   30

SECOND PART
TRAPPIST AT SCOURMONT AND CALDEY (1935–1955)

The Abbey of Our Lady of Scourmont and
    Dom Anselme Le Bail   35
Novitiate   38
A Military Interlude   44
Ora et labora   46
Student in Rome   49
Under German Occupation   57
The Luftwaffe   58
In Bethany with the Farm Brothers   63
Gestapo   66
After the War   71
In Caldey with Dom Anselme   74
Master of Novices   78
Love Lost for Lady Poverty   83
Father, Father, Why Have You Abandoned Me?   85
Crossing the Desert   87
To Dom Anselme, for the Fulfillment of Long–Held Hopes   92
Paris   96
Languages and Cultures of India   100
Caldey   106
Nothing is Working Out   110
Providential Intervention   115
Farewells   122

THIRD PART
INDIA, FOUNDATION, AND TAKING ROOT (1955–1968)

Elephanta	127
A Little Detour to Ranchi	129
Shantivanam, the Forest of Peace	134
Dazzling Syriac Experience	138
Farewell to Monchanin	143
The Prodigal Son and Motherhouse	148
Pushpagiri	152
The Mountain Fallen from the Sky	157
Rain and Wind, Bless the Lord	162
Gropings in the Darkness	168
Turning Point: Pilot–Village and Indo–Swiss Project	173
A Community of Brothers	180
That All May be One: The Separated Brethren	185
In Pursuit of the *Penqitho*	187
The Evolution of the Catholic Church	195
A Modern Agricultural Enterprise	198
Among the Mountain People	203
The Liturgical Project	209
Monastic Vesture	215
Visitors and Early Friends	221
Growth Crisis	224

FOURTH PART
KURISUMALA ASHRAM, ITS INFLUENCE (1968–1988)

An Interrupted Sabbatical Year   237
To the Himalayas   246
First Foundation: Shantivanam   252
Encounter with Hinduism   256
Congress in Bangkok   266
The Community at the Beginning of the 1970s   271
A Second Foundation: Thirumalai   276
Gheeta Bhavan   282
Around the World   288
The Operation   297
Shantivanam Emancipated   304
Prayer with the Harp of the Spirit   311
Silver Jubilee   316

FIFTH PART
FULFILLMENT (1988–2001)

A Visit from the Lord   323
Slow Apprenticeship of Rest   325
Cistercian Approaches   333
Albano   341
Incorporation into the Cistercian Order   346
Lourdes: Dom Francis Mahieu-Acharya   354
At the Gates of Sheol   359
All is Blessing   366
Epilogue   370

Chronology   379

Bibliography   383

Index   389

FOREWORD

BEGAN WRITING this book in 1995 without suspecting how much work it would represent. It was a long quest, a patient piecing together during which I discovered interesting people and moving places. Often I felt that I had reached the limit of my strength and competency, but, like my 'hero', each time this happened, I found providential friends along my way, who slipped into my knapsack the maps and provisions that allowed me to continue along my road.

This work would not have been completed without the collaboration of many people.

My cousins Annie, Janine, and Ghislaine gave me all the family archives—letters and photo albums—kept by their mother, Marie-Thérèse Mahieu, who had been privileged to correspond with Father Francis for almost forty years.

Before they died, my father, Charles Mahieu, and my uncle, André Mahieu, told me the memorable episodes of their childhood in Ypres and in Normandy and of their youth in Brussels between the two wars.

The monks of Scourmont—Dom Guerric Baudet, Father Charles Dumont, Father Godefroid Leveugle, and Father Jacques Blanpain— willingly recalled their memories and let me examine precious documents. The late Father Gabriel Ghislain generously opened the abbey's archives to me.

The monks of Kurisumala, especially Father Mariadas and the late Father Mariabhakta, told me how they had experienced the beginnings of Kurisumala.

Many strangers from all parts of the world answered my letters, sometimes adding an old photo or an anecdote.

Mother Paule-Marie OCSO, the abbess of Soleilmont, Sister Pia Valeri OSB, a former secretary of AIM, Sister Marie-Bernard OCSO, a careful proofreader, Sister Marie-Benoît Meeus OSB, an historian, and Father Jean-Marie Van Cangh OP, an orientalist, furnished sources and sustained my work with their warm welcome, their judicious comments, and their constant encouragement.

Father Francis Mahieu-Acharya himself, after having given me all his personal documents without reservation, allowed me many interviews during my trips to India and read the text chapter by chapter, adding many details by correspondence.

Not least, Dom Armand Veilleux, abbot of Scourmont, has seen the book from manuscript to printed page and kindly contacted Cistercian Publications and arranged for the publication of the English translation.

In all this, I have the feeling, as did my uncle, of having been merely an instrument, moved by a sort of imperative inspiration: it was urgent to assemble and conserve these sources, to give an account of this history, so that its memory might be kept alive.

Marthe Mahieu

November 2001

PREFACE

URISUMALA IS AN EVOCATIVE NAME meaning 'the mountain of the Cross', a place of impressive beauty, an uncommonly successful inculturation of christian monasticism in India. Telling the story of Francis Mahieu Acharya's life means describing the birth and growth of the monastery of Kurisumala, and telling the story of Kurisumala means describing the greater part of the long life of Father Francis, who in his nineties continued to be a spiritual leader in his community.

India was the cradle of the most ancient monastic traditions known to history, going back to the Vedic epoch and even to pre–aryan India. Ever since those distant times, the indian soul has always kept a mystical depth, which predisposes it to meet christian mysticism. However, this meeting had to wait a long time.

The various experiences of the evangelization of India during the last centuries put the people of India in contact with the missionary communities' charitable and social works, but rarely allowed the indian population a hint of the spiritual and mystical richness of Christianity. The prophetic efforts of inculturation with indian thought by Roberto de Nobili at the beginning of the seventeenth century were admirable but isolated.

Father Jules Monchanin seems to have been the first to perceive that the closest point of contact between the great spiritual tradition of India and Christianity was at the level of a seeking, a thirst for the mystery of divinity, *advaita* for Hindus and adoration of the Trinity for Christians. A man of exceptional intelligence and radical poverty of heart, he quickly perceived that the monastic tradition was the common element between Christianity and Hinduism. Before his departure for India in 1939, he used to come to Scourmont to talk with Dom Anselme Le Bail at length about the importance of a christian monastic presence in India, which would assimilate the spiritual riches of Hinduism. Plans for a foundation were immediately made, but various events, beginning with the war, delayed and then rendered impossible a foundation in India by Scourmont Abbey.

When the Benedictine Henri Le Saux joined Monchanin in 1948, both men adopted the way of life of a hindu *sannyasi* [professed monk]. As Swami Paramarubyananda (Monchanin) and Swami Abhishiktananda (Le Saux), in 1950 they founded the ashram of Saccidananda, known as Shantivanam, on the banks of the sacred river Kavery, in Kulittalai in the diocese of Tiruchirappally.

Francis Mahieu reached Shantivanam in 1955. He was not a young monk looking for adventure but, rather, a mature man, having lived the monastic life for twenty years, formed at the school of Dom Anselme Le Bail, and having exercised the office of novice master at Scourmont and Caldey, Scourmont's foundation in Wales. He entered Scourmont in 1935, after hearing Mahatma Gandhi during his studies in London. Very early on, after Monchanin's visit to Scourmont in 1939, he developed a desire to go on the foundation to India. Since this foundation could not be made, after years of waiting, he obtained permission to go join the two *sannyasis* of Tamil Nadu. The year that Father Francis spent in Shantivanam in the company of these two great spiritual masters deeply marked him. He came to know Monchanin, especially, with whom he quickly established a relationship of disciple to spiritual master.

A good number of Europeans looking for spiritual experience had passed through Shantivanam, but disciples who wanted to stay were rare, and indian disciples did not come. In reality, the Church of India did not yet have the necessary vitality to produce its own christian *sannyasis*, and the hindu tradition of *sannyasi* is one of itinerant hermits rather than stable communities. What Monchanin and Le Saux lived at Shantivanam was admirable, but to want to make it into a stable community of the benedictine type was utopic.

Christian monasticism is profoundly linked to the Church. It ordinarily can develop only at the heart of a Church that is sufficiently alive, that has realized its own contemplative dimension. This is why, even though the very rich spiritual experience of Monchanin and Le Saux was a seed of christian mystical life planted on indian soil, preparing the possibility of a christian monasticism inculturated with the indian experience, the context of a Church in the syriac tradition, such as the Church in Kerala, which for centuries has been inculturated with the traditions of India, was a much more favorable milieu for implanting an inculturated christian monasticism. Kerala, from the religious point of view, represents a unique situation in India. Christianity has been present there without interruption since the first generation of the christian era. Tradition traces its origins back to the apostle Thomas.

When the possibility of Father Francis founding a monastic community in a diocese of Syro–Malankar rite presented itself in 1956, Monchanin was very favorable. He had lost hope in a monastic 'community' in Tamil Nadu and placed his hope in this syriac Shantivanam.

Father Francis Mahieu undertook the foundation of Kurisumala, accompanied by Father Bede Griffiths, who had come to join him after a failed attempt to transplant european monasticism in India. During the first year after the departure of Father Francis for Kerala and the foundation of Kurisumala, in which Father Monchanin placed much hope, the latter died, worn out by asceticism and illness.

Father Le Saux maintained Shantivanam as best he could during the following ten years, but his heart was elsewhere. Having decided to settle in Gyansu in the Himalayas, in 1967 he gave his ashram of Shantivanam to Father Francis, who accepted it and sent Father Bede Griffiths and a few other monks from Kurisumala. This was Kurisumala's first foundation. Until his death, Bede Griffiths maintained the character of this new Shantivanam as it had been during the time of Monchanin and Le Saux, that is, as a meeting place between christian seekers and hindu seekers, and especially a reference point for the numerous Europeans who at that time were traveling to India in pursuit of religious experience. Kurisumala and Shantivanam even today represent two complementary experiences of christian monastic presence in India.

Much has been written about the concept of inculturation. Some day someone will have to analyze how this was accomplished in an original way in Kurisumala, which succeeded in the inculturation of the christian monastic institution, whereas the experience of the two great pioneers Monchanin and Le Saux had, above all else, been their effort to live the encounter of christian experience and advaitic experience ever more deeply at the heart of their personal relationship with God.

Encounter with a religious tradition, as with a culture, is made especially through ordinary human contacts, in particular in the realm of work. For Father Francis and the Kurisumala community, inculturation meant celebrating the liturgy every day in an indianized Syriac rite and in translating its rich liturgical texts. It has also meant the adoption of eastern monasticism's stages in the gradual initiation of a candidate to monastic life. But in addition, it meant building a monastery with their own hands, together with local workers; developing sources of revenue not only for the monastic community but also for the local population, particularly by setting up a dairy cooperative; and, especially, receiving day after day the many indian or european visitors, whether hindu, christian, or buddhist.

The present work is not a reflection on the problems of christian monasticism's insertion into the religious tradition of India. It simply tells the personal story of a monk who lived this process of inculturation day after day for half a century. Nothing can better allow us to glimpse the demands, the challenges, and the difficulties of such an enterprise.

The author of this biography of Father Francis Mahieu Acharya,[1] Madame Marthe Mahieu-De Praetere, is one of his nieces. In her text we can easily sense her admiration for her uncle, whom she visited regularly in Kurisumala for many years. This unconcealed admiration has not prevented her from consulting all the available documents in Europe and in India and from listening to everyone who could help her to give a faithful and exact account of the events she describes. These events not only constitute the history of Francis Mahieu and of Kurisumala but also in some way form the background of the development of all christian monasticism in India for the last half century.

Father Francis was a cistercian–trappist monk when he left for India. A project such as Kurisumala, however, could not happen within the structure of the Order, with all its canonical requirements, especially at a time when people were not yet sufficiently prepared for this kind of inculturation. Therefore, it was done under the authority of the local bishop,

---

[1] Acharya is the name that Francis Mahieu took when he received indian citizenship in 1968. *Acharya* in Sanskrit means 'the Master', the one who teaches the disciples.

and Father Francis ceased to belong to the Cistercian Order during all the years of Kurisumala's development. He remained profoundly cistercian to the bottom of his heart. Through Kurisumala's full incorporation as an autonomous monastery of the Cistercian Order of the Strict Observance in 1999, the historical cycle came full circle.

In these circumstances, it is entirely appropriate that this biography be published in the collection of *Cahiers scourmontois* (*Scourmont notebooks*), after the *Life* of Anselme Le Bail, who was Father Francis' abbot, and the *Poems and Prayers* of Charles Dumont, who entered Scourmont shortly after him.

Armand Veilleux
Abbot of Scourmont

FIRST PART

CHILDHOOD AND YOUTH
(1912–1935)

CHILDHOOD AND YOUTH

A FAMILY DURING THE WAR

APRIL 1915. On the road from Ypres to Bailleul, at the border between France and Belgium, a large family was fleeing the bombings on foot, abandoning the family factory and their house near the canal. René Mahieu, the father, walked in front, carrying a large suitcase in each hand. After months of hesitation, he had decided to leave Ypres in order to shelter his family. With his loved ones he joined the column of refugees leaving the city early in the morning. His six children followed him: Marie-Thérèse, the eldest, the serious one who just turned ten, had the job of pushing the carriage in which little André slept, wedged between packages. Charles and Paul, eight and seven, each carried a little cloth backpack made by their mother, full of provisions. René's wife Anna was at the rear, holding a little one's hand in each of hers: Antoinette, aged five, and Jean (John), not yet three and a half. She had delayed this departure as long as she could, as long as she could stand it with children in the city ravaged by the shells that the german batteries, entrenched only a few kilometers away, had been firing for months on the main square, on the famous covered market, and on Saint Martin's Cathedral, which were now only blackened ruins.

These last weeks, buying food had been more and more difficult for civilians. Food items had been requisitioned for the armies, whose reinforcements came from the ends of the earth: Canadians, New Zealanders with upturned hats, Senegalese, Arabs in burnouses, and others. But what clinched the decision was the asphyxiating gas offensive launched by the Germans on allied trenches a few days earlier. If this chemical weapon spread in the city, how could people protect themselves? Gas masks were distributed to soldiers, but civilians could not obtain them. And the shelters, the basements where they had been living for almost a year, would not save them from a horrible death. Faced with this new threat, even the most stubborn citizens of Ypres resigned themselves to exile.

Anna thought about all this as she walked, no faster than the small legs of the youngest ones permitted. On the road full of holes, the rising sun projected their elongated shadows in front of them. From time to time, she prayed silently: 'My God, protect our family, protect our children.'

Jean was just a little more than three years old. This little boy, robust and happy, affectionate, always in motion, was not aware of the dangers threatening his family. Why should he worry? Mother was there, sweet and patient, always even tempered, and she was holding his hand.

The group of refugees stopped suddenly: coming towards them was a detachment of strange soldiers on horseback. They were Sikhs, lancers from India, whose regiments had come to join the British army on the Yser front. Bearded, wearing turbans, dark skinned, lances at their heels, banners fluttering in the wind, their passing caused an admiring shock. Little Jean watched them go by, fascinated.

Seventeen kilometers to the border. They said that in Bailleul the Red Cross took charge of refugees and directed them towards the safe regions behind the fighting. Where will they be tomorrow? Suddenly, with a sound like a motorcycle, a biplane appeared in the sky. From the column of Belgians cries arose, and people ran. Leaving the road, they dispersed in the fields. A french soldier on a bicycle, passing the civilians, shouted to them as he pedaled: 'It's a Rumpler, hide, do not remain grouped together!' The whole family plunged into the damp ditch, leaving the baby carriage and baby in the middle of the road. Charles opened one eye when the noise was the loudest, and behind his outspread fingers, he had time to see the german machine gunner leaning out of the cabin, with his leather helmet and his huge glasses. Whew! He did not shoot, he was getting further away. 'Thank you, Lord!'

At nightfall, they arrived in Bailleul. Red Cross trucks drove them to the station in Armentières, where english officers channeled the new wave of refugees. During the night, with only two loaves of stale black bread to eat, the family traveled by train to Rouen. Jean fell asleep on the varnished wooden seat, his head on his mother's knees while she fed the baby. A new life began.

ROOTS

René Mahieu was born in Clercken, near Dixmude, in 1871. His father worked a farm, where eighteen children were born and grew up. The two older sons took over the farm. After their school years, the others dispersed to find work, settle down, and marry. René had a modern and enterprising spirit. He dreamed of mechanical things: motors, automobiles, airplanes. He took a job in a shop repairing agricultural machinery and soon went to Ypres to join his sister Euphrasie, whose husband had just died, leaving her with two young children to raise and a small factory of gas engines to run. René's dynamism performed miracles. The business expanded, and he became the Associate Manager. He had just turned thirty, and the new century opened in front of him, full of promise.

On Sundays, wearing his black suit, he attended High Mass in the cathedral along with many other people. After Mass, with his sister, he walked along the ramparts, first in one direction and then in the other. The citizens of Ypres were faithful to this circular walk, a Sunday tradition, exchanging greetings and raising their hats to the neighbors they met. For a few weeks, René had noticed a young girl, small and thin, with brown eyes, dark hair tied up in a bun, walking with her two sisters, closely followed by an older man who must have been their father. René managed to turn in the opposite direction, observing her face. Finally he was bold enough to follow her and from a distance saw the whole family go into a large house in Dixmude Street. Yellow letters on the closed store proclaimed 'Colonial Foodstuffs'. His decision was made: he would ask for her hand in marriage.

The following Sunday, his new beige gloves in his hand, he resolutely pulled the wire attached to the doorbell. A servant opened the door and Mr. Vandelanoitte received him in the parlor. After introducing himself, he said, 'Sir, I have the honor of asking for the hand of your daughter in marriage.' 'Which of the three?' asked the father, smiling. René realized that he did not know the name of the young woman he wished to marry. Without becoming flustered, he answered, 'The smallest one, the one who looks like an Andalusian with pink cheeks and brown eyes'.

Was the master of the house won over by his self–confidence? He called Anna and introduced her to her suitor, who from then on was permitted to accompany the family to Mass and on their walk about the ramparts before sharing their Sunday meal. Their engagement lasted two years, and the wedding was celebrated at Saint-Martin on 23 November 1903. The newlyweds went to live in a house near the canal, outside the ramparts. They lived there until 1915, and that is where Jean was born on 17 January 1912.

Anna Vandelanoitte was a young lady 'from a good family', as they used to say at that time. Her parents had wealth and a good lineage; they were proud to belong to the middle class of shopkeepers of the city of Ypres, rich in monuments and traditions that dated back to the Middle Ages. Her brother would become burgomaster of Vlamertinge, the prosperous neighboring agricultural village. Her eldest sister would marry a pharmacist, and the second sister would marry a notary. The Vandelanoitte family was very christian. Anna's father yielded the place of honor to her uncle, a parish priest, when he came to dinner. Grace was said before every meal. The mother had died quite young, and the three daughters had been educated at the fashionable religious boarding school in the city, run by the 'Ladies of Roesbruges'. There Anna learned the catechism and studied Scripture, needlework, and manners, with enough literature and arithmetic to be a shrewd lady of the house. She especially developed a fervent personal faith, a particular devotion to Our Lady, and an absolute confidence in Providence. She manifested the qualities proposed as a model to the students: modesty, benevolence, patience, and devotion—all the more since she had possessed them naturally since her childhood.

She and René formed a united couple of which she was the quiet light and he the energetic motor that sometimes backfired, because his character was quick–tempered, irritable, even choleric. Anna let the storm pass, kept silent, or answered calmly without ever raising her voice. Above all, she was a mother. Her children were her greatest joy. She gave them all her time, nursed them until the age of two, and she would keep the baby on her knees while she told stories to the older ones. Two servants did the housekeeping under her benevolent direction.

When the World War broke out, sending his family into exile, Jean was barely a toddler. Replaced by André as the baby, he and Antoinette were a pair of daring little ones, always inventing something. All day their father was at the factory, Mother took care of the baby or the house, and the three older children went to school. They, the little ones, escaped to the attic or the garden, built huts, looked at picture books. Sometimes they went to their maternal grandfather's house for a snack. They played hide and seek between the bags of burlap rough on their cheeks, where exotic products and pungent spices were stored: tea, coffee, pepper, cinnamon, cloves.

Seventy–four years later, when Jean came back from India after twenty years of absence and visited his cousin Doom, he wanted to see the house near the canal once more. It—as well as the whole city—had been rebuilt exactly the same, after having been razed by four years of bombing. He looked at it for a long time: there were his roots.

THE BEAUTIFUL LADY FROM EVREUX

In France, the Mahieus were first housed by the municipal authorities in the 'Villa des Marronniers' (Chestnut Trees Villa), a large unoccupied building in Bihorel-lez-Rouen, at that time a semi–rural suburb of the old city in Normandy. Later they would move to Evreux, where René was asked to take over two farms and run them with the help of other refugees from Flanders. The owners and agricultural workers of the region were almost all in the military, that is, in the trenches. Ensuring the harvest was imperative: food for civilians and the army depended on it. This was 1916, and no one still believed in a quick end to the war. The front line had stabilized, and the situation could go on for a long time.

But from the Mahieu children's point of view, the war was only a subject of adult conversation. Their war was over, left behind in Ypres with the bombs, the sandbags, the rubble, and the wounded, nursed in the school by Sisters wearing wimples. In France, there were no alarm sirens, no curfews, no explosions. The rare uniforms they saw were the sloppy ones of local boys home for a furlough. For these children, war became a prolonged vacation. They spent a carefree summer wandering the countryside, eating apples, bringing in the hay, and fishing for crawfish for the first time with the village boys.

The old house in which they lived was surrounded by a large garden with trees and flowering shrubs with a vegetable garden in one corner. On

Sundays and summer days, they went to Guichinville and Huet with their father to oversee the farms. Jean marveled at everything. He observed the wild hyacinths, the bees, the flight of harriers, and the tiny trees growing up from acorns hidden in the ground. His mother taught him his letters and Flemish. From his childhood in Normandy, he would keep a very vivid sensitivity to nature and a slight french accent throughout his life.

In autumn, they had to return to school. Marie-Thérèse and Antoinette were sent to the Sisters' school, the boys to the Jesuits' preparatory school. They learned the Marseillaise (France's national anthem) by heart, the complete list of french departments with their capital cities, and the fables of La Fontaine. Two years later, the armistice was signed at Versailles. The bearded survivors came back from the front, very happy to rejoin their wives and farms, but René was in no hurry to return to Belgium. The news from Ypres was far from happy: the factory had been completely destroyed, all the city was in ruins, Euphrasie was going from one ministry to the other to try to obtain war damages. On top of all this, Anna was pregnant! Why not stay in France a little while longer? But they must find a way to make a living: they had no more savings, and an extra pair of hands was no longer needed in agriculture. Stay, yes, but doing what?

It was Anna who involuntarily provided the solution. She loved coffee and was sad that she could no longer find any at the grocery store. 'If at least we had chicory!' she lamented. Before the war, in Ypres, chicory as well as coffee had been roasted in her father's store. They had been mixed in varying proportions to make a family drink. But in France, there was no roasted chicory. That was all René needed to start a new enterprise. From a neighboring farmer, he obtained the use of an empty hangar, borrowed money to buy burners, hired a few freshly demobilized fellows, and started to produce and sell half–pound packets of roasted chicory. They were wrapped in blue paper and decorated with a sticker he had printed in the city. Under the picture of a pretty brunette sniffing curls of steam rising from a cup were the words *La Belle Ebroïcienne*, which mean 'The beautiful lady from Evreux'. Since real coffee from the colonies was not available, the chicory appealed to the people of Evreux, who adopted it with enthusiasm.

The baby was born in April and baptized Albert, in honor of the valiant king of Belgium. Three more years passed in the restored peace, the taste of cider, and the acrid odor of chicory. The family returned to their homeland in 1921.

Ypres was still in a pitiful state. Euphrasie was living in military barracks and overseeing the factory's reconstruction. Her fifteen year old son had died, and her daughter Marthe, Jean's godmother, had just married an industrial man from Brussels, Pierre Vandemaele, who was ten years older than she. The whole region of Yser was destroyed, and most of the schools were in ruins. For Anna, this question of schools was of primary importance. She wanted her children to have a good education. For this reason, they chose to move to the capital. René rented a three–story house on François Degreef Street in Schaerbeek, which at that time was a well–to–do neighborhood in Brussels. It was close to two excellent schools, not far from the northern train station, and opposite Saint-Servais church.

When the family moved into this city house, little Albert, examining the tiny yard covered with a glass roof and decorated with a heap of artificial rocks, without any garden, declared categorically: 'I don't like Belgium.' The other children, without saying so out loud, also missed Normandy. One night Charles and Paul ran away from the college of Melle, where they were boarders, to go to Ypres, hidden in a train of merchandise. Alerted by his sister, where the two brothers got off in the middle of the night, René went to get them at once and, without listening to their supplications, took them back to the college before dawn. Father Director interrogated the dejected runaways. He understood the difficulty they had in adapting and let them return without being punished, under the seal of secrecy. Won over by this unhoped for mercy, they later were very happy at the Josephites College, where they finished their humanities education.

RETURN TO BELGIUM

After settling in Schaerbeek, family life little by little got back to normal. Then a tragic event upset it. One Saturday, on de Haecht Road, Jean and André ran home from Holy Mary School. They ran across the church square and rang the doorbell of their house, impatient to put their leather schoolbags down and go have a snack in the basement kitchen, where their mother was waiting for them. Albert came to open the door for them. He was four years old and just tall enough to reach the latch by standing on tiptoes. Little brother was not happy today. He whined and complained that his throat hurt. His brothers and sisters tried in vain to distract him by reading stories to him.

During the evening, his fever rose. Mother sent Jean to get the physician from the next street. He examined the child, diagnosed a serious throat infection, and prescribed syrup. All night, the little boy's state worsened. Anna watched over him, rocked him, and cooled his forehead. On Sunday morning he had a choking spasm. René ran to get the physician, but he was not home. By the time he found another and brought him home, the child had lost consciousness. In the kitchen, the physician tried a tracheotomy. Too late. Little Albert had died of croup, in his mother's arms.

Anna remained seated straight on a chair. Someone took the child to lay him down on his little bed upstairs in his parents' room. She did not cry; she was numb. She tried with all the strength of her faith to overcome this separation. René, standing in the living room, his jaws clenched, hit his forehead against the wall. The children were immobile, frightened, disbelieving. Silence filled the house.

Jean was ten years old. He loved his mother more than anything. Seeing her so unhappy constricted his heart. He felt powerless to console her. Gently, he came to lean against her shoulder. She was the one who spoke first: 'My children, let us thank God. Albert is happy now, and our family has a little protector in heaven.'

Jean promised never to cause his mother sorrow. From this day on, of all the brothers, he would be the most helpful, the most generous. Just like his mother, he would have a passion for the Absolute.

COLLEGE YEARS

In September 1922, Jean was not yet eleven and began studying humanities at Holy Mary Institute. For two years, life went on quietly between home and school, only a few hundred meters apart. At this time, there were six days of class per week. All the teachers were priests. Every morning, the students began their day by attending 8:10 AM Mass at the Institute, unless they were altar servers in their parish, in which case they had to bring proof signed by their parish priest. In order to avoid encounters with the opposite sex, the beginning and ending times for classes were fifteen minutes apart from those of the nearby girls' school, the Institute of the Ladies of Mary, where Antoinette also began her first year.

Jean showed himself to be a good student, putting forth regular effort. His fellow student Louis Evely was the most brilliant, consistently the top student in the class. Jean remained in the top third during all his studies, without particularly shining.

Mother was the soul of the house. Winter and summer, every day of the week, she got up at 6 AM, revived the stove, set the breakfast table, and woke the children before going to Mass at Saint-Servais church. At 7:30 she had returned—it was only across the street—to have breakfast with them. They never failed to come and hug her before leaving for school. Their father also left home early in the morning, to walk to the northern train station. He represented and sold the english 'National' motors for all of Belgium and visited his clients by train. He had an office and showroom on Anvers Boulevard in the very center of Brussels. His sons sometimes went there on their days off.

But he was still co–owner with his sister of the Ypres factory, and every Tuesday he went there to discuss business with Euphrasie. They often argued, and René would return to Schaerbeek in bad humor. He took his wife to witness about 'Euphrrrrrrasie's bad faith', rolling his 'r's with his terrible West Flanders accent, made even stronger by anger.

At noon, the children returned to have lunch. Mother herself cooked all the meals. She awaited the students with her unalterable smile and steaming pots. At four o'clock, they were back, to have a snack with her in the basement kitchen with its painted furniture, warmed by the heat of the stove and the odor of the day's work: laundry, soup, or pastry. She listened to them recount their days and tell of their successes or worries; she would laugh at their jokes. Sometimes she gave advice, corrected a judgment, and always stopped gossip at once. And sometimes she told stories, like that of Father Vincent Lebbe, a compatriot from Ypres who became a missionary in China and who had just completed a tour of talks in Belgium that she heard about at the parish church. Just like his predecessor, the Jesuit Matteo Ricci, Lebbe completely immersed himself in chinese culture. He spoke Chinese, dressed like the natives, and pleaded for the consecration of chinese bishops, in opposition to his superiors. During the Boxer war, he took sides with the chinese rebels, which scandalized many people. This story pleased Jean very much. He asked his mother to repeat some episodes of it.

Anna did not punish and did not shout, but when she asked something she was obeyed without discussion. Her children respected her and felt her strength, her interior consistency. She was totally devoted—in the full sense of 'devotion'—to her mission of mother of a family, and in this she found her joy. She did not complain or boast about this. Each of the children felt loved, guided by her, and even secretly believed that he or she was the favorite.

After their snack, it was time for homework. A 'study hall' was set up upstairs, beside the parents' room. The three oldest each had a work-table. André, since he was the youngest—he was still in elementary school—could stay downstairs near Mother and open his notebooks on the kitchen table, while she knitted or mended clothing, sitting in her wicker armchair.

After supper, eaten by the whole family together with their father, the children read, talked, or played. Marie-Thérèse marked her status as the eldest sister by disdaining games in favor of crochet or needlework; she was already sixteen. In winter they played parlor games such as checkers, backgammon, or snakes and ladders. In summer, when the evenings were warm and the days longer, the boys went to Lehon Place to play pelota ball or badminton.

Sundays were different: everyone got up a little later, Mother went to Mass at 8 AM and then prepared the Sunday meal: a leg of lamb or a roast with vegetables in season, followed by a pastry. The children went to High Mass with their father. Sometimes uncles and aunts from Flanders came to visit. They were received in the main floor parlor, which was extended by the little veranda called the 'winter garden', where a trickle of water gurgled among the green plants and artificial rocks. After tea, the family went walking in Josaphat Park, and sometimes with cousins in sailor suits, they would go to the sandy fields bordering Lambermont Boulevard. They planted stakes, then traced lines to mark off the croquet course or tennis 'courts'. During the long summer holidays, real matches were organized, energetically directed by Charles and Paul, who learned their passion for organized sports at the college of Melle.

At the end of the summer, the family boarded the train for Oostduinkerke, at the seacoast. They rented a villa for the first half of September, less expensive than in July or August. The children and their father enjoyed swimming in the ocean, while their mother watched them, reclining in a lounge chair.

THE PRIEST'S TROOP

The next year, a new field of activity opened for Jean, one that would make a profound mark on his growth as a teenager: scouting. Father Etienne Hemeleers, who taught history, had just founded a scout troop at Holy Mary School. He was an enthusiastic and demanding, authoritarian and non–conforming teacher. He was passionate about his task as an educator, and his charisma had a strong influence on his students. He left no one indifferent. Tall, athletic, with a craggy face beneath a prematurely balding forehead, blue–green eyes with penetrating glance, the young professor either fascinated or exasperated. His students in general, and especially 'his' scouts, admired him without reservation. Etienne Hemeleers sought original methods to form character and personality. Preoccupied by what he perceived as a weakening of christian and traditional values, he mistrusted intellectualism and especially walking encyclopedias without practical experience. His teaching methods were alive. He tried to form his students' judgment, reflection, and questioning. He especially wanted boys who had a sense of effort, endurance, and self–discipline. He traveled to Russia to see Bolshevism for himself, and to England where he visited several renowned colleges. This is where he discovered the methods of Baden-Powell. As soon as he returned, he started to recruit scouts and, to this end, composed tracts for the students' mothers, in the following style: 'your son will come back dirty and tired but, believe me, this will do him good and will keep him far from the temptations of idleness.' The uniform was very important to him: first it was simply an orange scarf and a blue beret. It quickly grew to include a felt hat, khaki shirt and shorts, belt, ribbons, and various insignia and for the leaders, colored shoulder lanyards, not to mention pennants, oriflammes, and banners. In his 1923 class photo, Jean was one of the eight students out of twenty–nine wearing a scout uniform. The priest prohibited 'totems' (animal names given to scouts during a ritual 'totem' ceremony) because he found them ridiculous and degrading. But the boys wore white gloves for processions and parades down the street, always in perfect order. The religious ceremonies gathering all the students of the Institute several times a year were held at Holy Mary church on Royale Street, because the school chapel was too small. On these occasions the scout band, with its drums, bugles, immaculate gloves, and standards, led the procession.

This should not lead you to believe that these showy military–style occupations were the essential element of scout activities. At the weekly meetings, 'scout games' were practiced in the Soignes forest. The boys learned techniques of 'outdoor life', observation of and respect for Nature, and how to build furniture. The motto was 'Serve and Surpass Yourself'. The boys had a lot of fun because the priest used a fundamental pedagogical method, one that was not common at that time: children learn by playing and remember especially well what has made them laugh.

JEAN'S STUBBORNNESS MANIFESTS ITSELF FOR THE FIRST TIME

In autumn of 1924, everyone expected Jean to continue as a student at Holy Mary, where he was a good student and an enthusiastic scout. But he, at the age of twelve and a half, decided otherwise. He refused to become the student of Mister R., whom the students nicknamed 'Pietje'. He was a sarcastic teacher, who took pleasure in catching students out, trapping them, raking them over the coals, and humiliating them. Jean experienced this bullying on several occasions and rebelled. He was ultra–sensitive to injustice and irony. He was already, in advance, Pietje's pet hate. His younger age—he was a year ahead—short stature, and swaggering had designated him the scapegoat.

But that was not the only reason for his decision: despite appearances, he did not feel that he belonged in Holy Mary, a college attended by the sons of Brussels' upper middle class. He felt different. 'I was a little flemish working-peasant', he confided much later when recalling this time in his life. What his older brothers told him about the college of Melle, where history and geography were taught in Flemish and where, for the most part, students came from a rural or small town milieu, attracted him more.

After the end of the school year, he announced to his parents that he would not return to Holy Mary but wanted to attend Melle. His father did not agree. 'What is this? This boy is deciding instead of his parents? What are the reasons? The teacher is unjust? Well, that will teach you to keep quiet. You will see other injustices! This is only a whim!' fulminated René. 'And the expense! Have you thought of the expense? Do you think I have a donkey that lays gold coins?'

René was angry. Anna remained silent. She let the storm pass. She reflected. In her heart, she took her son's side. She understood his decision, and did not believe this was only a whim.

Jean maintained his position, simply, calmly, without yielding one iota, with an unshakeable and respectful determination, waiting for the adversary to wear down. He knew that his mother supported him, and that was his strength. He, the obliging young boy, kind, conciliatory, always in good humor, who ran or jumped more often than he walked and who always sang, had turned into a rock. If someone tried to argue with him, he said, 'I will not go to Holy Mary next year.' That was all. Father finally yielded, convinced by Mother.

When the family returned from their holidays near the ocean, the young boarder's trunk was prepared. He took the train on 16 September, after telling Father Hemeleers his reasons.

Jean loved Melle so much that he spent three school years there. What influence did the Josephites have on him? At that time, they practiced 'modern' methods inspired by anglo–saxon colleges: two hours of sports each day, 'self–control' and 'fair play' in all circumstances, and elders who were responsible to be 'tutors' for the younger students. At the beginning of every trimester, Father Superior reminded the gathered students that Melle students had three duties: a spirit of hard work, a spirit of discipline, and a spirit of piety. Besides sports, which took up a large place in their day, theater and singing were practiced all year long. Jean took part, often playing a leading role, in various operettas and plays, with varying success. Already at that time he suffered regular throat infections and sore throats, which imperiled his performances. He always had an understudy.

He stayed in contact with Father Hemeleers and participated in scout camps during the summer holidays. After three years at Melle, he decided to return to Holy Mary to study with Father Hemeleers and Father Eglem, an old–fashioned teacher who wore a monocle. That year, 1927–28, he was patrol leader and served the 32nd BP more than ever, with their chaplain.

Until the age of sixteen, Jean was a child without problems. Enthusiastically he developed the values of his family, his school, and his time, which were completely congruous: love of God and of the Church, service to neighbor, frugality, physical endurance, and self–forgetfulness. His intellectual formation was classical, the basic greco–latin–christian culture that every young man from a good catholic family received before the war. He integrated it without arguing but without really deepening it either. His world was, above all, his family: his mother, to whom he was bound by an unfailing tenderness and confidence; his father, who readily showed him anger and impatience; and his sister Antoinette, pretty, intelligent, unpredictable, and the favorite of their father, who indulged her. Jean sometimes could not stand this arbitrariness, but he loved his sister and shared discussions, dreams, and projects with her. Both had an adventurous spirit and aspired to live outside the beaten track. As to the four brothers, at that time they were truly one. In the neighborhood, they were called 'the Mahieu brothers'. They looked alike, shared a love of sports and physical exploits, their father's enterprising spirit, and a great love for their mother. Photos show them in football or hockey outfits when they are not in bathing suits, arms around each other's shoulders, laughing and muscled.

In appearance, Jean was no different from his brothers. No doubt, like many other adolescents of that time, he developed in secret his dreams of heroism, or even martyrdom. But nothing led anyone to doubt that he would follow the comfortable career that his parents, concerned about his future, prepared for him together with his godmother, and about which they told him during summer 1928, after Marie-Thérèse's wedding.

A CAREER ALL MAPPED OUT

February 1929. Wearing an oil–stained grey coverall, Jean, standing in front of the parallel lathe, adjusted the calibrated metal pieces one by one, with a screech that pierced his ears. The big clock hanging on the factory's iron beams showed 4:30 PM. 'Half an hour left', he thought.

For the past six months, he had arisen at seven AM, taken the tram each morning for Forest, and worked eight hours a day as a lathe operator in the Union Factory. He hated this work and felt humiliated by his new situation. His brothers were students at Louvain. Antoinette, his almost twin, his very dear rival, was a student of Philosophy and Letters at Saint-Louis Institute. But Pierre and Marthe, the rich cousins, the most respected persons of the family, had offered him a position for the future: to work in the factory and, after a few years of training, to become their associate and their heir. They did not have any children, and Jean was their godchild. Can one refuse such an offer?

Five o'clock! The siren goes off, the workers lower the circuit break-ers, the machines fall silent. Jean quickly removes his coverall and runs to catch his tram to Schaerbeek. He finds Antoinette in the kitchen, mak-ing herself a sandwich. She relates to him:

Do you know what happened in philosophy class? Two boys sat be-hind us, in the row that is supposed to stay empty behind the girls. There are only seven of us and we are supposed to sit in the front row. But they hid behind Yvonne, who is larger, and were passing notes to us! The professor didn't see anything. He is eccentric, lost in his thoughts. He is interesting, especially when he talks about preclassical Antiquity. He was talking about the sophists.

Jean was silent, listened distractedly, and smiled automatically as he pre-pared four sandwiches, which he would eat as he walked. These stories that Antoinette told him with such volubility made him envious. He was mortified that he had nothing interesting to tell about his day. 'I have to run', he replied. 'I have a class at seven.'

While he ate his supper, he walked across the Botanical Gardens to Saint-Louis Institute, where he took evening classes in the School of Business until ten o'clock: mathematics, accounting, general economics, and business law. None of it interested him at all. Sometimes he even fell asleep, worn out by his workday in the factory. The evening classes were part of the contract with the Vandemaele cousins, who were paying for them. His parents had accepted this proposition with relief: Marie-Thérèse married, Jean taken care of by his godmother, they still had four students to pay for. University cost a lot of money, and business was not going well. The Ypres factory never had regained it pre–war prosperity and would be sold the following year. The crisis of 1929 was felt in bel-gian businesses, and motors were not selling well. Even though their fa-ther did not talk about this in front of them, the children guessed that he was preoccupied by the drop in the family's income.

Ten o'clock, class ended. Jean left the auditorium and met a few neighborhood friends in a Rogier Avenue café. They were former fellow Holy Mary students, who led a joyous night life. Especially on Satur-days, libations and the tour of the bars continued late into the night. Like most students, they acted provocatively towards the 'bourgeois'—singing risqué songs loudly under the windows of fashionable Louis Bertrand

Avenue houses, unscrewing street signs or car radiators' caps, urinating in the mailbox of the elderly spinsters who owned the bookstore or, better, the 'Ladies of Mary' Sisters. Jean was the boldest, the wildest of the group. At least at night, he was a fulltime 'student'.

For the first time, at the age of eighteen, he resented his parents and suffered from it. He vaguely reproached them for what he perceived as their dependence on the rich cousins. 'My parents don't dare refuse my godmother anything', he told a friend, 'because she is rich. She rides in a car driven by a chauffeur. His seat is separated from hers by a glass window! She uses a telephone to talk to him. Imagine!'

For three years, Jean played the game: he obeyed his parents and loyally honored the contract that bound him. After his apprenticeship in the shop and a successful first year in commercial sciences, he was promoted to administration and exchanged his coverall for a three–piece suit. Interiorly he was torn: he was not indifferent to his patrons' luxurious standard of life, with which gradually he became associated. In 1930, he had the use of his own car and earned a comfortable salary, whereas his brothers and sister had a meager allowance. Flannel suits and english ties looked good on him, and he was successful with girls. But he did not subscribe completely to this milieu, this career. Something bothered him, left him unsatisfied. He sensed that the plan for his life was something else. But what?

During these three years, he led a frenetic life, or, rather, he led many lives simultaneously: the factory, evening classes, his friends, soccer, and responsibility for the new pack of cub scouts formed at Holy Mary and of whom, at Father Hemeleers' request, he became the *Akela* [leader].

He organized weekends, camps, and multiple activities for his boys. He had them play and sing, and in the evening he told them the Jungle Book story near the dying fire. His expressive blue eyes, strong voice, and precise gestures resurrected the inhabitants of the indian forest, Mowgli's exploits, Shere-Khan's ruses, Bandar-Logs' tricks, and the wisdom of Father–Wolf. The cubs were charmed. They would gladly listen to him all night.

Jean gave himself without counting the cost, with overflowing energy, never at a loss for ideas, never discouraged. He was closer than ever to Etienne Hemeleers. Every weekend he discoursed with him. In the vocabulary of the time, he seemed to have chosen the scout chaplain as 'spiritual director'. He spoke to no one about the content of these talks. Within his family, he remained a good son, more distant no doubt: he was never at home except to sleep. With his brothers, it was 'All for one,

one for all!' If one of the four was in trouble, the others ran to him. And some nights in the street there were pitched battles and stick fights between the 'Socialist Young Guard' and the 'Catholic Circle' youth. Afterwards, everyone went to a nearby café to bathe their bruises in cold water, downing many pints of blond beer.

At night with his friends, Jean sought out thrills. His radicalness, his love of exploits—of the extreme, as we would say these days—sometimes led him to excess. One night, amidst a frenzied debauchery, he suddenly had a sort of disgust and stood motionless. He looked around him. Everything seemed horrible, empty, disgusting. He went away alone, in the dark and deserted streets, overcome less by shame than by a burning desire for another life.

LONDON

One foggy afternoon in January 1931, Jean lifted his suitcase up the straight, narrow staircase of a house in Paddington. 'Second floor left', said his landlady, handing him the key. He repeated these three words silently to himself, to be sure he understood. On the second floor, he discovered a small room with little flowers on the faded wallpaper. He put his suitcase on the floor and, sitting on the bed, examined his new home: a table with drawers, two chairs, and behind a divider hung with pink upholstery fabric there was a washstand with copper taps. The french door opened on to a little concrete balcony. The neighboring buildings were very close. In the small garden, a huge tree's bare branches grew all the way to the roof.

What in the world was he doing in this anonymous room in a London suburb where he didn't know anyone? It was not his idea: this year–long stay was part of the training program drawn up by Uncle Pierre and Aunt Marthe, his 'godparents/patrons'. It was all organized by their broker: registration in the Polytechnic School, renting a furnished room by the month, with some meals included. With a map of London, a dictionary, a small Kodak camera, and a wad of pounds sterling destined to cover all his expenses for six months, shortly after the New Year Jean had boarded a mixed cargo at Anvers bound for Harwich. His parents had accompanied him to the quay. Mother hid her emotion at seeing one of her children go abroad for the first time, and for so long. She hugged him, told

him those stupid things mothers tell a son who is going away: 'Be careful, wear your scarf, write to us.' When he thought of it, Jean's heart
constricted. He was really all alone here, and his school English was not
even good enough to let him understand what people were telling him.
They spoke so quickly and with a 'cockney' accent besides! However,
when his godmother had spoken to him about this project, it had pleased
him. After two years working hard at the factory while taking evening
courses, it was a kind of reward: a year of studies in London! Freedom,
adventure, just school, no more factory work. And to know English thor-
oughly would be an advantage. He did not imagine that this language
would one day be his second mother tongue, in which he would think,
write, and give talks, very far from London, its banks and offices.

Six o'clock. Night had fallen. Jean was overcome by sudden nostalgia, thinking of all he left behind in Brussels: his cubs, Father Hemeleers,
his friends, the room under the eaves that he had shared with André for
ten years, the Sunday soccer matches with his brothers, and the basement
kitchen where they must be eating supper all together, teasing Mother,
who smiled, crinkling her eyes.

But his education had taught him not to allow self–pity. He got up
quickly, opened his suitcase and put his things away in the cupboard.
Among his shirts, he found the book that the chaplain gave him before
leaving: the *Life of Saint Francis of Assisi* by Jörgensen.

At nineteen years of age, Jean was confronted with solitude for the
first time in his life. It was winter. London was gray, cold, wet. At the
Polytechnic School, the classes were incomprehensible, and the students
seemed haughty, a bit condescending towards the little Belgian. He was
afraid of running out of money before the end of the semester and spent
as little as possible. Everything seemed expensive here. Often he went
without a noon meal, and not daring to let his classmates know the reason for this fasting, he avoided them. He felt poor and was ashamed of it.
He spent his free time walking around the city. Sometimes he took photographs: a rowing match on the Thames, horse guards, statues, monuments. There was no photo of him during these first months: whom could
he ask to take one?

His love of nature led him to the gardens. Soon he knew all the hidden corners of nearby Hyde Park. He fed the squirrels of Regent's Park
with the cookies from his desserts, explored Victoria Garden and Ken-
sington. At night, he forced himself to reread and understand his courses

by looking up in the dictionary the many words whose meaning eluded him. He thought a great deal. Until now, he had followed the way mapped out for him by his family. He had even thrown himself into a kind of extreme activism, as a real scout always ready to serve, to please, to rush ahead to bring back the pennant. Now, in the emptiness of this London winter, deprived of another person to whom he could talk, he found himself confronted with himself and taking stock of his existence. The book by Jörgensen touched him deeply. He recognized in Francis Bernardone the young man he had been the two last years in Brussels: he also was young, popular in his band of friends, promised to a good future as a comfortable merchant. Good looking, well dressed, he pleased the girls and enjoyed himself without holding back each time the opportunity arose. Is that the life he chose, the life he really wanted? He did not yet dare formulate the question in Francis' way: 'Is that what God is calling me to?' For many weeks, he turned these thoughts this way and that during his long walks. Did he speak of them in his letters to his mother or to Father Hemeleers? No trace of them has remained.

In the spring, his life changed considerably when in an inexpensive cafeteria where he sometimes had lunch, he met a young woman ten years older than he who introduced him to her family and group of friends. Her name was Amy Henn, and she would become Jean's lifelong friend. With her sister Ida and their friends Maurice and John (called 'Big John' to distinguish him from 'little John' Mahieu) they formed a happy band never at a loss for ideas: canoeing on the Serpentine, picnicking at Hampstead, exploring the zoo or the botanical gardens. During the Easter holidays, they went to the ocean at Torquay, Brighton, Southend. In Jean's photo album, many poses of smiling friends replaced the sculptures and palaces. He himself appeared, almost dandy, in three–piece suit and striped tie, legs apart, rounded torso. But his face was still a child's.

In July he returned to Belgium and spent his vacation at the seaside with his brothers and sisters. On 17 August he went to the military recruiting office in Schaerbeek, where he was declared 'apt to serve', and then he crossed the Channel again. But this time he was almost impatient to return to England, where his new friends awaited him. He was invited to spend a few days with the Henn family, who lived in a large house in Hampton Court. The excursions and parties started up again.

At the end of September, Jean returned to his classes in Polytechnic, where he was now much more at ease. His talents as a soccer player facilitated his integration, and his English improved. The first day of school, the autumn light was so beautiful that he decided to walk home through the park. At Knightsbridge, a gathering attracted his attention. He approached to see what was going on. Suddenly, a cry went through the crowd: 'There he is, that's him!'

The man Jean saw going down the steps of a Victorian building to get into a black limousine would profoundly influence the rest of his life. He was small, bald, thin, and tanned. He stopped a moment to look at the English through his little round iron–rimmed glasses, and he smiled. He was bare–chested, barefoot, and wore a white cotton loincloth. It was Gandhi.

Until December, the man the british newspapers called 'the half–naked fakir' would be the subject of many conversations in London. Spokesman for the indian party at the Round Table Congress organized to try to find a solution to the growing conflicts between England and her colony, he settled in a popular east end neighborhood, where he soon became the idol of the children, with whom he chatted in the streets. His secretary wrote, 'Thousands of children in England have seen Gandhi and, who knows? It is perhaps with their generation that we will be able to settle our lawsuits.'

Jean cut out from the newspapers all the articles about the man of non–violence. He was impressed by his way of presenting himself as poor, his indifference to the luxury and pomp of the empire, being admitted to His Majesty's receptions dressed as a pariah, an untouchable. When the young student returned to Belgium, he showed a growing interest for the country from which this extraordinary man, this 'great soul' came. In 1980, in Kandi, at the asian monastic meeting, Jean Mahieu, now Father Francis Acharya, would remember this meeting: 'For me, it was the victory of a man who incarnated poverty. It was the epiphany of a purely spiritual power and I dreamt of following the same path.'

IN THE 'SECOND LANCERS'

'Steady, Rintintin, steady, my boy.' In the stables of the squadron–school, Jean energetically rubbed down the steaming horse that snorted and wiggled its ears at the sound of his voice. He had just come back from the exercise course where he had performed flawlessly. 'Congratulations, Mahieu', had said the Sergeant Instructor, who usually was stingy with his praise. When Jean took his place at the edge of the track, he had time to see the admiring astonishment in the Sergeant's eyes.

When he had arrived, three months previously, he immediately had contact with the animal entrusted to him and gave himself completely to learning how to be a lancer. His sensuality, his daring, his build—1.63 meters (5 feet 4 inches) tall, weighing 65 kg (143 lbs)—and his liking for physical exploits served him well. He was among the best in the obstacle courses and dressage exercises that took place every morning at the nearby military training area. He was even prouder of this because, unlike most of his comrades, he had never ridden a horse before joining the army. It was his godmother who had organized everything once again: a major she knew interceded to have this young factory administrator admitted to this prestigious regiment, where generally only sons of wealthy upper class families were accepted.

On 25 July he joined his regiment of lancers at the barracks on General Jacques Boulevard in Etterbeek, for fourteen months of service. At the beginning, like so many recruits, he experienced military life as a parenthesis, an obligation to be accepted philosophically. But soon, perhaps because of Rintintin, he got hooked, and his success made him a candidate in the competition to choose reserve officers. If he had to participate in combat someday, he would prefer to be commanding. He remembered how he had admired his first scout leaders, young officers covered with decorations, heroes of the Great War. Or, more obscurely, did he still want to get even with his family, his brothers, his friends? He did not go to university, so be it, but he will impress them all as a captain in the lancers!

He obtained a mark of 14.85 in the theoretical exam, which placed him eighth out of one hundred. There were fifteen openings: he had every reason to believe that he would be chosen. The men were lined up in five rows, in impeccable uniforms. In front of the row of noncommissioned officers, the lieutenant read the names of the winning officers. Jean was not named. He did not understand. When he asked the sergeant for an explanation, he replied that there were really three marks: the exam, the horseback exercises, and the colonel's 'moral rating'. This mark was the decisive one. 'On what does he base this rating?' Jean asked. 'He has never seen me!' The sergeant replied, 'That doesn't matter: from your file, reports.' Jean objected, 'But I have never been punished, there is nothing bad in my file!' Again the sergeant replied, 'What do you know about that? You have never seen that file. In any case, the colonel gives his rating, he has his reasons and he is the boss.'

Jean was furious, bitter, at a loss. The world was unjust, the world's rules were rigged. He was only a little naïve scout, giving of himself with all his heart and all his strength. He had not yet grasped that the army had its own laws, that some names came before his own, that some fathers had more powerful connections than his godmother's major.

During the following weeks, he brooded on his distress, he lost his enthusiasm. At drill, distracted, he misjudged his distance and received a kick in the knee from the horse in front of him. For three weeks he was in the military hospital. There, one morning in March, he woke up at dawn. In the huge room lit by a night light, the others were still sleeping under their khaki blanket. In the top of the chestnut tree whose branches could be glimpsed behind the arched window, a single blackbird started to sing. Suddenly, as if a fraternal presence, as if his double, the image of Francis of Assisi came to his mind. He, similarly, had been immobilized in a sickroom for many long days after a military horseback escapade that had turned out badly. Jean smiled. In his spirit, little by little, he mulled over his life. The failures, dissatisfactions, and frustrations that he experienced were reverse signals, signs of a more absolute desire, a more radical quest. Women, money, popularity, diplomas, successes seemed to him to be trivial stakes compared to his thirst, compared to the strength he felt ready to deploy and place at the service . . . of what? of whom?

When Jean was discharged at the end of September 1933, he was certain of one thing: nothing that had been his life until then could fulfill his desire. He would seek the Completely Other One. Or is it the Completely Other One who chose him and called him?

THE ACCIDENT

The next winter an accident happened. It did not have great consequences, but it showed Jean's energetic character and his voluntarist and confident way of facing obstacles, the contrary forces that prevent him from continuing on his way.

After his military service, he resumed his activities: work in the factory, where he was more and more involved in management; sports; and family life. Fewer drinking parties; he gave scouting the best of himself.

He had just been named cub leader in the Federation of Catholic Scouts and participated in an *Akelas'* weekend in Liège. We have this account from his own mouth. The event left very clear memories:

> Our weekend ended around five o'clock in the afternoon. Baudouin Meeus, *Akela* of his parish troop, absolutely had to be at the New Year's Eve party with his pack. Happy to be of service, I took him in the Nash my father had lent me. About fifteen kilometers from Liège we skidded on ice and hit the shoulder of the railroad. The car bounced violently, turned completely around and landed on the other side of the road, with its two left wheels broken. Baudouin was anxious and panic-stricken. I entrusted him to a car that stopped to offer assistance. Left alone, I discovered that thankfully there were two spare tires. I replaced the rear one, but the jack was too short for the front one. I tried to force the bolts, the jack slipped and the car's front left side collapsed, tearing my left arm and almost cutting off the last phalanx of my ring finger. . . . Another car stopped: it was going to Liège and picked me up. We arrived around 11 PM, the parties were in full swing. Towards midnight, we were lucky to find a hospital still open. The surgeon cut the phalanx, pulled back the skin and sewed it on, bandaged my arm and hand. A mechanic I met in the waiting room took me on his motorcycle. He brought a good jack and together we replaced the second wheel. We parted, wishing each other 'Happy New Year!' and I went back to Brussels driving with one hand. At dawn on 1 January 1934, I put my father's car back in the garage.

Looking at his shortened left ring finger, he added, 'The surgeon had told me that the nail would not grow back. But you see: it grew back!'

THE DECISION

An adult now and freed from his military obligations, Jean was named acting administrator of the Union Factory. He was taking evening classes pursuing his third certificate in Business Sciences, when Pierre Vandemaele died of a heart attack. After Pierre's burial, the whole family went to 'Dudenia', the villa in Forest where Marthe would live alone with her mother. As often happens after the meal on the day of a funeral, with the help of good wine, the morning's long faces gave way little by little to animated conversations among cousins happy to see each other again.

Poor Marthe. She was still a child when she lost her father, her
   brother died young, and now her husband.
Luckily she has Jean!
Yes, he will keep the business going, that's for sure. He already
   has the necessary stature and authority.
He could even settle here: there is enough room for a family.
'Listen, he is only twenty–two! Let him live his bachelor life
   first!' Antoinette intervened.

Jean, at the other end of the table, guessed that they were talking about him. He remained silent. Euphrasie looked at him for a moment, with her piercing glance. Did the old lady guess something? But she turned, made a sign to the servant and told him quietly: 'You will serve coffee in the drawing room, with cigars.'

During the following months, Jean worked a lot, in a difficult context: he gathered his uncle's papers, examined them, made the urgent decisions. Marthe had never set foot in the factory. She was now the only proprietor, but it was her mother who intended to control everything, arguing her long experience in Ypres. As far as Euphrasie was concerned, her daughter did not understand anything about business, and Jean was much too young. Amid interminable discussions before every decision, he had to take his final exams. He passed and received his diploma in June.

At the end of July, the whole family gathered in Brussels again, but bright long dresses and pearl grey jackets replaced the black coats: Charles was getting married! The party was gay, the numerous cousins and friends joking, and the uncles singing. Antoinette recited the poem 'The Lion in Love'. 'And you, Jean,' his brother–in–law asked, 'now that you have a good job, when are you getting married? I suppose you have too much to choose from.' 'That is not part of my plans,' Jean answered. And after a silence, he continued, 'I am entering the Trappists.' 'The Trappists? As a monk? You mean in Orders?' All conversations stopped. Everyone turned towards him, astonished. One of the bride's uncles, a little drunk, teased him, crying to anyone and everyone: 'A good–looking boy like you would go and bury yourself in the cloister? You must be crazy! With the opportunities you have, all the money that is in store for you. . . .' Jean interrupted him dryly: 'Sir, you do not know what you are saying. Mind your own business.'

In the embarrassed silence that followed, the news circulated, murmured around the table, creating considerable surprise. Of all the young people, only Antoinette did not look astonished. Jean got up abruptly and went towards the garden, himself moved by the revelation of his secret. André caught up to him. 'Jean, are you serious?' 'I could not be more serious, little brother,' Jean replied. André persisted. 'When did you make this decision?' Jean paused before replying. 'It's hard to say. I did not really decide. It has been settling in me, little by little since London. On Hemeleers' advice, I went to visit the cistercian abbey of Scourmont, near Chimay. Last April, I spent a retreat week there. I talked to the master of novices. They accepted me. I even heard that the abbot is preparing a foundation in India. That would be my dream.' André continued to question Jean. 'What about the factory? And Aunt Marthe?' 'I can't stop thinking about that,' Jean admitted. 'That is not the easiest question. But I can't keep making boot hooks and zippers all my life because she is my godmother and she's a widow! No, you see, André, the factory never was my project. They placed me there when I was sixteen; I did not know what I wanted. Now, I know. As for the factory, someone else can do that.' André leaned forward and asked, 'Have you told Mom?' Jean smiled. 'She was the first to know. At least, the first in our family. I had talked about it to Hemeleers long before.' 'And what did she say?' André persisted. Jean smiled without answering. 'I am stupid,' said André; 'obviously, she is happy. That must have been her dream that one of us become a priest. So, a Trappist, of course!'

The warmth of that late afternoon attracted the wedding guests into the little enclosed garden with red rose border. Charles invited them to tour the house, where he had just opened his law office. Jean watched them come and go, laughing and drinking. They were his family, and he loved them. He was going to leave them, but he was happy. He would be in the world, but no longer of the world.

At first Marthe had to overcome a great discouragement. She felt abandoned again. But like the good Christian she was, in the end she accepted this vocation and even felt proud of it. To the priest, to her friends who asked her after Mass, 'How is your nephew?' she answered proudly:

'Did you not know? My nephew is entering La Trappe, the Cistercians of the Strict Observance.' Her friends were impressed, but they inquired, 'What will you do about the factory?' And Marthe would explain, 'I have another nephew, Paul, a civil engineer who is working in Spain. We will convince him to come back. Jean promised me that he would wait until we find someone to replace him. He does not want to leave me in the lurch. It will take a few months.'

THE TRIP TO THE ORIENT

The next spring, Jean found himself in strange company: in a linen suit and tie, with a pith helmet on his head, perched on a dromedary guided by a fellah in a burnoose, he was visiting the Great Pyramid of Giza. Aunt Marthe thought that, before shutting himself up in a monastery, he should see the world. 'I want to pay for a long trip,' she announced. 'Where would you like to go?' Without hesitation, Jean answered, 'To the Holy Land.'

They were on a cruise to the Near East, accompanied by a Benedictine from Ypres who knew these countries well. Father Chrysostome de Saegher was not a stranger. A friend of Aunt Marthe, he tried to recruit Jean for his order, inviting him to spend a week at Maredsous before deciding. In vain. Jean remembered having told his mother: 'It's not my style.' He wanted something more radical, more rugged. That did not prevent Father Chrysostome from taking him on the trip, and when they went to Rome, obtaining for him a private audience with the Pope and his blessing on this trappist vocation.

About thirty pilgrims gathered each morning on the deck of the Pierre Loti, to hear the Mass said by Monsignor Potard. In one of the drawing rooms each evening, the rosary was recited and Monsignor introduced the next step of the trip. There were many stops: Naples; Greece, where Daphni especially left a delightful impression on Jean; and Istanbul. They were sailing the Black Sea, where they glimpsed the russian coast. Jean met Françoise Courcoux among the group. The bishop of Orleans' niece, she was traveling with her mother and sister before entering the convent of the Little Sisters of the Assumption. Their similar plans brought the young people together, and they rapidly formed a friendship. Remembering that time, Françoise wrote to me much later:

One night, there was a little party on the ship and as I loved to dance, I invited Jean. 'No,' he said. And it was a staunch, energetic 'No'. I couldn't insist. He evinced a vocation already mature and strong. That impressed me a great deal. Jean was kind and pleasant with everyone. He was helpful but kept a certain solitude. He remained silent a long time looking at the ocean, so beautiful and majestic.

From Beirut the trip continued to Damascus by car, no doubt helping them to discover an Orient much more real than in books. They spent Palm Sunday in Jerusalem. In the Basilica of the Holy Sepulcher, among the crowd of pilgrims, Jean followed the holy week offices fervently. His soul, intoxicated with the incense and psalmody, exulted in the worship of God. Later, he would write to Françoise: 'In the West, we accentuate the passion and death of Christ. In Jerusalem, I was dazzled by the mystery of the resurrection.'

The last stage of the trip brought them to Cairo. He discovered the poor, the resourceful, ragged, happy, and talkative poor of the large cities in the south—a huge, bustling, organized poverty that had very little in common with the shame–filled, alcohol–drenched misery he saw in London. Poverty continued to question him, to haunt him. He would like to mingle with these people, to sit among them rather than drive in this honking taxi that brought him to the hotel.

'I will return,' he thought. He would indeed return, thirty years later, in pursuit of the seven–volume *Penqitho*, the voluminous treasury of choral prayers of the antiochan syriac tradition. With a Jesuit as guide, from Beirut to Damascus, from Jerusalem to Bagdad, he would find them at last in Mosul. But this, as Kipling says, is another story. Letting his godmother and her benedictine friend return to Belgium, Jean stopped in Paris to say goodbye to Antoinette, who was finishing her thesis at the Sorbonne. They spent three happy days talking about their plans, sharing their hopes, before separating for a very long time.

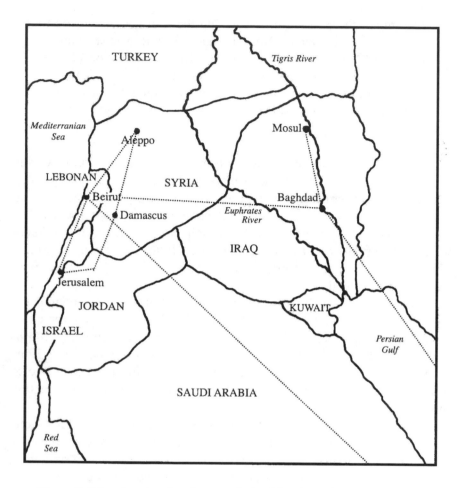

Figure 2. Map showing Jean's route during his trip to the Near East.

YOU SHALL LEAVE YOUR FATHER AND YOUR MOTHER

René still hoped, in the depths of his heart, that his son's monastic plans were not definitive. He thought it madness to prefer this imprisonment to such a promising career in industry. He did not understand. He felt rejected by his son. On François Degreef Street, the atmosphere was tense. Everyone avoided the subject for fear of an outburst. Jean had many details to settle before leaving: his successor with the scouts, commercial business with Aunt Marthe and his brother Paul, farewells to friends. When his father was absent, he discussed his vocation with his mother, what he perceived of Scourmont, his hope that he would go to India after his formation. Sometimes, alone in his childhood room, he went through moments of anguish. Leaving worldly life for the trappist monastery, 'I prepared myself in fear and trembling,' he told me one day.

When the day of departure approached, he decided to confront his father's disapproval. There were no outcries, no anger. René listened, then uttered this glacial, definitive sentence: 'If you do this, I disown you. I will never see you again.'

When Jean left the house, 14 September 1935, his father refused to say goodbye to him and went upstairs without saying a word. Anna bit her lip in Marthe's car on the trip to Chimay. Jean regretted his father's attitude, but his determination was not shaken. He was happy to start along the radical road of love of God and detachment he chose. The novice master was waiting for him. At Vespers, they celebrated the Feast of the Exaltation of the Holy Cross. Eight days later, his head was shaved, he received the white habit of a novice, and he was given the name of Brother Francis.

SECOND PART

TRAPPIST AT SCOURMONT AND CALDEY
(1935–1955)

TRAPPIST AT SCOURMONT
AND CALDEY

THE ABBEY OF OUR LADY OF SCOURMONT
AND DOM ANSELME LE BAIL

I N 1935, the Abbey of Our Lady of Scourmont was not yet one hundred years old. Founded in 1850 by a few Trappists from Saint-Sixte priory in West-Vleteren, near Poperinge, it experienced a difficult beginning on the marshy plateau offered by the Prince of Chimay. Auguste Malengreau, a nineteenth–century chronicler, wrote, 'Witnesses worthy of belief say that three farmers in succession had come to lose everything in this place of misery and desolation. Seven hectares of cleared land had been transformed into a very poor prairie that produced only reeds and moss. More than one peasant, seeing the religious with their hand tools working that earth, perhaps untilled since the creation of the world, did not believe they would succeed.'

The first years were heroic. The monks lived in a humid barn in Wayères and worked simultaneously on building the church, clearing the land, and collecting funds throughout Belgium and the neighboring countries. The beggars brought back more than money from their peregrinations: many postulants followed them, so much so that from the original seventeen members, the community grew to eighty monks in 1861. Ten years later, the Scourmont trappist monastery was raised to an abbey. It would extend its domain and consolidate both temporally and spiritually until the First World War.

In 1913, Dom Anselme Le Bail, who would later have a great influence on Jean, was elected abbot. He was only thirty–four years old. A native of Morbihan, with a degree in philosophy and letters, he entered Scourmont at the age of twenty–six, and within eight years rapidly was promoted to secretary, novice master, sub–prior, prior, and finally abbot. He was a cultured, very spiritual man, and at the beginning his severity was feared. In 1914 he was mobilized as an officer in the french reserve and sent to Compiègne as a military chaplain. The four years during which he was confronted with the terrible realities of the Great War were to change him profoundly. Demobilized in 1918, he returned unannounced to his abbey in his officer's uniform and toured the cloister incognito. No one recognized him! Dom Anselme returned to his abbatial duties with a series of reforms: a return to the original spirituality, deeper intellectual formation, and greater personal freedom within the community. Emphasis was placed on the interior life, on seeking God beyond the observances and the expiatory penance that had dominated cistercian culture during the nineteenth century.

The course of studies he developed included philosophy, history, and law. He increased the library considerably. At the end of his abbacy, it would include more than eighty thousand works. He also created an archive service. He built up a qualified corps of professors for the novitiate by sending several monks for diplomas at the Gregorian University. He even decided that all the novices who were capable would also go to Rome to study theology and philosophy after their first two years of monastic formation in the abbey, which was not the common usage at that time.

In the temporal order, he revealed himself to be an imaginative and prolific builder. Under his direction a scriptorium, guesthouse, and sepa-rate novitiate were built. The abbey was surrounded by a wall with turrets at its four corners; the main building's windows were framed with neo–gothic reliefs. From 1920 on he was seconded by another monk whose personality was exceptional: Dom Godefroid Belorgey. A former cavalry officer and veterinarian in the french army, Dom Belorgey converted and entered the Trappists against the advice of his family, which renounced him and considered him crazy. These two men soon gathered more than one hundred monks around them. Dom Anselme dreamed of a foundation in India. With this vision, in 1929 he accepted to take back the priory of the island of Caldey in Wales, where he settled a dozen of his monks. In the abbot's mind, since India at the time was a british colony, the welsh priory would serve as a forward base.

The great prestige and influence in all of northern Europe that Scourmont enjoyed at the time, brought it many vocations. In 1932, Dom Belorgey became the auxiliary abbot of Cîteaux. 'I have given you the best of my sons', wrote Dom Anselme to the Abbot General. He named Father Corneille Halflants prior and Father Albert Derzelle, who had a doctorate in theology, master of novices. Each in his own way, these three men were to have a profound influence on Jean, who was admitted to the novitiate under the name of Francis.

Father Corneille was an imposing man with a welcoming air and a liberal spirit. He was affectionate and sensitive, attracted by mysticism, and with a great knowledge of Saint Bernard. He spoke according to his heart and listened benevolently. Father Albert was more reserved. A certain physical fragility about his appearance struck one at first, but very quickly he revealed himself to be extremely generous. He was mild, but also a demanding idealist. Above all, he was an educator. His novices perceived that very quickly and all their life remained deeply grateful for this charism, conscious of the limitless devotion he manifested in his duty as novice master. As for Dom Anselme, his visionary side found an enthusiastic response in Francis. He quickly appreciated this energetic and very resourceful young man who was able to plan multiple projects and follow up on them. Besides this, the interest that the new recruit manifested for India gave the aging abbot the premonition that he had perhaps found in him the son who would give flesh to his old dream of a foundation in Asia.

Several caricatures and humorous notes witness to the bond that grew between Dom Anselme and Francis. Often after Compline, the abbot kept the novice in his office, asking his help to imagine constructions and make plans. One can guess the jealousy that insinuated itself into the soul of the other monks when, crossing the dark garden, they saw this little rectangle of light and the silhouettes of the two men discussing animatedly late into the night.

NOVITIATE

He was but a young man of twenty–two. What ardor! What impatience! What impetuosity of desire! This strength, this vigor, this boiling hot blood, like misty wine, does not allow him to be stale or moderate.

(Bossuet, *Panégyrique de saint Bernard*)

November 1935. Two o'clock AM. The bell rang, muted by the fog. The nine novices were sleeping fully dressed, their blankets drawn up to their eyes. They got up noiselessly, put on their socks and their boots, and one by one sprinkled cold water on their faces at the sink near the door. No need for a comb; their heads were shaved.

The master of novices lived with them in this rectangular cinderblock building, built in a few weeks the preceding year at the abbot's initiative and furnished by the novices themselves: a dozen pallets with straw mattresses, a large table, a few chairs, and a coal stove that was lit only in winter. This *sancta simplicitas*, dear to Saint Bernard, suited Francis perfectly. The uncomfortable dormitory made him as happy as did the frugality of the strictly vegetarian meals. That was what he was seeking. 'For him, the harder the better!' said his friends.

In single file and always in silence, the novices crossed their garden where the leeks awaited harvesting and a few chrysanthemums were still blooming. As he often did when he went outside at night, Francis raised his eyes and tried to identify one or another constellation, to find the planets, remembering the long dialogue where Job, exasperated, harangues his creator and hears himself respond, 'Who is this that obscures divine plans with words of ignorance? . . . Have you fitted a curb to the Pleiades, or loosened the bonds of Orion? Can you bring forth Morning Star in its season, or guide the Great Bear with its train?' (Job 38:2, 31–32).

Each novice put on his cape of ecru wool, pulled back his hood, and took his place in the choir where the professed monks awaited. In the bare white church, with few lights, everyone prostrated and in the night, the modulations of gregorian chant rose from fifty men's voices.

Here Francis was like a fish in water. In a few months, Scourmont became his home, the brothers his family, Dom Anselme his father, and Father Albert his teacher. A little before Christmas, around five o'clock in the afternoon, on a day when the weather was horrible, he was reading in the scriptorium. A brother came to get him. 'Your father is at the gatehouse, asking for you.' Intrigued, vaguely worried, Jean went there and found René soaking wet. René embraced him and nonchalantly said, 'I was in the neighborhood, I missed the bus, so I thought you could maybe give me shelter here'. Few words were exchanged, and no one ever knew what had caused René to change his mind. We can guess that Anna worked patiently at this reconciliation while allowing her husband to save face. Whatever the cause, this visit was followed by many others.

During the two years that followed, Francis applied himself to liturgical chant, communal prayer six hours per day, and silent prayer with equal fervor. He worked in the bakery and each week baked three or four batches of more than one hundred loaves of bread. He prepared the dough leavened with yeast, shaped it in the pans, and put them in the wood stove at the appropriate time.

He was enthusiastic about the program of studies: christian spirituality, liturgy, rule, customs, Holy Scripture (especially the Gospel of John, which he would always prefer), and monastic history (with a leaning towards the eastern Fathers). The three hours of *lectio divina* went by too quickly. 'It is in the Scourmont novitiate', he confided much later, 'that I really learned to read, to appropriate the masters' thought as my own through reading, comparing, and writing syntheses. There in the silence I developed a taste for intellectual work. I even remember', he added with a grain of malice, 'that the novice master showed us how to turn the pages of books without harming them and without making noise'. His teaching was centered on Saint Benedict and his Rule of life. This Rule is presented modestly even by its author as a 'handbook for beginners', but for one thousand years it has established itself among all the monks of the West who, in this century, introduced it to the four corners of the earth. In fact, it offers a remarkable environment for 'ascetics living in community, under a rule and an abbot'. It is recommended as a 'school of the Lord's service'. It trains young people on the paths of the Gospel, on the roads that Christ himself traced for his disciples to lead them to 'the beatific vision'. It initiates them to a life of asceticism and prayer in communion with the Church and also imposes thoughtful duties towards those whose life they share. Finally, in its epilogue, it exhorts to the highest aspirations, nourished by the reading of Holy Scripture, the Fathers of the Church, and the sayings and lives of the Desert Fathers.

Francis would often quote a few sayings of one of them, Evagrius Ponticus, rediscovered and rehabilitated this century as an authentic spiritual master:

The monk is one who is separated from all
but in communion with all

The monk is one who is united with all
because he sees himself constantly in each

If you are a theologian, you will truly pray
If you truly pray, you are a theologian[1]

For Evagrius, the theologian is one who, after being purified interiorly, surpasses contemplation of beings to contemplate God.

But the course that caused Francis the most enthusiasm and that he was to recall with emotion a long time afterwards was the course on Saint Bernard. He recalled it in a letter written in 1996:

Every Monday morning, our prior came to the novitiate for a commentated reading of Saint Bernard's works, read in Latin. First, the treatise on the *Steps of Humility and Pride*, where the young abbot of Clairvaux commented for his monks on the famous chapter seven of the Benedictine Rule leading to the free-dom of the spirit. The twelve degrees are restructured by Bernard into a triple seeking of truth: truth about oneself leading to humility, truth about one's neighbor, awakening compassion, truth in itself leading to God, known only by those who approach him with a pure heart. 'Blessed are the pure of heart for they shall see God' (Mt 5:9). The treatise *On the Love of God* followed, with its three degrees: of the servant who loves his master, in view of the salary that awaits him; of the son who loves his father but also hopes for his inheritance; and finally of the bride which is pure gift to the bridegroom.

---

[1] *Chapters on Prayer*, 124, 125, 60, in *Evagrius Ponticus: Praktikos and Chapters on Prayer*, pp. 76, 65.

But of Saint Bernard's works, the one Francis found most charming was his *Sermons on the Song of Songs*, eighty–six sermons given by the prestigious abbot to his monks during some twenty–five years of an other-wise very eventful monastic life. He comments on these biblical wisdom poems, which sing of the mutual love of a Beloved and her Lord, their encounters, separations, seeking, and union. The conclusion comes to us from the Beloved's mouth, revealing the nature and ardor of her love:

Set me as a seal on your heart,
as a seal on your arm;
for stern as death is love,
relentless as the nether world is devotion;
its flames are a blazing fire.
Deep waters cannot quench love,
nor floods sweep it away.

(Song of Songs 8:6–7)

'It's beautiful!' he wrote at that time in large letters under his notes. One senses that the very restrictive behavioral drill that the cistercian noviti-ate was for these young people was brightened and illuminated from within by sensual metaphors, effusive and powerful mysticism, the joy of a loving encounter of the soul with God where their masters lead them, following Saint Bernard:

I let myself be carried by desire, not by reason (*desiderio feror, non ratione*). I beg you, do not accuse me of boldness, as long as passion drives me (*ubi affectio urget*). Of course, modesty ex-claims, but love triumphs. . . . I ask, I beg, I entreat, 'let him kiss me with a kiss of his mouth.' For many years, for his sake, I make myself live in chastity and sobriety; I continue in reading, I resist vices, I apply myself diligently to prayer, I keep watch against temptations, I think over my past life in the bitterness of my soul. I believe that I do not seek conflict in my conduct with my brothers, insofar as I can; I am subject to my superiors, com-ing and going at the elders' orders. I do not covet the goods of others, on the contrary I have given mine and I give of myself. By the sweat of my brow I eat my bread, but in all that, there is nothing but routine, nothing that is consolation.

(Sermon 9.2)

No one could deny the spiritual as well as the literary grandeur of this passage. The subject who speaks is at the same time the spouse of the Song of Songs, an anonymous monk, Saint Bernard himself, and every attentive reader. This message contains the admission of a burning desire, a passion exacerbated because it is insatiable:

> There are not many authors who dare to say that an exemplary ascetic life is not sufficient to lead a truly spiritual life. We can keep all the commandments and still barely survive on a land without water. This desert can be irrigated only by the desire for God, seeking his presence, a passion that expresses itself in sentiments of protestation and thanksgiving. The truly spiritual soul is led by desire and not by reason. Reason lets itself be tempered by prudence and reined in by modesty. It considers the King's majesty rather than the Spouse's benevolence. It thinks that it is better to adore the Father in heaven than to embrace the incarnate Word. Reason has more sobriety but love has more beatitude.
>
> (Verdeyen and Fassetta, *Sermons sur le Cantique*,
> vol. 1 [Sources chrétiennes, no. 414], pp. 36–37)

Obviously, Jean encountered obstacles in seeking the 'perfect life'. They did not come from austerity or fasting, or tiredness from the long night vigils, or from concentration in prayer. They were rather found in obedience and humility. He recognized this in a letter written from Rome to Father Corneille in 1938: 'Please pray for me, dear Father Prior, to obtain for me a little humility. I notice every day that this is what I lack most. . . . Christ would need to come at Christmas and tear me away from myself to drag me after him, because my powerlessness is truly evident to me.' During his entire lifetime, he would have to rein in his tendency to be the best, to be the leader, to glory in his successes, even successes in devotion or piety.

But the three who guided him were men of quality who knew how to form him to an authentic spiritual life, turning his willful and dominating character to good account without breaking it. All three loved him as a son and even, some murmur, as the favorite son in whom great hope was placed.

After Francis had become Acharya, he summed up his first years of monastic life in these words: 'At Scourmont I was a very happy novice.' Happy people do not have a history or stories, it is said. In fact, there are very few written traces of this period: three letters addressed to Father Albert from the Bourg-Léopold military camp in 1937; the comments written in ink in the margins of his course on the Song of Songs; and the annotations in the *Novum Testamentum graece et latinae* given to him and inscribed by the novice master (*ad usum f. M. Francisci, per ducatum Evangelii pergamus itinera Eius*). The underlined passages are found in the greek text, which he preferred to the Latin because they were closer to the original.

The few extracts reproduced here reflect his state of mind, the personal accents that he introduced into this monastic language where French and church Latin were intermingled and into which he rapidly immersed himself. On the endpaper of his copy of the Gospels he recorded, 'From one end to the other, the Gospel is a call to liberality. It is the handbook of free men, free creatures and liberal creatures, that is to say, everything is about love.' About Saint John the Baptist he noted, 'Joy—Austerity—Holiness—Energy'. Luke's reflection (Lk 4:24–27) on the help given by Elijah to the widow of Zarephath in pagan territory at a time of famine and the healing of Naaman the Syrian by Elisha when there were many lepers in Israel, was interpreted in a very personal way: 'Terrible lesson for the privileged souls who might let themselves be invaded by lukewarmness or indifference.' Beside the 'The Son of Man did not come to earth to be served but to serve', in red capitals, he wrote the scouting motto: 'Serve'. In the margin of his course on Saint Bernard there appears: *Non est quo immiscat vanitas, ubi totam occupat charitas* [Vanity finds no place where love occupies all the place] and, further on: 'Reread XIX, 7, advice to novices full of natural ardor':

> But this spiritual doctrine. . . judges this indiscreet vehemence which I have had to repress in you more than once, and which is much more an opinionated intemperance. You do not want to be content with the common life. Nothing is enough for you, the fasting called for in the Rule, the ritual vigils, the imposed discipline and the prescribed moderation in clothing and food. You prefer your own austerities to those of our Rule. Since you have entrusted your life to us, why are you meddling in governing yourself ?
>
> (*Sermons on the Song of Songs*, 19.7)

A MILITARY INTERLUDE

While the monastic life was following its serene course at Scourmont, the political situation in Europe was deteriorating. At the end of the 1930s, governments worried about Hitler's military parades and the rise of Nazism. The belgian state decided to organize exceptional maneuvers in Bourg-Léopold and to experiment there on a war footing with newly acquired weapons. In March 1937, Brother Francis was called back to serve for two weeks, with the entire 'class of 32' and the two classes currently serving. There as elsewhere, he would give free rein to his 'natural ardor'.

His superiors allowed him to spend Sunday night with his parents, who had just moved to a smaller house after André's marriage and Antoinette's departure for Brazil. One can imagine his mother's happiness, organizing a big family reunion with his brothers and sisters and five little nephews.

'Great excitement . . . an excellent evening', he wrote to Scourmont. But he seemed not to have any nostalgia: 'I HAD to pay a visit before reaching home.' No doubt the family was proud to show the cousins and Aunt Marthe 'our Trappist', as he was now called by the family. With kindness, he went along with this, but it seems that it was the others who considered this a notable event.

He disembarked Monday noon at the Bourg-Léopold military camp. The very next day he told Father Albert: 'There were trains from every station in Belgium, so their arrival was a great scramble, all the more so since the troops on horseback, motorcycle, half–track or tractor were arriving at the same time. There are still beds, mattresses and blankets missing. There were interminable exchanges to find equipment the right size for everyone, and to form combat groups. Later we will go get our horses and weapons.' As soon as he could, he went to the chaplaincy, found a fellow Trappist, Father Vincent Delférière, and fraternized with the chaplain. It was the end of Lent, the week before Palm Sunday. Francis tried to maintain a minimum of monastic life and reported to his novice master: 'I will be able to attend the first Mass regularly. Maybe I will also be able to do some reading, but the better part of the day I will have to be content with yearning for Scourmont, as the deer longs for running streams' (*sicut desiderat cervus ad fontes aquarum*).

A few days later, he seemed to find pleasure in the military and sporting events, which he described in a second letter:

Our group of lancers, in a defensive position in the fir plantation, was attacked twice. The first time was on horseback, which we easily repelled, the second came from armored cars, to which we opposed the new canons 4.7. The result was the same because they did not succeed in dislodging us from our positions. It was a triumph! The king with his staff was at the top of a dune dominating the whole plain. We could see him following the maneuver with the greatest interest. They say he left very satisfied.

Between two rounds, our gunner Francis did not fail to contemplate nature and marvel at it, because he added, 'We were flooded with sunshine and penetrated by the strong vapors rising from the heather.' What he did not write, no doubt because he wanted to keep it a surprise, was that during the steeplechase that ended the cavalry exercises, dashing off and clearing all the obstacles, he took first place. On his return he gave the abbot the cup of golden metal that he received. Dom Anselme kept it in his office for a long time.

Saturday afternoon during a few hours leave he went to Brussels with Father Vincent, to attend a matinee performance of Paul Claudel's play 'The Tidings Brought to Mary', from which the novice master had read excerpts to his novices. The two friends were enthusiastic about Claudel's text, remarking, 'It was a four hour long meditation'.

The second week was less exciting. It rained, and the exercises of 'terrain organization' were fastidious. It was Holy Week, and the young monk missed liturgy in common. 'Sometimes, I recite an hour of the office. I read the Nocturns. Often there are a few minutes during the marches or the exercises, to recollect myself and that does me immense good, like a drop of living water that comes to me from Scourmont and quenches my thirst in my desert.'

Francis measured the distance between him and most of his comrades and was moved by their existential void. 'Have a prayer for all those here, please', he wrote. 'There are so many who are hardening themselves in a very miserable situation.' On Holy Thursday he received a letter from Father Albert and despite his imminent return, immediately responded. In this letter he expressed his affection for his new family, using bernardian metaphors such as 'precious perfume' and 'treasure chest': 'I opened your letter as one opens a flask of precious perfume, because I did not want to lose any. You cannot imagine what pleasure that can cause. . . .

Yes, perhaps in thinking that I received it as a treasure chest containing the most charming souvenirs of the house'. He signed the letter, 'Your very affectionate son'.

The last days dragged, as there were not many exercises. Francis passed the greater part of his time at the chaplaincy, where he found old friends and made new ones. One night, he walked with a seminarian by the light of the moon and taught him to recognize the constellations. Finally on Saturday he was liberated: he returned to Brussels by motorcycle to get there faster and arrived at Scourmont for the Easter vigil.

ORA ET LABORA

The sun was already high in the sky when the nine novices climbed up on the wagon with side rails, dragged by two huge horses from the Ardennes with their slow steps towards the pastures where hay, mown the previous day, was drying. Brother Noel, standing on the shaft, drove the horses. No one spoke. And until the bell for Sext, Francis, perched on the sweet–smelling bales that he was rapidly piling up, climbed ever higher, his work robe tied back by cords around his stockings. When the work required some communication, they did so by signs in the silent cistercian language. Of course, for each of the newcomers, they invented a sign to serve as his proper name. For Francis, it was the scout salute.

At noon, they returned on foot, in indian file, one behind the other, each with a wooden rake on his left shoulder. Sext, meal, siesta; the exhausted young men who had been up since two AM did not need any urging to take a nap. After the brief office of None, they went back to put the wagon's contents into the hayloft, amid a cloud of golden dust, in the stifling heat of the loft. Euphoria seized them, making their eyes shine when they signed to each other: 'Let's go!' Because of this fraternity of manual labor, the scent of the warm grass, the task, the work . . . they brought in all the hay before the storm. A short break gathered them at snack time, around the honey rye bread the cellarer brought them in a wicker basket. A few big pitchers of the light beer brewed by the abbey refreshed their dry throats.

In summer, agricultural work dominated the novices' schedule: no reading, no classes, no housework. Their diet was augmented by a little butter and cheese. But prayer, day and night, unfolded its sacred chant, the unceasing 'work of God', which takes precedence over everything else.

A few times each year, during the summer, Francis and the other novices were allowed to receive a visit from family. Those Sundays were the best days of the whole year for his mother. One or another of her sons drove her in his car, and she would be in her glory when Jean guided everyone through the fields along the river. Photographs were taken. Women could go only to the parlor and the guesthouse refectory, not the church. When they stayed overnight, it was at the edge of the property, in a small house called Bethany.

In July, the cubs and scouts put up their tents and their flags in the meadows. The novices took advantage of this to play football and leap-frog. For Francis, it was a joy to see his friends again, to see his little cubs grow, to attend their promises and sing his repertory of rounds and sacred songs, marching songs, and campfire songs in a loud voice.

That fall, on 3 October, he made his simple vows with Maur Standaert, who entered the monastery the same day. Prostrate in the choir, surrounded by his brothers, he answered the questions his abbot posed in Latin:

> Brother Francis, what do you ask?
> The mercy of God and of the Order.
> Rise, in the name of the Lord. Do you wish to persevere in your
>   vocation?
> Yes, Reverend Father, with God's grace. I promise you and all
>   your legitimate successors, obedience according to the Rule
>   of Saint Benedict in accordance with canon law.
> May God grant you eternal life.

The abbot blessed his son and embraced him. The latter went towards the little table that held the schedule of his vows he had carefully written by hand the previous day. He read it out loud and signed it under the eyes of the community. In it he made vows of obedience, stability, and conversion of manners, which meant that he committed himself to a continuous trans-formation of his soul, in a total abandonment of his own will to God's will. On this occasion, exceptionally, the family was allowed to attend the ceremony from the tribune. Anna squeezed Marie-Thérèse's arm. Neither of them held back their tears.

At chapter that evening, Dom Anselme gave a talk in which he revealed his freedom of thought and the modernity of his pedagogy. In fact, this homily was his response to a letter that Francis and Maur had addressed to him a few weeks earlier. Torn between Father Albert's approach, centered on the Rule, and Father Corneille's, centered on the Spirit, they felt a little ill at ease and asked him to enlighten them, to be a mediator for their interior conflict. Through the abbot's response, we can see the trace of his personal experience during the war. We can also see a sort of premonition of Francis' destiny, of his uncommon vocation. We reproduce the beginning of this text, written down on the fly, copied and kept at Scourmont.

(Notes taken during Dom Anselme Le Bail's talk for the simple profession of our brothers Maur Standaert and Francis Mahieu, 3 October 1937)

Saint Bernard had to adjudicate this controversy, namely, which monk is the most observant of the Rule. The question is not only applicable to Bernard's time, it is valid in every time, because it touches what is properly human. It is the question of knowing whether the body forms and rules the spirit, or rather the spirit rules and informs the body. Let us note that the question is not about the respective dignity of the body and the spirit, but it consists in knowing what should prevail in the formation of man, exterior discipline or discipline of the spirit.

Discipline is made up of palpable things: rules, observances, environment, behavior, which all contribute to forming the soul. Should it come first in education, or is it the spirit that should form the body in its image? If the spirit is good, will it lead the body?

This question will always be controversial. It was already posed at the time of Our Lord Jesus Christ. Is it the Law that makes a man just, or the spirit?

For the first monks, our eastern Fathers, the first opinion was by far the most important. The best monk was the one who held perfectly to the letter of the observances, who broke the records of fasting and mortification.

Saint Benedict answers rather by the second opinion: to temper austerity, exterior discipline to put the soul at ease, not to crush it, to give it freedom of spirit.

The following winter, Francis, wearing his black woolen cloak, walked up and down on the platform of the train station to warm up. The train from Brussels stopped, and a frail young man with dark skin got off: an Indian from Pondicherry coming to join the Scourmont novitiate. The novice master, knowing Francis' interest in all that came from India, sent him to Chimay to fetch this strange postulant. The boy had never seen snow! For a first experience, he was well served. The snow was at least thirty centimeters deep along the entire five kilometers of woods that separated the last houses of Chimay from the Poteaupré hill. He hid his hands in his sleeves and opened his eyes very wide! Let us bet that along the way Francis could not resist asking him about his country, his life. Does the rule of silence apply in such unusual circumstances?

Antoine Tamby was not as young as his slenderness and smooth face indicated. He was already over thirty years old. Born in Saigon of french–speaking Tamil parents, he received a christian education in French at Pondicherry, a french concession in southern India. He began to study medicine before entering the Company of Jesus, which he left after two years to enter the diocesan seminary, where he studied theology and was ordained a priest. An admirer of monastic life, he wished to see it established in his country and decided to devote himself to this mission. This is why he entered the cistercian monastery of El Latroun in Palestine, but, having heard that the abbot of Scourmont was preparing a foundation in India, he obtained permission to go to Scourmont to finish his novitiate there. He would make temporary vows at Scourmont in 1940, but would not see the realization of his desire: of fragile constitution, he endured the harsh climate of the Ardennes with great difficulty. He fell ill and was sent to Aiguebelle, where despite the Provençal sun, he died in 1943.

His funeral talk given by Dom Anselme at Scourmont, ended with these words: 'It is certain that his death was offered for the great idea that inspired his whole life, that is, the establishment of the contemplative life in India. If this work is to be realized, the sacrifice of his life will have played its part.'

STUDENT IN ROME

At the end of October 1938, eight monks in temporary vows got on a train at Hirson, the french station near Scourmont, bound for Rome to study theology. When he gave them his blessing, Dom Anselme told them to come back the following summer with results that would make the community proud.

After two years of novitiate and one year of philosophy apart from the world, the trip itself was quite an adventure! At the end of the afternoon, having changed trains several times, they arrived in Frontenex in Haute-Savoie. They would spend the night at Tamié Abbey. The cellarer awaited them, driving a pickup truck. The ascent was heroic, according to Brother Francis' account in a letter to his abbot:

> It had snowed that morning, and it started to snow again as soon as we started up. Father Guerric was settled comfortably in front near the driver [sitting, he said later, in a puddle of water], while we seven were standing up in the truck amid the suitcases and improvised seats, hanging on to the wood of the carriage and bent over under the snow that fell on us in avalanches. On this zigzag road, which goes from one hundred fifty to nine hundred meters elevation on a stretch of a dozen kilometers, it was quite something. From time to time, we did not succeed in bending over soon enough, and pine branches and apple branches full of fruits and snow hit us in the face at the speed of the truck. With all that came down from the sky, it was really a lot and many of us arrived at the abbey with snow all down our necks and hoods. Father Gall, very distressed by this little game, but always very valiant, had finally put his glasses down at the bottom of the truck and his face was dripping with water but full of joy.

Tamié Abbey seemed austere to them, a little somber, 'less joyous than Scourmont'. The wild site, surrounded by mountains and forests, 'makes us forget the flowers in our gardens'. The travelers attended Vespers and Compline, and even the Night Office on Sunday morning. Francis was a little distracted from his prayer because his eyes and ears were keen to compare the performance of Tamié with Scourmont: 'In the church, the dove is suspended a little high. The voices are no better than Scourmont, but there is more unity despite the rapidity and a higher tone.' After the *frustulum* of bread and black coffee according to the Rule, the group left again before daybreak, with two young confrères from Tamié added to their number. They were ten boarding the train for Turin. After

Mont Cenis, on the italian side of the Alps, the sun welcomed them and did not leave them. The transfers were not ideal; they traveled all night and arrived in Florence at dawn the next day. They began by going into the famous *duomo*; Mass was in progress, with 'two monsignori and three canons singing the office with ardor'. A contrast, no doubt, to cistercian simplicity? We shall see that at the Vatican, they would be drawn to other splendors that they would not disdain. The train for Rome did not leave until 4 o'clock, and they used the time to visit a few convents, of which Francis left a colorful description:

> This allows us to pass a few hours contemplating the canvasses of Fra Angelico in Saint Mark. The miniatures are truly unique. We discovered an exquisite Annunciation and also his large crucifixion where he represents all the great founders of orders at the foot of the cross: Saint Benedict, Saint Bernard, Saint Francis—which is lovely—Saint Dominic, and others. At noon we left for Fiesole to contemplate the panorama and the city stretching along the Arno, and there we had one of the most beautiful impressions of our trip. All the little florentine convents are so pretty with their roofs of round tiles, their open bell towers, their vines and olive trees, but none is more welcoming than the convent of Saint Bernardine of Siena at the very top of the mountain. There we were received with enthusiasm by a very tiny Franciscan who ran in front of us and showed us every corner. They were all charming: the XIVth–century cells with their little window on the valley, a few planks for a bed, a kneeler, a few old devotional books or antiphonaries, the lovely little cloisters. You have no idea of the beautiful things they were able to do with almost nothing: wooden ceilings, round tiles, a few very simple little columns, an old well.

In Tuscany, where his dear Saint Francis had traveled and which had not changed since then, Francis was moved by the alliance of great simplicity and a search for the beautiful, by the naturally beautiful landscapes, patiently embellished by flowers and cultivation. Everything is there: the river and mountains, vines, olive trees, simple and beautiful objects made with little cost, seeking God in joyous vitality.

Now after three days of wandering around, it was time to go to the Order's Generalate, on the Aventine, which gathered in a sort of temporary community all the Cistercians from Europe and America (at that time, there were none in Asia or Africa) who were studying in Rome. Father Anthony Daly, from Roscrea in Ireland, who welcomed them would be their 'student master'. The very next day, while Theodore brought Francis to buy the famous conical black hats that all the students attending the Gregorian had to wear, Guerric and Gall went to get the schedule of courses. As his choices, Francis selected Hebrew, which he immediately began to study on his own, and 'Introduction to the Mystical Body', given by Father Tromp. On Saturday morning, classes began with the *lectio brevis* and Mass of the Holy Spirit. Francis was impressed:

> One feels very small in the midst of this mass of students from all different countries. All the groups from Germany, England, Scotland, France, the United States, Spain, Latin America, youthful and lively. One is happy to belong to a family that manifests such vitality and which inspires such great hope. That was clear when we left the Gregorian en masse to go to Saint Ignatius for Mass sung by the whole assembly of about two thousand five hundred people. The voices were so strong that at certain moments the huge building felt shaken by them.

After a few weeks, this enthusiasm of a 'jamboree' was shaken. The constant exercise of conversations in Latin (the compulsory language of the students among themselves) was more painful than he imagined. He was more attracted by the Italian that he heard in the street. The courses were disconcerting to him: the subject matter was not defined, the expectations not precise, the professors not all equally good. One day, when with great effort he had prepared a whole chapter in advance, the professor simply skipped over it and went on. He was very disappointed. His Hebrew professor, Father Galdos, had expectations that seemed impossible to him, and he gave up writing that exam. Later, he would discover that there were ways to obtain dispensations, but all that had not been explained clearly. He missed the ambiance of Scourmont. Here the offices were said as quickly as possible; studying was the priority. Here he found nothing of the monastic teaching from master to disciple that he loved. In his letters, he evoked this with nostalgia:

Here, there are no chapter talks about Aelred, Isaac of Stella, Baldwin of Ford and the others. . . . No more Sunday sermons about self–governance, no more Saint Bernard, but always definitions, *prenotanda, distinguo,* and *subdistinguo, argumenta*. . . . Saint Thomas Aquinas's *Summa* itself appears to me now to be a juicy fruit compared to these treatises on supernatural criteriology or the examination of liberal and modernistic theses in the *De Ecclesia.* I am a little like the soldier who has to remain on the front line of the battle with only dry biscuits for food!

He seems almost angry, but remembering his vow of obedience, he adds immediately: 'Do not believe, Reverend Father, that I am complaining. I am ready to eat dry biscuits for as long as you wish and rather I thank you for allowing me to see all that I encounter here.'

There were also good moments: Father Rosadini, 'whose Latin is so well accented that we think he is singing'; the 'Moral Theology' course with Father Hürth; Father Tromp's course on 'The Church as Mystical Body of Christ'; the beauty of the eternal city whose secrets Father Gall, very keen on archeology, disclosed to them; playing volleyball on the terrace; and, especially, the friendship of his companions. The approach of Christmas revived Francis' frustration. On December 19, he wrote to Father Corneille:

Advent was spent distinguishing the act of scientific faith from the act of divine faith, and analyzing the theories of Sabatier, Harnack, Goguel, and a few others! And Saturday it will be Christmas! . . . I remember now, when you were sick and I went to see you in that little room lost under the roof of the infirmary, I had understood all of a sudden that Christmas is truly an incomparable mystery, when you quoted the beautiful sermon of Saint Bernard for Christmas vigil: *Sonet vox laetitiae in cordibus nostris* [Let the sounds of gladness ring in our hearts]. Thank you for all that. These memories help me to get through these programs for which I am discovering that I do not have much disposition.

During the second trimester, Francis regretted even more not being in Scourmont, as Father Jules Monchanin, leaving for India, went to give a conference to the community. 'What bad luck!' he wrote. 'I will pray for him and for India.' What he did not yet know was that Dom Anselme had spoken at length with Monchanin privately, he had invited Father Albert to join their talk, and that it had been agreed that Albert Derzelle would join Monchanin in Tamil Nadu the following year, after six months of Sanskrit in Paris, to help prepare a monastic foundation. Did Anselme judge that Francis was still too young? Was he thinking of him to join the team later, when he had finished his studies? We will never know, because the war turned these projects upside down.

In the meantime, in the month of March 1939, Rome was at the center of the news: Pope Pius XI died suddenly, Cardinal Pacelli was elected after three days of conclave and took the name of Pius XII. Long live Pius XII! Rome was effervescent, and this fever spread to the Generalate. On the day of his coronation, the young Cistercians left their house in the middle of the night. They walked along the Tiber. Every bridge was guarded by groups of 'blackshirts'. Further, the roads were blocked, reserved for the official procession. Francis and Theodore left the group that hesitated and, lifting up their robes with both hands, ran in the darkness through a maze of narrow streets, coming out under the colonnade of Saint Peter's Square. Francis later wrote, 'The sky is reddening but Venus remains suspended over the river'. On the immense square, the compact silent crowd waited. Finally at six o'clock, the doors opened and it was another rush that led the two friends into the center nave, against the railings that contained the audience. The sumptuous procession would arrive at 9 o'clock. The next day, a dazzled Francis sent his Father Prior six pages:

> How could I delay any longer to communicate the fervor, admiration and joy that fill me all these days. Yesterday, I experienced one of the most glorious days I will see for a long time. I have the impression of turning a momentous page in history and I feel like the explorer who has just returned from a trip where he made great discoveries, and to whom all things now seem renewed.

After a long description of the ceremonies, homilies, songs, blessings, and the procession, he concluded, 'When this morning I found myself once again studying *De Ecclesia*, I asked myself, why all these laborious analyses and arguments? Aren't the Church's heartbeats more luminous and convincing than an erudite description?'

In July, after having passed the first year exams—a postcard sent to Scourmont detailed the marks received by the 'Romans' in the various subjects—Francis returned to Belgium alone. He finished his exams later than the others by the luck of the draw, and with Father Prior's permission, he went by way of Switzerland to visit his former teacher, Etienne Hemeleers, who had been hospitalized for three months in a sanatorium in Montana. He got off the train at Assisi, not able to resist visiting the places where the Poverello had lived. Before returning to his abbey, he visited his family: a trip to Gand, where Marie-Thérèse's three little girls climbed on his lap; an evening in André's young household; and especially a few hours with his mother, who was having trouble getting used to living without her children. For her, the all–too–rare meetings with Jean were a true feast. To be closer to him in thought, she started to say the cistercian breviary, and planned to become an oblate, if René accepted. She spent several retreat days at Scourmont at Easter with Amy Henn, who came to spend her vacation with the family of 'little John', who had become 'Brother John'.

Francis returned to Scourmont at the end of July. The newly mown meadows were fragrant under the sun, the garden was full of flowers, and his heart dilated, singing with his brothers in the big white church. He was very glad to be back with his three spiritual fathers. But the joy of this return was soon tempered by rumors of war. Dom Anselme sent Francis and Theodore back to Rome a little earlier than anticipated. This was a good thing, because a few days after their departure, twenty–four monks, including Corneille, Maur, and Guerric, were mobilized. Legally residing in a foreign country, Francis escaped the 'strange war', and with determination he attacked his second year of theology. As had been his experience in London, the second year was less difficult. He was no longer a greenhorn; he had adapted. To tell the truth, the general situation in Europe and the arrogant fascism that he witnessed every day in Italy preoccupied him more than his courses. He worried about his mobilized brothers. In January 1940, he learned that Guerric might be demobilized very shortly. At once he tried to find the dispensations that might allow his friend to finish his fourth year in one semester. But he waited for him in vain: a swollen knee prevented Guerric from going to Rome.

On May 7 1940, he wrote to Father Corneille, telling him of his joy at knowing that he had returned to Scourmont and speaking about many things: his family; classes; and the celebrations at Saint Peter's. He feared difficulties during the return journey, but did not seem to be aware of the imminence of the war that would begin in Belgium three days later. The next week, things happened quickly: belgian and french religious were expelled from Italy, but a delay of eight days was granted to write their exams! Francis wrote all his second–year exams in three days and, because of this special session, obtained his bachelor's degree in theology. In mid–May, in the midst of the german offensive, he and Theodore boarded a train that was never to arrive in Paris. Shortly past the swiss border, near Dijon, the way was blocked, and the travelers had to get out of the train in the open country. The roads were bursting with refugees. From time to time, german airplanes machine–gunned them from low–flying planes, just as it had been in Ypres in 1915. But Francis did not remember. He had been too young.

In the midst of this disaster, the two monks providentially were able to get to Cîteaux, where they spent a few weeks. As soon as they received the news that the Scourmont monks who had not been mobilized had found refuge in Thymadeuc, they rejoined their brethren there. The abbey had been transformed into a shelter: every corner was full of refugees, illegal immigrants, orphans, homeless of all kinds. Dom Anselme's sister, who managed a large agricultural concern a few kilometers away, offered to house the young monks from Scourmont. They spent the summer there in a joyous chaos and tried nevertheless to sing the offices. Once again, war became a vacation on the farm for Jean Mahieu! At the end of September, France and Belgium were occupied, the armistice was signed, and the line of demarcation [between occupied and free France] traced. Scourmont had been evacuated for a few weeks. The community went back and worked to repair the degradations and damage from looting. To return to Belgium, the brothers bought an old rickety pig truck from a farmer and piled into this unpretentious vehicle, which caused unending jokes among the monks.

Despite the occupation, Dom Anselme tried to restore a normal monastic life. He set the date of October 24 for the solemn profession of Francis and Maur. Because the war forbade any communication with Italy, he obtained permission from the Abbot General to send his monks to study at the University of Louvain and registered them there. For two years, life would continue almost normally at La Trappe, which would hide more than one jewish child and would help more than one member of the resistance to cross the french border.

UNDER GERMAN OCCUPATION

February 1941. The worst winter of the belgian war. The abundant snow and the bitter cold that continued until March added to the rigors of the occupation. Rationing was severe for everyone, but it broke records at Scourmont. The monks' diet became miserable. For weeks, in fact, they ate only potatoes harvested in autumn, after their return from Brittany. All the summer harvest had been lost because of the sudden evacuation. The brewery was inoperable for lack of fuel.

Despite all this, Francis continued his religious studies at the Catholic University of Louvain. Several times a week he stayed over at the College of the Holy Spirit for seminarians. But his lack of enthusiasm for academic teaching made him skip classes. The difficulty of travel caused by the war were good excuses, and then he spent peaceful hours in the abbey's beautiful library, studying and reading in silence. He posed his questions to Father Thomas Litt, who taught him philosophy after his novitiate. This passionate philosopher, interested in science, was the brother of the rector of the university. For Francis, a half–hour discussion with Father Litt was worth three hours of public lecture given in an auditorium, whether in Rome or Louvain. Still curious about India, he registered for a course on the *Upanishads*. There also he was disappointed by the Europe–centered approach of the professor, who pointed out the omissions and weaknesses of the vedic religions compared to Christianity, rather than conveying their richness and their own spirit in their cultural and historic context. The project of a foundation in India was suspended because of the war. All communication, even by letter, was cut off, God only knew for how long. Caldey also was relatively isolated from the continent. No more canonical visitations, no exchange of novices; each was blocked where the war overtook him, and crossing the Channel had become an exploit. Francis, however, continued to prepare himself interiorly for what he believed more and more to be his vocation. On October 12, 1941, Bishop Delmotte, the bishop of Tournai, ordained him a priest. At his first Mass, the organ played scouting songs. His family was there in the tribune, and the Sainte-Marie troop was in the church. On the memento card with a photo of him consecrating the wine, he had these simple words inscribed, 'Lord, bless and keep my family, my friends and all who did me good out of love for You.'

Summer 1941 brought an improvement to material life because of the work of the community that resumed the cycle of agricultural work. Relations with the *kommandantur* [commanding officer] of Chimay became more normal and personal. The commanding officer was a cultivated man, courteous with the monks whom he respected and sometimes questioned about their activities and their life. Dom Anselme trusted Francis more and more and made him an associate in his many enterprises. In these difficult times, he appreciated the daring character of his young monk, his practical sense, his knowledge of foreign languages. It was Francis who was asked to oversee the workers repairing the church, to negotiate with the Germans, who was sent to the neighboring farmers to borrow agricultural material, or to the mother abbey in West-Vleteren to obtain food, fodder and seeds on credit. (There he used his father's Flemish accent and was received with open arms.)

On All Saints Day, 1 November, he started his second year of licentiate in theology, but unexpected military events would once more upset the program.

THE LUFTWAFFE

April 12, 1942. A black sedan, driven by a german soldier, stopped in front of the main gate. An officer, followed by his batman, pushed open the little shutter and ordered the brother porter to go get his superior. He saluted Dom Anselme by clicking his heels together and handed him the order requisitioning the monastery. 'May I?' The abbot took the paper. To the brother porter, whose eyes did not leave him, he made the scout salute and a gesture of his chin, meaning: 'Go get Francis, quickly!'

'Order of the headquarters. Luftwaffe. Install here FLAK', said the German. 'For how long? A long time?' The officer shrugged his shoulders with an evasive gesture. Then, stiffening, he continued in an imperious tone of voice: 'Evacuate by Sunday night.' His index finger in the black glove showed the date on the document that Anselme was still holding in his hand. Francis came running. 'Ask him for more time', urged Anselme. 'We can't evacuate the community in three days. There are the sick, the elderly, and we don't even know where to go!' Francis discussed in German, made jokes, and was able to sway the officer, who telephoned his superior from the porter's office. Three additional days were granted.

Dom Anselme asked the princess of Chimay first. She agreed to house the monks in her castle's outbuildings. But there was not enough room, and the chapel was tiny. They had to find somewhere else. Before a decision was made, Francis was sent to reconnoiter Scourmont. Had the abbey really been transformed into an anti–aircraft base of defense? He came back to report that the occupiers were building military barracks in the large pasture behind the church. Machine guns and radars were installed at the top of the plateau. The whole domain was guarded by sentries. There was material warehoused in the sacristy. They had to face the evidence and for the moment give up returning to Scourmont.

Dom Anselme started to look for a refuge that would allow them to reorganize regular life. At Momignies, about fifteen kilometers from Scourmont, he found the Saint-Jean-Baptiste de la Salle boarding school, run by the Brothers of Christian Schools. Before the war, this establishment had almost five hundred students, mostly french, who received a catholic education that had become rare in the north of France. But since the invasion, its boarders had left. Negotiations began, and soon the community could settle in this large white building at the edge of the road leading to the France–Belgium border.

During the whole summer, little by little, thanks to the *ausweiss* [pass] obtained for a few monks, they evacuated all the precious things from Scourmont: church vessels, liturgical ornaments, books, and archives. They also transported to Momignies all that was necessary for daily life: furniture, bedding, work implements, provisions, stock of beer, and other like items. Francis participated in all the moving. He drove the truck that the glass factory at Momignies lent to them from time to time or, failing that, the cellarer's wagon, pulled by two workhorses. With his confrères, he packed, lugged, hoisted, and unpacked many loads during dozens of trips. Sometimes Brother Theodore's old gas generator truck came to their rescue. 'It doesn't take much gas, but generates a lot of trouble,' the young people joked. At the end of May, the temporary settlement was almost completed. Dom Anselme freed Francis from material tasks to allow him to study and write his exams at Louvain for a licentiate in theology, which he obtained in June. Summer 1942 saw no haying or harvest for the Scourmont monks. As in 1940, their harvest was lost. Dom Anselme brought Francis to the *kommandantur* of Charleroi to try to obtain permission to harvest. Commander Doctor Meiborg received them very courteously but gave them no authorization. 'I'm very sorry.

The FLAK reports directly to headquarters. We can do nothing here. Try asking the *oberfeldweber* at the abbey. He will transmit.' But there also they came up against a refusal: 'Military zone. It is forbidden.' In the boarding school's playing field, they planted potatoes for winter.

The brothers' chapel was a little too ornamented for cistercian taste, but it was large enough to contain all the choir members, and the rhythm of the offices punctuated community life once more. In November, three young men came to join Father Albert's novitiate. The elders described Scourmont as a promised land. 'You will see when we return after the war.'

March 3, 1943. Night fell. The deserted abbey was dark and cold, except the guesthouse kitchen, barely warmed by the oven. A dozen monks ate with their abbot around the oilcloth–covered table. On the menu was whatever Brother Yvon had been able to find in the neighboring farms, without worrying about the monastic customs: a roast and cheese. Because he had not had time to bake bread, he made pancakes with flour and milk. The ambiance was not according to protocol. They were telling the abbot, who had arrived from Momignies a few hours earlier to check how the work was coming along, about the events of the last few days.

In mid–February, when after ten months of exile the monks were resigned to patience, a phone call from the *Kreiskommandantur* of Charleroi allowed them to return. 'We don't need your buildings any more. You can move back and cultivate the land. Only you must scrupulously respect the military orders: *ausweiss* for those who work in the fields, blackout, curfew. The *oberst* there will explain everything to you.' At once, Francis was placed in charge of organizing the return. He chose about ten companions, the strongest, to help him clean and then transport everything in improvised trucks.

The monks told the story of their return to their abbot with enthusiasm: 'Father, do you remember when we arrived with you the first day? What desolation. The church was vandalized, the altar relics chiseled out, the tabernacle's silk cut up.' 'Yes, I remember. It's the second time we were pillaged. But the important thing is that we were allowed to come back. The others will arrive the day after tomorrow.' 'With Father Marc', Robert said, 'we spent four whole days cleaning the church and sacristy. And nothing is repaired yet.' 'And the scriptorium', added Désiré; 'it's a disaster. There is mud and sawdust everywhere. They must have used it as a workshop. But everything is clean now, the desks are in place. Only the books need to be re–shelved.' 'I don't believe the Germans are responsible for the pillaging', said Francis. 'The *oberleutenant* seems ok to me. I spoke to him several times. One of the soldiers asked me if he could go to confession and another if he could attend Mass.' They all shook their head, suddenly silent. Francis resumed the story with a half smile: 'We worked without stopping. On Sunday, Pascal and Désiré even rebelled! They were saying it was the Lord's day, that Father Prior had promised them a day of recollection, that we were transgressing the Sabbath rest and what else!' Pascal continued, somewhat embarrassed: 'It's true, Father, we couldn't continue. It was no longer the life of a monk but of a convict.' The abbot laughed. Ghislain, the farm brother, returned to serious matters: 'That's all well and good, Father, but we have to start plowing and then plant without delay. We're late. May we ask the Champenois farm for help? If Joseph comes with his tractor it will go three times as quickly as with horses.' 'We will see about that tomorrow morning', said Anselme. 'You have worked well, my sons, the rest of the community can arrive. We have one more important thing to do early tomorrow morning: reattach the bell ropes. I want them to hear them ring as loudly as possible from the road. And now, I have a surprise for you.' From his large pockets, he took out the bottle of cognac and the cigarillos that his family brought him the week before at Momignies. 'One must take the rough with the smooth!'

That night, the men remembered that before becoming monks they had been students, workers, soldiers. That night, laughing fraternally in their house they had regained, they drank, with their abbot's blessing.

March 15, 1943. The entire community was in the refectory, eating their noon meal in silence. For a week, monastic life had regained its normal course: offices, silence, and other observances had been taken up again. The new lenten schedule had been posted. At the desk, the weekly reader continued to read the *Life* of Saint Stephen Harding. Suddenly, his voice hesitated; he was distracted. A brother came to speak to Dom Anselme in his ear. He got up and quickly left the table. As he walked by, he made the sign: 'Continue to read!' A few minutes later, he came back in, his face tense. He stood in front of his plate where his soup was growing cold.

The reader stopped, and after a long silence, Dom Anselme announced, 'We have just received the order to evacuate the monastery by Wednesday at noon. The order came from the

Forges Commune. We must always be ready. We will begin moving immediately.' The abbot was visibly upset. He went out, then changing his mind, came back in and said, 'To avoid any discussion, I will say that this is probably another consequence of war. It seems that the german soldiers have been ordered to their quarters. They told me a letter would follow.'

Everyone was thunderstruck. Grace after the meal was recited in the refectory, and then Father Sub–Prior distributed the work and they began to load. On the Champenois's chariot they loaded the desks and bedding, on the truck, the ten tons of coal they had just brought from Forges. Despite the harsh news, moving took place with great serenity.

(Extract from the journal kept by Father Francis between February 18 and May 21, 1943, at the request of Father Colomban Bock, archivist)

The team of movers started again to do its work, like ants. This time, they emptied everything. Even the washstands were taken out. The monks divided up the cattle and part of the furniture among the neighboring farms. It was the third evacuation since the war began. Wednesday night, Dom Anselme was the last to leave. The car that came to get him stopped in front of the porch. He then told the *oberst*: 'Push me out yourself, because I am not leaving here of my own free will.' The officer understood. Respectfully, he pushed the abbot's back with his two hands to make him cross the threshold.

Three days later, Dom Anselme took Francis to Herr Doktor Meiborg in Charleroi once again, with the pretext of returning the ten *ausweiss* that had become useless. In reality, he hoped to obtain two things: explanations about the reason of their last expulsion; and permission to cultivate the lands. Francis reported in his diary:

The conversation took place in German. Meiborg asked us to show him precisely on a map the boundaries of the domain and the location of the various buildings. He examined all that with attention, then telephoned Brussels in our presence, and finally obtained a compromise: a small number of workers could cultivate the farm, but they had to live at Bethany, outside the militarized zone, and scrupulously follow all the orders.

Reverend Father then ventured to ask whether the new expulsion had been ordered by the Gestapo.

'Certainly not', replied Meiborg. In fact, it seemed that an
unfavorable military report had been sent by the Luftwaffe's
feldwebel. 'Something about lights in the night or something like
that. This report had been sent to Brussels and then to a superior
officer of the army in Holland. They decided that you could not
remain. I suppose they were afraid of espionage.'

Doctor Meiborg then asked us a few questions about our way
of life, the monastic contemplative life. He asked what the words
'Trappist' and 'Cistercian' meant. He knew the Benedictines.
We answered his questions eagerly.

Before going to Cîteaux for the meeting of the abbots of France and
Belgium, Dom Anselme designated Francis the leader of the small group
that would live at Bethany. He would bring Brother Ghislain for the
fields and Brother Yvon for cooking and the house. Other religious
would come occasionally as needed.

IN BETHANY WITH THE FARM BROTHERS

Tuesday 30 March 1943 (continuation of Francis' diary).

Brother Ghislain drove a hay wagon to which a full dump truck
was tied. I followed him with a manure spreader pulled by Bijou.
We left Momignies around noon, in very bad weather. Brother
Ghislain's two horses were tired. Once we arrived at the 'Four
roads' we stopped at farmer Lousberg's to take back a few tables
we had left there. The horse Diane was really exhausted. On the
hermitage hill, we had to stop about twenty times. We tied her to
the manure spreader and continued with Josette and Bijou
pulling the hay wagon. Brother Ghislain rested a bit on the
spreader and I took the wagon. We arrived at Bethany around 4
PM. Brother Yvon was happy to see us. We continued right away
to the monastery. It was humid and gloomy. We were soaked
and caked with mud. I went to see *Feldwebel* Raabe. He received
me very kindly. I suppose he was impressed by my traveling

clothing and muddy shoes. He told me that we could walk around
the monastery grounds from 7 AM to 8 PM. We must always have
our pass. The stables, cowsheds, barn and other outbuildings are
at our disposal. He asks what we will cultivate: wheat, oats,
barley, beets, horse beans, etc. To conclude, he held out his hand
to me but I found mine so dirty that I held out only my little
finger. That seemed to amuse him. Meanwhile, Brother Ghislain
untied the horses and took care of them. We unloaded the hay
above the stable, put everything in its place, locked up and
walked to Bethany around 8:30. There Brother Yvon was waiting
to have supper with us. We still had to blackout, put everything
in order. We went to bed exhausted around 11 PM.

The first days, it rained so much that they could not begin to cultivate
the fields. The three monks used the time to organize the house and supply
it. Brother Ghislain had run out of steam. He had trouble accepting this last
evacuation. He worried about his horses overextended by the moving and
who had twenty–five hectares of land to till, sow, roll. The storm winds
howled. They waited for the seed that didn't come on the promised day.
And they still had to go get the supplies that had been divided between the
neighbors and repair the fences that had been damaged by the military
convoys. Francis hoed the rhubarb plot in the chapter garden, without regard for the rain. He thought about how to encourage his little band. Little
by little, life got organized. He established a schedule and created rites
adapted to their particular situation. Up at 5 AM, they spent the first two
hours of the day in prayer in common and meditation. From 7 AM until 8
PM, field work was interrupted only by two pauses for a brief prayer, followed by a meal in the field. In the evening, after supper, he inaugurated
the 'spiritual break': a page of the Gospel was read, and each one shared
what the reading suggested to him. The laybrothers greatly appreciated this
time of sharing. Before going up to bed, all three sang the *Salve Regina*,
standing in the dining room where the flame of a household candle flick-
ered. Francis alone stayed up a little while longer, to write the chronicle of
the day in a little canvas notebook.

Sunday was a day of rest. Sometimes they returned to Momignies by
bicycle to share the community life. Sometimes a few fathers came to
them, to sing Mass at Bethany. The afternoon was spent reading, writing
letters, or taking a walk.

An officer of the *Feldgendarmerie* came one morning to investigate the damages and pillaging of the buildings that occurred during the 1942 evacuation. He made note of what Francis described and went to see for himself: door latches, faucets, electrical wires, and sockets had been removed, as well as several valuable paintings. The great organ had been damaged and innumerable windows broken.

Several more times subsequently, thieves entered the empty buildings during the night while the three companions were sleeping at Bethany. During a visit to Charleroi, Francis learned that it was Doctor Meiborg who ordered the investigation and who had signs posted on all the abbey walls forbidding access under penalty of military sanctions. He came himself a little while later to see the damage and was very surprised to learn that german soldiers who had come to buy straw took away brewery machinery! He promised to document all that and to obtain war reparations.

In April, neighbors came to lend a hand and additional horses. In the pale spring sun, five teams of horses worked together to sow and roll the fields. But on Wednesday of Holy Week a disturbing piece of news came. Brother Yvon ran to tell Francis, standing on the sower in the middle of the field: 'Father, two officers and three soldiers are at the monastery. I don't understand what they are saying, but they are measuring the buildings.' These men were veterinarians, and they told Francis that the army had decided to transform Scourmont into a veterinary hospital for horses. Three hundred sick or injured horses would be arriving soon if the building was suitable. That is what they were examining. The next day, workers arrived, cleaned the guesthouse and the stables and began to hang numbered signs everywhere: 'Stall 1, Stall 2. . . .' Francis hurried to Momignies right away by bicycle to warn Dom Anselme. They had only one hope: Doctor Meiborg! Unfortunately, when they got to Charleroi, they learned that he was on vacation until May 4. His substitute, Hauptman Apel, received Corneille and Francis in Mons the next day and informed them: 'Ach! If you knew what a file we already have on your monastery! We have tried everything to allow you to return, but we are powerless!'

The two monks, disappointed, dined on a piece of bread in the college garden, before boarding the train back. An anti–aircraft base was bad enough, but the idea of seeing their abbey transformed into a horse hospital left them dismayed.

On their return, they found the veterinarians settled into the guest-house, in the bishop's quarters. Sickened, they joined the community in Momignies for the Easter celebrations. The next day, the atmosphere was heavy, the work interrupted, again they experienced the uncertainty, the climate of evacuation. 'We must always be ready,' the abbot said. They waited for the decisive visit from the cavalry's superior officer.

Thursday 6 May. Again it rained buckets. Still no visit. On Friday, a subordinate came to announce they had received the order to abandon the project. It was too far away from the train stations, the stables were too small, there were problems with fodder for the winter. Whew! He asked them to take the keys back. We can imagine with what eagerness Francis did so at once.

With relief, the fieldwork was resumed, despite the rain and strong wind. Towards the middle of May, fine weather began. Brother Ghislain was exhausted, so Francis took upon himself the hardest work. They still had four hundred kilos of potato plants to plant in the Boucher pasture that had been plowed along the wheat field. Désiré and Théodore came to help.

At the end of May, after returning the borrowed machinery to the neighbors and placing the animals in pasture, the three monks returned to Momignies with the others. The planting was finished and Francis finally found time to read and study until harvest.

Summer 1943 passed quietly. Dom Anselme finally decided to entrust the harvest to the neighboring farmers, who in exchange kept half of the proceeds. They prepared themselves for a second winter as refugees. But a few weeks before Christmas a new dramatic episode struck the community. This time it was not the reasonably accommodating Wehrmacht but the Gestapo who burst in.

GESTAPO

That morning of 9 December 1943, darkness still reigned over Saint John the Baptist boarding school. It was not yet eight o'clock. About fifty soldiers from the Chimay garrison silently took position in the inner yard.

Even though the monks were already assembled for *lectio divina*, everything seemed to be sleeping in the blacked–out buildings. Calm was interrupted abruptly when a plain–clothed police officer burst into the scriptorium with a machine gun in one hand and a flashlight in the other.

He was accompanied by soldiers who were also armed. He cried out immediately: 'Erhaus! Refektorium!' Taken aback and frightened, the monks complied. Not fast enough, no doubt, because the police officer threatened Brother Ursmer who was seated at the back and seemed to be taking his time. At the same time, another police officer entered the children's wing in the same way.

In the monks' quarters, the man from the Gestapo was already on the second floor. He asked for someone who spoke German. Father Francis stepped forward. 'Bring me to your superior!' the Gestapo demanded. Francis led him towards Dom Anselme's room and knocked at the door. The police officer moved him away and broke down the door, but he hesitated on the threshold. The room was plunged in darkness. The abbot was resting in his alcove. Francis wanted to warn him, but the police officer went ahead of him and tore open the curtain that protected his bed, training his flashlight on the sleeper. With an abrupt gesture, he tore off his blanket as well, shouting, 'Refektorium!'

The operation was led with such brutality that all resistance seemed useless, maybe even imprudent. The monks were gathered in the refectory, each in his usual place. The police officer was surprised at their small number. He decided to search the upper floors. On the third floor, he made Brother Bernard, in his work apron, come out of an 'occupied' bathroom. His full beard occasioned a comment that was meant to be ironic. They found Father Columban in his room, working with Father Gerard. They dragged the infirmarian, Brother Baudouin Meeus, exhausted by his night watches, out of his bed as well.

In the refectory, where the second police officer joined the first, this time with a 'house' interpreter, they made note of the monks' identities. The buildings continued to be searched, and all the documents found in the abbot's office were taken in a crate. At around ten o'clock, the operation was finished.

From a list that he found in a file, the police officer lined up the following religious: Fathers Le Bail, Herman, Litt, Schuon, De Vinck, De Haene, Delférière, Vaillant, and Meeus. He accused Fathers Litt and Schuon of being Jewish. He then declared to the nine men that they were arrested. They could go get dressed and bring food for twenty–four hours. Father Albert Derzelle then stepped forward and bargained with the German: he offered to replace the abbot, an aged man suffering from heart disease and whose presence was indispensable for the community. The man from the

Gestapo hesitated a moment, then, perhaps a bit disconcerted, accepted with a movement of his chin and changed the list of names.

A truck came into the yard around 11:30. The monks and their packages climbed in. Before his turn to go onto the truck, Father Litt made a sign to Brother Charles, a novice, to come closer and told him: 'My notes for logic are in my drawer.' The soldiers left at the same time as the truck.

Consternation was complete. In chapter, Dom Anselme declared soberly: 'Regular life will continue. We will continue to sing the office and High Mass.' But they did not do nothing. Francis took the 2 o'clock train to Brussels. He went by way of Louvain to warn Maur and Robert, who were very surprised. No, the Germans had not gone to the College of the Holy Spirit. Francis and Robert spent the night in Louvain (it was 11 PM) and took the 5 AM train to Brussels. Francis went directly to Uccle to meet the pastor of Notre-Dame of the Rosary, Canon Vanderelst, who, it seemed, had connections in Saint-Gilles prison. After Mass, the canon brought Francis to his home, where Francis told him the whole story. Vanderelst was the diocese's delegate to deal with the Gestapo. He was well able to help Scourmont. In fact he recognized the police officer immediately by Francis' description. The man's name was Zeck, a former Wehrmacht officer, in charge of surveillance of the belgian and french ecclesiastics of the north.

In Momignies, neighbors advised that Father Leon and Father Noel had been arrested at Beauchamp farm and led to Saint-Gilles prison also. Everyone was convinced that the origin of all this was an oblate from Luxemburg, Brother Hildebrand Zelle, who lived at the abbey from 1938 to 1942. He had had a brush with the abbot and novice master. This would in some way be revenge. If this could be proved, the accusations would no doubt be dropped. But of what were the religious accused? Canon Vanderelst would learn this on Saturday the 11th, from Zeck himself: that they collaborated with escaped prisoners, hid Jews, and publicly read a letter from Monsignor von Gallen, bishop of Munster—all anti–german actions. The facts were unfortunately true, and the proof would have been easy to assemble if the police had searched Father Colomban's room. As a good secretary, but very imprudently, he had noted and kept a record of the movements of escaped prisoners who stopped through Momignies, of help given them to cross the border, and even the inflammatory letter of Monsignor von Gallen. And besides, hadn't they named the pig they were fattening in the yard Adolf, an unpardonable insolence!

Yet, Canon Vanderelst seemed optimistic. Through his intervention, Father Francis was permitted to bring regular packages of food to the monks imprisoned at Saint-Gilles. Their lot was not an enviable one. Thanks to Mr Leger, a lawyer incarcerated at the same time as they were and liberated shortly after, we learned that the religious were not separated but locked up with eleven other prisoners in the former sewing workshop of the prison (a room eight meters by five), that they had individual mattresses, seats (chair or stool), a cupboard, and a shelf. Someone swept three times a day and emptied the latrines twice. The prisoners quickly organized themselves: Father Litt gave conferences on astronomy, Father Schuon on Mesopotamia, and Brother Baudouin Meeus on Morse code. They were allowed to read the german newspaper *Brusseler Zeitung* and the french newspaper *Le Soir*. They even made a chess set and could ask for library books. Life would be endurable but for the anguish that worried them: they knew that every sentence of longer than six months was to be served in Germany.

Francis was their link to the community. During the following months, in addition to his new work as novice master, replacing Albert Derzelle, several times a week he went to comfort his brothers in prison. Thus, on 22 December, to obtain permission to give the prisoners Christmas parcels, he went to the Gestapo headquarters, in a luxurious hotel on Louise Avenue. He went into office 31 at 1:15 PM to find Officer Zeck with Father Albert collapsed in an armchair, his face pale and drawn. After verifying Father Francis' identity, Zeck asked him half joking: 'Aren't you on my list?' and pretended to consult a file. 'No. . . . Do you know that your prior does not tell the truth?' 'That seems absolutely impossible', answered Father Francis. Albert spoke up: 'Ask Father Francis what he knows about your man Hildebrand Zelle.' The prior was escorted out, well guarded, and Francis was interrogated at length about the oblate from Luxemburg. Zeck admitted that the man was unbalanced. 'That does not mean that the accusations are unfounded!' he corrected at once. 'And, the letter from the bishop of Munster, do you deny that it was read in the refectory in 1941?' 'That is completely ruled out', affirmed Francis. 'Your Father Thomas however admitted that it had,' came the accusation back. 'In the refectory, we read only sacred texts. You know that,' answered Francis without becoming flustered.

There, Father Francis was gambling. He knew from Canon Vanderelst that Zeck had been a seminarian. The officer smiled but said nothing.

Turning towards his secretary, he dictated a letter authorizing the prisoners to be given ten packages. But Francis, who understood German, told him quietly: 'May I point out that there are eleven?' 'Brother Baudouin will be released for Christmas', announced Zeck, who continued, 'tell your father abbot that we will not cut his monks' heads off and that no doubt we will return a few to the convent after the preparation of the case.' In fact, during the month of February, in small groups and without explanation, all the religious were to return to Momignies, except Thomas Litt and Albert Derzelle who were released only on March 15. Did they look like leaders?

During one of the trips between Momignies and Brussels, Francis continued to Gand and arrived unannounced at the house of his sister Marie-Thérèse (called Rithé). She had been recently widowed and was raising her six children alone. It was late. They insisted that he spend the night. And in the blacked–out old house, after a frugal meal, Uncle Jean spent the evening singing with his nieces, who had just joined the girl scouts, the entire repertory of scout songs that he knew by heart. Fifty years later, they remembered that evening as an unmixed joy, an unplanned celebration of love in the midst of their life saddened by war and their father's death.

For two more years Francis, acting as *socius* [assistant to the novice master] would continue to help Father Albert with the novices, before replacing him definitively in 1946. During the summer of 1944, the abbot sent him to Scourmont often to settle business with the german garrison or with the farmers who rented the monastery's lands and took care of their cattle. He still had his *ausweiss*, which allowed him to inspect the abandoned buildings. Sometimes he spent the night alone at Bethany. One morning, he woke before dawn as usual, parted the blackout panel a bit, and saw the sky begin to turn pink at the horizon. Quietly he opened the door to breathe the night air and look at the last stars.

Suddenly, with a terrifying noise, a burst of machine gun fire rained on the wall all around him. Fear seized him. He stayed there a moment, petrified, asking himself if he were dead. Miraculously, not one bullet hit him. He saw two silhouettes and heard them scream 'Halt! Wer da?' Quickly he closed the door and shouted through it: 'Ausweiss! Trappist!' The others ran to it, hammering the oak door with the butt of their weapons. Francis opened the door a crack and saw two young soldiers. The taller one put his watch under Francis' nose and shouted, 'Five o'clock!

Not authorized to go out until SEVEN o'clock! Order to shoot on anything that moves here!' The announcement of the allied landing no doubt made them nervous and made them see spies everywhere.

The next day, with the order to retreat, they received the order to blow up all the munitions stored in the abbey's basement. In a hurry to leave, they prepared to set fire to the crates where they were. Immediately Francis perceived the threat. By many negotiations, he obtained permission to transport the shells into the field himself, with Brother Ghislain's help. The extent of the fireworks let them imagine the destruction that the conflagration would inevitably have caused.

At the end of August 1944, the south of Belgium was liberated. There was jubilation. The monks returned to their abbey, for good this time. They found it in very poor state after twenty–eight months of being abandoned to the humidity and the looting. The community was impoverished by the war but, under Dom Anselme's energetic leadership, set to work immediately to restore the buildings, restart the brewery, and cultivate the land. All of that would take several years of intensive work. Everyone, choir monks and laybrothers, would contribute.

AFTER THE WAR

In Scourmont as elsewhere, the years after the war were marked by an intense effort of reconstruction and modernization. They started by re-painting the church completely white, as Saint Bernard wanted. *Sancta simplicitas*, but complicated work! Armed with long poles with a brush at the end, the more agile monks wearing a woolen robe and floating scapular—work overalls were not yet worn—climbed on improvised scaffolding where, hanging on with one hand, and bending forward or backward for hours, they managed to paint the vaults' corners and ribs. *Domine, dilexi decorum domus tuae*, wrote Francis on a photo showing him in action.

The abbot was preoccupied by temporal worries. The coffers were empty. He sent Francis and Maur first to Westmalle, then to Aiguebelle in France to try to borrow money. But they came back empty–handed: all the abbeys were impoverished by the war. Then they decided to restart beer production whatever the cost. During the war, some machines were damaged, others stolen. It was an opportunity to rethink the whole process and acquire more modern equipment. With Father Corneille, Francis was charged with organizing this revival. His training as a commercial engineer and his experience as a business leader before he entered the Trappists were placed at the monastery's service by an abbot who, as a good leader, knew how to discern his men's abilities: each one, according to his talents, served the community's project to the maximum. He had to discuss with entrepreneurs, calculate costs, oversee the work. Francis discussed this with his father who had come to visit, and who was very interested in the project. René was reconciled with the Trappists for good!

In a renovated brewery, our engineer/monk took his place amid the teams of religious in leather apron and wooden shoes taking turns to bottle, cap, and label in rhythm, while Father Noel, bearded and punctilious, watched the stills in the huge basement. It was also the monks who took turns to deliver the beer to Charleroi in the old gas generator truck that had to be 'fed' an hour previously with a good measure of chopped wood.

One afternoon in February 1945, Francis went alone to make a delivery. At the top of the hill, when the descent was beginning, the brakes failed. He veered onto the grassy side of the road to reduce the speed, tried to 'break on the motor', but the heavily loaded vehicle continued down the hill. A providential embankment stopped it, in a clatter of broken branches. The driver, a bit shaken, got out to inspect the damage: the truck's cabin was so bumped, rusted, and holey in places that it did not make much difference. The bottles were intact, that was the important thing. A glacial wind swept the plain. Francis lowered his hood and rolled himself in his cloak. He could do nothing but walk back to the monastery and come back with help to tow it away.

A fine snow began to fall, but something else was bothering him. As he walked, his thoughts turned to India. Dom Anselme never spoke of it any more. He was busy with the abbey's construction and reorganization. He had to borrow money and mortgage land to finance the new brewery. The debts would have to be repaid before thinking about making a foundation. For perhaps the first time, Francis felt weariness and doubt rise within him. It seemed to him that for years the community's main preoccupations had been of the temporal order. During the war, that was to be expected; they had to survive, and protect the buildings and crops. But now, they were speaking only of the brewery, building a crypt, and buying tractors. He had always been willing to work hard, to serve in the front line, but for the past few weeks, he felt a vague dissatisfaction, a sort of rift between his daily life and his monastic dream. Night had fallen when he first saw the abbey's pointed bell tower. He joined his brothers in choir and, as always, singing Vespers revived his soul, but a hidden crack remained.

The next day as he unpacked a box of used books sent to the monastery by a donor, he found the book *Le Pèlerinage aux Sources* [*The Pilgrimage to the Sources*] by Lanza del Vasto that had been published two years before. This book, which recounted a Christian's first trip through India, from Ceylon to the Himalayas, captivated Francis immediately. Its precise, vivid descriptions of daily life alternated with colorful presentations of hindu philosophy and mythology to culminate in a meeting with Gandhi and a stay at Wardha, his village school.

In the freezing scriptorium, Francis put down his book and closed his eyes. He saw himself, also, welcomed by the mahatma, following him along the rice paddies on his morning walk, listening to him speak to his disciples in the evening, crouching like them on the packed earth floor. The youthful enthusiasm for Gandhi that Jean Mahieu had felt in London awoke in a more mature Francis enlightened by his spiritual formation. More than ever, it seemed to him that for this hindu people, so naturally inclined to seek God, to simplicity of life, to fraternal charity, the best way to encounter Christ would be through contemplative monks, as the Holy Father called for and as Gandhiji himself desired. In the meantime, he hid the book in his desk. From then on, he would bring it everywhere with him, as a talisman.

In June 1945, Father Maur, who had continued his studies in Louvain in spite of the war, received his doctorate in theology. At the festive celebration, humorous short plays in Latin written by Francis were performed. They featured learned men in the manner of Molière. Unfortunately, the text has been lost, but let us bet that the author used his fellow novice's academic success to poke fun at this university theology that he definitely disliked. The most memorable part of this little party for the monks, who told us about it some fifty years later, was the exceptional snack at the end. They served military biscuits with hot chocolate! What an event! Especially the chocolate, which was still very rare and which they had not had at all during the war.

IN CALDEY WITH DOM ANSELME

The Island of Caldey (Ynys-Pyr in Gaelic) was inhabited by hermits or monks from celtic times, before roman colonization. A benedictine community lived there for almost a thousand years, in the old medieval priory whose ruins can still be visited. In 1532, Henry VIII suppressed all the monasteries of his kingdom, and the expelled Benedictines left the country. The island was sold and occupied by individuals. Some were interested in discovering and restoring its historical ruins, others simply exploited its pasture lands or enjoyed its quiet in summer. In 1906 anglican Benedictines bought it to live there. A few years later, converted perhaps by the spirit of the place, the entire community joined the Catholic Church. Its abbot, Dom Aelred Carlyle, recognized by Rome, then began to build the present buildings in a somewhat surprisingly spanish style: a kind of white castle covered with pink tiles, with little towers and surrounded by terraces made of small varnished baked earth tiles. This building, together with a private house and a chapel, was only the first part of the work in Dom Carlyle's grandiose project, and was not destined for the monks to live in. It was going to be a sort of abbatial boarding school for boys that would have provided an income for the community at the same time. But the college project never happened. The abbot's plans were too grand, and he did not take finances into consideration. When he suddenly went to Canada in 1921, he left a deficit of twenty thousand pounds sterling. The community was bankrupt!

His little community, distraught, joined the abbey of Prinknash on the mainland, abandoning this island that was windy and very isolated for most of winter, without much regret. The Catholic Church would not have wanted this monastic land to be purchased by laypeople, or worse, revert to the Anglican Church. The Holy Father himself, judging that Cistercians would no doubt be the most apt to endure the harsh climate and isolation of Caldey, bought the island, its castle, and debts in 1925, and asked the Abbot General to send Trappists there. Scourmont was approached to send monks because their community numbered almost one hundred. Dom Anselme accepted all the more willingly in that he saw an opportunity to establish privileged contacts with England and, beyond, with India, which at the time was a british colony. According to the custom of foundations, he sent thirteen monks led by an 'elder', who by coincidence was named Aelred. On 6 January 1929, Dom Anselme established the cistercian life in Caldey. He visited the monks several times in the thirties and welcomed there asian novices who were asking to join the order, from China, India, and from Senegal. But the war interrupted all communication, and Dom Aelred Lefevre, promoted to prior in 1934, died prematurely in 1942.

Since the liberation, the community had been waiting for a canonical visitation. The previous one had been in 1938. At the end of 1945, when peace had been reestablished and the monastic rhythm of life returned to Scourmont, Dom Anselme decided to go visit his english daughterhouse. He chose Francis to accompany him, and in January 1946, both boarded the Ostende–Dover Malle. Francis was happy to travel with his beloved and revered abbot, happy to discover Caldey, happy to lean against the rail of a huge sailing ship. They stopped at Downside abbey in Somerset. Their benedictine brothers welcomed them warmly. They enjoyed the white bread, cheese, jam, and butter cake. They had not tasted those in a long time, and Downside seemed to them a delightful oasis of abundance after the years of war and severe rationing on the occupied mainland. After a few days of rest, they both took the train for Tenby, where the priory's motorboat, steered by a brother in a sailor cap, was waiting for them. The weather was calm, and they took the opportunity to load it with oil and a few cases of food. Only grass, gorse bushes, and a few trees twisted by the wind grow on Caldey. The monks lived off a dairy farm, where they made cheese, chocolate, and caramels. But the balance sheet showed a deficit, especially since the war, which had paralyzed commerce and reduced tourism to nothing. The gift shop, run by the monks near the quay, and boat rides, of which they hold the monopoly, had been an additional resource that they hoped to regain.

While Anselme listened to his sons talk to him at length about their troubles and hopes, Francis explored the island, suggested a few technical improvements to the dairy farm, and took intense pleasure in walking along the cliffs, breathing the salty air deeply. All his life he would be very sensitive to nature, marveling at creation, a lover of trees, mountains, ocean, birds, and stars as well as rain, insects, wind, and storms. As he himself wrote about Saint Francis: 'Everything in creation was for him as a finger pointing towards the creator. To praise God was both the duty and the joy of every created thing.'

Before he left the island, the abbot wanted to reassure this cosmopolitan and energetic community, but also to recall it to order: during the war, left to themselves, forced to rule themselves, they took a few liberties. Before all else, it was important to find a good superior for the community, who could show both firmness and diplomacy. 'Francis', he said, 'let's go for a walk, I need to think.' 'Gladly, Reverend Father. Would you like to go up to the lighthouse?' 'Let's go!'

Anselme walked silently for a long while. The young monk took his superior's pace, slower, heavier. He stopped, short of breath, to sit on a half–crumbled stone wall. The air was mild for the season, a light wind chased the white clouds towards the Gulf Stream, and between the clouds, a few pale rays of sun glinted on the pastel facades of Tenby. 'What if we proposed Father Albert to them?' he asked suddenly, continuing aloud his inner train of thought. 'He would bring his uprightness, his sense of the Rule, his spiritual vision.' Francis replied quickly: 'It would certainly be an opportunity for Caldey, Reverend Father. And an onerous task for Father Albert. Have you considered that he speaks almost no English?' Anselme persisted, 'He will learn quickly.' 'And who will replace him in the novitiate?" probed Francis. 'You, of course!" came Anselme's answer; 'How old are you?' 'Thirty–four yesterday, Reverend Father!' Francis responded.

Anselme continued to think aloud. 'That's one year too young! But we will easily obtain an indult dispensing with the age requirement. Especially since you have been *socius* since 1943 and you have already replaced the novice master during his arrest by the Gestapo. . . . What is it? I can see that something displeases you. You can tell me everything, you know that.' Francis confessed, 'Reverend Father, forgive me, but I am still thinking about that foundation in India. If I become master of novices, does that mean that you will keep me at Scourmont?' Anselme explained, 'We are not there yet. First, we have to revive Caldey, which, as you have seen, has been tried. Then consolidate Scourmont, which is recovering from the war very slowly, despite the community's courage. Do not forget that we are completely bankrupt. Worse than that, we are in debt. The day we have the necessary resources, if you still desire to leave, we will find someone to replace you. But we have time to think about that!' 'Thank you, Father', replied Francis. 'Whatever happens, I will obey you.'

At tea–time—because at Caldey, the english Cistercians who joined the community did not compromise about tea–time—Francis questioned the novices from India and Ceylon about their life, their country, the christian communities they came from. 'Are there contemplative monasteries in your region?' he asked. 'Yes, buddhist ashrams, groups of hindu hermits.' 'And Christians?' he continued. 'The Christians build schools, hospitals. We need contemplatives. Indians know only about the active, charitable, socially effective aspect of Christianity. That is fine, but for them that is not what is essential about religion. The hindu religious *sannyasi* is, above all else, a "renouncer", a seeker of God, detached from material goods, vowed to prayer, fasting, silence. . . . It is for this reason that we have come here: with God's help, we can perhaps begin the monastic life in our country after our profession.'

Many weeks more passed in negotiations and various reorganizations. Father Albert was finally elected on February 12. When a telegram from England brought him the news, he asked to be left alone all the following day, to digest this terrible news.

On the return voyage, Francis thought about the form most suitable for an indian foundation. He could see it similar to a hindu ashram, with monks who would live simply from the product of their work. Certainly they should not build a replica of a western monastery, with a neo–gothic church, stalls, a refectory. What Francis would like was to pursue the action begun by Father Vincent Lebbe in China and Roberto de Nobili in India. When the time came, he would speak to Dom Anselme about it. But beside him, the abbot dozed, rocked by the jolting of the wagon. Francis looked out the window at the welsh hills and tried to imagine what a christian ashram in India might look like. At the same time, in his silent prayer, he entrusted himself to the Lord to lead all this in His ways.

The following summer, returning from Achel where he participated in the ceremonies of the centenary of that abbey, Dom Anselme spoke about his admiration for the noble and powerful community of Achel. At chapter he reminded the community that Scourmont's centenary was approaching in 1950. He recalled the work accomplished by the monastery during its hundred years of existence and ended by expressing regret that he had not yet been able to join to the foundation of Our Lady of Peace and Our Lady of Caldey a foundation in India. Francis jumped at this last phrase. Did he hear in it a hope, or on the contrary the expression of a definitive abandonment? The same night, he was officially named novice master of the choir novices, because the indult granting him a dispensation on account of his age and length of profession had arrived.

MASTER OF NOVICES

An elder who is skilled in winning souls (*RB* 58:6)

Beyond techniques, the most refined psychological processes,
the efforts of wisdom and prudence, isn't the best way to honor
Saint Benedict's request to be 'an elder skilled in winning souls'
to be oneself a man fascinated by the mystery of God? If the novice
master 'truly seeks God' in all the truth of his life, is he not able
to make a life completely given to this infinite seeking the
Lord's face seem desirable? The connecting thread of our life
might be the history of our profound and vital desire through all
its evolutions. Man is a being who desires. That is well known.
His sanctification will be the slow and progressive conversion of
his attraction, of his attachment: *aversio a creatura, conversio ad
Deum*, [turning away from creatures, turning toward God] Saint
Augustine used to say, until he recognizes that only the face of
the risen Christ, in whom all beauty is summed up, is worthy of
his love. In this sense, the novice master's role is that of a leader,
a trainer of men, and goes beyond that, of course.
     (Vuillaume, 'Un ancien qui soit apte à juger les âmes', p. 3)

The novice master is a professor, a boarding school teacher, spiritual director, elder brother, and something more than all that. The father master,
as he is called, directs two separate novitiates: the future priests' and the
laybrothers'. Assisted by two father sub–masters, he organizes the life of
the novitiate, sets the summer schedule—from Easter to mid–September,
the time of agricultural work and extra nourishment—and the winter
schedule, time for study and the long monastic fast. He establishes the
content of instruction and, in consultation with the abbot, the subjects of
the weekly conferences. The instruction or 'lectures' were the courses
that roughly followed the program outlined by Dom Anselme at the end
of the 1914–18 war: monastic spirituality; usages (the customs and habits
that must be observed in the monastery); monastic history; Rule (of Saint
Benedict, called R.B.); cistercian spirituality (especially Saint Bernard);
psalms; and liturgy. The lessons and practice of gregorian chant were
held every afternoon. Written and oral exams, in the abbot's presence,
tested the knowledge acquired.

A weekly conference was organized for the whole community. The novices and students (of philosophy) were present, as well as the lay-brothers. The subjects were varied, religious or secular, linked with current affairs. The speaker was sometimes from outside: a visiting abbot or priest, more rarely a lay expert in some subject. Often, it was a monk from the community who shared with his brothers the fruit of his reading, research, or recent experience.

Thus Francis, on his return from Caldey in February 1946, gave a conference on the monastic island where he had just spent two weeks: he presented its history, geographical site, the economic context, and the multicultural and multilingual community. The father master lived in the novitiate with the young people, in a building separated from the monastery by a small garden:

It's a small building (20 meters by 6) in cement block, covered with corrugated sheet metal, without a second story or attic, without interior rough–cast or paint, just bare cement. It would be a mere garage if fifteen large windows did not bathe it in light, because the walls' glass surface is much larger than the cement surface. Everything is poor, but everything is happy, with light, flowers, good taste and especially joy. And thanks to God the novices do not lack joy. Everything is transformed: the cement softens amid the tulips, geraniums, dahlias, chrysanthemums, the cloister wall itself little by little loses its forbidding air and will soon disappear beneath the honeysuckle and the climbing roses.

(anonymous typed text from Scourmont archives)

On 15 May 1946, this building was unusually bustling: all of Father Albert's former novices were gathered to bid him a formal goodbye before his departure for Wales. Father Pierre spoke on the theme 'Dom Albert, spiritual master and especially spiritual friend'. Albert, very moved, answered, telling him the novice master's affection for all those he had directed, in whom he had witnessed God's action, penetrating and transforming souls (*liber lectionum*). The next day Francis began his instruction, choosing as his subject 'the early monks' prayer'.

We have found no letter from this period 1946–49, no personal trace of Francis' interior growth. We know that he lived in the novitiate, that he had a corner there with his worktable and a small white wooden cupboard where he stored his books and course notes. On the inside of the door, he attached a picture of Father Lebbe, in chinese clothing. It can be noted that of his eighteen years of trappist life in Scourmont, he will have spent less than four—between 1941 and 1946—in the community buildings. After his own novitiate and his studies in Rome, the war, stays in Momignies and Bethany, replacing Albert during the Gestapo episode, and then as novice master, all these events kept him relatively apart from community life. Does this partially explain the difficulties he would encounter later?

Our only written documentary source for this period, besides the abbey's annals, is the *Liber lectionum in cella novitiorum*, that is, the book of talks given in the novitiate from 1945 to 1950. It is a sort of logbook where Francis wrote in chronological order, beside the date, the name of the person giving the talk and its subject. In addition, at the end of the volume, he gathered the weekly schedules and various sheets of advice and rules on manual work, personal reading, the good use of 'intervals'. A glance at these sheets tells us, for example, that:

Twice a month, Father Francis presided over the Chapter of faults.

8 September 1946. F. Augustin Vercruysse received the habit, Dom Anselme gave a talk on 'Contemplative Life and the Missions'. The abbot was still interested in a monastic foundation in what was still called 'mission lands' at that time. They did not speak of the 'third world' yet.

25 September 1946. Father Francis: 'Spirituality of the Pagan World'. We do not have the text of this original talk. Did Francis lean yet on the theory of the 'Seeds of the Word'? Did he take his examples from Hinduism?

4 October 1946. Mr. Ravoet: conference on beer manufacturing. (The abbey's principal resource was and would remain 'Trappiste de Chimay' beer, sold in small bottles, which began a lucrative career after the war.)

26 November 1946. Father Francis: 'Saint Athanasius' "Life of Saint Anthony" and the 'Spirituality of Saint Anthony'.

2 December 1946. Father Francis: 'Saint Pacomius'. His spirituality was to occupy the instructions until 7 December.

Francis continued with 'Desert Spirituality' and 'Letters from Macarius to his Sons'.

9 December. Father Gall gave an ethnographic conference on 'The Red Skins'.

March was devoted to Cassian and April to Saint Benedict. In the meantime, of course, the Rule, the Usages, the history of Cîteaux, the Psalms and all the other classical monastic studies were part of the program.

24 April. Francis gave a conference on 'The Eastern Incarnations of the Monastic Idea'.

In February 1948, Dom Clement Lialine gave several conferences on orthodox theology. Who invited him? This was the era that saw the birth of the ecumenical movement.

In January 1949, the East was featured again: Ignatius of Antioch, Origen, Anthony, and Pacomius. Francis presented the 'Letter of the Churches of Vienna and Lyon to the Churches of Asia'. Father Sub–Prior gave a conference on 'The Eastern Church'. At Christmas, in his annual pastoral letter, the Abbot General, Dom Dominique Nogues, had asked for prayers for the chinese cistercian brothers and all their martyred Church.

In February, Francis spoke to his novices about the sayings of the desert Fathers, unceasing prayer, Saint Macarius, and Saint Basil. However, modernity was not forgotten: during the same month Father Thomas Litt gave two philosophical conferences: one on existentialism and the other on Gabriel Marcel.

Three Testimonies

To complete this objective but dry enumeration, we have asked three of Father Francis' former novices, some fifty years later, what memory they have of their novice master. Each in his own way, this is what they answered us:

Father Charles Dumont: 'Francis was an energetic, demanding master. We could feel he was seeking new ideas, sometimes strange ones, from the desert Fathers or the eastern monks. For example: daily confession, which he decided one day to require

of us, but which was found to be inappropriate and was abandoned at the end of eight days. He taught us very conscientiously
about Saint Benedict and his Rule, but we could sense that his
heart was leaning more towards the eastern Fathers: Saint Basil,
Saint Ephrem. He was also interested in Saint Seraphim of Sarov,
the "Prayer of the Heart". He remained an idealist, a spiritual
man more than an intellectual. Marked by scouting, he kept a
"heroic" mentality. At that time, he was dreaming of exploits, of
radical ascesis. He was faithful, through everything, to his
monastic vocation, to his indian project.'

Father Godefroid Leveugle: 'He was a teacher, a real master,
demanding and generous, who gave the example and gave of
himself. Very strict, even sometimes authoritarian, he was always
concerned about our monastic formation. In the morning, he
prepared his instructions in the library. In the afternoon, he
worked with us. He was strong, well built, very effective during
the haying and harvesting. With him, we had to be punctual. He
insisted on personal reading, on *lectio divina*. Even when there
was a lot of work, we had to interrupt everything precisely at
4:30 and resume our reading. He also insisted on diligence in the
chant lessons. He himself had a beautiful voice. At the evening
chapter, he explained to us the spiritual concepts of the Rule of
Saint Benedict.'

Father Jacques Blanpain: 'I remember the course on the Usages,
which bored me. One day, Father Francis had had to be absent
for a few weeks, and when he returned, he could not remember
which paragraph had been the last we studied. I told him: 'Fifty–
three.' But in reality it had been forty–three. At least we got out
of that much, I told myself. At the beginning he believed me, but
later he noticed and reviewed everything we had skipped. He
scolded me a bit but he laughed. One day when I made a fire, a
big bonfire with the little branches of a tree we had cut down, he
came to help me and at the same time he questioned me, whether
I was all right, while he stoked the fire. He used to speak freely
with us, we could tell him everything, we could sense his trust-
worthiness.'

Francis loved his task of novice master and gave himself completely to it. Those three years were no doubt happy ones, even if a thousand signs revealed that he was continuing to prepare himself, almost in secret, to be a monk in the East. He still was waiting for Dom Anselme to resume contact with Father Monchanin, of whom they had not had any news since his visit in 1939, or with some local bishop, to start this foundation they had been talking about since the twenties. And now that Dom Albert was in Caldey, who, if not Francis, would be in charge of leading this project?

What were his sentiments when in 1947 he learned about India's independence? How did he react to the news of the terrible massacres between Hindus and Muslims, which cast a shadow over this victory, and worse still the news of Gandhi's assassination by a hindu fanatic? Was he aware that this new nationalist regime would make it very difficult, if not impossible, to found western christian communities in India? We do not know.

LOVE LOST FOR LADY POVERTY

The war had been over for more than two years, but despite its efforts, the community was in greater and greater debt. It got to the point of mere survival: in December 1946, they no longer peeled the potatoes, in order to have more to eat. They heated the buildings only slightly. The chronicle for Sunday, 26 January 1947, suggests, not without some humor, what must have been the night office in winter: 'The weather is freezing, it's minus twelve degrees and the northeast wind is glacial. In church, the temperature is siberian. The cold pours in through the forty–two holes, sixteen windows, twelve doors, without counting the deadly whirlwind near the unfinished deambulatory. We sing the night office but because of the cold, there is no chapter.'

That year a Savings Committee was created, made up of Anselme's trustworthy assistants: Corneille, who had been cellarer since the war; Guerric, the prior; Maur, the sub–prior; and Francis, novice master. In each sector, the four monks examined the bills, studied possible savings and checked them. Beer was no longer served in the evening, radiators and electric heaters were removed, and additional food was reduced to smoked herrings. Paper was rationed. The envelopes from incoming mail were cut up to become notepaper. They even went so far as to organize a public sale of the surplus agricultural implements in April, but the result was disappointing and left the brothers sad to see the old familiar work tools go.

In January 1948, they had to acknowledge that the financial situation was worse than ever. When Guerric presented the 'state of temporal affairs' for the year 1947, the expenses were twice the income. Saving more was impossible. The conclusion was clear: income had to increase. Agriculture operated at a loss. Their hopes rested on the brewery. That evening, Dom Anselme spoke about the doctrine of 'holy abandonment'.

At the end of 1948, one year later, an examination of the accounts revealed a true miracle: the brewery's revenues quintupled! The benefit was substantial, despite the cost of the investment. At the same time, they were able to reduce the daily cost per monk from 53 francs 25 to 48 francs! Father Prior concluded his presentation of the accounts, the chronicler says, 'by exhorting us to reduce expenses even more and especially to thank Providence who had come to our aid'.

Was it Providence that inspired the saving idea? In March, the brewery launched a new product: the 'small bottle' of 33 cc. Its conical shape and blue sticker with the Trappists' coat of arms was a resounding success. The 'Chimay' beer, light or dark, with 8 or 10 percent alcohol content, would bring an end to the destitution in which the community lived since the war, and even plunged it into real opulence, without a transition. The brewery worked full time; they even hired a few boys for the warehouse. They could scarcely fill the orders, and the novices often worked until supper, to the detriment of prayer and reading.

This sudden commercial success fell, if one can put it that way, on a fragile community. The occupation, the uprooting to 'Momignies crossroads' as the 1946 chronicle put it, and the misery that transformed temporal affairs into an obsession weakened the community's spiritual impetus. During the war, like everyone else, they practiced tricks and were very resourceful, engaging in all sorts of little arrangements that are permitted by exceptional or dangerous situations but that do not favor spiritual seeking or the elevation of souls. The sudden riches that the success of the small bottle brought in a few short months, in fact, constituted a new trial, a more insidious one. Whereas misery endured renders voluntary poverty difficult, easy money is a formidable enemy for the cistercian soul. Francis was among those who worried about this. He did not share the euphoria that overcame the managers. Plans for construction, transformation, more comfortable buildings—they were already talking about installing central heating—seemed to him to be contradictory to the lifestyle they had chosen. And he foresaw the worry and distraction that these works would entail for years, whereas he aspired only to be freed from the 'temporal', to finally think of something else. In his favorite book by Lanza del Vasto, he underlined this motto of Gandhi's 'Let us stamp out misery, let us cultivate poverty'.

In August, he once more accompanied his abbot to Caldey, where difficulties were multiplying: Albert was ill, the new boat sank, the community was divided. Dom Anselme was burdened by the material worries that he had been facing for more than eight years, despite his best efforts, and that kept him far from the spiritual seeking that he wanted to pursue in peace during this last stage of his life. One evening, seeing Albert return from the fields in work clothes, thinner than ever, his face drawn, emotion seized him and he murmured, 'My poor child'.

Francis vaguely sensed that now the indian project was abandoned. Anselme no longer had the resilience necessary for such an enterprise that India's independence made even more complicated. The joyful foundation—sending a group of monks led by Albert and Francis to India, blessed by their abbot, duly mandated by the Order and with solid support; that dream as Francis had pictured it during the 1939 visit by Monchanin and that he had kept since then through all that had happened—finally crumbled. Everything became dark; the future seemed unclear. Providence was preparing in secret something more fitting, more unprecedented, more simple, which was not accessible to the winning Francis, the leader, the triumphant Francis. First he would have to go through the great trial, purify himself in the fires of the desert, die to himself in solitude and suffering.

If 1948 marked for Scourmont the beginning of prosperity, it was the beginning of the great crisis for Francis, and this, no doubt, was not a coincidence.

FATHER, FATHER, WHY HAVE YOU ABANDONED ME?

A little before Christmas, Francis was stricken by a strange illness: he could not open his left eye, his mouth was twisted, speaking and eating were difficult. The doctor from Chimay diagnosed facial paralysis and treated it with massive doses of vitamins. After a few weeks the symptoms disappeared. This episode remains quite enigmatic even today, and we will not try to interpret it, but in the context, we cannot help thinking it might be a psychosomatic manifestation. His general state of health remained precarious; a double mastoiditis prevented him from accompanying the abbot to Caldey at the end of January 1949. He returned at the beginning of March, visibly strained. That is when catastrophe struck.

On 14 March, at the beginning of the afternoon, when Father Colomban went into the abbot's office, he found him lying on the ground unconscious. Dom Anselme had a cerebral hemorrhage and remained in a coma for several days. Where were Francis' thoughts during those long nights when he watched in silence over his unconscious abbot, with Maur Standaert? Was he measuring the isolation in which he would find himself from then on? It was the end of one stage, and the next stage had not yet begun. He knew only one thing: he would leave. When, where, with whom? He did not know. The words of Psalm 13 that he recited at dawn seemed to come out of his own heart:

How long, O Lord, will you forget me?
How long will you hide your face?
How long will I make projects in my soul?
How long will my heart be afflicted?
Look at me, answer me, Lord, my God.
Enlighten my eye lest I fall asleep in death.
Let my enemy not say: I have prevailed over him.
Let not my adversaries exult if I waver.
As for me, I trust in your goodness.
My heart will exult because of your salvation.
I will sing to the Lord for the good he has done for me.

When the abbot of West-Vleeteren, Scourmont's Father Immediate, arrived a few days later, he exhorted the community to remain united and confident. 'Obey your prior', he enjoined them, 'as if the abbot were away on a trip. Later, we will see, depending on his health'. In May, the neurologist called to consult the physician treating Anselme drew up a report of his health, noticing 'amazing but limited improvement' in the patient's state. He prescribed complete rest: 'The abbot must have no worry, every problem must be avoided'. Practically, Dom Anselme had become an invalid, totally incapable of speaking, paralyzed on his right side and mentally handicapped. 'Sometimes his comprehension is complete and at other times, it is diminished. It is not possible for those around him to know his thoughts' (from Doctor Descamps' report in the Annals of Scourmont). From that time on, the abbot would remain in the infirmary, under the devoted and jealous care of Baudouin Meeus, who had become his infirmarian. Incapable of writing, speaking, or signing, he was completely unable to take part in the governing of the monastery. After a few weeks, it became clear that Dom Anselme's health would not return and that he would remain incapable. The physicians were certain of this. However, the abbey could not remain without a leader. The juridical and administrative void ended on June 5, when a pastoral letter from the Holy See named Father Guerric Baudet 'apostolic administrator'. The annalist mentioned without comment that the letter was read in chapter and that Father Guerric had immediately stood up to go sit on the abbatial seat. A few days later, Guerric moved into the abbatial room, but decided that in church, Dom Anselme's stall would remain empty, to recall that he retained the title of abbot. In August, Dom Dominique Nogues, the Order's Abbot General, came to comfort the monks and visit Dom Anselme.

After the end of the war, Francis could not find the joy he had previously found in the monastic life. His abbot's accident was the last straw to plunge him into despair. At the same time, he had lost his spiritual father and the only support for his indian project. He entered into a 'dark night'. It was on August 21 that the chronicles mention for the first time that 'Father Francis is ill'. In fact, for weeks he had been enduring a veritable martyrdom: a herniated lumbar disc was crushing his sciatic nerve, and the long periods of standing during the offices caused him sharp pain. He could no longer stand it. No doubt he had come to the point where he was fed up, his body was screaming in his stead, 'brother ass' had let go.

CROSSING THE DESERT

Francis opened his eyes. He directed his gaze slowly towards the window where a feeble light filtered through the closed drapes. His head was spinning. Was it evening? Morning? How long had he been there? His whole body hurt.

It was at the end of September that Doctor André Ferrière, his former classmate at Sainte-Marie, had brought him here to his small private clinic in Ottignies. Called to help Francis, the doctor first had tried to reduce the hernia by a plaster corset, but that only proved to be an additional torture. Then he asked a neurological surgeon from Louvain for advice. He operated on Francis right there, in conditions that appear to us today very primitive. An error in transfusion worsened the shock of the operation, and the patient was just barely saved from death.

As soon as he could sit up, his first action was to write to Father Guerric, his superior and former fellow student, who came to stay with him the first night himself, without telling the community.

Reverend Father,

Since I began to revive a bit this morning I am aware that I must first thank you for staying with me Monday night. And then I must reassure you about my state. The shock must have been severe because until last night I felt in a state of total debility. My legs had no more substance than my shirt sleeves, my scar burned and the lower half of my body was as if constantly undergoing nervous shocks that gave me the impression that I was going to break into pieces like a piece of baked clay between a hammer and an anvil. The first two nights, despite all kinds of injections, were without sleep, or perhaps a short hour of dozing. I could drink only clear water and yesterday it seemed to me I had reached the end. Finally, thanks to a new combination of drugs, injections, etc. spaced throughout the night, I was able to rest well. I no longer feel the dislocation. I am regaining a bit of strength along with my appetite and my mind is returning to normal. I believe that the worst is past and I have hope. I am glad to be able to tell you this. As you may guess, care is not lacking, nor visits. I will need to limit the visits at certain times. I was able to pray a little each day, very little Tuesday and yesterday.

A cordial thanks to all those who sent me their encouragement and wishes, especially the novices.

Cum sincera et humili dilectione [With sincere and humble affection]

F.M. Francis

At the beginning, the operation seemed to be a success: Francis could get up and walk, and the sharp pain in his left leg diminished a great deal. But his general state of health remained of concern. In fact this hasty surgical operation on an organism probably weakened by too much physical labor and prolonged malnutrition left him broken. The wound was not healing. After three weeks it was still suppurating. André Ferrière obtained permission to bring his friend to his home, in the large villa near the clinic, where his wife Cinette and their three young children surrounded Francis with affection and solicitude. They were fervent Christians, seeking ecumenism. Francis said Mass every morning in their oratory and the rest of the time remained lying down, drowsy. Despite his weakness and against the doctor's advice, he returned to Scourmont for All Saints Day. Ferrière wrote to Guerric: 'I can no longer detain him here, but we cannot consider him cured'. He insisted firmly that the convalescent must avoid all fatigue (no staying on his feet or profound bows!), must remain warm, be given a diet with additional protein, etc. Were these recommendations followed? It is difficult to imagine Francis asking for them. The chronicles mention only that, in preparation for his return, the infirmary was heated!

The winter did not bring much improvement, because the check–up visit to Louvain in February 1950 revealed 'residual pain and severe anemia'. Heating pad, lombostat . . . nothing helped. Francis tried to fulfill his charge of novice master despite everything, but strength often failed him.

In April, two young Indians who were pursuing their novitiate in the benedictine monastery of Saint-André-lez-Bruges came to spend a few days in Scourmont. Father Bénédict Alapatt, who accompanied them, was originally from Malabar. He had left the missionary Sylvestrins of Ceylon to prepare a benedictine contemplative foundation near Madras. In chapter, he spoke about India and monastic life there. His project of transplanting western benedictine life to Tamil Nadu did not attract Francis.

On July 26 the solemn celebration of Scourmont's centennial took place with sung Mass followed by procession, meal, and speeches in the presence of prestigious guests including the bishop of Tournai, the prince of Chimay, and abbots of many other monasteries. Torture no doubt for Francis who, in addition to his usual back pain, was now suffering severe ophthalmic migraines. He left discreetly after the office of None and from his bed listened to the Schola of the Children of the Cross sing under the pavilion set up in the garden, facing the VIP stand. His thoughts and prayers turned to Dom Anselme, whose absence presided over the celebration and put a damper on the general joy. No one noticed that Father Baudouin had pushed his wheelchair near an open window from which he was also listening to the concert, looking delighted, nodding his head.

In October, Francis' state worsened. They considered a shortwave treatment—a novelty that was in style then—but finally they chose X–rays administered in Ottignies in a dose of thirteen minutes of radiation every two days. At least he was once again staying with the Ferrière family, where it was warm and where he was stuffed with substantial food. At the end of November, at the doctor's advice, he was sent to Aiguebelle as Antoine Tamby of Pondicherry had once been, to spend the winter in the sun and promote his convalescence. In the new Plymouth 'station wagon' that had replaced the gas generator truck a few months previously, he was driven to Brussels. From there he went the eight hundred kilometer trip to Provence by bus! The chronicle does not tell us in what state his vertebrae got off the bus.

He remained in Aiguebelle for five months, unable to work or to participate regularly in the divine office. In January 1951 he suffered pulmonary congestion, had a high fever, and recovered slowly after a sulfamide treatment. The rare letters he sent to Scourmont that winter reveal the mental crisis he underwent. They reveal a discouragement, a disenchanted tone that is not typical of him. Until then, he had resisted interiorly, he had kept his optimism no matter what, trusting in Providence and his own strength. But constant physical pain, exhaustion, separation from his community, and no doubt also a kind of emptiness and routine where his monastic life was stagnating for months plunged him little by little in a quasi–depression. Doubt and thoughts of death haunted him. He evokes several times the 'feeling of division' that he feels. Was he not a victim of *acedia*, like the Desert Fathers?

> Humility makes a man rise up to heaven
> and disposes him to join the chorus of angels
>> (Evagrius of Ponticus,
>> 'Treatise on the Eight Capital Vices')

The summer of 1951 saw Francis go from one place to the other without settling down, and he was not well anywhere. In March he prepared to return to Scourmont after begging Guerric to discharge him from the task of novice master: 'not that I would not be happy to return (to the noviti-ate) but it seems to me that I would also be happy within the community and maybe I would be better there?' He continues by giving him news of his health: 'God leaves me my attacks of neuralgia. I am to find joy with them. The liturgy helps me do this when it asks, *qui macerantur in corpore delectentur in mente*, that is, Those whose bodies being consumed, let them rejoice in spirit. A fitting seasoning as Lent begins'.

He had nightmares, and the lack of sleep left him all day 'in a state of mindlessness'. They offered him the post of chaplain to the nuns of Chimay, but finally he found himself in June with Dom Belorgey at the nuns' monastery of Igny. In August he spent a few weeks at the home of his sister Marie-Thérèse, who had moved with her family into a villa in the Brussels suburb near the Soignes forest, where he walked a little every day. There for the first time in two years, he felt a little better. He prayed constantly—according to Evagrius, it is the only way to repel demons—and read 'The Monk in the Church of Christ' that his faithful friend Maur sent him from Scourmont at his request. But finally in Campine, where he spent the month of September in an isolated castle transformed into a retreat house, peace returned to his soul.

'I spent two delicious days in the library of the Ruusbroec Genoot-schap', he wrote to his prior. In the texts of the Admirable, he found once again two living sources: his mother's accent that brightened his child-hood and the mysticism of his monastic youth, which introduced him to the 'Kingdom of those who love God'. His physical strength returned little by little and allowed him to take solitary walks on the nearby moor, 'accompanied by a friendly book', as long as the corset that he never went without was tied tight. In this countryside he appreciated the 'at-mosphere that brought peace to my nerves and rest to my unbalanced joints, because everything is very flat'. However, he still dreaded partici-pating in community life and dreamed of prolonging this beneficial rest as long as possible. He was looking for some quiet chaplaincy and sent a request to this effect to Cardinal Archbishop Suenens. In the letter where he tells his superior of this step, he added, 'unless you judge it as well that I return to Scourmont.'

Apparently that is what was judged best, because the chronicles men-tion his presence in November. We find no trace of his activities during winter 1951–52. It was as if he had melted into the anonymity of the community. The personnel list from the end of January 1952 mentions him as novice master of both novitiates, that is the one for future choir monks and the one for laybrothers. The number of persons entering had greatly diminished: four in 1951, five in 1952. The number of brewery workers, in contrast, grew from four to twelve. At Caldey, it was the opposite: the novitiate flourished, and the financial deficit increased.

For Francis, India was very far, like the dream of a man asleep, like a buried jewel, like an extinguished fire. But it is well known that fire can smolder a long time under ash. An unexpected, perhaps providential, spark can revive it.

TO DOM ANSELME, FOR THE FULFILLMENT OF LONG–HELD HOPES

One morning in February 1952, Guerric went to the novitiate, at the time for *lectio divina*, and handed a small greyish brochure, printed on cheap purple paper to Francis, saying, 'This might interest you. Someone sent it from India for Dom Anselme. I showed it to him, but he did not react.'

Francis examined the small volume, entitled *An Indian Benedictine Ashram* by J. Monchanin and H. Le Saux, five hundred copies printed at St Joseph Industrial School in Tiruchirapalli. He turned the page, and his heart beat faster when he read the dedication: 'To Dom Anselme, for the fulfillment of long–held hopes, Jules Monchanin.' During the following days, the novice master took every opportunity to immerse himself in reading these hundred pages that localized, concretized, and dynamized the desire he still held vaguely for the monastic life in India. Much more than in Dom Alapatt's projects or those of the ceylonese novices in Caldey, he found here the sketch of a christian ashram as he had always imagined it, in the perspective of Gandhi and de Nobili. On page three, he noted, 'Though it is praiseworthy to try to develop an ashram in the benedictine line, we must not forget that the life of the ashram and *sannyasa* can not in any way be enclosed in the compass of any of the present western christian monastic traditions' and further, in the foreword written by Monsignor Mendonça the indian bishop of Tiruchirapalli: 'to make the church indian as Paul had made it greek or roman, from jewish as it had been at the beginning. Christianity continues to be seen in India as an imported religion, a vestige of the days of foreign domination. The best way is to begin with contemplative life.' Further on, Le Saux wrote, 'The christian *sannyasi* must, like Saint Benedict himself, refer above all to the Fathers of the desert, their life, their teachings. To start again, from the Rule itself, not to reproduce in India one or another western monastery. To start again from the trunk or even from the roots, not from the branches' and further: 'scrupulous attachment to the indian ways of life must be considered essential to the institution proposed here'.

From that time on, Francis resolved to prepare to leave alone, join the two hermits, and help them to make of Shantivanam, with God's help, a true monastic community. An article by Monchanin, recently published in the periodical *Église vivante* [*Living Church*] comforted him in his projects. But he first had to resolve the interior problem that this departure posed: was it compatible with his vocation, his profession, his vow of stability? In April, to his great surprise, he received a letter from Father Le Saux, addressed to him by name! One of his former cub scouts, Jacques Tombeur, now a priest and a member of the SAM in India (the Society of Auxiliaries to the Missions, founded by Father Lebbe in Louvain and to which Father Monchanin belonged), had been the instrument of this providential acceleration. He had gone to visit the hermits and showed them a letter he had just received from his former *Akela*, in which he talked about his desire to join Shantivanam. Le Saux, very much on the lookout for reinforcements for his enterprise, took note of this unknown monk's name and address and took the initiative to write to him: 'Come, we need you!'

In June it was to Father Albert, whom he considered his spiritual father since Dom Anselme's accident, that Francis wrote to outline his project. He did not hide his scruples from him and asked him to enlighten him. At the beginning of September, Albert left Caldey to go to the General Chapter in Cîteaux. He stopped at Scourmont on his way and talked at length with his former novice.

> Father Francis, I read attentively your long letter, and I looked through the small indian book you sent me with interest. I was also touched by the dedication which reminded me of the interview with Father Monchanin in 1939, in Dom Anselme's office. That was a long time ago! Father Guerric seems to think that Caldey inherited this foundation to be made in India. And it's true that with my three—soon to be four—ceylonese novices, I could envisage founding something in Ceylon.

In Ceylon? Why not? When do you envisage starting?

In two or three years, perhaps, when a first core of young people
  has been formed. You could go with them, lead them.

I would be very happy to. Do you have a precise idea about
  implantation, contacts, a location in mind?

No, nothing specific yet. You know, my community has been
  growing constantly since the war, it is difficult to govern, with
  these different cultures and many young people who are
  sometimes unruly. The material worries are heavy, I have
  little help. I have even encountered a certain hostility from the
  elders. I don't have time to take care of the concrete details of
  a foundation. But it remains present in my thoughts.

I'm sorry, Father, I feel that I have added another worry to your
  already heavy burden as prior.

No, Francis, do not apologize. It is your duty to speak to me
  about this and mine to try to enlighten you. You see, I am
  amazed to see how these young eastern people adapt easily
  to our usages. They have started to learn Latin and are faithful to manual work. We would have no trouble with them, to
  implant monastic life there according to the Rule, with a
  minimum of adaptation that the local customs would require.
  Besides, that is the point of view of Bishop Selvanathen as
  we heard last night in chapter: the indian bishops are
  counting on us to bring a solid and tried christian monastic
  tradition to their country. But I hear the bell for Compline:
  we will continue talking about this tomorrow.

After this first conversation, Francis became aware that Albert's project not only was vague but also, especially, was considerably different
from that of Monchanin and Le Saux, towards which he felt himself attracted. The next day he spoke with Albert again:

Father, I thought all day about what you described to me yesterday. I would obviously be happy to serve the monastic cause
  in India under whatever form it takes. But if several paths
  open, it seems to me that the call I received from Father Le
  Saux corresponds best to my own vocation. Remember,
  when I arrived in the novitiate, you were the first to whom I

confided my India project. This christian ashram, which goes back to the original poverty and asceticism in a local way of life, that is what I would like to live.

I agree, Father Francis, I recognize your stubbornness, your enthusiasm, I could also say your temerity. But in this case, what do you do with your vow of stability?

That is certainly the most difficult point to discern, I agree. I also foresee that if I leave the Trappists, many will view that change as an infidelity. But that is not my sentiment. It was you yourself, Father, who taught me that Saint Bernard advised to change monasteries if one could no longer accomplish the promises made to God in the place of one's profession!

Do you find that that is the case for you in Scourmont?

No, I am not saying that. But all the same, since the war, I experience the desire for a more radical life, a greater need for asceticism. It seems that my going to the ashram would be somewhat equivalent to what going from Cluny to Cîteaux was in the Middle Ages: going back to the origins of the Rule.

I understand. It is a fact that stability, while being an authentic cistercian value, is not the last word on monastic perfection. But why India? You are not an orientalist, as far as I know. You could ask permission to lead an eremitical life here, in the Ardennes, for example?

This is another question, that has nothing to do with Saint Bernard but is linked to the crisis the Church is experiencing in mission countries: the bishops are calling us to spread the christian contemplative life in these countries, particularly in India. It seems to me that I have been called to this task for a long time. Many years ago I read in a book about the Desert Fathers that there is a particular form of *apotaxis* [renunciation] called *xeniteia*, that is, a vocation that leads you to exile in a foreign land, far from everything you had, far from all that you are. Reading that, I was moved, as if those words were addressed to me.

Listen, Father Francis, you are posing a problem that I have never encountered. We must take time. I admit that there can exist this kind of special vocation in the Church. But I can not give my opinion on the value of yours. I know you well. You have always had some degree of impetuosity, excessive. . . . We must wait, pray, examine that from all sides, be sure that this is not an escape, an infatuation with a fad, a thirst for personal glory. On the other side, your superiors must check whether a cistercian community has the right to let one of its members go to consecrate himself to that kind of mission. Let us speak to Father Guerric about this without delay.

The two monks separated, making an appointment to talk again at Christmas. Father Daniélou was to come to preach a retreat to the community at the end of December. That would be the opportunity to submit the entire question to him: his advice certainly would have great weight in the decision. Albert promised to be there. He recommended that Francis pray and reflect.

PARIS

Along the Boulevard Jourdan in Paris' 14th arrondissement, the University City spreads its forty hectares of gardens, roads, and many buildings of various styles. One September evening in 1952, Francis arrived at the Belgium-Luxemburg pavilion with his little bundle of clothes. He had been sent to Paris for a month to follow a new medical treatment: the well–publicized microwave sessions performed only in a few large university hospital centers, from which they expected the complete healing of his persistent back pain. A preliminary examination revealed the first effects of the arthritis that was to cause him so much suffering later on. The treatment that justified this trip was only every two days, for two hours. This left our Trappist a great deal of liberty, and he took advantage as much as possible from the situation, exploring the extraordinary concentration of resources where he found himself for a few weeks. On 9 September 1952, he wrote to Father Guerric:

> The setting, in the University City, is pleasant and peaceful. It is also very cosmopolitan. The french Union (Africans and Asians) is largely represented. I have also met a ceylonese monk, professor in Colombo, who came here to do a doctoral thesis in the Institute of Indian Civilization. He showed me his licentiate thesis which

will soon be printed, on the history of Buddhism. He is very likeable and interesting. You can guess, no doubt, that he makes my mouth water when he speaks to me about his monastic life, courses and his professors at the Institute. It was here also that Father Monchanin studied before the war.

His new friend introduced him to the circle of indian studies scholars and introduced him to Olivier Lacombe, a specialist in questions of indian philosophy. He gave him advice on the readings and courses that would be helpful to prepare him to go to India. Francis took notes, borrowed course notes, bought books, and began to learn Sanskrit. He obtained an additional sum of money from Guerric to purchase more books. 'These are not whims', he pleaded, 'but classical texts. One of them was published by Budé. The textbook *Classical India* by Renou and Filliozat, published by Payot in 1947, would also be one to acquire. Professor Lacombe advised me to get these.'

From his student room, he wrote his first letter to Father Le Saux, a long epistle of five typed pages. He spent several evenings and was very careful.

Reverend Father,

You had perhaps begun to think that your letter of April awakened only a few echoes in me. That is not the case, of course. On the contrary, it filled me with joy, fulfilling my waiting much more than I had hoped and finally giving consistency to very old aspirations. Why then such a long silence? You will guess that a monk who has spent seventeen years in a trappist monastery, leading the cistercian life there with enthusiasm, while fulfilling the task of novice master for the last ten years or so does not go to India as would a traveler who is free to come and go as he pleases. It was good for me to retreat, to ask myself if truly I could begin to 'build this tower' or 'wage this war'.

He gave a few details on his studies and abilities, described his project, and evoked the difficulties he foresaw about his 'stability'. He summed up his talks with Father Albert and continued:

What are my dispositions now? I do not disagree that I could lead an edifying religious life in the church as a Trappist, whether at Scourmont or in India if I were sent on a foundation. However, I am afraid that this would not allow me to pursue as completely this desire for a second conversion, which is impelling me towards the ashram. I recognize that this aspiration must be the object of a serious spiritual discernment and it is to this end that I am writing this letter. Inasmuch as I see clearly, it is a question of the conversion of those who *bene extructi fraterna ex acie, ad singularem pugna heremi, sole manu vel brachio, Deo Auxiliante, sufficiunt* [going forth from the rank of their brethren well trained for single combat in the desert, they are able, with the help of God, to fight single–handed without the help of others]. I do not imagine this at all as a pleasant adventure, but I am preparing myself 'in fear and trembling', as I did when I wanted to leave secular life for la Trappe. This signified for me a concrete perspective of a poorer, more ascetic life, whose witness is perhaps more in the line of the primitive monasticism of Saint Pachomius, of the Sayings of the Desert Fathers, and of Cassian whom Saint Benedict taught me to love.

This does not prevent me from feeling that in many respects I am letting go of something solid to grasp a shadow. I am very conscious that at my age one is more attached than one realizes to western culture and customs, to the benedictine and cistercian usages that flourish here and that helped me discover the meaning of monastic life. In the novitiate I was especially interested in the spirituality of the Rule of Saint Benedict and of the golden age of Cîteaux. I am extremely attached to its movement as a return to the sources: return to the integrity and purity of the Rule and through the Rule to the Bible, the Fathers and early monasticism, all of which culminates in a very deep mystical current in which I find the fulfillment of my interior life. The basis of my under-taking is a thirst for the absolute, a desire for a sort of spiritual exploit, if I dared I would say a spiritual parachuting. The years spent in Scourmont seem to me to have been years of prepara-tion, formation. Would it then necessarily be temerity to desire, at a time of spiritual maturity and in full clarity, to sell what one

had acquired, abandon everything to which one was attached, to
sow seed in newly plowed soil?

He dated this letter 4 October, the feast of Saint Francis of Assisi, and
sent it on the 8th, keeping two carbon copies: one for Father Albert and
one for his superior Father Guerric.

This text seems to indicate that it was during his stay in Paris that
Francis made the decision and ripened his project to go live his cistercian
life in India, alone if he had to, as long as his superiors gave him permission. From this time, all his energy and intelligence would be used to
remove all the obstacles. Immersed in his readings about India, he truly
fell from the clouds when Father Thomas Litt came from Chimay to tell
him, beaming, that Scourmont was planning to make a foundation in the
Belgian Congo! A decisive consultation of the community was to take
place the following week. 'It would be difficult for me to hide from you
the dismay I experienced facing this unexpected prospect', he wrote to
Guerric that very night. 'Is it really a new and decisive orientation? I
don't know what to think of it'.

At once he returned to Scourmont to participate in the community
meeting that was to decide about the foundation to Kivu. He would play
the role of devil's advocate. He drew up a passionate speech for the
defense in twelve handwritten pages, and gave it to Guerric. This incisive,
polemic, and sometimes excessive document could be seen as a desperate
attempt to have the community renounce the project in the Congo. In it, he
denounces what he deems to be the 'colonial character' of the undertaking.
He deplores the fact that the manpower and financial resources that
Scourmont can offer are not being put at the service of Dom Anselm's
indian project—that had become his. He doubts that the african culture
could be favorable to the implantation of monasticism: there will perhaps
be many postulants, he says, but of what quality? How many years will it
take to form these young black men from 'primitive populations'?

The second part of the text is more interesting, and more personal:
Francis recalls 'at the risk of making the debates reactionary and to become the scapegoat of the adventure' that for more than twenty years
'Dom Anselme had turned us towards India', and that this foundation in
Kivu 'takes away from us the merit of pursuing the work of our venerable Father Abbot who is still living'. He enumerated all the meetings,
the invitations, the contacts established, Antoine Tamby's coming and

his death. Finally he showed how the cultural and religious milieu of India, which had developed monastic life even before the christian era, was more fitting than Africa for a contemplative foundation. He concluded, 'This sudden infatuation for the Belgian Congo seems so out of proportion to the twenty–five year vocation that calls us to India. We would find effective poverty there, to which too much prosperity or at least too great an involvement in temporal affairs has taught us to aspire.'

We do not know what effect this note had on Father Guerric. In any case it did not influence the vote that took place the following day, which revealed a 'moral unanimity' (?), according to the chronicler, in favor of the african foundation. Was Francis the only one to vote against it?

LANGUAGES AND CULTURES OF INDIA

> Are you called or is it you who call yourself ?
>> Is it because you thirst to undertake, accomplish, sacrifice?
>> That is very laudable, but is it you who thirst?
>> Is it on your own intelligence that you are counting,
>> on the resources of your nature, on your many gifts, on your
>>> courage?
>> Then, know that all that will be useless.
>> Ask yourself: is it God's will or mine?
>> Because that is the only important point.
>>> (Gandhi's answer to Lanza del Vasto)

At six o'clock in the morning, by a dark night with a new moon, a hooded cyclist crossed the Saint-Michel forest by the flickering light of his headlight. He pedaled steadily to reach the great descent that leads to Hirson, just past the border marked only by a double sign. A small nocturnal animal, scared, ran before his wheel and disappeared in a crackling of dead leaves. Fifteen kilometers from Scourmont. Francis left in this way each Monday before dawn. Up at two o'clock, he sang the night office, said his Mass in the crypt, and quickly ate breakfast before getting on his bicycle. At Hirson, he took the seven o'clock train for Paris. It was barely daylight when he got off the train at the north station and hurried to catch the subway to the School of Advanced Studies, where he attended five courses during the day: 'yoga and Veda', 'factors of indianness', and 'indian civilization and culture', given by Masson-Oursel; 'yoga–sutra of Patanjali' and 'buddhist idealism of Asanga' by Olivier Lacombe; and 'darsana upanishad' by Jean Filliozat. At about six o'clock at night he took the train home, where he studied unless his third–class compartment was too crowded with noisy card players. He got back on his bicycle at Hirson and this time went uphill in the dark of evening, up to the long straight road that crosses the Forges plateau, where the wind blows all year long. He would discreetly put away the old bicycle and go to the kitchen where supper leftovers awaited him. Guerric allowed him to go to Paris in this way every Monday, and both agreed not to let the word get out to the community.

The prior no longer hoped to convince Francis to associate himself with the undertaking of the Mokoto foundation in Kivu. On Francis' return from Paris, Guerric listened to him without allowing him to guess his own thoughts without suggesting precise directions. Formed by Dom Anselme, Guerric intended, like his abbot, to leave the monks free to develop their own charism. He did not share the view of his novice master: the project of a foundation in the Belgian Congo seemed to him so much more reasonable, surer, more serious than the fantasies of Father Le Saux, whose prose had not inspired much enthusiasm. But he did not want to prevent Francis from pursuing the 'narrow way' that he had chosen. As long as the cistercian constitutions allowed it and the community was not suffering from it, he agreed to Francis' requests, without giving him a mandate to do it or committing himself to support it.

At Christmas, Father Daniélou came to preach the community's retreat. He developed his vision of the Incarnation by painting a grandiose picture of the history of salvation from the beginning. Francis was won over by this enthusiastic and eloquent Jesuit. There was one shadow however: Albert had not arrived from Caldey. 'Until the day before Christmas, even up till the evening of the feast, I had hoped you would arrive', Francis was to write to him a few days later. 'You would have loved this retreat.' He compared the preacher to Saint Bernard himself, 'so versed in the art of breaking spiritual bread for his monks without letting them remain hungry'.

The founder of the Saint-Jean-Baptiste Circle in Paris that gathered Christians open to ecumenism and foreign cultures, Jean Daniélou (whose Brother Alain, a musicologist and historian of indian music lived in a palace on the banks of the Ganges in Benares) knew India well. Francis went to find him in his room during the time foreseen for private talks, and talked with him at length about his project. One can imagine the encouragement shown him by the man who was to write a few years later:

> The believers are all those who, in whatever degree, receive knowledge of the divine name. There are many degrees of this knowledge, from explicit to implicit. For many, it will remain vague. An enormous mass of people will meet only a fragile and fugitive footprint, on dark and out of the way roads, but they will have kissed this footprint with love and been inflamed with a holy desire. . . . The World still resists. Many reasons argue in favor of this resistance. The great masses of ancient civilization belong to very old religious traditions: Buddhism, Hinduism, Judaism, Islam, the importance of which we in the west are tempted to under-estimate. These religions formed immense peoples for long centuries. They implanted wisdom, principles, and habits, compared to which our western activism seems barbaric and depraved. Rare are the missionaries who, like Lebbe, Foucault or Monchanin, have brought the presence of Jesus Christ to the contemplative and silent mode that penetrates the eastern soul.

Francis found here a choice ally. 'Father Daniélou', he wrote to Father Albert 'obviously did not reveal to me by a light from above that such was indeed God's will for me. But, beyond what could appear to be unfaithfulness to Scourmont or Cîteaux, he did not hide from me the orthodoxy of these aspirations and their coincidence with what has all the appearances of a present action of the Holy Spirit on the missionary and monastic Church. Father Daniélou knows Father Monchanin very well. It is he who published his texts in *Dieu-Vivant*. He will publish another one soon. He also follows with much interest the missionary efforts that are tried at present in India. No doubt, he did not give his opinion on my capacity to lead the life of an ashram. But he thinks that this is an orientation of monastic life providential for the conversion of India.' Later, he concluded, 'These are the dispositions in which I live. By this openness of heart will I deserve that you tell me what you think of it? Certainly Father Daniélou's approval is precious to me. All the more since you have delegated him, in some way, to decide about my future. But it is not for him to give approval. Approval from the one who formed me to monastic life and followed me every day for the first ten years, this is the blessing I ask from you, with religious and filial affection.'

During the few days he spent in Scourmont, Daniélou spoke with Guerric about Francis' project, told him about the good he thought of it. He insisted that he be given two days a week in Paris and even offered to lodge him in a Jesuit house. Guerric consented to everything. From that time on, Francis could add to his program a well–researched course given by Filliozat at the College of France, on the topic 'Two hundred years of indianism'. He also took a course of elementary sanskrit grammar at the Institute of Indian Civilization and a course of Tamil at the School of Oriental Languages. It was an indian student who was replacing professor Meile at that time, and Francis was very happy to hear him relate his encounters with Monchanin at the Alliance Française of Pondicherry.

During the winter, the community was learning about Kivu: the Superior of the White Fathers of Africa came to speak to the Chapter; Maur and Corneille took an exploratory trip. Francis spent all the time left from regular life and the novitiate on his new studies. He wrote to the hermits of Shantivanam:

These courses are more than sufficient, as you can imagine, to keep me spellbound. They contribute very effectively to discipline and stimulate my own work. I must say that this first acquaintance with the language and texts is very ascetical, in the narrowest sense of this word. The text of Patanjali that I am beginning to read in Woods' translation, outside of the course, is extremely interesting. But my progress seems so slow compared to my desire. I was able to acquire most of the books that you recommended to me and I have reserved a place for them in this already very full schedule. These studies obviously contribute a great deal to keeping up and strengthening my hope. But I am still waiting for a definitive decision. You will understand, however, that I can obtain this decision only by respecting my superiors' delays. It seems to me that this patience together with a burning desire must be acceptable to God. My monastic life owes Dom Albert so much that I cannot give it this new orientation without receiving his blessing. I asked him for it in my last letter. As soon as I have received it, I will present my request to Dom Guerric again, asking for a three year exclaustration. I would very much like to know your advice on this subject, and I would receive with gratitude all the suggestions you might wish to make about my studies and preparation.

On 15 March, Francis was seated in the train that was about to leave the Hirson station in a few moments. The stationmaster blew his whistle, and through the window Francis saw Guerric and Maur running on the platform, looking into each compartment. Quickly he got off the train as it started to move away. 'What is it? Are you looking for me?' he asked. Guerric caught his breath. 'Francis, it's sad news.' 'What? What happened?' Francis asked. 'Your mother died during the night, of a heart attack. They telephoned the abbey this morning and I thought it best. . . .' 'Thank you', Francis replied; 'really, thank you'.

Francis did not return to Scourmont with them. He went in the opposite direction, northwards. He went to comfort his father, to be with his sister and brothers. It was he who prepared the funeral liturgy and composed the text that recalled the memory of his beloved mother. What was he feeling, beyond the words appropriate to the occasion? Anna had gone so gently, after a smooth and right life that had led her so close to God, that the journey to eternity must have been very natural. The most unhappy one was René, who lost the woman who had been his companion for forty–nine years and who now had to face the loneliness of daily life.

Once back at Scourmont, Francis returned to his unrelenting rhythm of instructions to the three novices, personal study, and courses in Paris. He was still waiting for Father Albert's response to his 'openness of heart' and the blessing he so hoped for. A little before Easter, an envelope from Caldey finally arrived. On it he recognized his teacher's handwriting. He opened it with joyous impatience, and his deception was equal to his anticipation. It was an answer like that of Pontius Pilate: do what you believe to be your vocation. I am not opposed to your project. Dom Albert added, 'I cannot speak like Dom Le Saux and tell you that I think it is the Lord himself directing your footsteps'. He left it up to the superiors and left Francis alone to face his choice. No approval, no blessing. Worse: he told him to be on his guard against 'his character, his heredity'. Was he alluding to his father's quick–tempered character? Francis absorbed the blow, reflected, and prayed intensely. It was Holy Week, Passion Week. He waited several more days, and when his calm had returned, he answered,

After these weeks of waiting and prayer, I can thank you (*corde et animo*) for having reminded me of the obstacles that you see on my road. All the difficulty of 'character, temperament and heredity' could not fail to make an impression on me. Who can say that he is free of these? But was this problem not posed more crucially before my entrance to the Trappists, since I lacked any experience of religious life? I remember that my parents and occasional directors often spoke to me about this at that time. And like then, after this last Lenten retreat, I believe that I see that, with God's grace, this is exactly what I must convert to God and immolate more deeply.

This desire for the 'singular combat of the desert', as extra-ordinary as it is in our day, as you remind me, seems to me to be the expression of a deep aspiration, deep desire, as we require for a religious vocation. Is it not tested by a prolonged stay in the *coenobium* as the elders asked? This stay, has it not always been accompanied by a desire for a more ascetic life with respect to temporal things, more demanding in terms of spiritual seeking?

To all of this the ashram seems to me to be the providential answer, accomplishing in addition another long–standing desire, to lead the contemplative life in a mission country. To now re-fuse to see this as God's answer would seem to me to be an eva-sion that I could not put up with. After having severely examined myself once again, I do not discover anything in me that indicates that I am giving in to weariness or some desire for adventure or human success. You know that at Scourmont I had found the hidden treasure, the pearl for which I had given up everything, but for which also the Lord has not ceased asking me to abandon more and more. It is to say yes to this invitation that I believe I have to turn to the ashram.

Was it the state of exhaustion Dom Albert found himself in that made him delay his answer several times? We can imagine the difficult moral dilemma that his disciple posed him, if we recall that Albert him-self had met Monchanin at Scourmont in 1939 and had promised in front of Dom Anselme to go as soon as possible to explore the possibilities of a foundation in India. But that had been with the abbot's blessing, before the war, before Mokoto.

Conscientious, obedient to the point of self–sacrifice, in 1953 Dom Albert could not bring himself to support his disciple's project, or to be responsible for what appeared to be a personal adventure perhaps doomed to failure, if not to death. At the end of May, he wrote to Dom Guerric: 'I can't do any more. Three more postulants have arrived, the community is murmuring against me. Take the novices to be formed at Scourmont or send me someone solid here to take care of them.' A short while after, he had a nervous breakdown and was sent to a rest home in London for a prolonged stay. Dom Godefroid Belorgey, who had recently resigned his office at Cîteaux, was free. He had always had a soft spot for Caldey and agreed to take charge there during Albert's illness. But the latter was right: they needed someone to take care of the novitiate of about a dozen young men, some of whom had come from far: Scotland, Norway, Senegal and even a Chinese from Hong Kong. Dom Godefroid gave Dom Guerric an up–to–the–minute report. There were only two novices in Scourmont, and one of them was going to join the regiment. They decided to send Francis to help Caldey: he was an experienced novice master and spoke English fluently. These qualities would be enough to choose him, but there was another probable reason: they were not sorry to get him away from Scourmont where everyone was preoccupied with preparing the foundation in Africa. His indifference, if not the silent reproach of his presence must have irritated many. Francis obeyed. The courses in Paris had ended. Enrollment for the next school year remained to be seen. They spoke of a stay of 'a few months'. Would the island finally play the role Dom Anselme had reserved for it, a 'trampoline to India'?

CALDEY

On 31 July 1953, Francis was welcomed to Caldey by Dom Godefroid Belorgey. After the muddy Thiérache and the gloomy refuge of Momignies, Caldey seemed to him a wonderful place, not only an enchanting island but also a well–known sacred place from the origins of celtic monasticism, to which the small church of Saint David especially was a striking witness. Without delay, he went to the novitiate, where he gave regular instruction. He found there a dozen young people full of life, a heterogeneous international group, sometimes rowdy but much more interesting than those he had known at Scourmont since the war. These exceptional recruits were not stimulated enough: the novitiate had no books except for a few classics, in latin and french translations. No serious program had been followed for months, and the schedules were eccentric. The new novice master sent letter upon letter to Scourmont, asking for choir books, graduals, gospels in english translation, works of patristics, spirituality, and even music stands. His novices did not know Latin well. He tried to teach them Latin, but in the meantime, they needed books in English.

Despite the zeal he showed in his new mission and the pleasure he experienced working at Caldey under Dom Belorgey's guidance, Francis secretly hoped that this interim assignment would not continue beyond the two or three months Dom Guerric had asked, because that would delay a departure that he continued to hope would be soon. In October, however, he had to resign himself to seeing his mission prolonged: Dom Albert's health caused serious worry, and the London physicians started a six–week course of shock treatments, a therapy very fashionable at that time in England. On each visit, Francis found him numb, as if absent. They foresaw several months of rest after the treatment, which delayed his return to the community until after Easter. Regular visits to his former master, for whom he still felt deep affection and a sort of veneration despite the rift caused by his last letter, allowed Francis to undertake various steps in London towards his departure. First, he had to take care of administrative affairs, both the civil and ecclesiastical ones: official permission from his superior, support by the local bishop in Asia, and especially a visa from the indian government, without which all the other steps would be in vain. Henri Le Saux sent him long letters in which he wove in practical recommendations and addresses of resource persons with stories of what interested him: his eremetical stay with the hindu *sannyasis* of the Arunachala mountain, disciples of the recently deceased great wise man Ramana Maharshi.

It took a long time at the indian embassy. The simple request that Francis made in Brussels when he left Scourmont was refused without comment. Following the advice of Father Le Saux, Francis submitted to the embassy in London, called India House, a more elaborate request, based on a file of recommendations that took him several months to draw up, with the help of his professors of indian studies in Paris. He added a letter in which he insisted on the private nature of his stay, on the interest he had in indian history and philosophy; he defined himself as a simple monk–student, not calling himself a priest and still less a missionary. It was difficult for christian religious to get a visa from the new government in India, because they were considered agents of the western powers from which the newly emancipated country intended to break away. From time to time Francis went to India House to inquire. He waited for hours, sitting on the leather benches in the hall, contemplating the mythological engravings and exotic landscapes that adorned the walls. The receptionist in a sari came to recognize him and softened her always–evasive response with a smile: 'No news, Sir. Next week, maybe?'

In the middle of December, as a surprise to everyone, Dom Albert returned to Caldey, against the physicians' advice, announcing that he was taking everything over. At first, Francis was glad to see his former novice master recovered and hoped that he would soon be freed of his charge. But things did not work out as he had hoped. Dom Albert did not yet feel very solid. He insisted that Francis stay with him, and had him promise to help him for another year. But the responsibility for the novitiate was not clearly defined. Many other things were unclear there as well, which irritated Francis. Was it the magic site of this lost welsh island at the very end of the world? Was it the more than one–thousand–year–old influence of celtic lack of discipline, or the more recent influence of anglican 'comprehensiveness', or the uncertainty of the sea's capricious nature? At that time at Caldey, nothing worked in a very orthodox manner. In the refectory, they were reading *The Little World of Don Camillo*. Every afternoon there was tea–time with cake and pleasant conversation. The twenty–fifth jubilee of foundation, 6 January 1954, ended with a film festival during which the community watched a spy film on the secret of the atomic bomb and a war film telling the story of the escape of three english officers. The prior's decisions changed from day to day, and the elders took certain liberties with the Rule. All this was done in a good–natured atmosphere where everyone assured each other, and especially the prior, of his affection and 'loving support'.

Francis would gladly have put a little discipline in all that, but he was not the boss. He suffered from Dom Albert's procrastination, hesitations, and changes of orders. He could not understand that a man who had previously been so rigorous was now speaking of interspersing sessions of free discussion between the instructions to the novices. He was afraid that the electroshock treatment in London had deeply shaken Albert and transformed his tendency to be a little too literal and persnickety into permanent and anguished hesitation. When later he would speak about his former master, he would often call him the 'Lamb', seeing in Dom Albert an innocent sacrificed, destroyed little by little by missions beyond his strength: first Caldey, then Mokoto—both of them missions that Francis avoided, moved by a reflex of self–preservation as much as by the conviction of a higher call to the East. At the end of his resources, he finally wrote to Dom Guerric at the end of January, awaiting clear directions from him. He started his letter with good wishes, with a hint of reproach for the founders of Kivu.

> I echo the hope that Scourmont must feel in these last preparations for the departure to the Congo. I ask God for all the graces they will need to implant the contemplative life in the heart of Africa. If I let myself be impelled towards other skies, where for a long time I had hoped to see Scourmont go, I do not for all that ask the Lord with less insistence that he give the seed you will sow there the growth promised to the mustard seed.

The rest of this long letter described in detail the last incidents he experienced at Caldey and continued, 'this community's great suffering seems to me precisely to be the gulf that is being dug between the leader and the flock.' He concluded, 'I feel that I cannot give Dom Albert the support, the help, the advice he hopes to find from me. Everything here is going at a rhythm with which I have difficulty harmonizing, a sort of mysticism of fraternal charity, elbow to elbow, universal adaptation against which my monastic fundamentalism can only bristle and which drives me more and more to find salvation in the "narrow way" of Shantivanam.'

To Maur, in a letter dated 15 January for his feast day, Francis confided, 'I join myself with all my heart to the last preparations for the Congo departure and I entrust the work of the founders to the Lord. I myself am in waiting, more so since Dom Albert decided to return. Now it is only a question of obtaining a visa. But this is not easy. I hear that every side is blocked: Brussels, Paris, Saint-André de Bruges. I keep up my hope but I ask you for your prayers.'

On February 4, in the siberian cold, the Scourmont community celebrated with much solemnity and emotion the departure of the *pusillus grex* [little flock] of founders to Kivu. Father Charles took advantage of some family business to deal with in Belgium to be present for this great event. It was he who recounted it to Francis in detail at his return.

After the High Mass sung by the founders, everyone had dinner
    in the guesthouse.
Why the guesthouse?
It was so cold in the refectory!
But you observed silence?
Yes. They read some very beautiful texts, one of which was an
    article by Dom Quatember on the participation of monks in
    missionary activity, and there were the speeches of the Father
    Immediate and Dom Guerric. He was quite moved, so, you
    know him, he took a playful tone and was even ironic at times.
    After the thanksgiving, there was a 'reception' in the great hall.
    Everyone wanted to embrace the travelers, encourage them,
    tell them a last word. Around three o'clock, the entire com-
    munity assembled in church. Even the workers were there.
    They recited the prayers for the journey and Dom Guerric
    gave Father Corneille the foundation cross, the relics for the
    church, a Bible and a Rule of Saint Benedict.
That must have been moving. How did they leave?
They were led to the door in procession. In the meantime they
    had put on their travel clothing. Dom Guerric took the wheel
    of the Plymouth and the whole group got in with him. I went
    in the car with the abbot of Saint-Sixte and Jacques Blan-
    pain, your former novice, who is serving in the military in
    Brussels and who had to return that very evening. He asked
    me to say hello to you. All together, we went to Melsbroeck
    to see them off.

Francis remained thoughtful. Even if he continued to regret the choice of
Africa, he was sensitive to the emotion of this departure, this monastic
fraternity, these rituals where the holy objects full of symbolism are
transmitted to those who are going far away.

NOTHING IS WORKING OUT

For the second time, Father Francis was refused a visa for India, despite
the file full of prestigious recommendations in which he had placed great
hopes. Must he give up the idea of joining Monchanin and Le Saux in

Shantivanam? He considered settling for a neighboring country, which would at least allow him to get closer to them and perhaps to start a similar contemplative ashram somewhere else. He started a vast operation by letter, sending dozens of letters, establishing contacts all over the place, telling everyone about his project, men or women, religious or lay, in Europe or Asia, anyone who might possibly help him or give him information. For example, he corresponded with the Benedictines of Saint-André-lez-Bruges, who recently had sent two monks and a group of novices formed in Belgium to Siluvaigiri, near Madras. He exploited all the contacts he could find in the countries neighboring India: Pakistan, where he knew one Capuchin; Chittagong, where someone gave him the address of canadian missionaries; and Ceylon, where the Caldey novices had relatives. Monchanin and Le Saux were also very disappointed by the second visa refusal and briefly considered creating an 'annex' of Shantivanam in Pondicherry, still french territory. But they soon gave up that idea, because of the political instability in the former trading post of Dupleix. To tell the truth, all three of Francis' reference points at that time—Scourmont, Caldey, and Shantivanam—were going through a difficult period.

In Scourmont, the new Congo foundation was at the center of their preoccupations and kept excitement going. Dom Guerric made several trips, leaving the governing of the abbey to Maur, who was sub–prior and recently promoted novice master or, rather, master of the one novice. The decline in number of postulants was beginning to worry them.

Shantivanam was in neutral. The two hermits rarely were there together: Le Saux often stayed in the Arunachala caves, and his spiritual search for non–duality as experienced by hindu sages occupied him almost exclusively. He was writing *Guhantara [Going Into the Cavern]*, in which, from his notes taken while on the mountain, he tried to describe the spiritual apperception of Hinduism, which would require a rethinking of the Trinity and Creation. Monchanin admitted that he was touched by the undertaking but remained skeptical about its validity. Every time that his companion agreed to babysit the ashram, he went to Bangalore or Pondicherry to fill up on reading, philosophical meetings, and classical music. He tried to approach the archbishop of Delhi to obtain a visa for Francis, but received an apologetic answer: 'I'm terribly sorry, but. . . .' The archbishop heard himself answer that now only doctors, nurses, or 'experts' in some field were granted visas. Monchanin added, 'We find ourselves clearly facing a determined desire to stop the visas. Entreaties bounce off this wall fruitlessly. If cenobitism is impossible, eremeticism remains. Despite everything, I believe in Shantivanam (but I don't believe in Arunachala).'

Francis knew that the two hermits had abandoned hope of welcoming him. One of the belgian Benedictines of Siluvaigiri, Father Dominique van Rolleghem, wished to join them and undertake a more austere, more radically indian life. He accompanied Father Le Saux during one of his stays in Arunachala, awaiting authorization from his superiors in Bruges. Monchanin wrote to Le Saux, in January 1955: 'Happy to know Father Dominique is in his element. May he replace Father Mahieu here.'

In Caldey, the situation was the worst. Dom Godefroid Belorgey, who had the habit of thinking out loud in the presence of an interlocutor, engaged Francis almost every day in a dialogue while walking when the weather permitted, as Dom Anselme used to do.

How are the novices doing, Father Francis?

Rather well, I think. The books Father Maur sent us from Scourmont and those I brought back from London give them good reference works and reading. These young people are promising, eager to learn, they are progressing rapidly in the spirit of religion. The irish officer is a bit crazy, the Dominican is sometimes disconcerting, no doubt because of his previous immersion in another spirituality. I think the young Scotsman will not stay. He is having a hard time enduring our way of life.

Good. And with Dom Albert?

You know yourself how difficult that still is. The changes of schedule and the ambiguity still create difficulties for the novices. They don't know who is directing them any more. They are told white in chapter and black privately. These 180 degree changes feed rumors, regrettable gossip, that turn against Dom Albert himself.

I wrote to Dom Guerric yesterday, but I wish you would report to him from your point of view. I approve the way that you are leading the novices and how you protect Dom Albert, but this cannot continue like this.

Shortly after this, Francis fell ill. A stubborn infection felled him, and the fevers and painful neuralgia that he already had experienced left him without strength for several weeks, apart from the community and its problems. As soon as his state allowed, he was sent to London to a bacteriologist, who suspected that the illness originated in his teeth. They extracted four, but follow–up treatment involved regular injections in a hospital. This was a good excuse to move to London temporarily, to Sacred Heart convent. The sisters gave him lodging in exchange for light chaplaincy duties, which left him time to follow a few courses of Tamil and Sanskrit at the Oriental School and to visit his childhood friends, Amy and Ida Henn, who became enthusiastic hearing of his projects.

At Caldey, during this time, the void in authority became more pronounced and tension grew. After new misunderstandings and despite the charitable and elegant attempts of Dom Belorgey to save the situation, the infuriated community had asked the Abbot General to send them a Visitor to whom they could express their grievances. They were asking nothing less than the resignation of Dom Albert. Dom Guerric arrived by airplane to take the prior back to Scourmont.

Francis would never again meet his novice master to talk about their indian project. Albert would be transferred to Africa, where he would be prior in Mokoto for a time. He would finish his monastic pilgrimage in Kivu, as chaplain of la Clarté-Dieu, a community of nuns entrusted to Scourmont.

In September, after the General Chapter, Dom Albert's resignation and his replacement by an irish monk, Eugene Boylan, were announced. The new prior was a physicist who had published a thesis on atomic energy in the 1930s at the University of Vienna. He would start his functions in January on his return from Australia, where he was finishing the installation of the first cistercian foundation on that continent: Tarrawarra, daughter of Roscrea, which would cross Francis' path in a providential way some forty years later. In the meantime, Caldey was once again fatherless. Dom Belorgey took up the interim, helped by Francis.

Tourism had picked up in Wales in the summer of 1953. The community began to make perfume, honey candy, and ice cream. Three young belgian women came to spend the month of July in the guesthouse. One of them was Claire Vellut, the cousin of Father Marc Marcq of Scourmont (nicknamed Bismarck). She recently had obtained her medical degree and joined the ALM (Lay Mission Helpers). As a member of this international women's organization, begun in 1938 in the movement of Father Lebbe's Samists, she was getting ready to leave for India.

The three young women were entrusted with selling the ice–cream, but during their breaks accompanied the monks walking around the island, where sometimes they ran down the flowering fields to the beach where the waves broke. They sat in the sand to catch their breath. Claire found herself naturally with Francis, and each time their conversations turned to India, where their hopes converged. The doctor, who was leaving in a spirit of medical and social service, was impressed by the knowledge her interlocutor had already gathered about the country's history, religions, languages. Both were especially preoccupied by the difficulty in obtaining a visa.

Doctor Vellut would leave in the spring with a three month tourist's visa and a letter of recommendation from Professor Maisin of the University of Louvain. In Delhi, presented to the indian ministry of public health by Father Jerome D'Souza, she would obtain a resident's visa through his intervention and would be sent to Pollambakkam, in Tamil Nadu, to start a center for combating leprosy. At once she was to write an enthusiastic letter to Caldey: 'Our center is not far from Shantivanam or from Ceylon. I await your visit soon!' She wrote to Monchanin remembering her meeting with Father Mahieu: 'His faith is too strong not to succeed despite everything.'

In the meantime, this faith was put to the test. Francis continued to exchange letters with Ceylon, Lahore, and Chittagong. He tried to determine the chances of success of a foundation in one or another of those regions. The bishop of Lahore—who was Flemish from Belgium—wrote him a very personal letter, affectionate and enthusiastic. He put sixty hectares of land at his disposal and assured him of the diocese's active support. The problem was that the population was 95% Muslim, and that probably would reduce the monastery's activity to witnessing, without great hope of the inter–religious dialogue Francis sought, following the path Monchanin had traced. Chittagong presented the same situation. Ceylon, with a buddhist majority and a solid christian community that already was ancient, offered a better environment. But the archbishop of Colombo showed no interest in the implantation of the contemplative life in his country.

Francis could not decide, no doubt because none of these destinations fully satisfied him. It was India he wanted, to meet the indian people and hindu monks about whom Le Saux passionately continued to tell him in his long letters from Arunachala.

PROVIDENTIAL INTERVENTION

Huge storms, weather conditions this time rather than storms within the community, shook Caldey that winter. Communication with the mainland was suspended. The west wind was so strong that it was dangerous to go out even on foot. In his cell where the hurricane shook the streaming window, Francis turned and turned in imagination around a triangle of three thousand kilometers per side: Lahore? Chittagong? Ceylon? In the center was a small dot, inaccessible: Shantivanam. It was time to choose, time to clarify his canonical situation. He sat in front of his typewriter and composed a text outlining the situation for his superior.

What did he want? To join or create a hermitage in the subcontinent. Where? Since India remained closed, he had to look elsewhere. Several bishops desired to have monks in their diocese, especially in Pakistan whose government easily granted visas. He had to choose. 'Although we must first and foremost entrust ourselves to the Lord for him to make the mustard seed grow as tall as a tall tree, we should not refuse to examine the various qualities of the soil where we are called to sow.'

Why a hermitage rather than a classical foundation? First, because the eremetical life corresponded to the eastern religious culture and its conception of the monk, that it was favorable to a return to the sources in the tradition of the Desert Fathers. Then, because hermits under the local bishop's authority would arouse less suspicion in the current political situation than a foundation, which was juridically under a western religious order. Finally, because inter–religious dialogue presupposed adaptation of the Rule and lifestyle to local customs, and such delicate work would be done best by a man alone rather than a group, which would be tempted always to reproduce its usual ways of functioning.

In the last paragraph, for the first time, he stated specifically what he expected from Scourmont: moral support (permissions, recommendations, introduction of a request for exclaustration to Rome) and effective support (that is, financial support) for the trip and beginning. Not much in total. Where would further funds to continue come from? Friends, family, Mass intentions, and, as soon as possible, from his own manual work there.

Dom Guerric did not answer immediately. All of that required reflection. Charles came to spend a few days at the mother house. Guerric asked him how much it would cost to build a hermitage in Pakistan! Charles, who had not the slightest idea, asked Francis on his return. At once Francis took up his pen to reassure his superior: 'Everything will be very modest. In fact, for the time being, it is only a question of the cost of the trip by boat.' Guerric then gave his complete consent to Francis' requests. He was happy, he wrote, to see what he considered Scourmont's third foundation taking shape and gladly gave his permission and tuition fees for a trimester of courses at the University of London. He pressed the future hermit to choose his destination, because the request for exclaustration must be backed up by a letter from the bishop of the diocese where he would settle.

Francis made a last round of consultations before deciding. Dom Eugene leaned towards Lahore, as Dom Belorgey had before him; the bishop seemed so friendly, so enthusiastic. Claire Vellut knew the bishop of Chittagong and assured him that he would be received with open arms. Dom Guerric, while telling him that he knew nothing about these countries, came round to the advice of Le Saux and Monchanin, who had advised Ceylon, more open to the monastic spirit.

Francis had decided, but on his way to London to request a visa from the Pakistan embassy, he made a detour to the benedictine abbey of Prinknash to meet Father Benedict Alapatt. He had declined his superior's invitation to join Siluvaigiri, a foundation of Bruges, and was getting ready to bring Father Bede Griffiths to Bangalore to found a new monastery. Since one was an indian citizen, the other a member of the Commonwealth, they had no problems with a visa. Learning of their confrère's tribulations, they suggested he go to Goa with a portuguese visa. As soon as that territory was linked to India, which would probably be soon, the residents would automatically be permitted to stay in India. They proposed that he meet them in Bangalore to reinforce their small group. Francis thanked them without committing himself. Was he afraid of being absorbed by the Benedictines, of whom he had once said, 'This is not my style'? Was he skeptical about the chances of the Goa strategy? Or simply did he prefer to keep his hands free to discover for himself, once he was there, the possibilities that would open up? In any event, he did not neglect to maintain good relationships with all those who tried to live the christian monastic life in Asia.

We have to go through London before leaving, would you like to come with us?
Willingly.

'I want to say goodbye to "Mother Toni" before going to Southampton', explained Bede Griffiths.

'Who is this religious?' asked Francis.

She is not a religious. She is an elderly lady, a remarkable person. Her real name is Mrs Antonietta Sussmann. She is a jungian psychoanalyst of italian origin, married to a Jew. She converted to catholicism and is continuing her spiritual journey through Hinduism. She and her husband fled the nazi regime in 1938 and like Sigmund Freud, found refuge in London. She gathers around her a group of indian scholars of whom are several religious, university professors and also free seekers. Would you like to come there with me tomorrow night?

I would be very interested.

This is how Francis discovered the large house in Gloucester Square, where Mother Toni taught and meditated, surrounded by her disciples and statues of Shiva, Vishnu, Ganesh, and Hanuman. They prayed, and practiced yoga, sitting on the ground or on low seats. It was a sort of foretaste of India, and he would often return during the few months before his departure.

The next day, he accompanied the two Benedictines to the quay, where they embarked for Bombay. When the gangways were drawn up and the horns sounded, he felt very nostalgic. When would his turn be? And to which port would he go?

He returned to the train station by foot, in the maze of docks among the merchandise, riggings, the scents of tar and gasoline, and the gulls' piercing cries. Back in London, he went past India House—noticed the young lady in the sari was not there—and filled in the form for a simple tourist visa. At the question 'reason for the trip', he wrote, 'to go to India to visit a few friends before going to Lahore'. They can't refuse him that, surely!

His courses at the Oriental School began in April. This time he chose history of Buddhism and the Tamil language. He could no longer lodge at the Sacred Heart convent. He found a place in a rectory on Ogle Street, not far from the university. The parish priest was sick. Francis would replace him. One morning, shortly before Easter, he found two similar envelopes in the mailbox: one had Pakistan's coat of arms, the other the familiar India House address. The government of Pakistan gave him a residence permit, but the indian embassy laconically communicated their

third refusal. Even the simple transit visa was not granted! Francis tried
to overcome his disappointment, to accept this third refusal as a trial sent
by God. He returned to the City to get his Pakistan visa and then, without
knowing exactly why, went by way of India House, as if to see for a last
time the only portion of indian territory he was allowed to enter. Was it
nostalgia that impelled him, a mysterious intuition guiding him, or an
angel who took pity on him? He wandered for a while in the great hall,
sat on the green leather bench, then, not recognizing any familiar face,
went out and stayed on the sidewalk a few instants.

'Hello, Father, how are you?' Two indian women in sari gently
approached him. He recognized the embassy employee whose smile had
brightened his long waits the year before. Her mother was with her. The
conversation started. The young girl had heard of Shantivanam. One thing
led to the other. Francis told them his troubles, the succession of refusals,
dashed hopes. They listened, smiling. Finally the mother told him: 'Father,
if you will permit me. This is not how business is done in India. You have
to know someone in high places. Files, the hierarchical way, that does not
work.' 'My friends in India asked the archbishop of Delhi to intervene but
nothing happened', Francis responded. The mother elaborated, 'You have
to aim higher. Why do you not address a personal request to the
ambassador, Mrs. Vijaya Lakshmi Pandit? She is the sister of our Prime
Minister Pandit Nehru, she loved Gandhi very much. She is very
intelligent, very open. Perhaps she will see you. Try, ask for an audience!'

Francis returned to Ogle Street and wrote a letter at once, sending it
that very day. One week later, he was summoned to the embassy, but it
was Mrs. Pandit's secretary who saw him. 'Sir, it is not up to me to make
a decision on your case. But I believe your project might interest Her
Excellency. I advise you to write as completely as possible why you want
to live in India. I will give her your document and it is possible that she
will invite you to meet her.'

Full of energy, Francis perceived that he was playing his trump card.
His whole future depended on this text he was going to send her. He
wanted to reread Le Saux's letters, be inspired by *An Indian Benedictine
Ashram*, check precise references. All his papers were at Caldey. He re-
turned to the island, shut himself up in his cell for three days, and wrote a
seventeen–page text that he entitled: 'The meeting of Hinduism and
Christianity in monastic life'. In his haste, he did not even keep a copy.
He sent the text as someone might cast a message in a bottle into the sea.

Less than two weeks later, he received a telegram: 'Mrs Vijaya Lakshmi Pandit wishes to receive you next Friday'. On Thursday, April 21, he took the train to London, in clergyman's garb as it was the custom in Great Britain for traveling religious. In his bag, he took his cistercian habit with him, because he wanted to be dressed as a monk to see the ambassador. A lady and her daughter, on retreat at Caldey after a long stay in India and who kept the souvenir shop, advised him to bring a gift. They themselves prepared a lovely wrapped basket containing small pottery items, dried flowers, and bottles of lavender, all products of Caldey.

Very cordially received by the staff this time, Francis was ushered into the antechamber, where he changed his clothes before sitting down. He felt like a student in front of the door to the examination hall, but his heart swelled with hope. The interview would remain one of the most beautiful memories of his life: this great lady, sitting very straight behind a long mahogany table on which was the text he sent her.

'Please sit down, Father. May I introduce Doctor Rozario, secretary of the Educational Department. He is catholic like you and I invited him to participate in our meeting.' Francis was immediately won over by Mrs. Pandit's graciousness, intelligence, and attentive benevolence. He answered with clarity and simplicity, giving her the clarifications she requested. 'Really', she concluded, 'I am astonished that you were refused this visa. I express my regrets to you. I will inform my brother in Delhi today. You will receive news soon.'

Before leaving, Francis gave her his gift. He was already in the staircase, when she called him back to tell him how much she appreciated the contents of the package, which she had opened immediately.

Francis did not leave Ogle Street and kept watch for the mailman. He wrote to Dom Guerric, to tell him about the providential events. Finally, on May 16, he received a message inviting him to the consulate to get his visa! Brother Jacques Blanpain, who was staying with him a few days before returning to Caldey, accompanied him into the city. When Francis left the consulate, he could not contain his exuberance. His happiness was overflowing. He skipped in the street, ran with Brother Jacques, and jumped onto the platform of a moving bus to go directly to make arrangements to take the boat. The first available cabin was on a ship that left September 30th. All the others were booked! But they let him hope for a cancellation, and he extracted their promise that they would give him the first available place. He wrote to Dom Guerric immediately to obtain the eighty pounds for the ticket and ask an additional thirty pounds for a slight (!) detour by train to Ranchi at the foot of the Himalayas, before going to Trichy. Fortunately for him, Guerric's knowledge of the geography of India was not very clear, and once again he consented to everything. Not a minute to lose. He urgently needed the exclaustration for the diocese of Trichy. 'Do you still have the letter that Monsignor Mendonça sent you in 1953? I am writing to him right now to tell him what has happened and to tell him of my arrival.' Francis' heart had wings. He redoubled his efforts. At the Oriental School, he changed his registration and took up with renewed zeal courses of Sanskrit and Tamil. A few days later, the travel agency phoned him to tell him there was a place on the *SS Carthage* June 24th. Yes, he would take it! It was his feast day, Saint John the Baptist! He had one month left to pack his bags and say goodbye. He wrote to Dom Guerric that he would go to Scourmont on Pentecost weekend to say goodbye.

An Indian Tale

In his dream, a monk had seen a faraway city, full of marvelous temples, where many men sought God. He dreamed of completing his life of adoration and detachment there, what they called *sannyasa*. He went by foot, doing all kinds of work to earn enough to survive along his way, saying his prayers and purifying his soul. The trip lasted twenty years. The city, recovering from a long war, was surrounded by a thick wall with three gates, guarded by soldiers. They looked at the stranger with mistrust. Our monk went in all simplicity to the first gate. He had no knife or subversive books. He had only a piece of cloth around his waist, another to cover his shoulders, a walking stick and a little iron cup tied to his waist with a string. The guards pushed him away roughly without even searching him or questioning him. He meditated for a little while, fasted, then he went to the second gate. This time he had prepared his story.

Hello, guards, I am Francis, a friend of Filliozat and Lacombe from Paris, a great city in the West where wise men cultivate knowledge and love for your city. I come from even further to pray in your temples.

Without a word, the guards stepped forward a pace, crossed their lances and looked at him menacingly. He went away into the forest to pray and meditate again. A little later, he went to the third gate at nightfall and said:

Officer, sir, I am a simple traveler, crossing this country. I have been told of your temples. May I spend the night with you before continuing toward the North?

But the guards did not let him enter.

We have no use for vagabonds of your race, cried one of them. Go away.

Then he went away with a great deal of sadness in his heart, because he had exhausted all his resources and tried every gate. He sat near the river, abandoned himself to God's will and fell asleep. Before dawn, he was awakened by a murmur of voices and soft laughter. Two women, dressed in shimmering cloth, each carrying a copper jug on her head, were standing in the moonlight at some distance from him and looking at him with curiosity. He smiled at them. They came closer and wanted to know what he was doing there. He told them his whole story. These women were the servants of Lakshmi, the sister–wife of Vishnu, the goddess of chance and prosperity. They told their mistress the tale of the monk Francis, and Lakshmi's heart was moved. At once she transported herself to the river and her luminous apparition dazzled the monk, who bowed as he greeted her.

It is I who rule over this city, she said. Come with me, because I know your purity of heart.

Immediately she changed into a swan, and carrying on her back the radiant pilgrim, she crossed the ramparts with a single flap of her wings. In the sky, a few stars were still shining. Francis chimed out their names with jubilation. Lakshmi landed on the temple esplanade where thousands of small oil lamps were going out, and having let her passenger off, she transformed into a peacock and went away majestically through the gardens, in the pink light of dawn. Francis gave thanks to God.

FAREWELLS

Francis got off the train at Hirson station just in time to catch the last bus to Chimay. He was happy to see Scourmont again after a two year absence and to share with his brothers, Father Maur and especially Dom Guerric, his joy at having obtained a visa at last, and his hope of bringing to eastern soil the monastic fervor he found here twenty years earlier. On the road to Poteaupré, he sang an old scouting song as he had done before. 'I will arrive just in time for Vespers', he told himself, walking a little faster. He went in without being seen, found a cowl in the cloakroom, put it on and hurried along the long hallways towards the church. The others were no doubt already in choir. He passed in front of the abbot's office. The door was open. He stopped, knocked two short knocks on the door frame and poked his head in, smiling. 'Here I am, I caught the last bus, you won't have to come and get me at the station!' Guerric looked embarrassed. After a silence, he said, 'Take that cowl off, Francis. I prefer that you not appear in community. Go to the guesthouse. I will send someone to tell you what to do.'

Francis did not understand. He obeyed without saying anything. He had not imagined such a thing: to be refused access to his own house, to be kept away from the choir where his brothers were singing the divine office. He went to the guesthouse. That evening, a brother brought him food, with a message from Dom Guerric, asking him to go say Mass the next day at the Chimay racecourse, where an automobile race was taking place. He was to stay there all day, to ensure a priest's presence in case of an accident.

Sunday evening, light–headed, deafened by the sound of the motors and the crowd's excitement, he fell asleep in the guesthouse after begging the Lord to deliver him from the bitterness that assailed him. On Monday morning, after a short visit from Father Maur, who brought him the books he had asked to take with him, Guerric asked him to come to his office to see him. He gave him the money for the trip and two cistercian habits made of light cloth; no doubt some of those that had been made for Mokoto. 'Farewell, Francis. May God protect you.'

Twenty years before, Francis left his childhood home, abandoning the career traced for him by his father, who denied him and refused to embrace him. Today, he was leaving his second family, alone, without escort and without explanations. He thought he had come to say goodbye, as to old friends; to kneel in front of Dom Anselme, to embrace his brothers, his former novices. Not for a second had he thought that his request for exclaustration might forbid him access to the community. And Guerric just wanted to do things correctly, canonically. Surprised by his arrival, ill at ease, he could not find the words to explain this to him. Pentecost 1955 would remain a painful memory for a long time.

But the euphoria of his imminent departure submerged all the negative feelings at the moment. From the abbey of Clervaux where he stopped on Monday night, he wrote to Guerric: 'I thank you for the hospitality you showed me at Pentecost despite the upset my arrival caused you. Thank you also for all you have done to facilitate my trip.'

The warm welcome he received at Clervaux confirmed the interest the abbot had in the Shantivanam experience. Francis took with him books and messages for Father Le Saux, and went to Paris where other friends awaited him, among others a couple of artists who created liturgical objects for Asia. They gave him a chasuble embroidered with a cross planted in a lotus blossom, a worked ciborium, and a folder of sketches, outlines, projects, all inspired by indian art. He put all that in his suitcase, promising himself that he would show them to Mother Toni before giving it to Father Monchanin. A few days in Brussels to visit his elderly father; a round of visits to brothers, sisters, nephews and nieces; a quick hop to Ypres to Aunt Marthe, with a stop in Bruges to see the abbot of Saint-André; and Francis returned to London for his vaccinations and last preparations. He bought several iron trunks that he filled with books and a portable typewriter. He returned to Caldey on June 15 and left it again on the 21st for Southampton. Father Charles helped him to carry his suitcases on the plank wharf of Prior Bay. At the moment when the boat was approaching, Francis asked him, 'Sincerely, what is your opinion of my enterprise?' Charles answered him as a man from Normandy would: 'If you succeed, everyone will agree with you. If you fail, everyone will deny they knew you.'

The big motorboat sliced through the waves. On the wharf, the silhouette of Charles waving his hand was already fading in the fog.

From Southampton, the P & O Company's *SS Carthage* had to begin by crossing the channel to stock up with supplies at Calais because of the english dockers' strike. But Francis did not care: his trunks of books were on board, that was the essential thing. The six 'fathers' were together in one cabin and at one table, but he was the only Catholic priest.

The others were Protestant missionaries going to Southeast Asia or China. For them, Bombay was only a stop between Aden and Singapore. For Francis, it was the end of a patient voyage and the beginning of a new life. He prayed the canonical hours alone on the upper deck. Each morning he said Mass for the catholic passengers and for the Goan crew members. He started a liturgical innovation: a time of 'prayer of the heart', in silence, after a short reading from the Gospel. He started a conversation with a professor from Trichy, and asked him to have him memorize a few phrases in Tamil every day. The other accepted willingly: everyone tried to keep busy during these nineteen days of travel. On 11 July, it was announced that they would arrive in Bombay the next day before dawn. As soon as it left the Red sea, the tugboat was shaken by the monsoon. At two o'clock in the morning, they started the maneuvers for docking. In their narrow cabin, the six religious pressed their noses in turn against the one porthole. But they could see nothing but torrential rain pattering in the darkness. At daybreak, the passengers disembarked. Dom Le Saux was there, in saffron clothing with a black umbrella, waiting for Father Mahieu.

THIRD PART

INDIA, FOUNDATION, AND TAKING ROOT
(1955–1968)

INDIA, FOUNDATION, AND TAKING ROOT

ELEPHANTA

FATHER MAHIEU HAD SCARCELY MOVED into Saint-Xavier college, when Dom Le Saux brought him to Elephanta, a well–known sacred place of shivaitic spirituality. The monsoon was so strong that the little tourist boats that sailed between the island and the 'Gate of India' several times a day stayed at the wharf. Only a government official was getting ready to do a tour of inspection in the bay and proposed bringing the two monks in his motor launch. 'I can let you off at Elephanta around four o'clock, Father', he offered, 'but I can't come to get you until tomorrow at noon'. 'Is it possible to find lodging on the island?' queried Francis. 'There is no hotel, but the guardian is alone during this season. He will no doubt be happy to have some company.' 'Let's go!' said Francis, lifting his robe to step over the ship's rail. Le Saux tried to shelter him under the large black umbrella that he held at arm's length, while lifting onboard a heavy cloth bag. 'What are you taking that is so heavy?' asked Francis, shaking his soaked hood. 'It's a surprise', Le Saux replied mysteriously.

This was Father Le Saux's first visit to Elephanta as well. He had seen many photos of the large temple cut from granite, and for a long time he had desired to see it. He had prepared this visit for his companion

127

as an enthronement feast, a sort of ceremony of initiation to Hinduism, maybe as sort of a test as well. The fact of spending the night on the island gave his plan a still more exciting dimension.

The guardian–conservator was a young man, jovial and cultured. He went before the visitors up the steep staircase invaded by a colony of monkeys and brought them into the huge room cut in the rock. At the entrance, Shiva Nataraja, his eight arms spread out, danced the world. Shiva Yogeshvara was sitting on his lotus flower, eyes half closed, indifferent to the goddesses flying about around him. Francis looked at everything and listened attentively to their host's explanations. Le Saux was no longer with them. Sitting at the back of the room in the shadows, he was plunged in contemplation of the enormous three–headed Shiva. He later explained, 'When my eyes met those lines, those curves, and especially those eyes, the shock was such that I had to lean on a column. The conservator continued to explain but I was no longer listening to him. He proposed to make supper, give me a room for the night. As for me, I was thinking of only one thing: to stay there, seated, in the middle of the cave, in front of, in communion with this Maheshvara, sunk in this presence.'[1]

Francis, impressed, sat at some distance from his confrère and gave himself to silent prayer. Hours passed. Darkness was complete, and the stone's relief was no longer distinguishable. The Benedictine had not moved. Francis decided to go back down. He got up without making noise, stretched his stiff limbs, went back to the guardian's house, and shared his vegetable curry. After the meal, the two men spoke at length of the religions of India and the place that the Catholic Church occupied there.

The next day at dawn, Francis noticed that his companion had not reappeared, and went up to the cave without waiting. Henri Le Saux had placed on the ground, between the giant columns, facing the three–faced statue, a flat altar with a paten and chalice, lit by two small candles. He was sitting cross–legged on the ground, eyes closed, smiling. Francis was astounded. 'Good morning, Father'. ('So that was what was so heavy in his bag', he thought!) With a gesture, Le Saux invited him to take a seat beside him. *Introibo ad altare Dei. Ad Deum qui laetificat juventutem meam.*

What Francis would remember of this unusual excursion was the meeting with the conservator and the morning Mass under Shiva's triple gaze. In his journal, Le Saux spoke only of his ecstatic night, without

---

[1] Le Saux, *La montée au fond du cœur*, p. 138.

mentioning the presence of Father Mahieu. The two men were decidedly not on the same wavelength. Had Le Saux hoped by this spectacular production, to sweep Francis along in his slightly fanatical quest for *advaita* and to make of him his disciple? Had Francis had a premonition about his companion's suffering, the interior division that tore him apart more and more between his belonging to the Church of Christ and his attraction for the hindu way of fusion in the Brahman 'Supreme transcending all limits'? The Cistercian had come to India to live the simple life of a christian hermit and eventually start a monastery, a contemplative community, if he found the necessary support. These projects no longer interested the Benedictine, who a few days later wrote in his journal, 'The incompatability of character with Father Francis Mahieu makes my departure from Shantivanam necessary. I will do so without regret. I must go far from these attempts at monastic life, whether I remain a benedictine monk or not. All the questions will come up in a few months: where to go? In what capacity?'[2]

Francis, for his part, wrote to Dom Guerric on 2 August: 'I regret that the step (of exclaustration) must be taken so quickly, before I have had a chance to assess the ashram's (Shantivanam's) chances for survival. My contact with Dom Le Saux has not put an end to my hesitations.'

A LITTLE DETOUR TO RANCHI

Francis was in no hurry to go to Shantivanam. He was experiencing this fabulous India he had been studying for three years in books and sacred texts, of which he had been dreaming for more than twenty, through every one of his senses. He gave himself to it physically during an improvised journey of more than ten weeks which would lead him by small stages to the Himalayas before descending again towards the extreme south of the peninsula.

The first week with Le Saux, he visited the buddhist caves of Kanheri, Ellora, and Ajanta, vestiges of the great monastic establishments of the first centuries. But there was no connection between the two men. The hermit of Arunachala's somewhat fanatical talk, his superstitious scruples—one day he refused to say Mass because his altar stone was

---

[2] Le Saux, *La montée au fond du cœur*, p. 143.

cracked and he saw in this a sign, a punishment—left his companion perplexed and reserved. On the other hand, Francis' cistercian fervor, his unconcealed desire to found a monastic community that would participate completely in the indian culture and Gandhi's ideals but would nevertheless be unambiguously in the christian tradition and ecclesial structure, provoked the condescension of Abhishiktananda–Le Saux, who was more and more attracted by the shivaitic conceptions: 'I am afraid that Father Mahieu's enthusiasm for Buddhism is especially joy at finding here his dear cistercian monastic conventual life. . . The hindu monk has neither *sangha* [community], nor *Dharma* [Rule] nor Buddha to give himself to. He lets himself be swallowed up by the Absolute. . . How could collaboration be possible between one who received his illumination in the solitude of Arunachala, from a guru who does not show himself, and the one who received it from a flesh and blood master in the chapter room at Scourmont?'[3]

Le Saux soon joined Doctor K. Metha, a parsee guru, founder of a 'nature cure' society, who guided his disciples on the way of meditation and detachment in his Bombay and Poona centers. Francis went to Ranchi alone by train to meet belgian Jesuits who had been living there for decades. He was charged with a message and was happy to meet Father Quirijnen, originally from West Flanders also, and who had just spent several years as a hermit in a village of Bihar. After that, he planned to go straight south towards Tamil Nadu, to join Monchanin. But the indian hospitality and enthusiastic welcome from the Jesuits would lead him, on the contrary, ever further North, to the Himalayas. He would let himself be swept along willingly, marveling, captivated, transported by the discovery of India. Monchanin, learning that his future disciple had become a yoga enthusiast, told Father Le Saux about his reservations towards these practices. Indulgently he concluded, 'The first contact with India is certainly intoxicating.'

We have found the letters the traveler sent to Europe at each of his stops. They form a journal.

---

[3] Le Saux, *La montée au fond du cœur*, p. 138.

Bombay, St. Xavier's College, 19 July 1955

I am still on the threshold contemplating the profound mystery of 'Mother India', Yes I love her. That is not new. I did, before I left, when I knew her very little.

The change, for someone arriving from London or Paris, is so evident, so striking. The atmosphere is so different: peaceful, silent, dignified. How can I put it? I have the feeling that people here are closer to the way of the Beatitudes than we are back home. The poverty is immense. It appears everywhere in the streets, trains, buses. But there is such a reserve of patience, kindness, veneration for all forms of religion.

Allahabad, Bishop's House, 26 July

When I was in Bombay, a friend from the College took me to the caves of Kanheri. It is one of the most beautiful monastic sites one could dream of. We had to leave the car five kilometers from our goal and walk up the side of the hill on a path crossed by streams—it's the monsoon season! The caves were dug in the rocky face, all on the same side. They dated from the first centuries AD On the lower level, the abbot's cell, the guesthouse and a Caitya, a large rectangular temple similar to our christian basilicas from antiquity. From there, we went up to the top by a narrow cornice. We were climbing from one cell to the other. It reminded me of the *carceri* of Assisi. All the caves are linked by staircases carved in the rock. We even found the 'chapter room' (Dharmasala, place of the Rule, it's the same meaning as the chapter room in our monasteries), a beautiful square room with a stone bench along three walls, and in the middle the superior's seat, recognizable by its sculptures. I really had the impression of seeing the monks with my own eyes, the *bikhu*s assembled there, as we did, to listen to the teaching of their master on meditation, asceticism or love. I heard them accuse themselves in front of the chief of the *sangha* of their failings to the Rule, as it is prescribed in their Vinaya Pitaka. And all that in the midst of wild nature, with forests all around and very far on the horizon towards the west, there is the sea. Overhead, the sky where a few kites circle, very high. On the terrace leading to the Dharmasala, I sang None and it was as if the skies opened. . . .

On 22 July, I arrived in Sanchi, the fourth stop on my indian pilgrimage. It is there that the largest and oldest buddhist monasteries of India are located. The great stupa of the emperor Ashoka (240 BC) is still in excellent state. There, I met a young buddhist monk from Ceylon, 28 years old, a student of Rev. Rahula who guided my first steps in Sanskrit three years ago in Paris. We had a very long conversation, until my train's departure at 11 o'clock pm. He already had a good experience of meditation, with this great gentleness characteristic of the 'Middle Way'.

There is so much to see also in daily life: traveling by train in third class in India, day and night, would give enough material for a whole book . . .

God has been so good to me thus far, and everyone I met so kind. . . . He must have in store a few different experiences, otherwise it would be too easy.

Ranchi, St Stanislas College, 2 August
(to Dom Guerric)
Dear Father Prior,

I have arrived safely at the belgian Jesuits. The missions I visited to break up the trip all revealed to me how much monastic life is awaited here. If the Jesuit fathers themselves are unanimous, is that not convincing? . . . They have a flourishing mission but it is restricted to the aboriginal tribes. They think that the monastic life is the only way open for them to be admitted by the Hindus. . . . How I wish you could spend a month in India to see how this need is real and how firm the foundation stones set by Hinduism and Buddhism.

My plan had been to go south from here to Trichy, passing through Calcutta, but Father Quirijnen is urging me to go as far as Kurseong first, where the scholasticate is. It is a cultural center in a very monastic area. I think I will go there at the end of next week.

Ranchi, 6 August. Feast of the Transfiguration of Our Lord.

I love this feast: to contemplate and marvel at the glory He calls us to share. This mystery has always deeply impressed me. No doubt is it tied to my secret inclination for eastern spirituality. . . . More and more I abandon the organization of my trip to divine Providence! It is above all an interior pilgrimage. It sometimes happens that our spiritual quest must be pursued in a particular country. It is the case, I believe, for me, in this country that I am learning to know and love. Everywhere I find such a warm welcome, not only from the Jesuits but also from the people I meet on the trains. They offer to share their dinner with me, served on a banana leaf!

At Bodh Gaya, where the (Buddha's) tree of illumination is, I visited chinese, burmese, tibetan, and sinhalese monasteries. I spent a week with hindu *sannyasis* (professed monks) who invited me to their *mutt*. This is a community of life and prayer, very similar to our monasteries although more free.

Goom, Himalayas, 31 August 1955

From Calcutta, I was led to Kurseong: 5,200 feet, at the foothills of the Himalayas. En route, I visited Nalanda University where buddhist monks from all of Asia come to study. Interesting meeting with a cambodian monk. This morning, we got up at two o'clock to go to Tiger Hill at 8,200 feet. From there, we saw the sun rise over the snowy tops of Kanchenjunga and Everest. Just as the sun was rising, I sang Lauds.

What a difference here, when we come from the plains: the countryside, the people, the climate, everything is different. At Kalimpong, I was able to meet tibetan monks and spoke with them about our respective ideals and the roads to meditation. This afternoon I discovered a young man from Nepal who lives as a hermit in the midst of the Darjeeling bazaar. I spoke about meditation with him also. It is now time that I go to Trichinopoly and start to meditate myself rather than speak of it with a lot of people. . . . I am starting to yearn for a hut on the bank of the Cavery.

Puri, Orissa, 7 September 1955 in the train.

My journey in the North is drawing to an end. I left Calcutta last night to go to Madras. This morning, we are held up by floods. I hope to be able to say Mass in the station. . . .

The spiritual life, like breathing, like the heart's beating, is made up of two alternating movements. The first is a time of retreat within ourselves, of silence, meditation, like Christ on the mountain, Saint Anthony in the desert, and all the spiritual masters of India. The second is a movement of love, generosity which pushes us outside ourselves towards others, to cooperate with them and serve them. This alternating is for me the essence of seeking God. . . . (Now the train is moving again, but in the opposite direction! This will perhaps allow me to see Bhuwaneshvar and its jain temples again?)

Madras, 18 September 1955, Archbishop's residence

This wandering is both a journey of thanksgiving and a pilgrimage. In Orissa, I crossed flooded villages. The earthen houses with palm roofs had been swept away in a few hours. Before the torrential rains, the drought had lasted too long and burnt the paddy fields. The force of nature as well as the force of the crowds seems stronger and less controlled here than anywhere else. My heart was broken to see these people who had lost everything. Poor dear India. . . .

Pollambakkam, Tamil Nadu, 21 September 1955

For the last two days I have been working in this center of struggle against leprosy, founded by a belgian physician, Dr Hemerijkx, and where I saw Claire Vellut again. With two nurses, they visit the district's hundreds of villages by jeep. Several times a day, they stop under a tree to clean ulcers and distribute the medicine that cure or at least stabilize the illness. Everywhere, huge crowds follow them, as they followed Jesus when he healed the sick. . . . This is a complete change from the hindu *mutts* and the buddhist caves. Saturday, they will drive me to Shantivanam. At last!

SHANTIVANAM, THE FOREST OF PEACE

On 27 September 1955, led by Le Saux who had come to get him at Bishop Mendonça's house at Trichy, Francis arrived at Shantivanam. He met Monchanin for the first time, and at once found him 'welcoming and very charming'. He discovered with curiosity this site of which he had dreamed for so long. The very next day, he wrote to Father Guerric and drew a plan of the facilities with a legend.

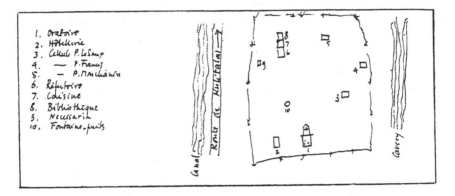

The hut they had built for him was tiny. The palm roof with its double slope almost touched the ground. It looked like a tent, with a bamboo pole in the middle of the entrance. The only furniture it contained was a small very low table and a thin mat of braided straw. The other huts were dispersed in the woods around a stone hindu–inspired oratory. Birds, squirrels, and monkeys inhabited the mango and palm trees' branches. It reflected a great simplicity, in keeping with the poverty of the surrounding villages.

Even if his stay in the *mutts* with the *sannyasis* in the north had made him somewhat familiar with the indian lifestyle, Francis had much to learn. His body had to get used to new constraints: sitting on the ground, sleeping on the brick floor, eating with the fingers of his right hand. There were no utensils, chairs, tables, or beds here. Food consisted of rice garnished with vegetables and fruits, with milk. The first week, he was sick and suffered from stiffness in his neck and back. But the idea of experiencing this eastern eremitical life he had desired for years kept his enthusiasm up.

Soon they began—at his initiative or in his honor?—to sing Mass and the canonical hours every day. 'That gives life a rhythm', wrote Monchanin to his mother. The rest of the time, a little manual work and long hours of solitude in his cell. Meditation, reading, yoga, prayer. At that time it was really the 'woods of peace' and Francis was profoundly happy. He gave himself without reserve to the 'Jesus Prayer'. Very quickly he abandoned his cistercian habit to wear the *khavi*, the saffron robe of the *sannyasis*, as had his two companions.

In mid–October, Le Saux brought him to Siluvaigiri, a benedictine monastery founded in 1947 near Salem by two indian capucin brothers who had recruited about thirty young people. The belgian Benedictines of Saint-André, near Bruges, agreed to sponsor them and send them two of their members: Father Dominique van Rolleghem and Father Emmanuel de Meester, named prior. This visit confirmed Francis' desire for a properly cistercian foundation. 'These Benedictines are a little too businesslike with their study of theology and philosophy', he wrote, explaining further:

> They have little time left for spiritual life. I have encountered this often here: India is awakening to independence, and the young people are preoccupied by lots of problems: social, economic, political. There is little energy or interest left for a deeper life. It's always disappointing for me to see, even in the ashrams and convents, how few are inclined to meditation, how few free themselves from attachments, images, desires, to develop a true search for union with God. Even those who embrace with courage and sincerity the evangelical counsels of poverty, obedience, and chastity rarely taste their mystical and spiritual fruits. I realized this still more keenly this week while re–reading the poems of one of our flemish mystics, Hadewijch of Antwerp. She consecrated herself to loving and singing her love on the most extreme mode, in ecstasy and suffering, plunging to essential destitution.

His life as a hermit at Shantivanam, in fact, was not satisfying him either. Had he ever seriously considered remaining there? As soon as he arrived in India, he had perceived this strong expectation of monastic centers, organized contemplative communities where priests, religious, social workers could come to recharge their batteries, where those who were seeking God from every religion could come to meditate in silence. Le Saux was right: he was dreaming of an abbey. After a few weeks, the two hermits' ashram appeared to him as 'a research institute into monastic things, without contact with the local clergy or Christians'. The absence of the means of self–support bothered him: after seven years of existence, Shantivanam still continued to depend exclusively on european charity, and that was not about to change soon. Very quickly, he realized that he would not stay there, even though he considered his stay there as an excellent preparation, a sort of 'indian novitiate'.

After Siluvaigiri and the studious Benedictines, Le Saux brought Francis to Arunachala, to the fervent Hindus. He wanted to show him his friends, lead him along in his discoveries, no doubt with some strategic ulterior motive: from there, they would send the Cistercian as an ambassador to two prestigious persons who had not yet come to Shantivanam, in spite of several invitations. First, Bede Griffiths, recently settled near Bangalore with his friend Alapatt. They had bought land and built a small monastery in the 'colonial bungalow' style, where they began regular life with two novices. But their foundation was encountering huge canonical difficulties, one of which was the proximity to Siluvaigiri. Francis found a good welcome there. However, he was asked to remove his *khavi* and to put on the white hooded habit of Prinknash, so as not to compromise the young community's reputation. He listened to his colleagues tell him of their tribulations; they remembered Mother Toni and London memories; and they promised to meet again at Shantivanam.

His second mission was to go to Mysore, further north, to meet Father Raimundo Panikkar, who at the time was professor at the catholic university in that city. People were beginning to talk about him as a daring theologian of inter–religious dialogue. But when he rang the doorbell at the address he had written on his notebook, it was a very hurried man who welcomed him: the theologian was getting ready to leave for Kodaikanal by motorcycle, where Father Heras, very ill, had asked for him. Pannikar, whose father was Hindu, was Spanish—more precisely Catalan—on his mother's side, which strengthened his friendship for Father Heras. He took Francis behind him on his motorcycle and drove him to the bishop of Mysore. He tried to explain:

Please understand me, Father Heras is critically ill, he is an old friend, the road is long. . . . I do not even know if I will arrive in time. The bishop can give you lodging and tomorrow morning you can catch the train back to Trichy. I will gladly see you another time. I am very sorry that you made this long trip for nothing.

After having briefly introduced Francis to the bishop, Panikkar adjusted his glasses, climbed onto his motorcycle and disappeared in the dust, without knowing to what extent his departure would be providential.

DAZZLING SYRIAC EXPERIENCE

Msgr René Feuga, bishop of Mysore, was delighted to spend the evening
with a francophone and began the conversation:

So, you are a Cistercian?
Yes, from the Scourmont trappist monastery in Belgium. It is
    very close to the french border.
And what are you doing in India?
I would like to found a contemplative monastery.
Ah! Very good. We need one here. And your abbey sent you?
Not exactly. Let us say that I left as an explorer. If I find land
    and the protection of a bishop, it is not impossible that they
    would send reinforcements. While I am waiting, I am
    sharing the hermit life with Fathers Monchanin and Le Saux
    in Shantivanam.
Your project interests me. The diocese has several pieces of land
    not far from here, and if I did not have to leave tomorrow
    unfortunately. . . .
You are going on a trip?
Oh, not very far. I am going to Malabar,[4] where the syrian
    Carmelites are celebrating their hundredth anniversary. They
    have invited representatives from the other churches in a
    laudable desire for rapprochement. Do you know Malabar?
Not yet, but Father Monchanin has contacted several bishops on
    the west coast. He thinks that transferring Shantivanam into
    one of their dioceses would bring better recruitment.
He is probably right. Half of the Catholics in India are Malabars!
    It's a very old church that goes back to the apostle Thomas,
    they say. The most lively are the Syrians. In each of their
    families there is at least one priest and one nun! But why not
    come with me? You would meet all the bishops and all the
    heads of the institutions at the jubilee celebrations. And be-
    sides, the road is magnificent: we cross the Nilgiris range, the

---

[4] The malabar coast, the principality of Travancore, and part of the district of
Madras would be joined to form the indian state of Kerala a few months after this
episode.

blue mountains, the tea plantations, Travancore. . . . There, it's settled, you will come with me.

Thank you very much, Monsignor, but I am afraid I cannot accept. I have already spent more than two months travelling through the north of India. I have been at Shantivanam only a few weeks. The Fathers are waiting for me, I must return.

As you wish. It is late. Good night, my son. Father Jean will show you your room.

After he had gone in, the secretary closed the door and remained silent a moment.

Excuse me, but you are new, I must explain to you. I think you cannot refuse the bishop's invitation. Here, in India, that is not done. It would be taken the wrong way. He is doing you a great honor by taking you to introduce you to the syrian bishops. You risk offending him by disdaining his offer.

But I am not disdaining anything! Believe me, I am dying to accept. I just don't think I have a right to, that's all.

Listen, it is the bishop of Mysore who is inviting you. Everyone will understand that you could not refuse. It would be a faux pas.

Francis was easily persuaded by Father Jean's arguments. The next day at dawn, instead of taking the train back to Trichy, he went north towards Ootacamund, comfortably seated at the back of the episcopal limousine. The road climbed through the forest where the coconut palms gave way little by little to denser stands of silver oaks, white and red sandalwood. The car passed several elephants dragging tree trunks of the precious wood. Higher still, the mountains covered with tea and coffee plantations reached more than 2,500 meters. The tumultuous Peryar river was crossed by a hand–cranked ferry. The freshness of the air was a pleasant surprise after the more than thirty degrees centigrade day and night year–round at Shantivanam and in the cities of the plain. They stopped to eat lunch and to stay overnight in one or other of the many convents or catholic colleges that dotted their itinerary. Yellow or pink buildings with smooth cement floors, with glassless windows decorated with ornate grills or simple bars, with flowered gardens where the bishop and his retinue were received with kindness and simplicity. Between the stops, conversation turned to the countryside, customs, and the compli-cated history of the christian churches of India. Amiable and talkative, the bishop initiated Francis into the subtleties and susceptibilities of the various groups coexisting in the region:

> Those called Jacobites are in fact orthodox. They belong to the patriarchate of Antioch, but some of them, led by their bishop Mar Ivanios, rejoined Rome in 1930, while keeping the Syrian rite. They form the Syro–Malankar Church, whereas the more numerous latinized Syrians form the Syro–Malabar Church. These Little Sisters of Mount Carmel, where we had lunch yesterday, belong to the Latin Church, the more recent church, as I do. It was Saint Francis Xavier who founded it in the sixteenth century, not without trampling on the eastern traditions that he judged to be heretical.
>
> Their church is very 'portuguese' in style: the white stucco, baroque and colorful statues, the bloody Saint Sebastian.
>
> Yes, I imagine that it clashes with your cistercian sense of esthetics! But tonight we will come to Alwaye where the jubilee will be held. You will see, it's different. They are Syro–Malabars.

At the house of the CMI (Carmelites of Mary Immaculate), the jubilee's pomp unfolded: solemn masses, sung processions, golden parasols, homilies, and testimonies. The ecclesiastical habits were varied: the latin bishops' white cassocks with red belt, the Syro–Malabars' black cassocks with purple belt, the Jacobites' stuffed turban, the Syro–Malankars' black satin hood embroidered with silver crosses. Francis, with his saffron khavi, awakened curiosity. They often asked him, in that insistent manner that sometimes seems rude to westerners: 'What is your name? Where are you from? To what Order do you belong?' But not everyone looked upon him with goodwill. Msgr Lucas, internuncio in New Delhi, spoke his disapproval out loud, 'How can a catholic priest wear sadhus' clothing? It's a dishonor for the Church. These Hindus are depraved, irremediably corrupt.' Turning towards Francis, he added, 'If you want to do serious work here, stop these undesirable eccentricities.'

At the end of the 1950s, many of those in positions of authority in the Church, whether in Rome, in the religious orders, or in the local hierarchy, shared the opinion of the internuncio. India certainly needed contemplative communities, they thought, and besides, the pope had reminded them of this several times. But they desired a powerful western congregation, able to transfer here the models that had been tried in Europe and more recently in America. They were wary of everything eastern, especially hindu monasticism, which was considered immoral and scandalous.

These several days were very instructive for Francis. He understood better why Shantivanam was stagnating, despite the high intellectual and spiritual quality of its founders: the distance between it and the local christian community was too great. The majority of the Church of India was not yet sensitive to the 'signs of the times' disseminated in Europe by visionaries such as Daniélou, de Lubac, and Teilhard. At the same time, he discovered the great vitality of the Syrian Church of Malabar: more than one hundred vocations each year! Receiving invitations from all sides, he spent the week visiting seminaries, university colleges, girls' and boys' schools, hospitals, exhibitions, and even the bank created by the diocese to shield fishermen, small–scale farmers, and artisans from usurers. He was welcomed by several families: K. V. Thomas Potten-kulam, who owned huge tea plantations in the mountains of the back country; and Zacharia Mar Athanasios, the malankar bishop of Tiruvalla, who showed him much kindness and ardently desired to see a monastery in his diocese. With him, Francis was to live a decisive experience, a sort of liturgical 'falling in love', which would crystallize and precipitate the concretization of his monastic project.

This 24 December 1955, each christian house had a large luminous star made of colored paper. Night fell, the car was climbing on a winding and bumpy road, crowded with cyclists, carts, men, and women carrying packages, jugs, and tools. Mar Athanasios was taking Francis to Kumbala-ndanam, a small mountain parish where he would celebrate Christmas Mass. In the forest, houses were rare, but everywhere groups were walking, carrying lanterns. Children lit firecrackers and dispersed, laughing.

In the church lit by oil lamps, about forty families were waiting. The men on one side, the women on the other, they were sitting, in silence, on mats in the nave. The bishop sat down in their midst and started to talk to them in Malayalam, a dravidian language, close to Tamil, spoken in southwest India. They recited the three nocturns of Lilio.[5] There were many children, calm and attentive, in the congregation. Young mothers fed

---

[5] *Lilio* is the syriac equivalent of Vigils, the night prayer that began at 3 AM at that time. Since the 1970s it has started at 4 o'clock.

their babies, shielded by a fold of their sari. Dialogue was constant among the bishop, the deacon, and the congregation. Everyone knew the hymns, psalms, and responses, some said in Syriac, by heart. The chants were repeated in chorus. Towards four o'clock, a noise of small bells and drums was heard outside: the shepherds were climbing towards the church, their resin torches piercing the starry night. Everyone followed them to walk around the church. The bishop lit a large fire that crackled high and clear, illuminating the faces of the recollected people. It was the blessing of the fire. After the homily, they listened to the readings of the Old and New Testament through the sweet–smelling bluish haze of the incense. The bishop then went up to the choir and disappeared behind the gold–tinged hanging that acted as an iconostasis. When the curtain opened, he was wearing an ample green cope to celebrate the *Qurbana* [Mass] in the very language of Jesus, according to the venerable rite of Antioch, conserved almost intact in these isolated communities from the first centuries of Christianity.

The horizon was pale when the parishioners filed out one by one, the women carrying sleeping children, to receive the final blessing. The bishop placed his hands on each head, repeating the ancient formula.

Francis was amazed. He gave thanks, and a kind of jubilation filled his soul. He seemed to have found among these simple people, in this sacred drama celebrated with splendor and dignity, the fervor and faith of the eastern Fathers, still living, that he knew only through his reading.

On the road home, when Mar Athanasios invited him in a very official way to found a cistercian monastery of the Syriac rite in his diocese, his heart said 'yes' even before he had weighed the words for his answer. This community liturgy, bearing adoration and praise, eastern in origin and indianized so long ago, corresponded very closely to his dream of returning to the monastic sources.

Back at Shantivanam, he made a detailed account of his stay in Kerala to the two hermits and invited them to share the offer that had been made to him. But from then on, Le Saux aspired only to following the way of the wandering *sannyasis* and was preparing to leave for the Himalayas. Monchanin, already ill, hesitated to change rites. Learning Syriac seemed to him to be beyond his strength. In March 1956 he wrote, 'Father Mahieu seems to have a taste for this semitic world. Maybe he will be the founder of the syriac Shantivanam?'

FAREWELL TO MONCHANIN

Lent 1956, which Francis spent at Shantivanam, was more than any other Lent a time of silence, retreat, prayer, and the slow ripening of his project. He felt and was distressed by this powerful calling to restore monastic life in the Syriac Church that had resounded in him since Christmas. After the whirlwind of visits and meetings his stay in Kerala caused him, he enjoyed the peace and silence of his little hut. He knew that this would not be his home. 'It is the house of the pilgrim', he wrote,

> the house of God: poor, bare, but filled with Him. The pilgrim knows that God is with him all along the road. He was in the forests of Mysore, on the heights of Ootacamund, in the lagoons of Malabar, and the three seas on which the sun sets at Cape Comorin. Yes, he was there in the crowded trains, in the dust of the buses, among these crowds who walk around in the streets at night. . . . He was in the smile of children and the look of beggars. But here, I can almost see him, standing on the threshold, waiting for me and looking at me with a Father's tenderness.

Francis resumed reading the *Philocalia*, and reciting the burning strophes of Hadewijch of Antwerp: 'Hate luke–warmness, risk the adventure of losing everything to gain everything.' His *lectio divina* was guided by the syriac breviary. 'Never had the reading of Scripture inflamed my heart as much as during this Lent.' Every morning, he spent long hours in meditation and practiced yoga. Father Monchanin, a skeptic, teased him about this: when at the end of March Francis caught an ear infection aggravated by an eye inflammation, Fr Monchanin suggested that his illness was caused by too much *sirsasana*, a posture in which one made a headstand.

For Easter, the hermits went to help at the Kulittalai parish. They sang offices on Good Friday and held an all–night prayer vigil. They returned to the hermitage Saturday night, and on Easter morning, at the instant when the first ray of the sun touched the horizontal stone of the altar in the little sanctuary, the song of the *Exultet* rang out.

That very evening, Francis took the bus to return to the west coast, to Cherpunkel, where he arrived on Tuesday after covering six hundred kilometers of mountain roads. The Sainte-Croix community was a vast campus of terraced buildings along the Meenachil river: schools, parish buildings, lodging for about ten priests who lived in community, and an enormous church where the absence of seats, the illuminated iconostasis, and the purple curtain separating the choir from the nave created an impression of mystery. Pandit Thomas Kochayankanal was professor of Sanskrit and a Syro–Malabar priest. The previous January he had met Francis at Alwaye and had proposed that he could give him courses in Sanskrit during his college's school holidays. The place pleased the new student right away: the river where they bathed, the gardens and hills that the monsoon's strong rains made green again in a few days, the rhythm of the chanted prayer, the serene and studious atmosphere. He marveled at all of this. The pandit showed himself to be a merciless master! Eight hours of intensive study per day, interrupted only for the offices, Mass, and meals. The method was simple and Eastern: learn everything by heart! Francis rebelled interiorly. He would have preferred a progressive grammatical structure and orderly syntax. His desire led him towards the East and indianization, but he was forty–four years old, and his intelligence had been formed by Greek, Latin, and thomistic philosophy. 'The effort that this study demands of me is considerable', he recorded. 'Never has so much been required of my memory or my brain! At times, it seems a real chore. I have no time for anything else, not even correspondence. Luckily my master shows me great kindness and boundless patience. Then I resume my task with courage. But it seems to me that I do not retain things as easily as I did in my youth.'

One morning, saying Mass, he was overcome by emotion reading the collect, as if the text was addressed to him directly: 'O God, grant your people the grace to love what you command, and to desire what you promise, so that in the midst of the instability of the things of this world, our hearts may remain fixed where true happiness is found.' Suddenly the image of his Scourmont community came to mind: his brothers and his former novices. He remembered with pain the reproaches some of them had made to him about his departure for India, considering it as an escape, as unfaithfulness to his vow of stability:

And I prayed to God in tears, I begged him to keep me faithful to my profession. It is good to be criticized by one's friends, that purifies the heart as acid cleans copper, as Thomas the skeptic became a believer once again through Our Lord's reproaches.

Each word of this Mass struck me as Moses's staff struck the rock, and my tears were flowing. O Lord, you called me into this life and you blessed it marvelously in the good earth of Scourmont and Caldey. Do not let this little seed, now thrown into the red earth of India, be carried away by the storm. Do not let it dry out for lack of moisture, lack of this good water of common life and fervor. Please let it bear fruit a hundredfold by the grace of your love.'

On his return to Shantivanam at the end of June, he found the atmosphere strained. He even started to fast, to escape the uncertainties and divisions. Painful discussions about theological questions as well as practical problems were occurring more and more often between the two founding hermits. Le Saux was getting ready to leave definitively for the Himalayas. In August, he left to follow a retreat with his new hindu guru Gnanananda. Monchanin was affected by what he considered a defection. Ill and weak, he nevertheless went to Parakunnu to see his samist colleague Jacques Tombeur, and then spent a few days in Trivandrum with the Syro–Malankar archbishop Mar Gregorios, whom he found 'handsome and majestic like an oriental prelate, affable towards everyone and with a lively intelligence'. He wanted to explore by himself the chances of what he called 'the syriac life raft'. Back at the hermitage, he conversed with Francis at length about the future prospects of Shantivanam and the eventual eastern rite monastic foundation. At the beginning of September, an educated indian priest, Father Dharma, arrived and turned Shantivanam towards a kernel of apostolic work for the diocese's clergy and laity, who would there find an atmosphere conducive to prayer, dialogue, and research. This was far removed from the cistercian foundation Francis dreamed of. Monchanin found many advantages in the syrian prospects: an archbishop and bishop who were enthusiastic and open, a liturgy in the vernacular, an ancient monastic tradition, asleep on indian soil, certainly, but whose texts, customs, and rituals could be found in the Near East and adapted to India, thanks to hindu monasticism, which would furnish complementary resources.

Meanwhile, Francis immersed himself in *Hermits of Saccidananda* (the french translation of *An Indian Benedictine Ashram*) and in *From Aesthetics to Mysticism* (the stromata of Monchanin collected by his friend Duperray, published by Casterman and sent immediately to India).

Monchanin devoured the contents of the box of syriac books sent to Francis from Caldey: the *Didache* and the *Homilies* of Philoxenus of Mabbug.

It was during that summer that Francis truly discovered Monchanin and established with him a deep bond of filial love, from disciple to master. Both spent long quiet afternoons talking under the mango trees, while monkeys and birds chattered in the high branches. They talked about their current reading: Saint Ephrem, Philoxenus, Tauler, Mircea Eliade. Monchanin was developing his thought without wearying, happy to communicate the unceasing movement of his mind to an attentive listener.

In September, news came from the neighboring Benedictines, and it was not very good. All the indian monks had left the Siluvaigiri community. Some had returned to Europe, where they had made their novitiate. The Europeans remained alone with a small group of postulants. Hard lesson. In Kengheri, Bede Griffiths and Alapatt had just received the news they had dreaded: Rome refused them permission to make a benedictine foundation so close to Siluvaigiri. The two men proposed to help Francis in his foundation in Kerala and invited him to come discuss it. Mar Gregorios joined them, and after several days of very diplomatic exchanges, they decided that Father Alapatt would return to serve the diocese—Francis made it clear that he did not desire to take him along—and that Bede Griffiths would go with him to begin a monastic foundation in the Syriac rite in the diocese of Tiruvalla. The archbishop took it upon himself to find a house for the beginnings. Francis judged this meeting providential: a real monk, from the family of Saint Benedict, English-speaking, graduate of Oxford, and passionate about Hinduism—what more could he wish for as a companion to start? And the archbishop himself was smoothing the corners, finding Father Alapatt a new job, looking for a house. Father Bede was manifestly very courteous, with a calm and agreeable character. He expressed certain reservations, however: he did not intend to become a Cistercian or to go along with 'eccentricities' of clothing or food Shantivanam–style. In 1956, he was still quite conservative and classical. But he recognized the authority of Father Mahieu as prior and conceptor of the project that he was joining and offered him his collaboration to begin. For Francis, that was quite sufficient.

At the end of October, everything moved quickly. Mar Athanasios let them know that a property called Pushpagiri (meaning 'Hill of the Little Flower', in Malayalam, after Saint Therese of Lisieux in Kerala) awaited them. It was a former episcopal residence, empty for several months. He also proposed to assign a priest from his diocese for their liturgical initiation.

Francis began at once to pack his only goods: his books. He gave several to Monchanin, who was always short of something to read. On 18 November, at sunset, he took a last bath in the Kaveri, then went up the bank to the portico that marked the entrance to the hermitage. The swami was waiting for him on the bench. A long conversation then took place, or rather a monologue, which would remain for Francis a very strong memory, one of those from which he would draw strength at difficult times.

The priest, with his characteristic detachment and generosity, far from complaining or trying to retain his disciple, told him of his approval, his satisfaction at his departure. Better yet, he truly sent him on a mission, to pursue in Kerala the work begun on the banks of the Kaveri. He said,

> I have confidence in your work, it will bear fruit. God is sending you to open the way of a truly contemplative life to the young people of Kerala. India, I am sure, will one day respond magnificently to God's call. Be confident, go ahead. God has given you a deep sense of the monastic life. He will show you how to share it with others.

Francis was moved. He discovered the fruitful bond that linked him to Monchanin, the strength of which he had not measured until then.

The next evening, it was raining. Francis set his cloth bundle down in the small guesthouse where the swami was waiting to say goodbye to him. He knelt down to receive his blessing. Monchanin placed both hands on his head without saying anything, then, suddenly, himself fell on his knees. Both, hands joined, face to face, prayed there in silence, like children, with a strong consciousness of the Holy Spirit's presence.

It was with a burning heart that Francis went away in the humid darkness, along the sandy path along the Kaveri, to the Kulittalai station. He was taking with him Monchanin's dream, Dom Anselme's dream, and he was eager to give them form and consistence, with all his strength and with the help of God.

THE PRODIGAL SON AND MOTHERHOUSE

The correspondence that Francis exchanged with Scourmont during this exploratory period reflected both the maintaining of fraternal relationship and the permanence of a misunderstanding. For months he hoped, against all reason, that his motherhouse would sponsor him, support him, and officially sustain his foundation. He persisted in the idea that, even though this was not a canonical affiliation—the conditions for that were obviously not fulfilled—the monastery he was preparing to found would be recognized by the Order as being completely Cistercian, since he himself defined himself as completely Cistercian. Until 1957, he continued to ask that they send men, experienced monks, to help him. 'It would only need three or four monks to start. All the rest: vocations, land, would come from here and would flourish rapidly. But the question is: who will try?' (to Father Maur, November 1955).

He sent Dom Guerric several long letters in which he described his life and his meetings and detailed the pressing invitations bishops made to him, as well as the exceptionally good reputation the Cistercians enjoyed. He insisted that his superior come to judge all that for himself, so that he could see to what degree the Church in India thirsted for contemplative foundations. He received no response.

At Scourmont, things were perceived from another point of view. Francis' original enterprise aroused the interest and sympathy of some of his brothers: Father Godefroid, his former novice, wrote him long letters to keep him up to date with what was happening in the abbey. Father Maur, his fellow monk now become sub–prior sent him without grumbling the books and periodicals he asked for. Father Thomas Litt, his former professor of philosophy, tried in every way to find Mass intentions for him. But the community as a whole remained very reserved. Mokoto had priority, so there was no question of committing themselves elsewhere. Francis left alone, they reasoned; let him take responsibility for his decision. Father Colomban, longtime secretary to the abbot, the one who no doubt had been the most hostile towards Francis' indian project, died of peritonitis a few months after his departure. But the discredit he had cast on the 'fugitive', the 'rebel', did not die with him. It was Father Maur who decided to clarify the situation a little at the beginning of 1956:

You do not seem to consider how difficult it is to send Europeans to India at this time. You yourself obtained a visa only by a sort of miracle. But this is not the only obstacle or the main one. Our congolese project took more men than Dom Guerric had thought. If Scourmont were to envision a second foundation, it would have to go through a chapter vote. I have the impression that at the moment, the vote would not be in favor. The historical circumstances of your departure for India would no doubt contribute to this outcome.

Francis answered by return mail:

Your letter fell like dew on parched earth. All these feasts of Christmas and the New Year without a sign from Scourmont seemed very hard to me. Thank you for lifting a corner of the veil to let me glimpse the reasons for the unexpected reserve I found at Scourmont during my last visit. I heartily desire to learn more. What is it that in the 'circumstances' of my departure aroused this coldness that I felt without understanding it? Was it the principle of the decision? Or one of the circumstances accompanying it? In any case, if I hurt someone, it was against my will and I ask forgiveness. During all these years that prepared the decision—five years of struggle, research, prayer and illness—I always wanted to remain faithful to my monastic profession as a monk of Scourmont. And still now, living here, I am conscious of remaining faithful to it while giving it a new expression. Be reassured, my step is not a formal one, it does not require a vote. Simply, it would be a source of peace for me to know that Dom Guerric, you, Father Albert, and others understand my situation and that you do not object that I remain a monk of Scourmont in the preparatory work which is presenting itself to me here.

The wound from Pentecost 1955 had not yet healed, and the most painful thing for Francis remained the lack of explanation, his inability to understand why he had not been allowed to enter the church, why they had refused to let him celebrate the descent of the Holy Spirit with his community.

His letter reached Scourmont at the same time as his indult of ex-claustration for three years. He tried everything to delay or prevent this decision. He did not tolerate well no longer being a full member of his community; it was as if he had been sent away from his family. He pleaded the formula of 'detachment', but the Abbot General wisely con-sidered that exclaustration was the canonical situation best suited to the daring experience into which Francis was plunging himself: to be depen-dent upon a superior as geographically far and be subject to the detail of the Rule, especially in another rite, presented too many difficulties. It would be preferable to place oneself under the authority of the local bishop.

It was Father Maur who sent the copy of the indult to Shantivanam: 'I can guess that this will cause you pain, but I believe it is the least bad solution. In three years, you will have the time to study, observe, to clarify certain things. It is not impossible that after this time a project of a foundation in India could be envisaged here. Meanwhile, you will remain a Cistercian and a monk of Scourmont.' Francis grieved. 'This makes my heart heavy', he wrote to a friend. As when Father Albert had refused his blessing, he remained six weeks without answering, 'as one leaves the mash to rest so that it clarifies'. In his response, he asked for explanations for the reasons given by the Abbot General and tried once more, neverthe-less, to obtain a sort of moral guarantee, at least a *nihil obstat*, that would allow him to answer the bishops' appeals as a Cistercian, approved by the Order, if not mandated by the Order. To this end he wrote a sixteen–page memorandum, a kind of defense in which he went over his discoveries, actions, the offers made to him, his plan, and his requests methodically, one by one. He sent the text to Dom Guerric, who asked Father Maur to write an answer as invariable as the request: 'no.'

Francis felt misunderstood by his own. The abbot of Mount Saint Bernard in England, to whom by chance he had written asking for help, wrote to him: 'I am astonished to see you break so radically with our way of life in order to then pretend to desire to return.' Francis took Maur as his witness: 'How can I explain to him that what seems to him to be a break with the past is in reality for me a "going beyond", and that what seems to him a return is only a response to the clear calls I received here for the cistercian life? I regret that I had a part in a sort of scandal, but I hope more than ever that it will turn to the glory of God.' He added with determination: 'For me, in any case, that seems to me the providential way, and I am waiting only to see how to concretely realize the practical details that are not yet clear.' And he ended with a very pragmatic P.S.: 'Please could you send me the syriac grammar by L. Costaz? Learning Syriac is not difficult, except if one only has a grammar in the malayalam language'. In the same breath, he asked that he also be sent the *Collectanea Ordinis Cisterciensium Reformatorum* 1, 'to keep in contact with the Order'.

A little later, he received an affectionate letter from Father Thomas Litt. Advice for the organization of his future novitiate, opinion on the advantages of an autonomous situation: the philosopher exposed with humor the hidden traps in sending cistercian reinforcements: 'I believe that what you need is not a Trappist. As you know, there are very few religious capable of teaching in our Order. But there are other reasons as well: I would be afraid that the abbot who would let you have one of his subjects might choose one he was eager to get rid of, for reasons of character, for example. Finally, suppose a Trappist who is a good philosopher and theologian falls to you from the sky, one who has an open spirit, whose soul is Indian, with a great capacity for work and an excellent religious, then I would fear that he might have a strong personality, that he might already have or soon acquire his own ideas on the foundation to be undertaken, and that you might not get along with him. On the contrary, a secular priest lent to you, or even a Franciscan or some Redemptorist or other, would be more likely to feel that you are the one in charge.' The same week, he confided to an indianist friend interested by Francis' latest news: 'If I were ten years younger, I would ask to go join him.' A laconic message from Dom Guerric put things in place once and for all: 'Begin alone. Do it. Then it will be up to the Order to determine with you whether your foundation is Cistercian or if it has another spirit.'

On 1 October, Francis learned that Dom Anselme had died on 25 September. He remembered that that was the day that Dom Bede Griffiths' offer of collaboration reached him, and he couldn't help seeing a sign in that.

The day before Advent began, at Pushpagiri where he had just moved in with his new companions, he received the news of Dom Guerric's election as fifth abbot of Scourmont. He wrote at once to give him 'homage of humble and faithful dilection'. He renewed his vow of obedience in writing, in Latin, *usque ad mortem*, and added 'if the work for which I believed I could offer myself here does not inspire confidence in you, if you judge that to save my final perseverance in monastic profession it would be better that I return to Scourmont, do not be afraid to recall me. I never had the intention of shaking off the yoke of the Rule to be freed of it.'

On his side, Mar Athanasios was asking the Holy See for its *nihil obstat* for a cistercian foundation in the Syro–Malankar rite, and Francis asked Dom Guerric and the Abbot General for letters of recommendation for the Sacred Congregation for the Eastern Churches, which at that time was presided by a french prelate very interested in the Syrian churches of India, Cardinal Eugène Tisserant.

For Christmas, he wrote to his eldest sister: 'My text awoke little interest from the Cistercians in Europe. I do not yet have an answer from Dom Guerric on this subject. My companion is thankfully an excellent assistant, with all the qualities I lack. But faced with the great responsibility that awaits me, I feel alone and sometimes crushed. I am starting to lack resources. Most of the time, I find a solution only in prayer, being brought to my limits without ever receiving any assurance for the next day. It is a constant source of asceticism and purification. Everything is now suspended, awaiting the necessary permissions. The coming weeks will be decisive.'

PUSHPAGIRI

'I let myself be reintegrated in an *acies fraterna*,[6] scarcely a small patrol, to tell the truth. But we live a regular life, just as in a monastery.'

(To Father Maur, November 1956)

The former bishop's residence where Mar Athanasios settled 'his' monks had nothing luxurious about it. Abandoned for six months, it was even in a piteous state. Situated not far from the small city of Tiruvalla, separated from it by rice paddies and banana groves, the house was called 'Ceru Pushpagiri'.

Francis began by organizing the work teams: spring cleaning, whitewashing the walls, building partitions for the cells. They hoed a vegetable garden and put a cow in the stable to supply the daily milk. But from the very first day, amidst the brushes and tools, they recited the Liturgy of

---

[6] 'Army of brothers' : allusion to St Benedict.

the Hours according to the *ordo cisterciencis*, which Francis quickly interspersed with a few hymns from the Syriac Church and a few hindu texts from the Rig–Veda.

The small disparate group became a community little by little through *ora et labora*. Two indian postulants were accepted. Six others requested entrance, but they were asked to wait for the project to consolidate. Francis and Bede tried to learn the language of Kerala, a complex dravidian language with an alphabet of fifty–four letters and eighteen vowels. With their new companions, they applied themselves especially to the study of the syriac liturgy, tradition and texts for several hours each day, under the guidance of the Syro–Malankar priest assigned to them by the bishop.

They discovered they had a growing passion for this eastern church whose history went back to the beginnings, and which was at the time very little known in the West, outside of specialized circles. Even today, despite a resurgence of interest manifested by several recent publications, the near eastern churches remain unknown by ordinary people who divide Christianity into three main groups: the Roman Catholics, the Greek and Slavic Orthodox, and the Protestants scattered into many families. They rarely suspect the existence of a fourth christian world, semitic in culture, whose sacred language is neither Latin nor Greek but Syriac, which is the Aramaic spoken by Christ, the apostles, and the first Christians in Jerusalem, Antioch, and Damascus.

From the first Councils, before Byzantium separated from Rome, many of these churches situated in the asiatic borders of the roman empire and even in regions governed at the time by Persians, had constituted themselves in autonomous patriarchates tending first to Nestorianism then to Monophysitism.[7] Their complicated evolution into many branches— Jacobites, Chaldeans, Syrians, Armenians—is hard to follow. Beginning in the seventeenth century, each of these gave rise to a 'uniate' Church reattached to Rome and thus Catholic, while keeping its eastern rite.

The first generations of 'persian' Christians were very active missionaries, spreading the Gospel to the East. Along the silk route that led their caravans through the Sin-Kiang, they brought Christianity all the

---

[7] Nestorius was a monk in Antioch at the end of the fourth century. His doctrine emphasized the humanity of Christ, and he was condemned in Ephesus in 431. Monophysitism accentuated the divinity of Christ and precipitated a schism at the council of Chalcedon in 451.

way to China. They were present in the south of India as early as the third century. The story is told that even Saint Thomas the Apostle had come to preach and had been martyred there. His tomb in Milapoore, near Madras, is presently a site of pilgrimage.

The syrian christian communities of Malabar perpetuated themselves down the centuries, isolated from the western world and the ups and downs of the roman papacy. Until the arrival of the Portuguese in the sixteenth century, they were organized into parishes led by a priest, assisted by deacons and catechists. Bishops came every year from Seleucia in Persia to ordain the new priests and confirm the baptized. But the churches had a synodal structure, presided by an archdeacon. Thus the traditions of the first churches of Asia were preserved intact, nourished by the Holy Scriptures and the teaching of the eastern Fathers: Ephrem of Edessa, Narsai, and Isaac of Nineveh, as well as the Fathers of the Egyptian Desert, were held in great esteem, especially Evagrius Ponticus.

Francis had discovered and loved some of those masters from the very beginning of his monastic studies. From now on, he would never cease to study them, translate them, meditate upon them, and live them. What he loved in this spirituality was that it appealed to the imagination and the heart more than to reasoning or argument. It was a poetic and narrative theology, with a colorful liturgy, a true production of the mysteries of faith, which spoke to the senses through the scent of the incense, the shimmering colors of the cloth, the gleam of the silver crosses, the tinkling of the little bells and the flabelli, and the psalmodic recitation of the hymns.

But the more he advanced in his syriac studies, the more Francis realized that the indian clergy did not know the origins of their own liturgy; by reproducing it faithfully, defending it fiercely, its deep meaning had been lost. He then began work that he would pursue for years: from sources that he went to look for in the Near East, and with the help of european eastern scholars, he patiently reconstituted the monastic life of the Syriac Church, by establishing it in the cistercian perspective and in the indian context: liturgy of the hours, calendar of eastern saints, lectionary, hymns, ritual of admission, and receiving of the habit, proper of feasts, etc. He wrote to Father Khouri–Sarkis, rector of the Syrian Church of Paris, who was happy to give him a subscription to his new periodical *L'Orient Syrien* [*The Syrian East*]. He also asked advice from a belgian Jesuit he had met at Kurseong, Father Hambye, who became a good friend and an enthusiastic supporter of the project. 'Do not hesitate to use me', he wrote as early as 1957; 'you are making one of my most persistent dreams come true: a cistercian eastern rite foundation in India! What I admire in you is your calm, your daring prudence.' As for Father Maur Standaert, he was asked to find and send the four volumes of the hymns of Saint Ephrem published in 1856 in Malines, Belgium, by Monsignor Lamy.

The preparations for the foundation were not limited to the vast syriac world, as captivating as it was. They had to drum up vocations, find land, collect money, and, especially, obtain canonical status for the work to last. Francis as well as the bishop desired a cistercian spirit foundation in the Syriac rite. This presupposed that he could obtain the Order's patronage and a special indult from the Holy See for the adoption of the rite. Francis headed back to his typewriter and developed a complete description of his project in about twenty pages, entitled 'A Cistercian Ashram in Malabar'. He first described syriac Christianity in India, its fervor and dynamism, its expectation of a monastic foundation. Then he sketched the current state of his nascent community and the angles he was pursuing, being careful to find arguments in the words of the very persons he had to convince: Eugène Cardinal Tisserant, prefect of the Sacred Congregation for the Eastern Churches and the Abbot General of the Cistercian Order, Dom Gabriel Sortais:

> If the rites of the Church are not only a collection of liturgical singularities but the totality of the artistic forms and symbols in which the christian community expresses and lives its faith, it is evident that the Latin rite, notably its language, its austerity and gregorian chant, will never succeed in accomplishing this function in India. Hence the importance of the present roman directives in favor of the Syrian–rite churches in India.
>
> (Msgr E. Tisserant, in *Église vivante* 7 [Louvain, 1956])

> It could be that to truly implant itself in a country, the contemplative life would have to take a new form and give birth to a religious family quite different from those that already exist in the Church. Without in any way being in a hurry to abandon a Rule that has proven itself elsewhere, the Superiors must not refuse a priori to examine such a possibility.
>
> (Dom Gabriel Sortais, Function of the contemplatives
> in Mission countries, Westmalle, 1953)

To prevent any hint of post–colonialism, he quoted Gandhi himself as a witness, recalling the esteem and admiration of the father of the indian nation had professed publicly on several occasions for the trappist monasteries he had visited in South Africa and Italy: 'Their monastery was a model of beauty, a true garden. A pacifying silence filled the atmosphere. These men profess *ahimsa, aparigraha, brahmacharya* (that is to say, love of God, voluntary poverty, chastity). It would be an ideal for me to found such an institution.'

Francis concluded (and this was going to cause him some trouble): 'The foundation is known here presently as a cistercian ashram, without further title. We insist on awaiting the approbation of the Holy See before placing it under a title of the Virgin, who is patroness of Cîteaux and so dear to our jacobite brothers.'

During January 1957, this defense was sent to Dom Gabriel, Cardinal Tisserant, Dom Guerric, Dom Wilfried Upson of Prinknash, and a few others for information. In May, an english translation was circulated under a slightly different title: 'A Syrian Cistercian Ashram in Malabar'. The indult from Rome authorizing their practice of the eastern rite would reach the two monks on 12 August, with an affectionate and encouraging letter from Cardinal Tisserant. It caused great joy in Pushpagiri that evening, shared with the bishop and all the friends. The patient liturgical restoration they had begun received the go–ahead and was going to be able to be pursued legitimately.

But a problem remained. If we consider the english title of his last memorandum as well as the authors he chose to quote, we see clearly the three threads that from this moment would cross to weave Francis' project:

1. Syrian, for the eastern liturgy and spirituality;
2. Cistercian, for the Rule of Saint Benedict and the reform of Cîteaux; and
3. Ashram, for the immersion in the indian way of life and the example of hindu ascetics.

Ashram received a posthumous blessing from Gandhi and the support of the local populations. *Syrian* the same, from Mar Athanasios and the Holy See. But it was *Cistercian* that would cause trouble.

In January 1957, an indiscreet person forwarded a copy of the memorandum Francis had sent to his superiors to two english catholic newspapers, the *Tablet* and the *Catholic Herald*, who then published articles inspired by it. In these articles, the foundation was presented as a cistercian monastery, and, in a very journalistic style, the accent was placed on the most exotic aspects, with subtitles such as 'Bananas and snakes'. The cistercian Abbot General did not appreciate this. He felt that he was being confronted with a fait accompli and was being made to support disturbing novelties, in spite of himself; novelties that had not yet received any endorsement from the Order. Learning of this new misunderstanding, the two monks of Pushpagiri were distressed and protested their good faith. Bede demanded the right to respond in the London newspapers. Francis sent a last supplication in which he displayed his rhetoric and conviction in many pages, beseeching that his ashram be considered 'if not as a daughter, at least as a cousin of Scourmont, under the patronage of Cîteaux'. It was no use. After an exchange of letters with Dom Guerric, Dom Gabriel Sortais, the Abbot General, officially told Francis that he was not mandated by the Order and was not authorized to present his ashram as a cistercian foundation.

In the first 'Christmas Chronicle' that he sent to his family and friends at the end of 1957, Francis would use the expression 'sons of Saint Benedict' to describe the spirit of his community, but he could not help referring a little later to his 'cistercian roots'. The name faded, but the reality remained buried for forty years, long enough to make the desert bloom.

THE MOUNTAIN FALLEN FROM THE SKY

Many people had already proposed to offer Francis land for his foundation. The place he was brought to visit one day appeared particularly interesting. It was not a plot of land; it was a mountain, a terraced plateau of one hundred acres, about forty hectares, that rises to 3,500 feet in the Cardamom chain of mountains on the border of Kerala and Tamil Nadu. The donor, K.V. Thomas, was a syrian christian from a large family in the region, the proprietor of several tea plantations, and open to every enterprising idea. In 1952, he represented the indian government in the United States for the 'Sixth International Grassland Congress'. As soon as the monks arrived in Tiruvalla, he came to visit them and told Mar Athanasios of his desire to offer land for the future monastery. On the second Sunday after Easter, he brought the three religious to the mountain by car. The road stopped at Vagamon, a small, very poor village bordering the abrupt slopes where tea was grown. The four men continued by foot, sheltered under black umbrellas to protect them from the April sun, which was already burning hot. But the wind and the altitude made it a pleasant walk.

When Francis discovered the site that heaven sent him, he believed more than ever in the action of the Holy Spirit, and his heart leapt with gratitude. An immense horizon, a wild and very beautiful site, brown and purple mountains as far as one could see, and due south, against the light, like an enormous elephant's back, a grey granite hill surmounted by a cross at its summit: its Kurisu–mala, the Mountain of the Cross, where for more than a century, the bishop told them, Christians had been going up in pilgrimage on Good Friday, carrying a block of granite on their head as a sign of repentance.

'This countryside is truly grandiose', Francis thought, 'exactly what is needed to raise the soul toward God'. Bede Griffiths was less enthusiastic. Contemplating the impenetrable dales, the bare rocks, the uncultivated expanses, he murmured, 'It's beautiful, but terribly isolated! No one will ever come all the way here.'

On the return trip, they raised practical questions. The bishop asked the owner, 'What would you recommend that they grow on this land?' 'There are several possibilities,' he replied. 'The land is obviously not the most fertile. One could raise tea. It pays well, but the harvest requires a lot of workers.' 'We are not yet very numerous', Francis said. 'Where could we find help?' 'Oh, around here there are many workers' families, recruited in tamil country to work in the plantations. You could ask in Vagamon'.

From the very beginning, this idea displeased Francis. He had heard that in the 'tea estates' the workers—often women—were badly paid, exploited, picking tiny leaves on steep hills for a few rupees per day. It was not surprising that the communist party, very active in Kerala, recruited many of its members among them. He countered, 'And besides tea, what enterprise could one start?' 'If the land is worked in terraces, you could raise vegetables, pineapples or bananas,' the owner suggested. 'The monsoon is very violent on this exposed western slope. This gives a lot of water, but the water streaming down tends to erode the soil. To tell the truth, this land is rather propitious for cattle: the only thing that grows naturally in abundance is grass.' Francis promised himself to study all these possibilities and to do more careful research from the area's farmers.

He had more questions, however. 'And for the buildings, how will we do this without an access road?' 'You need bring only cement and timber,' came the reply. 'That will have to be carried in on foot. As you can see there is no lack of stones. The granite can be cut right there, after a block has been blown up with explosives. And the Meenachil river which flows at the foot of the mountain, provides sand. Good artisans can be found in the plain, a few kilometers from here. But you will need an architect to direct them. Do you know one?' Francis thought about Mr Ingle, the friend of Monchanin, whom he met several times at Shanti-vanam and who lived in Kodaikanal, not far from here. 'I will write to him this very evening', he told himself.

The following weeks, his thoughts took a very concrete turn. The future ashram now had a setting, and what a setting! If they wanted to move there before the end of the year, they would have to draw plans, survey boundaries, even start to plant.

At the beginning of May, Mr Thomas went to the bishop's palace to sign the act of donation. Mr Ingle agreed to draw up the plans. He came to examine the land and took a few photos. Francis wrote a small brochure in English to make known the work in India. Illustrated with photographs, with numerous quotations and references, with a saffron–colored cover, its title was 'Kurisumala Ashram, by a Cistercian Monk'. We can't help but notice the combination of obedience and stubbornness this title reveals.

In Belgium, they counted on Marie-Thérèse (called Rithé), the eldest of the family. With her two daughters, she formed a sort of 'central office', sending out letters and chronicles and gathering financial contributions. Some were unexpected: Louis Evely, a former classmate of Francis in Brussels, became a priest also. The director of a large diocesan college, still brilliant, he was also a successful preacher and had just published his first book *Notre Père* [*Our Father*], which was selling very well. He told Rithé that he would give all his royalties towards the construction of the ashram. For his part, Bede Griffiths contributed the royalties of his auto-biographical book, *The Golden String*[8] (which told about his youth in Oxford and his conversion and had been published just before his departure) as well as the gifts from his family and circle of friends. They decided to concentrate all the proceeds into one account in the new central

---

[8] Griffiths, *The Golden String. An Autobiography* (1954).

bank of Palai, the nearest town to Kurisumala. Dom Guerric let them know that since official filiation was lacking, the new foundation could count on material assistance. 'I encourage you to continue in the way that seems to be opening in front of you. You can always count on Scourmont's sympathy and effective help.' Francis insisted that when he traveled to Mokoto, in east Africa, his abbot cross the indian ocean and come see for himself the work accomplished and especially the local church's welcome. After Dom Guerric had at first accepted, he finally decided to not make the detour. In June it was Mar Athanasios who, visiting Rome, continued to Scourmont. The abbot received him very courteously, and, with Father Albert, who was on his way to Mokoto where he was sent to be prior, they talked at length about the monastic project that had been undertaken.

If the material preparations were proceeding well, the learning of languages was progressing more slowly than anticipated. The difficulties of Syriac had discouraged the oldest of the postulants. To intensify the linguistic and liturgical training, beginning in September the small community spent time at Holy Redeemer ashram, with the Fathers of Bethany. This order, founded in 1930 by Mar Ivanios, the jacobite bishop who rejoined Rome to form the Catholic Syro–Malankar Church, actively contributed by its social and apostolic work to the reunion of the separated brethren. It was there that Francis learned that Father Monchanin had died in Paris on 10 October, worn out by illness. More than ever, he felt called to make the seed sown by his friend in the soil of India germinate.

After a few months at Holy Redeemer, the daily attendance at the offices and immersion in a Syriac–rite community gave the 'trainees' sufficient ease to preside over the ceremonies. At Christmas, Francis celebrated his first *Qurbana* in Syriac. 'It was quite laborious!' he confessed to his sister in a letter, 'but a great joy, despite the tension of the first performance'. Bede Griffiths did not yet feel ready and continued in Latin for the time being. At Epiphany, one of the postulants on the waiting list was accepted. The founders were now ready for the departure, which, together with the bishop, they had set for 21 March, the feast of Saint Benedict. Their professor of Syriac was authorized to go with them; he was a native of the area who spoke Malayalam fluently and knew the region well. As the months progressed, he had developed a great friendship for his students, and their project was dear to him. He asked to stay with them during the first months of settling in. His help would prove valuable.

In the shops of Tiruvalla, Francis carefully chose the sacred vessels and liturgical ornaments they still lacked. He also bought a few objects necessary for housekeeping: stainless steel plates and cups, pottery pitchers for drinking water, and a pot for the rice. Bede began to pack their precious books in metal trunks.

Meanwhile, having obtained all the authorizations, from Rome and the benedictine and cistercian religious superiors, the monastery was canonically erected by Mar Athanasios on 3 November 1957, the Sunday of *Quodosh Itho* [Consecration of the Church], which marked the beginning of the liturgical year. The document signed on that occasion constitutes a sort of founding and legitimizing charter for Kurisumala ashram:

Considering the reiterated exhortations by the Holy See to ensure that the austere and contemplative life be introduced and spread by the establishment of monasteries among the eastern peoples naturally inclined to the life of solitude, prayer and contemplation, and desiring to ensure for our people the inestimable source of edification that a contemplative monastery can bring to our brothers, separated Christians or Hindus, we have called two monks belonging to the benedictine family and have entrusted to them the foundation of a contemplative monastery in our diocese. . . .

The main objectives for this foundation are four–fold:

1. The solemn and complete celebration of the liturgy and the Prayer of the Church—which is presently only partially celebrated in our parishes by the clergy and religious more and more engaged in active work.

2. The consolidation and development of the Syrian rite, so venerable and rich, but exposed to becoming a hybrid of the dominant Latin rite.

3. Welcoming clergy and laity for prayer and retreats developing the spirituality of the eastern Fathers, their asceticism and mystical theology.

4. Kurisumala ashram will be especially dedicated to the unity of the separated brothers.

The life of the community will be organized according to the cistercian tradition and the antiochian Syro–Malankar rite. The

ashram is called to witness to the strict demands of the monastic
life, most perfect flower of the christian life.

(Given at Marygiri, Tiruvalla,
Quodosh Itho Sunday in the year of grace 1957.
† Mar Athanasios, bishop of Tiruvalla.

On 8 January 1958, Francis wrote to his family:

Soon we will leave this plain to go to our mountain. Only then will
the seed truly be planted, and I count very much on your prayers
for God to let it bear fruit. It is especially through vocations that we
can expect this. Many are appearing on the horizon: we are
awaiting a priest, a religious, a seminarian and a young indian engineer who graduated in London. But each of these has obstacles to
overcome and bonds to untie. Besides the problem of vocations,
there is the problem of facilities. The last administrative formalities
for the acquisition of the land are still pending. The site is worthy
of the cistercian tradition but its isolation and its absolutely uncultivated state will require efforts that more than one wise man calls
foolhardy. I myself, when I catch myself considering the poverty of
our diocese—the poorest in Kerala—our destitution and the
fragility of our roots here, I can only find refuge in abandonment to
the ways of God who has brought us here.

RAIN AND WIND, BLESS THE LORD

21 March 1958. Feast of Saint Benedict and 860th anniversary of the
foundation of Cîteaux. Five men walked along a steep rocky path in the
western ghats of southern India. Francis, energetic, walked first, followed
by Bede, a tall silhouette. They were barefoot and wore saffron robes that
Mar Athanasios had blessed and solemnly given them the day before. During the same ceremony, he had given them the titles of prior and sub–prior
of Kurisumala ashram. Each one carried a narrow wooden table with long
legs on his head: this was his altar. That is what they brought first, and a
few days later they began construction of the church. God was served first.
Behind them, Sylvester and Vargheese, the indian postulants wearing
dhoti, and the young professor of Syriac in his cassock carried the liturgical

necessities and a few household utensils. A little past Vagamon, the road became impassable. They had to leave the oxcart on which their goods were piled up. They forded the Meenachil river, with water up to their knees. Now the day was declining; the Cardamom mountains projected their purple summits on the pink sky. Francis stopped a moment. Straining his eyes, he could make out the silhouette of the chapel built on the Mountain of the Cross in the last century. It was said that two medals of Saint Benedict were sealed in its wall. He promised himself that he would climb there as soon as possible. In the west, in a clearing, he could see the plain below them and one could guess that the arabian sea was under the golden horizon. 'Beauty is favorable for prayer', he told himself. 'The monks' praise will naturally rise to God.'

Now they were on their land, of which no one exactly knew the boundaries: the surveying, extremely difficult on these wild escarpments, was not finished. A group of huts in ruins, the remnants of the tea cultivation that had been abandoned by the donor, sheltered them for the night. Two men appeared in the darkness, escorted by a few boys. The children were carrying torches made with half a coconut holding a wick in some oil. The men were carrying a jug of milk and a small pot of rice with vegetable curry. They were neighbors, two fathers of large families who cultivated their small plot of land nearby and kept a few half–wild cows. They saw the swamis arrive and were bringing them an offering of their supper, along with their *namaskar*, their smiles.

After they had sung Compline, the five companions spread out their mats on the ground and got ready to sleep. Francis went out one last time to look at the stars. Venus was especially bright. The familiar constellations seemed to welcome him in the warm night. The silence was complete.

The following days were spent transporting the rest of their material along the three kilometers of path, in many return trips, to organize the 'base camp'. In a few hours, the neighbors, with the help of a few workers from the tea estates, set up a large hut using the local technique: large bamboo risers, walls made out of woven palms, grass roof. The ground was covered with cow dung, which protects from crawling insects. The space, about thirty square meters, was divided in two by a green curtain, with a red silk cross, surmounted by an icon of the Mother of God, painted and given by Father Emmanuel de Meester, the benedictine prior of Siluvaigiri. This delimited a 'chapel' where, from the beginning, the monastic offices were chanted in Syriac and the *Qurbana* was concelebrated every morning. In the other half, an iron trunk—the one Francis had bought in London—contained the books. Another sheltered the liturgical objects and vestments. Food was cooked outside on a wood fire, and they ate on the ground, using their fingers in the indian manner. At night, they unrolled mats to sleep, with their cotton shawls wrapped around them. Francis had experienced this kind of life at Shantivanam for a year. For Bede, it was his initiation. Perhaps it reminded him of the ascetic and community experiences of his youth, in the Cotswolds with his Oxford companions.

The building of the modest ashram began. 'It will be a miniature monastery', wrote Francis in a letter. Mr Ingle chose the spot—the church choir facing east—and traced the outline on the ground. A dozen or so men were hired to begin by leveling the land. An engineer from Kerala came from Trivandrum with cartridges of dynamite and blew up a few areas of rock below in the west. Each morning at dawn, when the monks standing in their hut sang the office of *Sapro* [Lauds], the first hammer blows of the workers breaking the blocks of granite into stones could be heard. The walls of the small church were rising, surrounded by bamboo scaffolding along which the thin black local masons climbed with agility. Others formed a human chain passing materials from one to the other all day long, carrying them on their head: water and sand from the river, logs sawed by hand in the nearby forest, cement and sheet metal that yellow trucks decorated with sacred images in bright colors unloaded at Vagamon.

The monks and their companions worked hard at clearing the rocky soil to assure their future subsistence. Of the ten acres that they had planned to sow before the monsoon, they were able to turn over only five: one for the vegetable garden, two for pineapples to be sold, and two for a nursery of 'casuarinas', an australian tree that grew relatively quickly and would provide shade, wind screen, and wood to burn. The tasks necessary for survival absorbed a great deal of energy: getting water, dead wood for the kitchen fire, and provisions. What could not be found in Vagamon—paper, ink, certain utensils or products—had to be purchased in Palai, eleven hundred meters lower, a real trek in the mountain. It took about three and a half hours to go down and more than four hours to go back up, laden with packages, along an uneven shortcut seventeen kilometers long. Francis, forgetting all his problems with his vertebrae, would often make this trek during the first years, until the new road that linked the plain to the high lake of Peryar was finished in January 1962.

One afternoon in April, in the heavy pre–monsoon heat, the workers were starting to raise the walls of the community building. Bede, whose stomach had been causing him suffering for a while, was working in the hut translating the syriac breviary into English. Francis and the postulants were sweating, hoeing the dry earth, from which they constantly had to remove large pieces of rock. They saw a majestic silhouette dressed in black, with an embroidered hood on his head, walking along the path. It was Mar Athanasios coming to visit them. The old bishop had left his car and chauffeur in Vagamon and had taken the path alone, like a shepherd seeking his adventurous sheep, carrying a gourd of water, a camera, and a few pieces of fruit to share. His was a paternal visit, followed by financial help and a command tinged with affectionate worry: 'You must eat appropriately and give your young people substantial food, otherwise you will see their health suffer.'

The small community hoped to move into the stone buildings before the monsoon. But it came earlier than anticipated. One morning in May, Vargheese went to look for wood on the slopes towards Teekoy. Francis was sitting on the ground in front of the hut, reading the mail he brought back from Vagamon. Suddenly the sky darkened, and in a few instants they were caught in a downpour. From afar he could see the young man, bent over under an enormous load of kindling, run towards them, then stop, blinded, soaked, searching for his way. The hut was flooded. They had to lift the precious trunks up on rocks and blocks of wood and take the mats outside to dry at the end of the day, when the sun managed to dispel the thick mist that enveloped the mountain. Rats made their appearance. Traps were set, a sort of rustic cage with a spring door. That year the rains were particularly violent. Building slowed. In June, Francis went down to Palai to withdraw the workers' pay from the Central Bank. Their savings had melted away: the materials, fifteen hundred pineapple and casuarinas plants, salaries, daily food, even though it had been reduced to the vital minimum, had exhausted the diocese's donations and the savings scraped together in Pushpagiri. Francis climbed back, asking himself where he could find money to continue. He walked under the rain, praying and thinking. Borrow from the bank? It was not easy. The priest who accompanied them had warned him that the socialist government of Kerala, urged by the communists, was resistant to the mortgage system. The lands were not accepted as guarantee. Ask Scourmont to bail them out? He would wait until he had no other option. He would begin by writing to his sister, to try and gather a few donations from Belgium. Providence would not abandon him, he was sure. The downpour redoubled when he arrived on the plateau, and the wind blew in gales that drove the rain almost horizontal.

The following night, when the brothers got up to chant *Lilio* (Vigils), Francis did not move. Perplexed, Bede went close to him, spoke to him: no answer. He touched his forehead and realized that his companion was burning with fever. They tried to make him stand up. He swayed and fell back. All day he stayed lying down, prostrated, half–conscious. They tried to give him water to drink. The next day, his state worsened: shaking, inert, he murmured words that made no sense. Sylvester and Vargheese went through the mountains towards the tea plantations, where on certain days a dispensary was staffed by a nurse or doctor. Bede watched over the sick man during a long night where he feared for his life. At noon, Sylvester brought back a doctor with his emergency kit. Not knowing what he would find, he had brought a maximum of instruments and medications. He carefully examined the european swami and left a few medications to give him.

Francis, who told us about these events much later, had only very vague, almost dream–like memories of this illness, from which only one precise image emerged: the black leather suitcase with chrome fastenings, which had been near his face and which had seemed enormous. The rest had been told to him after his recovery, which from that day on had been rapid. If this illness had a name, a diagnosis, it has been forgotten.

In July, the monsoon redoubled its assaults. The wind howled day and night; the mountain, streaming with water, seemed to be inhabited by Yahweh in his days of wrath, as the chronicle of 1958 evokes, 'The voice of Yahweh thunders on the waters of the river which rise in a few instants, sweeping away our little bamboo bridge and the materials collected on the banks. . . . The voice of Yahweh thunders in the water that pours streaming down, in the force and splendor of the mountain torrents. . . . The voice of Yahweh thunders, shattering the trees and collapsing the shelters.' However, their frail cabin held firm. In spite of these terrible climatic conditions, the walls of the dwelling were finished, and on 5 August, a corrugated sheet metal roof with a double slope was attached to the walls. The next day was Sunday: day of rest and reading in the hut, while outside the hurricane shook the mountain. Suddenly, the brothers heard an enormous crack, followed by a sort of monstrous groaning coming from the building site. They ran to it and discovered that an entire half of the roof, five thousand square feet of sheet metal, with the beams, purlins, and rafters, had been lifted up and folded on to the other half. Consternation. They all raised their heads, incredulous. Bede, the tallest, with a very british smile, pointed to an inscription stamped on the back of the sheet metal: 'Made in Belgium!'

The following week, the winds died down, the damage was repaired, and at the end of August the small group moved into a solid building, whose roof had been anchored directly into the ground. Only the main work was finished; there still were many small details to complete. The workers refused to continue if they were not paid. Francis sent a first distress signal to Dom Guerric, who sent fifty thousand francs.

On 14 September, the feast of the Exaltation of the Cross, Mar Athanasios visited Kurisumala for the second time. This time, he was expected with all honors: he came to bless the church and clothe the two young men with the *sadhaka* [novice] habit. He spent two days with his monks. It was the beginning of good weather, the sun shone, the sky was blue, and the novices were smiling in their new white habits, still starched. Three postulants were expected the following month, one of whom was a young indian engineer who had graduated in London. They were needed: there were many technical problems to be solved, of which the water supply was a priority.

One Sunday, shortly before Christmas, Francis was sitting on his mat, a small wooden board on his knees. He was writing the Christmas chronicle, in his even handwriting. He looked out the window at the blue sky where a couple of birds of prey were circling very high. Bede had gone to Tamil Nadu, to experience Arunachala with hindu hermits. The novices were hoeing the vegetable garden, where almost all the seeds had been carried away by the monsoon. The shoots that had resisted had dried up in November, for lack of water. They were starting again from nothing, but it was very late. 'The field of pineapples will also have to be fenced', thought the prior, 'because the neighbors' cattle come in and ravage it'. He continued to write his chronicle in French, to give news to family and friends in Europe. His niece would type it and circulate it. 'Hopefully it will bring us a few more donations', he couldn't help thinking. 'There are so many more buildings to put up. A small guesthouse, for example, to fulfill the monastic duty of hospitality while protecting the novitiate's silence.' He reread his text, where he retold the important points of these nine months spent on the Mount of

the Cross, and ended by expressing a hope in which the inspiration of the
Council and inter–religious dialogue could be predicted:

By the exterior and interior forms we give to our life, we trust
that God is guiding us to establish in India a truly contemplative
christian monasticism, one that is well rooted in this country. Each
person here is conscious of the void his absence would represent
in the life of the Church. Our attempt is still only a humble seed,
and we know very well that our growth remains at the mercy of
many storms. But those we have weathered since this inspiration
came to us give us confidence that God will make this seed grow
into a great tree that could extend its branches to the ends of
India. This country has a hindu contemplative tradition that goes
back to the origins of its history and that has left an indelible
impression on its culture. Even more, it is still living and could
be a considerable contribution for the world. At present, the
Church is such a stranger to this tradition that it seems scarcely
possible to establish true dialogue. We must first establish here
our own contemplative tradition. We hope to make a contribution
to this effort, as modest as it may be, and thus prepare for an
awakening when the Church enters fully into the spiritual inheritance of the East and when the East finds the fulfillment of its
history, thought and seeking for God in the living truth of Christ.

GROPINGS IN THE DARKNESS

Like a mist that hides the sun
Sometimes, without apparent reason
Dark night envelops the spirit
The heart must not be troubled by this
Or fall into discouragement
Let it patiently seek the light
In the writings of the Holy Fathers
Trying gently to pray
Turning its gaze toward heaven
Awaiting help from on high.
                    (Isaac of Nineveh [Syrian Father, seventh century])

End of May 1959. Humid air. Rain drumming on the sheet metal roof. Alternating chant of the psalms. The community—nine men now—was gathered in church for the night offices: *Lilio* (Vigils) and *Sapro* (Lauds). When the recitation was finished, they extinguished the oil lamps, except the one near the icon of the liturgical season, on the right. Time for silent meditation in the half–light. The rain had stopped. Only the intermittent mooing of a cow broke the great silence of the mist–covered mountain. The pink light of dawn was entering the cross–shaped chevet window when the sanctuary curtain opened. *Qurbana* was celebrated by the two european priest–monks. Another time of silence. Everyone was seated on the ground, on rope mats, turned towards the east. The serving brother went out the side door, silently. The muffled tinkling of the milk cups and plates of rice he was lining up in the hallway could be heard. The gong sounded. The monks went out in single file to take their first meal.

One of the peasants hired to help with the heavy work was waiting in front of the window. He made a sign: 'come, come and see.' Francis followed him into the rudimentary bamboo barn and found a cow lying down, her legs shaking with death throes. 'Black quarter?' Francis asked. The man said 'yes', with his head nodding sideways rapidly in the indian manner. He was a local boy, who knew animals but only a few words of English. Francis continued in Malayalam, 'What can we do?' The peasant made a resigned gesture. 'You think she will die too?' Francis asked. Affirmative nod of his head.

It was the second cow to die that week, after six calves. In a few days, the epidemic had killed more than half the small herd bought last November down in the plain. The boy stood up straight and suddenly talkative. 'We should have given them shots before the rains. Each year it's the same thing. At the first rain, many cows die. Those on plantations have veterinarians come from the city, but here, we are far from everything.' Francis tightened his lips and fists, and with this mechanical gesture showed a strong annoyance that he was trying to master. He had thought that with a little hygiene, supplementary fodder, he could make a herd prosper and obtain a decent milk production. He already imagined the slopes of Kurisumala covered with green grass where fat cows would graze, accompanied by their gamboling calves.

He had to think everything over, start from zero, he realized as he walked along the vegetable garden. Work more methodically. These mixed–breed cows in any case produced very little milk, at the most, two

liters per day. He had to find something else, better animals. He stopped to
examine the tomato plants. That was not going well either: they were
growing wild, without any fruits. 'Maybe the soil is not the right type', he
mused. 'The layer of humus is so thin. Maybe too acid? Should write to
Father Marc of Scourmont. He knows. And for the cheese, we should ask
him for some rennet, which cannot be found here.' The pineapple plants,
however, were developing well on the slope cleared with great difficulty
the year before. The first fruits should be harvested before Christmas.

Preoccupied, Francis joined his companions who were unearthing
and reassembling rocks to continue the pasture wall. He had been able to
persuade Bede to allow another month of intensive work and to start the
novitiate courses again only in June when the monsoon would intensify.
The Benedictine, a studious man, worked at teaching and publication.
This exhausting lugging of rocks weighed on him. He did not consider
that he would live here indefinitely. His temporary exclaustration from
Prinknash was coming to an end and might not be renewed. The set up of
the site and the building concerned him less than liturgical, spiritual, and
philosophical research, which was more in accordance with his own
journey. In any case, he was planning to return to Europe in September
to give a few talks in England and participate in the liturgical congress of
Nimègue in Holland, where he would represent the syriac Catholics.
Francis asked himself whether his companion would have the courage
after that to return to live in destitution. In Bede's absence, Francis' own
task would be even heavier, because he gave most of the classes: Patrology, Holy Scripture, weekly commentary of the Sunday Bible readings.
In addition, he willingly took care of the visitors, more and more numerous, to whom he explained the origins, the life, and plans for the ashram.

While carrying the rocks, Francis remembered the events of the last
months. They had fenced the vegetable garden, the pineapple orchard,
and the large pasture to protect them from leopards and wandering cows.
The first devoured several calves, the latter nibbled on their grass and
vegetables. It was enormous work. To resist the violent winds and torrents
of water, these low walls of stone had to be at least eighty centimeters
wide at their base and one meter twenty high. The larger blocks were
broken with a sledgehammer.

'It is not going fast enough', the prior concluded. There were more
than two kilometers of fence to build. They would need to hire workers:
they ask only 66 rupees per hundred feet. But the handsome check Dom

Guerric had sent in January (the money for the trip to Kurisumala he had foregone, as he wrote) had immediately been swallowed up in building a small guesthouse: a dormitory room and two cells. The sheet metal roofing had suddenly become impossible to find, and in order to put a roof on before the rains, they had to buy some on the black market at exorbitant prices. The worst was that these worries and problems occupied their minds and caused agitation, whereas calm is so necessary to the formation of the young. In addition, there was the matter of Asirvanam. A little before Easter the belgian Benedictines of Siluvaigiri who had just moved there had had enormous community problems. Father de Meester had called on Francis for 'consolation, guidance, and arbitrage'. Twenty–five hours on a train in third class, in heat of almost forty degrees celcius. On his return, he found that construction had been interrupted and the workers were on strike, fighting each other with knives. Once everything had been settled, he himself was struck down by a case of dysentery.

'Once more I saw my strength fail suddenly, body and soul, I felt I was sinking. And then, in faith, slowly, I returned to the surface.' He remained exhausted physically. 'I feel like I am crossing a period of darkness, after a long period of peace and blessing' (letter to his sister, September 1959). His consoler was Isaac of Nineveh: 'When doubt seizes you, roll your cloak about you and wait for it to pass.' Another consoling angel, very much living and sometimes mischievous, came to comfort him at Easter: his compatriot and friend Claire Vellut, who had just been given charge of the leprosarium of Pollambakkam, which Belgium had donated to the indian government. She told him about King Leopold's visit and the Mahieu family news she had gathered in Brussels in February.

The rain started to fall hard again. Everyone, without showing it or even admitting it, awaited the noon gong that would bring respite, if not comfort, since it was almost as humid in the monastery as outside. 'We will have to make a fire in the library's wood stove', thought Francis; 'the books must already be half moldy. And ask the family to knit and quickly send pullovers. The young people who came from the plains are not used to this climate: they are shivering.'

During the whole year 1959, Francis took care first of all to teach and spiritually consolidate a growing community that was giving rise to more vocations than it could accept. At the same time, he tried to lay the foundations of an agricultural enterprise to ensure their financial autonomy and their subsistence. But the major works of the facilities—

construction, leveling, terracing—in fact took the largest share of the money they were able to gather, and also their physical and mental energy. Without start–up capital or a european motherhouse, the prior was always trying to raise financing. The bishop was doing his best, but the diocese was poor. Scourmont sent a few substantial checks, faithful friends sent donations, and the family opened an account in Belgium, organized collections and knitted! Caldey regularly forwarded Mass intentions. But the needs were always more than the funds. In addition, the failures they encountered, both in animal rearing and in cultivation, showed the lack of method and practices adapted to the climate. Although these experiences were disappointing, they would yield fruitful lessons. If Francis lacked agricultural and, especially, veterinary knowledge, he mastered the general technique of enterprise. He was a tireless worker, led by a stubborn will and a great confidence in Providence. From the very beginning, he analyzed, evaluated, and measured the attempts and results with precision. At night, he kept a 'Diary of the Goshala' (journal of the dairy farm) where he jotted everything down: purchases and sales, the names of the fertilizers and seeds, and the number of liters of milk produced by each cow each day. From these data, after a few months he drew longitudinal observations, mini statistics. He set up a small library of agronomy and subscribed to periodicals. In this building without electricity, running water, or access road; isolated in a mountain drenched with water and shaken by the wind for six months every year, completely dried out for the other six months; on poor, rocky, steep land, he stubbornly kept trying to create conditions for good productivity.

His energy was sustained by the thrilling feeling of seeing his old dream take shape, with such poor means, in this grandiose setting. By prayer also, especially prayer at night, which he would always prefer. 'At the hours where one's conscience is the most vivid, that is in the silence of recollection and prayer, all the asceticism, all the physical, intellectual, or spiritual labor are marvelously transformed into peace and joy, confidence and self–abandonment. Are these not the most delicious fruits of the Spirit?' (Christmas letter 1959).

TURNING POINT: PILOT–VILLAGE AND INDO–SWISS PROJECT

Two decisive factors would allow the agricultural activity of Kurisumala to take off in the year 1960. The first was a material factor coming from external political initiative. A highway, built at considerable expense through the mountain by the Kerala government, little by little linked the high ground to the coastal plain and allowed motorized vehicles to come to the lowest point of the property. The monks would spend three months building their private road, one thousand six hundred meters long, leading to the buildings. The entrance to their property was marked by two stone pilasters topped by a syriac cross. In March, the three first trucks loaded with timber stopped in front of the monastery. The second factor was mental and relational, coming from Francis' initiative: his analysis of the preceding year's failure and planning of a more systematic approach would give rise to providential collaborations.

The beginning of the year was still marked by stumblings and by a few commercial misadventures. The first surplus of milk was put for sale on the market in Vagamon without success. Each family of workers had a thin cow and was content with her production. So that the precious liquid would not sour, ghee, a sort of butter used in all of Asia, was made. This ghee, judged of excellent quality by the visitors, did not find any buyers nearby. Are the people too poor? Do they make their own ghee? One day, a man came to the ashram and proposed that he would go sell the milk at retail in the surrounding area. Excellent idea. They agreed that he would buy the milk for .25 rupees per liter and sell it wherever he pleased, for the price he wished. With his thirty–liter jug on his head, this door–to–door salesman went by foot along the mountain paths, stopping in each hovel to fill the housewife's containers in exchange for a few coins. Alas, after a few weeks—during which of course they trusted him and did not annoy him by asking him to pay cash—he disappeared for good with the milk, the jug . . . and the money.

The pineapples that they began to harvest at the end of November 1959 finally were a complete success. The fruits were large, numerous, and succulent. The first one was solemnly offered to Mar Athanasios, who blessed it and cut it himself to share with all the community. With his long white beard and embroidered hood, he looked like some biblical patriarch offering the first–fruits of the harvest. They picked more than a thousand. They ate them, they really enjoyed them, and they even took photographs of them. But selling them was another matter. They realized too late that they should have taken them to a cannery in the plain. Without a passable road, how could they do this? One of the brothers tried his luck and stood behind a full basket of fruits at the Vagamon market. That evening, he had sold only two! The remainder was left with a shopkeeper who finally sold them for a third of the price before they were completely overripe. A commercial fiasco, no doubt, but an agricultural success, if the only one. The monsoon had drowned nine tenths of the nursery of young trees, and then the months of dryness saw the hundred rescued ones wilt. The vegetable garden suffered more or less the same fate, showing the absolute necessity of a water reservoir coupled with a drainage system. As for the few beasts that survived the epidemic and were not devoured by carnivores, they were sold, to be replaced by a small kernel of purebreds: a young bull fathered by an Ayrshire; and two Shorthorn heifers. These were provided by scottish tea planters. Living in Munnar, a small town they built on the mountain, about 125 km from Kurisumala, these planters were interested in animal husbandry and built herds known for their good milk production, from animals imported from Australia. Now it was a question of keeping these cows alive, ensuring numerous descendents, and seeing that they gave a maximum of milk that they hoped to sell more easily in the city because of the new road.

One night, after Compline, the prior retired to his cell, took a notebook, filled his petrol lamp, and sat on his mat, a small plank of wood on his knees. He wrote on the paper, until the hour for *Lilio*, his reflections on the farm, methodically, in three columns: dysfunctions, causes, and remedies. Little by little, things clarified in his mind, and the conviction emerged that only a dairy farm had a chance on such a site, to ensure their subsistence and financial autonomy. In addition, from there, they could be of most use for the local development of the neighboring population. Had Gandhi not recommended that ashrams perpetuate the tradition of *goseva*, reconciling this ancient 'service of cow' advocated by the hindu religion with increased milk productivity, which was indispensable for economic recovery? All efforts must be concentrated on this and, above all, to be sure of sufficient external help to begin working more rationally.

The day after the next, before dawn, with his saffron cloth bag slung across his chest and his black umbrella in his hand, Francis descended with long strides towards the bus stop recently built on the road. The rusty vehicle, heralded by its horn, was still half empty at this altitude. The prior sat near the window, on the men's side. The driver pulled the string that rang the bell, and they were racing down the slope towards Vellikullam. At each stop, men gathering up the tails of their *dhotis* and smiling women in saris sprang out of the jungle. They were carrying all sorts of packages: cans of petrol, baskets tied up with ropes, cylinders, vegetable baskets, even babies. When they arrived in Palai, there was not an empty cubic centimeter on the bus. The smells of sweat and kerosene replaced the fragrance of cardamom and wet leaves. Everyone got off. A more comfortable bus served the route to Trivandrum, the administrative capital of the state. The sun pierced the fog. They were traveling now along lagunas bordered with coconut trees where a lake–dwelling people bustled, getting from place to place by boat. The monk's franciscan soul marveled at such splendid scenery. He gave thanks for the sun, for the reflection of the green trees in the water, for the red flowers in the gardens, and for the young girls in yellow saris laughing as they washed their metal dishes on the shore.

It was almost two o'clock when Francis got off at the Trivandrum bus stand. He sat in the shade, recited his office, and ate his two bananas. A man approached, knelt down, and placed a small brown sticky bun at his feet. He was no longer astonished: everywhere in India, *sannyasis* were the object of this kind of offering. In the street, he looked at the shops, bought a wooden spoon and a pruning knife, and examined the display in the *ayurveda* pharmacy with its piles of dried leaves, seeds, powders and bottles. He went to the public service area and looked for the ministry of agriculture. It was an old building with peeling paint, in the middle of a yellowed garden. The doorman was drowsing, slumped on his table. Roused to answer Francis' query, he responded, 'Husbandry Department? It's on the second floor, Swami. Ask for Mr Kartha. It is written on the door.'

Mr Kartha was a middle–aged man, quite tall for a south Indian, and his eyes were kindly behind thick black–rimmed glasses. His office was cluttered with files, cartons, and cloth registers piled on the ground. On the wall, under the fan, hung a colored picture of Gandhi on a turquoise blue background, such as were sold everywhere along the sidewalks. He called a boy who brought them two glasses of tea, asked Francis to sit down, and then, after the usual preliminaries, listened attentively to Francis' story and request:

If I understand correctly, you are asking the government's help
to develop a private husbandry center in your ashram?
In a way, yes. But we are ready to offer a service to the population in exchange.
What kind of service?
By sharing the experience we gain, the techniques we used, the
seeds, we could be a center for demonstration, for information
on husbandry on the mountain. You see, although in the eyes
of the law we are a private group, our aim is not commercial.
We do not want to make a profit; it is important for us to keep
a poor lifestyle, similar to that of the neighboring peasants.
We wish only to take care of our own needs and, if possible,
be of social service, help development and health. One of
our projects, for example, is to create a dairy cooperative by
gathering the district's small producers into an association.
Hmm. I see. As a matter of principle, my department cannot sign an
agreement with individuals. But your project interests me.
Have you heard of the 'Key Village Unit Scheme'?
No. What is that?
It is a plan thought up by Pandit Nehru at the very beginning of
independence, with Gandhiji. I myself worked on the national level to put the concept into operation. The aim is to
improve the productivity of the livestock of India, from pilot
centers each serving a dozen villages. You know, no doubt,
that we have the largest population of cows in the world and,
despite this, the milk production is the lowest per capita.
And the production in Kerala is still lower than the national
average! This is due to several factors: the cattle are poorly
chosen, breeding is done by chance, and cows are poorly fed
and poorly cared for.
Yes, we had this experience last year. In the meantime, we bought
a few animals of good breed, but they need to be cared for
by a veterinarian. We also need to develop feed, plant good
quality grasses. For all this we would need competent
advisors and subsidies.
Listen, I have an idea. The first thing to do is to create a blood line,
a breed that has the genetic characteristics of good dairy
cows, and that can adapt to the climate in the high slopes. At

the same time, you need to grow the proper feed: clover, corn, what will take root best. And first, no doubt, you need to amend and fertilize the soil.

We have manpower: there are ten of us. And we are building a permanent barn for twenty–four animals.

Good. All that can be taken into account. But, what I need here in Kerala especially are good breeding stock. Your Ayrshire cross young bull is not bad, but a Key Village Unit needs something better than that.

Mr Kartha remained silent a moment. Francis waited, slightly annoyed, not seeing clearly where he was going.

I propose this bargain. You told me you are Belgian. You lived in England; you have colleagues there. What we would need here is one or two purebred bulls. Jersey bulls, for example. If you could get two and keep them on your farm, they would remain your property, I could create a Key Village Unit from there, based in Kurisumala. You would have a veterinarian and an assistant permanently, a monthly subsidy for the bulls' upkeep, experts to improve the livestock and the grazing plants. In exchange, your bulls would provide the semen for artificial insemination of the whole region. What do you think of that?

That would be wonderful! I will contact our brothers in Wales immediately. They know cattle; they themselves have a dairy farm on the Isle of Caldey. But they are not rich. The problem will be to find money. A Jersey bull must be worth quite a bit.

Think about it. May I come to see your facilities?

Of course, whenever you wish. I would be glad to show you our possibilities.

Francis returned full of hope. This time he took the train and arrived in Kottayam during the night. The first bus for Vagamon left at five o'clock in the morning. A few forms were lying stretched out in the station. He lay down near them, his cotton shawl rolled around his head.

Around four thirty, the police woke them up by hitting them with *lathi*, those long flexible sticks that they used as truncheons.

The next week, Mr Kartha went to Kurisumala by jeep and toured the domain with Francis. They visited the directors of the nearby plantations, whose cooperation they desired to obtain. The two men discussed at length the concrete aspects of the enterprise. That very day, Francis wrote to Dom Samson of Caldey to ask him if he could buy and send them two Jerseys. He reminded Dom Guerric of the gospel story of the 'unwelcome guest' told him about his talk with Mr Kartha and, showing him the issue of the Key Village Unit, asked *cum humili et sincera dilectione* whether he could send him the bill for the bulls.

The veterinarian service proper would not begin until 1961. The dairy farm, however, was doing better and better. The new cows gave almost ten liters of milk per day. Their calves were superb. They bought a dozen hybrid cows from the same breeder in Munnar. All of them, at night, when they returned from pasture, lined up in two rows facing each other in the new barn. The building plan, from Scourmont, was modeled on the Thiérache barns: a feed alley in the center; cement floor with a gutter along the walls. Each morning, the cleaning water mixed with the manure was gathered to fertilize the vegetable garden and pastures. Thanks to the road, the milk was sold daily in Eratupetta, the nearest commercial town, and began to provide money to buy food. One day, the cellarer brought back a few kilos of wheat flour. In a hastily built brick oven, they baked the first loaves of bread whose delicious aroma tickled the monks' noses pleasantly. Francis remembered that he had been the baker at Scourmont before the war, and as a connoisseur appreciated the bread served that evening. Kurisumala's bread, like its cheese, would soon have a reputation among all the Europeans in India.

That year they built a weaving workshop and sent four postulants to Tiruvalla to learn. They would live with the Fathers of Bethany—and thus would not lose their Syriac—and would follow the weaving courses at the technical school, to be in charge of making the pieces of cotton necessary to clothe the community: saffron for the monks; white for the novices and postulants.

At the end of August another setback occurred. When he was preparing the workers' weekly pay, Francis noticed that the tin box where he kept the monastery's money had only five rupees left. The next morning, with his cloth bag and umbrella as usual, he went to Vagamon to take the bus to Elapara, where the nearest branch of the Palai Central Bank was. He saw a group of excited people. From afar he heard their animated, almost shrill conversation in Malayalam. When he approached, he understood that the bank had failed. Should he believe them? In the bus, all the conversation had been about this news. 'That would be a terrible thing', Francis thought. 'All our money is in this account.' Indeed, in Elapara, the road was blocked by the police, who were putting seals on the building. The crowd was dense and rough. Francis left for Tiruvalla: only the bishop could help him out. 'Now', he thought while he waited for the bus, 'we don't have a penny left. God is sending us the experience of total poverty!' He was not really worried. He was used to empty coffers! Except that this time, it was the collapse of the largest catholic bank of the country. Practically all the religious institutions had their accounts there. All the diocese's cash was sealed! Mar Athanasios was able to find a few hundred rupees for the workers. The Palai bank was placed in liquidation, and finally Kurisumala was to recuperate its money many years later.

In November, a providential meeting would reinforce the dairy project. Jacques-Albert Cuttat, swiss ambassador to India, came to make a retreat at Kurisumala. In the political circles of New Delhi, he had heard about this strange eastern monastery founded by a belgian Cistercian and an english Benedictine on a mountain. That intrigued him, and during his next vacation he went there. Cuttat was a complex man. Passionate about the great religions' convergence, prudent as Monchanin was faced with the risks of amalgamation, he personally practiced various forms of asceticism and meditation. His first work, *The Meeting of Religions*, was about to be published. He was also a Swiss, a good manager, and a shrewd financier. Very quickly a friendship founded on a common spiritual approach and mutual admiration sprang up between Francis and him. 'This man understood immediately what we wanted to do here', Francis would say after the ambassador's premature death a few years later. Putting a governmental veterinary center in place opened multiple possibilities. It would facilitate linking the ashram to the huge 'Indo–Swiss project for milk production', one of whose promoters was M. Cuttat. His friendship and enthusiasm would provide useful guarantees with government officials (who had to be reckoned with, in a very bureaucratized India) and international organizations such as the FAO (Food and Agricultural Organization) of the United Nations.

After a week, the ambassador reluctantly left Kurisumala. Everything tried to keep him there: Francis' friendship; the mountain and its little walls of dry rocks that follow the land's undulations, as in his native Switzerland; the plans for creating a race of cows for high altitude. Still more, the spiritual experience dazzled him. Before leaving, he wrote in the new 'Golden Book':

The undersigned, who owes his return to his catholic faith to indian spirituality and *hesychasm* [Prayer of the Heart], leaves Kurisumala ashram with an immense gratitude and the pain of leaving behind a new spiritual fatherland. What I have found surpasses all I had hoped to meet: the mystical depths of India culminating in the *Totus Deus—Totus Homo* (Wholly God— Wholly Man) by the asceticism of the desert; the liturgy of the eastern church; and the pure monastic contemplation of the Church Fathers. . . . Here, our Christianity becomes indianized and our indianism is christianized. An immense future seems to me to be promised to the extraordinary synthesis achieved in embryo, but very truly, on this Mountain of the Cross. I think that on the day of Judgment, the Fathers of Kurisumala will hear Saint Benedict and Saint Bernard tell them: 'What we did for the West, you started to do for the East' (20 November 1960).

A COMMUNITY OF BROTHERS

From Scourmont to Caldey, Francis' indian project had a dream's out-line: go to Shantivanam to join the founding hermits Monchanin and Le Saux. Once there, month by month, disenchantment crept in. The life of a hermit, as desirable as it might have seemed from Europe, did not fulfill Francis' deep aspirations. His attraction for community life had revealed itself through scouting, the Second Lancers, but especially the novitiate. Henri Le Saux, the very type of the *gyrovague* monk, had noted with irony that 'Father Mahieu has only one idea in his mind, to found a cis-tercian monastery here'.

Francis Mahieu was a leader of men. He had the attraction for it and the charism. At Pushpagiri, it was he who took charge, established the schedule, directed the transfer and set–up. It would be the same on the mountain, as soon as the first hut was put up. If Francis had brought only Bede Griffiths with him, it would have been another experiment: two monks retiring into solitude. But he dragged postulants into the adventure, a kernel of the future community.

We can clearly see beyond the laborious setting up and the material tribulations of every sort—*primum vivere* [first, to live]—that the farmer–entrepreneur was also a true spiritual shepherd, solicitous for the flock in his care. Was he not named prior by the bishop? He never forgot it.

His first sheep were not chosen by chance. In two years the group grew, going from four to fifteen members. From 1960 on, can we speak of a monastic community? How are its functions divided? The prior, Francis, was Cistercian. The sub–prior, Bede, was Benedictine. Together with the Syro–Malankar priest lent by Mar Athanasios, they provided the priestly service as well as the rest: novitiate formation, spiritual guidance, teaching, accounting, secretariate, guesthouse, not to mention the farm work and construction. Of the many candidates who came, twelve were kept. Seven were now in the novitiate, and five were still postulants. Where did they come from? From all over: nearby villages, the cities of Kerala, and sometimes from further still, from Bangalore, Bombay, Poona, and Ranchi. Their spiritual origins were as varied as their geographical horizons. In spite of oneself, one thinks of the stories of the Fathers of the egyptian desert, when in the fourth century, young men came to them in Scete saying, 'Abba, make me a monk.'

Some of these postulants had been leading the religious life for many years and had answered the call to a greater detachment. Many had been born in the Syrian Catholic Church of India; some came from the Latin rite, or even from the separated Jacobite churches. They were well educated, had studied religion or science, or were experts in some trade such as weaving, basketry, baking, gardening, or bookbinding. They spoke Malayalam or Hindi, English more or less, sometimes a little Sanskrit, Syriac, or Latin. They had shaven heads, but only the *sannyasis* wore a beard: brown and bushy for Francis, white and thin for Bede.

The senior was the youngest: Sylvester was only twenty. Serious and intelligent, he had not been able to enter the Poona seminary. A companion from the heroic beginnings, it was he whom Francis was to send in 1960 to the Dairy Research Institute in Bangalore, to learn modern dairy techniques.

Vargheese left the orthodox Jacobites to become a catholic monk, for which his family never forgave him. Fervent and sensitive, this secret wound remained within him.

Andrew, past forty, was an indian Jesuit. He left the Ranchi seminary where he taught, to follow the narrow way. According to the course schedule, he learned about the Rule of Saint Benedict and the eastern Fathers with the other novices or joined the team of professors to teach Latin and English to the postulants. He was also, on occasion, assistant professor of thomistic philosophy. And through the courses given by Francis and Bede, he discovered hindu philosophy, of which he previously had only a superficial knowledge.

A young engineer from Bombay, a graduate of London, stayed for some time. Discouraged by the syriac liturgy, he asked to continue his novitiate . . . in Caldey!

Joseph arrived by foot one evening, bare–chested, his sparse baggage on his head. Knowing barely how to read, he left his family of peasants to become a monk. They put him to the test. He showed himself very concentrated in prayer and, after a few weeks, manifested an authentic religious spirit. Besides his talent for gardening, he had a very beautiful voice.

Philipose was really not tall. Francis wrote 'the little wise man' on a photo, which shows him smiling.

On a windy night, someone knocked on the door. A man of confident bearing stood in the doorway. He handed a wallet full of rupees to the prior, who was taken aback. In his suitcase were European–style clothes, and he spoke, 'It's for you. Take it all. I want to stay here.' 'Where does this money come from?' asked Francis in surprise. 'My father. It's to register at the University. But on my way there, I changed my mind. I don't want to go. I decided to stay with you, to become a monk.' Francis learned that the young man's name was Alexander. 'Go to bed, Alexander', he said. 'In one hour it's *Lilio*. We will talk about all of this tomorrow.' They sent him home with his suitcase and rupees. He returned, a few months later, with his parents, whom he had succeeded in winning over.

The influx of candidates was such that Francis hesitated. Should they enlarge, envisage fifty or sixty monks? In 1960, his decision was made: no more than about twenty. Later, he would say that he was inspired by his grandfather's family: two parents and eighteen children, working a farm with the help of a few agricultural workers. We may think that other factors weighed in the decision: lack of money, few able to provide formation. The number was reached in ten years. From 1968 on, the newcomers would compensate for the dispersal of the elders. According to the eastern custom, confirmed *sannyasis* would leave the house, in small groups or alone, to found ashrams in south India. This would be the way followed by Sylvester and Philipose. Others, like Joseph, would never leave Kurisumala, the founding kernel of a community spreading wider and wider.

At the end of March 1960, it was so hot that the water level in the wells began to go down. The monks had finally finished terracing and asphalting the access road. In a serene atmosphere, the instruction of the novices was going to start up again at a steadier rhythm. Francis sat outside with his group, under the casuarina trees, which were starting to give welcome shade for the young men sitting in a circle. Sylvester returned from Vagamon, where he had gone to get the mail. Crouching at some distance, his back leaning on the little wall of dry rocks, he held a large yellow envelope in his hand.

The class ended, and the novices' white silhouettes disappeared into the house: it was time for reading. Sylvester got up and went to Francis, who took the envelope and glanced at the printed return address: 'Sacra Congregatio pro Ecclesia Orientali, Via della Conciliazione, Roma'. He opened it with curiosity. These people had always sent good news.

This time it was a blow. Monsignor Coussa was worrying about Kurisumala's canonical status. Are you Cistercians? If you are, what is your motherhouse? As long as the monastery is not clearly attached to the Order of Cîteaux, you are forbidden to receive and form novices. The Roman assessor meanwhile wrote to Scourmont to obtain clarifications. Francis was aghast and did not understand anything of this change. For a moment, he began to hope that Rome's intransigence would force Scourmont's hand and favor its adoption of Kurisumala as a full foundation. Dom Guerric sent Rome a very benevolent report in which he summed up his brother's journey with his usual conciseness:

When Father Francis entered our abbey in 1935, my predecessor, Dom Anselme Le Bail, did not hide his intention of making a cistercian monastic foundation in India, and Father Francis manifestly desired to be part of this.

Various circumstances, of which the closing of this country's borders is not the least, prevented the carrying out of this project, while other favorable events allowed us meanwhile to make a cistercian foundation in the Belgian Congo.

Meanwhile, Father Francis did not lose hope of one day introducing the monastic life in India: this plan could not have had a better promoter. Father Francis has always shown a great firmness of character and tenacity judiciously enlightened by an extraordinary intelligence. His religious experience is solid, and he always enjoyed his superiors' entire confidence.

Answering your request, I think that in all conscience I can assure you, Monsignor, that it truly seems to me that my Father Francis Mahieu presents the necessary qualities and experience to bring about, if God wills, the monastic foundation envisaged in the diocese of Tiruvalla.

Dom Belorgey, who was consulted, qualified the matter as a 'great misunderstanding'. Dom Déodat, Procurer of the Cistercians in Rome, wrote to Dom Guerric: 'A matter that has caused many difficulties is that of Father Francis, who is in India. He had asked permission to receive novices. But at the end of the day we realized that he did not yet have canonical status. We will try to arrange everything for the best.'

Finally, Mar Athanasios, in a long letter, explained, with supporting references to the eastern canon law, that Kurisumala was a *sui juris* monastery of diocesan right, placed under his sole authority and without canonical link to Cîteaux. For him, all this upheaval came from the request for bi–ritualism introduced for the three postulants who had come from the Latin rite. Everything finally resolved itself. Rome accepted the *sui juris* status and granted permission to receive novices and use the Syrian rite. On one condition, however: that Kurisumala henceforth refrain from any reference to the Cistercian Order. A model of 'Typicon' [the eastern equivalent of constitutions or Rules] drawn up in Rome in 1958, was sent to Francis for the young community to 'follow the rules and ancient monastic traditions of the East'.

Francis remained perplexed. He wrote to Dom Guerric: 'In any case, this defines our canonical condition, and that is a good thing. It is too early to tell to what measure we can fulfill these directives. I ask your prayers that we be faithful in fulfilling the task the Church imposes on us.'

'THAT ALL MAY BE ONE': THE SEPARATED BRETHREN

Francis' energetic and optimistic character, as well as his 'providentialistic' perception of events, led him to use situations to further his project, while being open to giving them new accents. His meeting with buddhist and hindu monasticism was central in his eastern studies phase in Europe, during his initial trip in northern India, and during his stay at Shantivanam. During the first years in Kurisumala a new issue emerged: reunion with separated christian churches.

The six million Christians in Kerala at that time were divided into multiple sub–groups. Their dissensions, which sometimes took the form of sordid haggling, if not violent confrontations, were an object of scandal for the Hindus. It was not rare, on the occasion of a religious feast, to see one parish try to occupy the street first for a grandiose procession or, by using powerful amplifiers, try to drown out the rival church's singing. These quarrels, several centuries old, dated from colonialism. The proselytism of western missionaries who succeeded one another was not a stranger to this, placing the accent on differences of rite and culture rather than on questions of dogma and religious life proper.

The church of Kerala, which went back in history to Saint Thomas the apostle and was 'one' for fifteen centuries, in communion with the Church of Persia (The Syrian Church of the East or Chaldean Church), is today in an almost inextricable state of division as a result of the missionary movements that accompanied the european colonial conquests. The Syro–Malabars, the group that allied itself with the seventeenth–century Portuguese at the price of ruthless latinization, has not yet recovered its identity despite the Vatican's conversion to the oriental rites proclaimed in Rome from the time of Leo XIII at the end of the nineteenth century. Equally numerous and more influential with the indian government because they were considered as the most authentic representatives of Christianity in India are the Jacobites, also called Orthodox, who remained faithful to the collective oath not to submit themselves to the portuguese bishops. Almost a century later, still without bishops, they were successful in joining the patriarchate of Antioch, the Syrian Church of the West, whose rite they adopted. Besides these two large groups, there were more episcopal churches: pure Latins, Anglicans (Church of South India), and some 'Mar Thoma' Syrians reformed under the influence of the English in the nineteenth century. Kurisumala enrolled itself in the Syro–Malankar Church, a group of Orthodox who rejoined Rome in 1930. It is the smallest of the episcopal churches in India, but the one that kept the liturgy of Antioch in its greatest purity, unfortunately impoverished for use in the parishes.

Mar Athanasios, raised in a jacobite family and a convert to Catholicism, was animated with a vivid desire to see the churches in his country reconciled with one another. He started the periodical *Reunion Record* and encouraged all the initiatives that favored the reunion of separated brethren. He insisted on including the union of the churches in the founding charter of Kurisumala as an essential objective, convinced that monastic life, to the degree that it witnessed to an era before the dissensions, could constitute a center for reconciliation. Bede Griffiths, himself a convert from Anglicanism, was sensitive to this expectation from their bishop. As early as 1959, the Benedictine was a popular figure in the ecumenical movement in Kerala. He organized regular meetings of representatives of the four episcopal churches at the anglican ashram of Alwaye. The participants had three goals: develop a spirit of mutual comprehension rather than controversy; highlight their common heritage in Jesus Christ; and each express their repentance for the faults committed in the past. One of these days of exchange and prayer was held at Kurisumala, and the community instituted one day a week for prayer for the reunion of the separated brethren.

During the whole year, the guesthouse welcomed in turn eight bishops from various churches. Archbishop Mar Gregorios came to spend a few days of retreat and went so far as to share the monks' manual work.

'The dissidents, Jacobites or others, look with envy at the new foundation. Not with the envy which detaches and distances, but that which brings closer and incites to quench one's thirst at the same source of living water', wrote Father Hambye in the third issue of *L 'Orient Syrien* [*Syrian East*]. This belgian Jesuit, based in Ranchi, became a privileged partner of the monastery. He obtained permission from his superior to come teach for several months. Passionate about eastern Christianity and, especially, its liturgy, he was a specialist in syriac questions and in the eastern Fathers, enthusiastic to the point of sometimes annoying his northern colleagues, who teased him by calling him 'Mar Hambyos'. His competence and friendship would be a powerful encouragement for Father Mahieu.

IN PURSUIT OF THE *PENQITHO*

December is a time of good weather in Kerala. The vegetation, fed by the monsoon rains until October, is shiny, full, in bloom. The sky is clear, the sun shines, and the temperature is ideal. On one of those beautiful winter days in 1960, Francis went down to Kottayam with Father Hambye to correct the proofs of a brochure he was having printed on the presses of the Saint-Joseph School. This work took less time than they had allotted, so the two friends stopped in their favorite shop before taking the bus back. This was a shop open to the street, where the most diverse liturgical objects were piled on top of each other, as in an antique store: candelabra, censors, oil lamps, bells, stands, and bronze crosses of various sizes, those 'persian' crosses that can be found in the whole region. There is no corpus on it, the branches end in flowers, the foot plunges into four rivers, and the Holy Spirit as a dove with wings outstretched, head down, seems to be kissing with his pointy beak. Their conversation leapt from topic to topic and included their surroundings:

I am looking for a cross of this kind for our church, but one on a tall copper oil lamp stand, like in the hindu temples.

You won't find one here. This shop sells only standard items, such as we find in every syrian parish in Kerala.

These stands are well made. How much?

Eighty rupees. They are rosewood!

I would buy two. But we would need to travel by truck or jeep to get them up. That will be for another time. Those stands remind me of books. . . . Father Hambye, how is your research on the *Penqitho* [collection of the syriac liturgical texts for Sundays and feasts] coming?

I don't have any news. It seems that there is no complete copy of it here. The eradication of the Syrian rite was pursued very hard in India. At the synod of Diamper, in 1599, the portuguese authorities burned all the liturgical books, ornaments, and vestments. A bishop, they said, was able to save a few prayer books and took refuge in Rome. Later the breviary of Pampakuda, which you use, was adopted everywhere. It is an abridged version for parish use. The monastic liturgy was much richer. It filled seven volumes!

Since Father Hambye had come to Kurisumala, he had taken an active part in the monks' research to reconstitute the complete cycle of the syrian monastic office. Father Bede had already spent a great deal of time translating the syriac breviary of the ordinary into English. But for Sundays and feasts, the great liturgical cycles, they had only a simplified prayerbook, printed in India and lent to them by the Fathers of Bethany, who were insistently asking that it be returned. The Jesuit extended his search to the Near East that he knew very well because he had traveled there several times to study. He knew where the best libraries were. He wrote here and there but the answers were disappointing. He continued the conversation:

Many eastern monasteries abandoned their rite when their church rejoined Rome, joining existing congregations such as Benedictines, Carmelites, Franciscans. It is a great loss for the liturgical inheritance. Syria, Lebanon, Iraq, Turkey had dozens of Syrian– or Chaldean–rite monasteries. There are only a few orthodox for the most part. I wrote to Cardinal Tappouni, the patriarch of the Catholic Syrians in Beirut. I was told that my letter followed him to Rome where he is living at the moment. I have not yet received an answer.

What do you hope from him?

I am thinking about the major seminary in Sharfeh in Lebanon which is under his jurisdiction. There they have one of the best libraries in the world for all that concerns the semitic churches, those called 'minor churches'. If someone can help us, it's the librarian at Sharfeh, but to be correct, I want to go through their cardinal Patriarch and explain to him the reasons for our request.

All this is very slow. . .

What would you like to do? Of course it would be more effective to go and see for ourselves. Not only for the books, but to visit the monasteries, participate in their liturgy, learn about the sequence of the offices, the ornaments, accessories, chant. I would be happy to escort you there.

Father Hambye, you are making me dream. . .

We would be received with open arms. Those people are so kind and hospitable.

At this moment, I cannot envision leaving the ashram, but in a
few months, maybe, when the work on the barn is finished,
if the bishop agrees, if Father Bede is willing to take charge
of teaching. . . .
At the end of March would be ideal: we would have Holy Week
and Easter!
I have already followed the offices of Holy Week in Jerusalem
once, it was before entering the Trappists, in 1935, with my
cousin Marthe.

The bus stopped noisily in front of them, lifting a cloud of dust and
snatching Francis away from his daydream. During the trip, Father Hambye,
very excited by the idea of showing his colleague the Syrian rite's cradle,
listed out loud all the convents, patriarchates, bishops' residences, and
seminaries they should visit.

A few weeks later, it was decided. Mar Athanasios approved the project. For the money, they would see: the jesuit provincial at Ranchi, Father Moeyersoen, also a Belgian, would advance the necessary amount
for the plane tickets for both religious.

On 19 March 1961, they got on a Comet at Bombay-Santa-Cruz
flying to Lebanon. Francis, who was taking the airplane for the first time,
discovered the sea of Oman from the air, then, very quickly the sand of
the arabian desert. They could make out the flare stacks of the oil wells,
the palm groves of Bahrain, and already they were starting the descent.
In Beirut, Father de Gerphanion welcomed them and brought them to
Saint Joseph University, founded by french Jesuits in 1875. After black
coffee served in minuscule cups and accompanied by honey cookies,
they were shown to the library. A marvel. Francis did not have time to
make note of all the titles that interested him before another father came
to get them to take them to supper in the professors' refectory and show
them their rooms.

The next day began an adventure that would bring the two friends to
all the important places of semitic Christianity. Father Hambye was well
known for his work as an eastern scholar, and Father Mahieu, thanks to
his 'chronicles' and the articles published in *L'Orient Syrien*, was warmly
welcomed everywhere. Arab hospitality and catholic brotherhood, very
lively in these near eastern minorities, did the rest. At the patriarchate of
catholic Syrians, they were served a 'mediterranean lunch'—as Francis

called it in his travel journal, where he listed the menu: chicken with rice, arabic bread, salads, cheese, olives, grapes, dates, ksara wine. It was Byzantium after the austere indian mountain! That evening, the procurator brought them to visit the city: Beirut the sparkling city, Beirut before the fratricidal war, Beirut with its many churches, convents, and mosques living as good neighbors.

Each day they were invited somewhere: a chaldean bishop, a maronite parish priest, the olivetans of Kobbé, even the armenian patriarch who took them by car to visit Byblos and its little roman church built by the crusaders in the twelfth century.

On Palm Sunday, they arrived in Sharfeh. The syrian catholic seminary had just been renovated and welcomed more than a hundred pupils and students. One could feel the spirit of a return to the sources which, under the influence of a few precursors, contradicted the propensity of the 'uniates' [portions of the eastern churches who reestablished union with the Roman Catholic Church] to copy latin customs.

For the past few years, at least in the highest ecclesiastical spheres, eastern Christians, be they Greek or Arab, had not been considered with as much condescendence by the 'Romans', and they were even encouraged to rediscover their roots. Fifty years earlier, Pope Leo XIII had published his encyclical *Orientalium dignitas* (1894), which solemnly reaffirmed, 'The eastern catholic, joining catholicism, must remain in his rite.' On the ground, the rank and file had long remained deaf: local habits and prejudices are slow to change, especially when they entail questioning supremacy. But in these times of preconciliar effervescence, the climate was one of openness, welcoming minorities, and getting over old quarrels. The vocabulary changed. They spoke no longer of 'schismatics' but of 'separated brethren'. In the patriarchates, it was rumored that John XXIII intended to invite Easterners to the Council as observers, which had never happened since the fifteenth century. In Sharfeh, Patriarch Tappouni had the chapel transformed in the purest syrian tradition: worked chancel (railing that closes the choir), ciborium (canopy) above the altar, two sets of green liturgical veils, and ambo (stand for reading the epistle and the Gospel) in the middle of the nave as in the synagogues. The magnificent collection of icons, chandeliers, and silver and gold candelabras that multiply the flames of the lamps and candles—everything contributes to creating the eastern sanctuaries' atmosphere of sacred mystery.

The two friends participated in the Holy Week offices as connoisseurs. In the evening, Francis made notes and accompanying sketches in his notebook of what he observed in the church: the subjects and placement of icons, vestments of deacons and sub–deacons, frequency and direction of incensing, gestures of blessing, and movements at the altar. Does the service of God not require perfection of gesture, attention to detail?

Easter Monday, they were taken up the mountain to the convent of Sharbel Makhlouf, a maronite monk destined for canonization. The beautiful place that had been isolated for centuries had become a place of popular pilgrimage. Even Muslims went up, hoping for a miracle from the 'saint'. The boutiques of souvenirs and pious objects were everywhere. The Maronites invited Francis for a meal: Christ is risen, let us feast! These monks did not really follow the way of the Desert Fathers: they ate meat, drank wine, and after dinner they got together in the arabic way in a sort of *diwan*, with soft cushions to drink coffee while smoking small fragrant cigars. Francis did not let them see his reproving astonishment. As Palladius[9] says, 'wine can serve to exercise charity and humility, and it is better to drink wine with discernment than water with pride'. Before leaving, he went to pray on the tomb of Sharbel the simple. He prayed for Kurisumala, so that the ashram on the mountain might become a real monastery, by the grace of God.

During their stay in Sharfeh, the two travelers divided all the free time they had between offices and visits in the library. There they met Professor Arthur Vööbus, a famous estonian orientalist, a specialist in the ancient syriac Fathers, which gave rise to fascinating conversations. But no *Penqitho*.

> To my knowledge, the only edition of the *Penqitho* was printed by the Dominicans in Mosul at the end of the last century, in seven volumes. Before that, there were only manuscripts.
> Where would we have the greatest chance of finding a complete set?
> If I were you, I would go to Aleppo to the syrian patriarchate. Or to Damascus to the Jacobites. Mar Yacoub, their bishop,

---

[9] Palladius: a deacon in Constantinople (4th century) and friend of St John Chrysostom, author of *The Lausiac History* that tells the life of the Fathers of the egyptian desert.

would be happy to see you. He had been posted to Kerala a
few years ago.

They went to Aleppo by train. There again the french jesuits were
happy to welcome their belgian confrère and his monk friend. They
showed them this peaceful city with its old–fashioned charm, the *soukhs*
where the odor of spices, lamb, and soap mingle, the arab citadel at the
top of the hill, and the christian quarter that was still locked at night and
where Armenians, Melkites, Syrians, and Latins lived together. But, no,
they did not have a *Penqitho*. 'Go to Damascus, to the Jacobites', they
were told.

Mar Yacoub received them as brothers. Mass at the cathedral was
superb. He couldn't let them go before showing them the nearby *djebel*,
the very ancient churches of Maaloula, and the village on the side of the
hill where people still speak Aramaic, the language of Jesus. In the Saint-
Sergius chapel, built in the fourth century, Francis imagined the syrian
community that had prayed there, no doubt singing the hymns that
Ephrem of Nisibis had just composed. At Mar Mousa, he admired the
apse with a sort of cave dug in it, where the tabernacle was placed. This
would inspire him to transform Kurisumala's church. He went up on the
stone roof that formed a terrace and sat down, facing the mountain. On
the hillsides, the almond trees were in bloom. He gave thanks for everything. Mar Yacoub said goodbye, embracing them. He gave them gifts of
a syrian breviary and an icon of Saint Anthony. But no *Penqitho*. 'It's in
Jerusalem that you have the best chance of finding it', he advised. 'All
the churches there have a house, often an old house, and very rich libraries. The syrian orthodox library is remarkable. If they don't have it, in
any case they will know where to tell you to pursue your research.'

They went to Jerusalem by bus, traveling through Jordan. In the
Jacobite Church, Francis fell in love with the large repoussé silver cross
that hung above the tabernacle. He needed one exactly like it for
Kurisumala! In the goldsmiths' quarter, they found an Armenian who
agreed to make a copy. That would take several weeks. That was not a
problem; they left a deposit and promised to send someone to fetch the
order later. At the Holy Sepulcher, it was always the same mixture of
emotion and embarrassment. The basilica on these holy places is still the
object of petty rivalries and divisions, not only between churches but also
between religious orders. 'Here is where Christ died and rose again',

Francis told himself, 'and we are very far from the Gospel'. He attended the Mass of the Agony in the garden of Olives and prayed again, fervently, that Kurisumala live a truly evangelical life, that Monchanin's suffering and death give birth to a source of divine life through his successors' labors. At Saint Sabas monastery, one of the few orthodox monasteries remaining in the Holy Land, he asked the prior about the formation of novices, the schedules, and customs. But not the slightest trace of the *Penqitho*. 'You have one more chance. Go to Mosul in Iraq. This is where it was printed in 1896. There must be one left in a cellar. Go see Msgr Bacoz, in the chaldean seminary. He will help you.'

Francis made note of the names and addresses. That evening he went to the airport with Father Hambye, who was returning to Belgium. Left alone, Francis suddenly felt a great fatigue, a desire for silence after these six weeks of movement, intensive contacts, and multiple meetings. He went to El Latroun, the cistercian monastery in Palestine, and spent a few days of retreat with his brothers. There he found the atmosphere he had left six years earlier, that of Scourmont or Caldey, the offices, gregorian chant, silent meals, and the *Salve Regina*. He wrote in his notebook, 'Retreat at El Latroun. Life as it was before.'

A few archeological visits to the lavras of Wadi Pharan, a long solitary walk in the desert, and he returned to Beirut, where he found Professor Vööbus deep in conversation with Father Néophyte Edelby, who had just returned from Rome. The preparations for the ecumenical Council seemed promising for the eastern churches. The indian bishops had been listened to, the arab Melkites were intermediaries between Rome and the Byzantines, yet the latinized easterners disappointed. As interested as Francis was by this gossip, he was thinking above all about how to get to Mosul. The simplest way was to take the plane to Baghdad. Francis obtained a visa from the embassy of Iraq, but was warned that Mosul was in the security zone and that he would have to ask the army for special authorization to go there.

The day after his arrival, he was received by Msgr Bacoz, who asked his secretary to go to the military office with him. After a few discussions in Arabic and a long wait, permission was granted. He went to Mosul by night train, promising himself that he would visit the fourth–century chaldean monasteries he had seen on the map, north of the city. He got off the train early in the morning and went to the dominican seminary. Mass, introductions, exchanges, and visit to the gate of Nineveh.

'This time', he admitted, 'it's the last chance to find the *Penqitho*'. He decided to speak about it that very day to the librarian, Brother Lecomte, who advised:

> Hmm. For that, you should see Msgr Benni, the syrian arch-
> bishop. He has been here for a very long time. The archives are
> in the bishop's residence. I will try to bring you there tomorrow.
> But, if I may give you some advice, do not ask immediately.
> Here, we must take our time, establish contact, first go through
> the customary polite formalities.

Two days passed, filled by visits to the desert monasteries: Mar Mat-taï, Mar Elia, and Mar Hormiz. In the heart of the brown mountains was a striking vision: the huge monument to Sapor I, sculpted in the rocky wall, commemorating the victory of the Sassanid over the roman emperor Valerian in the third century, a victory that provoked the schism of the persian churches from the rest of Christianity. The rule of Sapor I was then marked by the persecution of Christians, most of whom fled to the East and came to strengthen the communities of southern India.

Francis spent Pentecost Sunday in the library, reading and copying texts, such as this one of Dadisho Katraya, a syrian Father of the seventh century:

> John the solitary said, 'There is no higher wisdom than that which
> consists in conquering one's passions and submitting them to the
> sovereignty of one's will. O my brother, if you want to live in
> solitude, you must fight and conquer the assaults of your passions:
> the burning memory of a woman, or a brother who made you
> suffer. Through these combats, you will attain purity of heart.

Francis' patience was rewarded. The following afternoon, Msgr Benni invited him to tea with a few priests from the house. Asked about the *Penqitho*, he confirmed that the only edition had been printed in his diocese. 'There must be a few in the shed. Come with me, we will look!' In a dusty junk room, behind a curtain, piled on the ground, they discovered not one but seven *Penqithos*. Seven times seven in–folio volumes, bound in tawny leather, damaged, but apparently complete. 'If they interest you', Msgr Benni offered, 'I will sell them to you. We no longer use them here.' 'All seven?' Francis was incredulous. 'Yes, of course. And these two small volumes of psalms in Syriac, do they interest you? I will quote a price for the whole lot. I have to discuss the amount with our librarian. Please come back tomorrow.'

The following day the bargain was reached. Francis was able to take a complete set with him. The rest would be sent by boat to Cochin. He had no money left, but promised to send the 72,000 iraqui dinars as soon as he returned. He carefully wrapped the seven precious books—the package was heavier than all the rest of his baggage!—and after expressing his gratitude to the archbishop, he took the train to Baghdad. We will see later that the adventure of the *Penqitho* did not end there. Before arriving in Cochin, the six sets sent by Msgr Benni would have to surmount many obstacles.

Meanwhile, Francis, who took the plane in Baghdad, arrived in Delhi with his cloth bag and his package of books. He took a taxi straight to the swiss embassy to show his treasure to Jacques-Albert Cuttat, who in return informed him of the latest developments in the dairy project. It was 23 May, and it was very hot. The prior was now anxious to return to Kurisumala and to take up the daily tasks once more.

THE EVOLUTION OF THE CATHOLIC CHURCH

For those born after 1960, it is difficult to imagine what the pre–conciliar Church was like; for example, in its attitude towards non–Christians. In 1950, participation in a ceremony in a synagogue or mosque was forbidden. In seminaries, *Ecclesia societas perfecta* was taught. Outside of Rome, it was taught, there is no salvation. The Jews are a 'deicidal' people. The Chinese, Hindus, Tibetans are 'pagans'. Buddhism, Hinduism, and Confucianism were associated with idolatry. Without being relegated to the idolatrous level, the Muslims were considered inferior, less civilized.

The Catholic Church gave itself the mission of evangelizing the 'pagan' people and of bringing back to its bosom and into its structures other, heretical and schismatic, Christians. This task was not always distinguished from the 'civilizing' mission of the West. The word *colonization* had a positive connotation. Most of the time, conversion to Christianity implied adherence to western culture, thought, and customs. Candidates for the priesthood, whether they were Africans, Indians, or Koreans, learned Latin and aristotelian philosophy and were supposed to mold their thought upon it.

It is almost impossible to describe this situation objectively now without a certain derision or virtuous indignation. However, we must re-call not only that it was almost impossible for the ordinary contemporary to see things differently but also that the religious who served the distant populations demonstrated good faith, good conscience, courage, devo-tion, and sometimes heroism. The fact remains that today we cannot read the missionary literature of that time without experiencing a certain embarrassment. But we are measuring the considerable revolution ac-complished by the Second Vatican Council between 1962 and 1965.

Of course, there had been Lebbe, Teilhard, de Lubac, Monchanin. Several centuries before, Roberto de Nobili in India and Matteo Ricci in China had possessed the intuition that the good news of the Gospel had to be translated into the local culture. Today they are considered forerunners, but in their day they were seen as dangerous dissidents. They were dismissed, or even forbidden to teach. Of course, there were already orientalists who studied Hinduism as a religion with a refined culture. But this was relatively recent, and confined to restricted university circles.

The rest of Father Francis' story—to a certain extent the Church's *aggiornamento* will catch up with him—must not make us forget that this is the context in which he left Europe. In India, he undertook the foundation of Kurisumala within a divided local church, marked by colonialism, where becoming a Christian still caused adherence to the western lifestyle, especially in the latin churches. It was Father Monchanin who told this anecdote: 'How can we recognize a Christian?' asked the catechist. 'He wears pants and eats meat', answered the Tamil child.

The Second Vatican Council, with the support of papal authority, introduced and disseminated radically new concepts: 'dialogue' was recommended, not only with the 'separated christian brothers' but also with the faithful of the 'other religions'. Not only the religions of the Book—those of the sons of Abraham—but also Buddhism and Hinduism, considered as authentic and respectable spiritualities that can lead to the experience of God. 'Inculturation' recognized the values present in indigenous cultures and encouraged Christians to live the Gospel and celebrate the liturgy in their language, their dress, and incorporating their customs. Theologians developed the theory of 'Seeds of the Word', according to which the Holy Spirit, who blows where he wills, was able to sow in the religions and wisdoms of the non–christian people elements of the Word of God. The sacred texts of Confucianism, Hinduism, and Buddhism, in this light appear to be a sort of asian Old Testament. For those at Kurisumala, all this was the 'green light' they had long awaited.

The 'revolution' inaugurated by the declaration *Nostra Aetate* in 1965 would arouse excesses in some places, resistance in others, and take several decades to reach the whole Catholic Church. New institutes, such as the 'Secretariate for non–Christians', founded in Rome in 1964, would contribute to this in a systematic way. Some individual events, heavily publicized, struck the imagination and caused reassessment. We think of Paul VI arriving in Bombay a little before Christmas of that year and who, after paying homage to India's spiritual heritage, publicly recited a prayer from the *Upanishads* to celebrate Advent (the *Upanishads* are the most ancient religious texts of India, belonging to the vedic literature, written more than six centuries before the christian era):

> From the unreal, lead me to the real
> From darkness, lead me to the light
> From death, lead me to immortality[10]

More discreet, but with a great influence on the monastic foundations and the processes of inculturation, AIM was founded in 1960. The three initials originally meant *Aide à Implantation Monastique*, Aid to Monastic Implantation ('in mission countries' was understood). Later it became apparent that this original name betrayed the europe–centrism that prevailed at the time—as if monasticism had been a western christian invention that had to be 'implanted' in other continents. Father Francis' procedure, following that of Fathers Le Saux and Monchanin, was the reverse: monasticism and asceticism had been developed by the Easterners earlier and more intensely than anywhere else, and western monks had much to learn in going to live among them. The AIM would keep its three letters, but in 1998 they were given another meaning: *Alliance Inter Monastères*. This became an extremely widespread network, which favored contacts and meetings between the small inculturated monastic foundations scattered throughout the world. Before, in spite of the exhortations of several successive popes

---

[10] This prayer is chanted every evening at Kurisumala.

(e.g., Pius XI in 1927 in *Rerum Ecclesiae*; Pius XII in 1957 in *Fidei Donum*) the number of christian monasteries in the third world was very small. There were fewer than thirty in 1960. It was no doubt under the impulsion of the Council and by the action of the Spirit that, twenty years later, there were 250. We might think that the intense activity of Father de Floris and Sister Pia Valeri in their small office in Vanves, near Paris, for twenty years, had much to do with it.

If scholastic theology is founded on reasoning and philosophy, monastic theology rests on personal experience of God and the contemplation of the Divine Mystery. This makes it a privileged point of departure for inter–religious dialogue. In this context, Kurisumala would appear to a growing number of Christians no longer as an exotic or eccentric experiment but as a vanguard, a laboratory for the new ecumenism, the new mission of dialogue among religions. However, they would have to wait until 1968, after six years of intense work, a few trials, and a new trip to the Himalayas for initiation and sabbatical to see the beginning of the new stage we have called 'influence'.

At the end of 1961, when Francis returned home from Mosul, the community was still fragile and its socio–economic anchor just beginning.

A MODERN AGRICULTURAL ENTERPRISE

'There they are! They have arrived!' Novices and monks, abandoning their silent work and usual reserve gathered in haste near the two yellow trucks that had just stopped in front of the barn behind the main building. 'Get back, they might be dangerous!' The group stepped back, with a murmur of voices and contained laughter, where the clear and clipped sounds of Malayalam surfaced. They unlocked and folded down the back of the truck, one of the workers jumped in, untied the rope, and, holding the enormous beast by the nostrils, made it walk backwards slowly on the ramp. With satisfaction, Francis contemplated the vigorous chocolate colored bull with its shining coat. He was scratching the ground with his hoof, looking at the monks with his head lowered, horns in front. *Deo Gratias*! May he multiply our herd like that of Jacob.'

Rajan and his suite had been awaited for a year. They had to negotiate with Dom Samson, the prior of Caldey. He charged Father Jerome, his cellarer, to choose and send the beasts. The cost of the trip was more than the cost of the animals! They sent the pedigrees to Mr Kartha at Trivandrum, and it took five months more to obtain the importation licenses from the central administration in Delhi. Father Jerome himself went to the Jersey Cattle Society's autumn fair to obtain the best animals at the best price. Two bulls and two jersey heifers finally boarded at Liverpool at the end of October 1961. Shortly after their arrival in Cochin, one of the two heifers died of a tropical fever. The other, pregnant, survived the illness but aborted the calf. The financing also was an adventure: the *Misereor* association of Aix-la-Chapelle, approached by Father Debatin, a german religious who had been a guest of Kurisumala in 1959, agreed to defray the costs. Presided over by the conference of german bishops and with a fair amount of money, this organization helps the missions. Francis, very happy, had already told Dom Samson that he could send the bills to them. But for reasons unknown, the germans pulled out at the last moment. Francis wrote his sister: '*Misereor* is dropping us! I don't know where to turn.' It was Dom Guerric, once again, who saved the situation. Francis wrote him: 'Thank you for your indefatigable help.'

Twelve hundred pounds sterling in total. At the time, 150.000 belgian francs were the equivalent of an average salary for a year. When we reminisced about this with him in 1997, and asked him why he had never gone to visit Father Francis, who obviously would have been very pleased, Dom Guerric answered with his mischievous smile: 'I sent him bulls instead. That was more useful to him than my humble person.'

The bulls' arrival accelerated the concrete realization of the Key Village Unit. The center for artificial insemination began its work. The monks built a small, square, two–story building facing the barn, and this is where the veterinarian and assistants lived. Their jeep would facilitate trips and transportation of merchandise. The number of persons and parcels that can be packed into a jeep in India is beyond imagining. Two stalls were built for the bulls, who had to be approached with prudence. All this was financed by the government, that in addition supplied a monthly allowance for the animals' feed and upkeep. Twice a week, Rajan's semen was sent to the farms of the district. Nine and a half months later, the first two calves were born at the ashram: everyone said they looked like their father! The cows were now producing more than ten liters of milk per day. The neighboring peasants sent their wife or son to carry their milk surplus to the monks, who paid them a just price, to re-sell it with their own production in the plain.

The absence of refrigeration limited freshness. Francis dreamed of substituting real cheese for the ghee. He wrote to Scourmont, asking them to send him some rennet. A belgian AFI (International Feminine Auxiliary), Simone Liégeois, stationed at Pollambakkam in Tamil Nadu, was approached to transport it. Willingly she agreed to bring the small jar, and easily slipped it into her suitcase. But when she arrived at Scourmont, they also gave her a scythe with its handle! Francis, who wanted to improve production on all fronts, had decided to teach the men of Kerala to scythe, instead of crouching down to cut the grass with a small sickle.

Miss Liégeois would remember that trip for a long time: she had to go through Switzerland before boarding at Genoa in Italy. Carrying two large suitcases, one of which was entirely occupied by the huge curved blade wrapped in cloth, the double handle on her shoulder, she endured questions, suspicion, and searches at each customs office!

The novice—who until that time had been making *ghee* in the manner of the region, sitting on the ground with his legs out in front of him, the container between his toes and the churn moved by a string like a diabolo—was converted to making a very much appreciated monastic cheese. But the scythe was soon relegated to the back of a workshop: the peasants quickly returned to their small sickle, with which they could go faster than with this awkward unfamiliar tool.

The anecdote reveals a problem in which the indian government was increasingly interested at the beginning of the 1960s: the poor agricultural yield of the country due to old methods, lack of fertilizer, and the anarchic proliferation of poor–quality cattle. During the first years of independence, Nehru, who admired the soviet model, massively supported heavy industry. Industrial efficiency was mediocre, while the problem of mass poverty and underemployment remained unchanged. Towards the end of the 1950s, Congress realized that in a country where 85% of the people were peasants, they had to give priority to agriculture. Several governmental plans were put into place to improve production, which led India to become self–sufficient in food fifteen years later. At the beginning, there were many obstacles. Social traditions, for instance: the redistribution of the land would be slowed by the *zamindars* (landowners of large properties)—that Congress needed, in order to remain in power—as well as by the peasants themselves, who trusted more in ancestral solidarities that bound them to their owners than in the promises of the government in Delhi. Another obstacle to overcome was ignorance of modern methods of fertilizing, soil amending, and husbandry. The creation of small local centers, which experimented with effective methods, showed their usefulness, and taught them to the local peasants, was strongly encouraged by the public powers. Kurisumala fulfilled this expectation exactly. Politically and socially, Francis' projects came at a good time. The indian government did not delay in sending civil servants to inspect there. They placed forty hectares of additional lands at the monks' disposal, and gave them technical assistance and funding to exploit the pastures more effectively. Tropical grasses—Hybrid Napier, Kikuyu—were sown, and the soil was amended and fertilized regularly—not only with cow manure, which was more and more abundant, but with well–researched chemical compounds. The results were better than they had hoped: grass grew two meters high and could be cut several times each year! Plants for fodder were experimented with: corn, clover, and soya. In contrast, the vegetable gardens required considerable infrastructure. The monks started digging trenches thirty centimeters deep in the rocky soil of the terraces they had made the year before, and by bringing in materials, reconstituted there a minimum of fertile soil: a layer of organic debris, a layer of manure, another layer of debris, and on top of that a small layer of sifted soil. After putting in drainage pipes destined to evacuate the overflow of monsoon water, they sowed the seeds. The results were clearly better, but for each square meter of fertile surface, it required hours of painful work, bent over double in the heat and the humidity, digging the rock, carrying in the materials by wheelbarrow, fitting the pipes together, and building the different layers of soil. The reward was cabbages, tomatoes, potatoes, squash, and manioc that would soon be harvested in large enough quantities to supplement the daily rice. The community was made up of about fifteen members, but with the workers and the guests who were more and more numerous, they fed at least thirty people every day.

Two crucial material problems were resolved between 1962 and 1965: the water supply system and motor force. The alternation of flooding and drought constituted a permanent menace. It would be overcome by the building of a veritable dam that held water, which allowed them to accumulate during the monsoon the ten thousand cubic meters of water necessary to survive during the dry season. They borrowed the money required to begin this work, hoping to complete it before the 1962 monsoon. But in August, they had to interrupt work: violent rains were falling, and money to pay the workers was lacking. Francis became stubborn: with a few monks, he himself went to work, building with bricks and cementing relentlessly, his clothing drenched. Brother Mariabhakta, who entered Kurisumala in 1960, remembered, 'It was too hard for us, who were not used to working at that speed. We had stiff fingers, we were shivering, we couldn't continue, so we went inside to dry off, to rest. But he did not stop. He continued all alone. Then we were ashamed, we went back to work, we took up our muddy tools. He asked a lot from us, but he himself worked more than anyone else.'

In October Francis fell ill. He wrote to his sister: 'For several months, Brother Ass moved only when prodded. A few days ago, he simply refused to get up. As it had been at Scourmont ten years ago: fevers, insomnia, neuralgia, violent lumbar pains have struck me down.' He was cared for with massages and vitamins. Mar Athanasios insisted that he accept the invitation of the Ingle family, who proposed that he go rest at their home in Bangalore. Arthur Ingle was the franco–english architect who drew up the first plans for Kurisumala. He had married a nurse from Lyons, Lucie Bose, a great friend of Monchanin, who had blessed their marriage in 1943 and had often come as well, to perk up in their home. In their large colonial–style house, surrounded by a wonderful garden, Francis regained his strength quickly. 'I am leading the life of a pacha here, clouds of servants satisfy my smallest wish. I am eating like four and rest all day long. It's a good thing that Father Hambye is at Kurisumala to help Father Bede with the young people.' He returned to the ashram for Christmas, all his symptoms gone.

At the beginning of 1963, a subsidy from Scourmont allowed them to finish the dam and install the pump. The monks themselves placed the five hundred meters of pipes that lead the water to the buildings.

As sources of energy for the first five years, Kurisumala used only kerosene, oil, or candles for light, and wood for cooking and drying, similar in this to millions of indian households. But these products were rare, especially wood, which they had to go quite a distance to fetch. An engineer from Delhi was beginning to be known in the region for having successfully installed equipment to produce gas from manure. Francis was immediately interested by this procedure, which corresponded with his community's values of autonomy, economy, and simplicity. In the garden behind the kitchen, they built a tank with a floating cover that rose with the accumulating gas. Rubber hoses brought the fuel to the kitchen and library, the only rooms where heating was permitted, as it had been in ancient abbeys. At the same time, negotiations with the government allowed them to extend lines for electricity from the neighboring village of Vagamon, which had just been linked to the network. India made a considerable effort to extend and reinforce the electrification of the territory: the national grid grew from 3,600 villages in 1950 to 44,000 in 1966. This would allow the monks to install a modern dairy with refrigeration, pasteurization, and sanitation, thanks to the finances from the Indo–Swiss project and the expertise of Brother Sylvester, with his recent diploma from the Technical Institute of Bangalore. Sylvester chose the material carefully and directed the workers. The large aluminum jugs were now lined up every evening on the dairy's cement edge and traveled by truck to Eratupetta and Palai during the night.

'All this is fortunate', Francis wrote to Dom Guerric in 1964, 'not only because we make our living, but also because hundreds of poor farmers who live near us obtain new resources.'

AMONG THE MOUNTAIN PEOPLE

Vagamon has a single sloping street, roughly paved, with shops and small dirt houses covered with thatch, and two small permanent buildings: the post office and the police station. On the higher side it has a kind of esplanade, where people wait for the bus, where the weekly market is held, and where the villagers gather on special occasions, such as today. In the far distance in every direction one can see chains of purple–brown mountains with, here and there, the green carpet of the tea plantations.

On this 15 August 1961, almost all the inhabitants for miles around were gathered. The men were wearing their best shirts and had tied their best *dhoti*s around their waists. The women were chatting and laughing in small groups, their babies in their arms. The grandmothers were watching the young children, excited by the music and unusual excitement.

The day before, a stand had been set up where India's orange, white, and green flag with its *chakra* waved beside the Communists' red banner. Pious images of Shiva, Ganesh, and Krishna were tacked up on one side, colored prints of the Virgin Mary, Jesus, and Saint George on the other. All around the stand, posts tied together by multicolored cloth garlands in shreds designated a field where, this rainy morning, young people participated in races, games of skill, and sports. It was the national festival. It was three o'clock, and the official ceremony was starting.

Francis had been invited by the president of the *panchayat* to sit on the stand with the local authorities: Doctor Kurup, the veterinarian of the new Key Village Unit; and Purush Pillai, the president of the *Grama Sevak* rural association. The national hymn, *Janagana–mana*, composed by Rabindranath Tagore, was sung in chorus, accompanied on a kind of portable harmonium. A drum roll called everyone to silence. President Kurian recited the hindu prayer to Paramesvara the Supreme, and as had been agreed during his visit to the ashram the preceding week, asked the christian *sannyasi* to give the opening speech. In English, Francis thanked the people of Vagamon for their welcome and for giving him the honor of opening this ceremony. He spoke about the Key Village Unit, its social mission; he told them of his hope of seeing the ashram contribute to the dignity and prosperity of this village and the whole agricultural region. He ended with a prayer of thanksgiving. People clapped, sang, and danced. Then an agricultural worker, a member of the *panchayat*, spoke in his turn. Then the local deputy started a long speech, from which Francis remembered only two things: the men of the village decided to build a primary school at Vagamon and proposed to keep up the two kilometers of road that led to Kurisumala, free of charge. After a new musical interlude and awarding of prizes to those who had won the games that morning, Father Chrysostom gave the closing speech in Malayalam. This indian priest, about fifty years old, had been received into the monastery's novitiate the previous year. With his graying beard, his white cotton shawl, and his local accent, he symbolized quite well the rooting of the cistercian foundation in the soil of these far–off mountains of India.

The social impact of Kurisumala was strengthened during the 1960s by the establishment of a hospital on its grounds. As early as 1959, Father Andrew, the Jesuit from Ranchi, set up a dispensary attached to the farm, where he cared for the neighbors free of charge: skin diseases due to undernourishment, infected wounds, snake bites, dysentery—all that could be treated with the modest means at his disposal. In December 1963, a middle–aged Englishman with a deeply lined face came to the ashram. Laurie Baker was looking for land to build a hospital to serve the poor. An architect by training, this man had finished his studies in England just before the war and had decided to spend a few years in China as a lay missionary. He had served as a nurse and then as a stretcher–bearer, but the civil war and growing xenophobia had forced him to flee. Crossing Pakistan during the massacres that followed independence, he had found refuge in northern India, where he had married a doctor from Kerala, who was in charge of a hospital there. They adopted three orphans. His widowed mother lived in Kashmir with her son. In 1963, the chinese–indian war was disrupting the border regions. The Bakers and their family—the youngest child was two and the grandmother seventy–nine—had to flee again. They crossed all of India in an old truck and temporarily lived with the doctor's sister in Kerala.

Laurie belonged to the Society of Quakers, also called 'Religious Society of Friends', founded in England in the seventeenth century. Egalitarians, pacifists, devoted to serving their neighbor, proud and independent, they raised their hat to no one and recognized no other authority than that of the Gospel and the Holy Spirit. Their worship is made up of silence. Francis and Bede had already made contact with the Quakers of Bangalore at their ecumenical meetings. Laurie was a man full of humor and with a pioneer spirit; imaginative, not easily disconcerted, and sometimes authoritarian towards subordinates. Very quickly he got along well with the monks and obtained permission to build his hospital on their land. He bought four hectares near the road below the monastery for his own house. Working with Quakers was not displeasing to Francis, and even less for Bede. In any case, a medical unit nearby was both a security and an additional factor of social development, without adding a burden to the community.

The hospital, very simple, was built in a few months. It was called *Mitraniketan*, the House of Friends. It was a one–story L–shaped building with an examination room, a delivery room, common rooms for about sixty patients, a laboratory for tests, and two offices. Everything was furnished in indian style, that is, with the greatest simplicity, and the whole was surrounded by a flower garden. A hundred meters away, the architect built a big house with a tile roof, in the local style, to lodge his family, and bungalows for the nurses. The hospital quickly drew a large clientele: the region's poorest came to be cared for, the farmers, and the agricultural workers who did not have access to the dispensaries on the tea plantations, the only ones in the mountains where a doctor's services were offered.

The Bakers were to remain only a few years, as their children were growing up and had to continue their studies in the city. In addition, Laurie had a new project: building prefabricated permanent houses at a low cost, according to a standardized plan he devised. With the help of the government subsidizing lodging, in twenty years hundreds of these 'Baker's houses' would be built in Kerala. The family moved to Trivandrum in 1969. Doctor Baker served the slum's inhabitants there while her husband supervised the building of his social housing. The hospital of Kurisumala was staffed by AFI: a german doctor, Hildegarde Sina, assisted by an italian nurse, Alina Cattani, would staff it together for more than twenty years.

These women were part of an international team sent to Tiruvalla to direct the hospital built by the diocese. But they ended their contract, judging that the project no longer corresponded to their ideal. They found it too comfortable, with ambitions of prestige and luxury. 'We had not come to India to serve the competition between churches, but to care for the poorest people', one of them would say recalling her youth. Alina was especially radical in her political opinions, and didn't mind criticizing the members of the clergy who had a tendency to display their riches, whether in India or in Italy. The monks of Kurisumala, as proprietors of land, did not escape her Marxist–inspired diatribes. This said, the hospital as the Bakers had left it—with its rudimentary buildings, rural situation, and the great poverty of its clientele—corresponded perfectly to their desires. Without awaiting the complete departure of the proprietors, they moved into a guesthouse built halfway up the mountain by the monks to welcome the families and single women—quite rare at the time—who went to visit the ashram. Later, with the nurses and indian nursing aides, they would live in the Bakers' large house, forming there a sort of lay community. On Sundays at the solemn *Qurbana*, the small church of Kurisumala was brightened by the colored saris of this group of women, most of whom were Christians.

During those years, the foundations of the organization that would make Kurisumala an important driving force for rural development were built. Until then, the region's economy rested essentially on the large–scale property owners' tea plantations. The workers were poorly paid and entirely dependent on the enterprise. They grew a few vegetables and raised a wandering cow for milk to supplement their diet. The children did not go to school. When they still were very young, they were hired to pick tea, which required small nimble fingers.

From the beginning, Francis refused to enter that system, which would have linked the monastery's prosperity to the sweat of the local proletariat. 'The monks must live from the work of their own hands and if possible contribute to the well–being of the neighboring people' (*Diary of the Goshala*, 1962). This was the Rule that prevailed both for the sons of Saint Benedict and for the communities founded by Gandhi, as opposed to the begging practices of the hindu eremetic tradition. To insure its own survival, the ashram began a process that in various ways would lead several hundred families to a better standard of living and greater autonomy.

At the beginning, the monastery simply created work, but skilled work: the young people who helped with the farm work learned horticultural techniques, vegetable garden techniques, amending of pastures, husbandry, and dairy. Later, the dairy cooperative allowed the small farmers who moved to the area nearby to sell their surplus, however small, to the monastery. Before daybreak, when dawn colors the crest of the cardamom mountains pink, villagers could be seen climbing up on all the paths. Sometimes they were children, barefoot, carrying their jug on their head. They would go back down with a few bills, sometimes with a bottle of oil, a packet of seeds, or medicine in exchange for their milk. The coop experienced difficult beginnings. Like the door–to–door salesman at the beginning, the milk sellers at first tried to take advantage of the monks or to make a profit without taking responsibility in the enterprise. 'The people of Kerala are intelligent', Francis said. 'They speak easily but they are often individualists and quarrelling. They had to train them, set up honest and interdependent commercial ethics.'

Parallel to its *sui juris* canonical status, also subject to tribulations and misunderstandings at the beginning, Kurisumala constituted itself as a 'registered charitable society', a civil status according to indian legislation, which gave the community a juridical personality in 1960. It was indispensable for establishing collaboration with public organisms, signing official acts, and obtaining bank loans. In 1967, the dairy coop also acquired an official structure, implying statutes and a code of ethics to which all the farmers who wanted to participate had to adhere: it was the 'Kurisumala Milk Suppliers Cooperative Society'. The partnership with the swiss embassy was in this context. But a few years later, without consultation, the cooperative's management was transferred to a government office in Vagamon and given to an official of the Indo–Swiss project. Ambassador Cuttat, meanwhile, had been the victim of a serious accident in Ceylon that had left him in a coma for several weeks, and he was no longer there to defend his friends. Francis was furious at the beginning, but soon came to think that this dispossession was also a liberation: the neighbors continued to bring their milk to the ashram, which, no longer responsible for the administrative and financial oversight of the business, soon became active in a new social field that required a closer and more educational relationship with the population.

In 1967, with the help of a youth movement in New Zealand, Kurisumala launched the 'family farm scheme' for raising cattle. Francis retold this experience in *Chronique des douze années: 1958–1970*, privately printed in 1972.

> Five young people, who had learned agricultural techniques for several years in the ashram's farm, had reached the age to marry. Each one was put in charge of a farm destined to become his personal property: twenty to twenty–five acres of prairie, a house with a barn and facilities for manure and irrigation, as well as ten head of cattle. These five farms were now in full development. Their milk production was placed in common with the ashram's for daily sale in the whole region. But a sixth of the proceeds of the sale is deducted towards the initial investment, and these amounts will serve to create new farms in the future.

In fact, a few years later, a large–scale enterprise for agricultural development was inaugurated. This time it would rest entirely on the monastery's resources. But in the same brochure, Francis notes again: 'Meanwhile we have had to keep in mind constantly that a monastery cannot be reduced to a model farm and the ashrams cannot be content to be pilot projects for economic development, even under Gandhi's patronage.' To Dom Guerric, who in 1963 sent him a 'monition' to put him on guard against 'an inclination to give too much attention to the things of earth rather than to the souls that must be led to God', he answered, 'That is perhaps the impression my letters give, but that is only one side of our life. You must understand that we had to ensure our survival in the midst of the uncultivated grasses that surrounded us. At present, the essential is done. It is important not only for us but for all the population in the district.'

FAMILY AND CHILDHOOD

1.

2.

3.

1. The Mahieu family in Normandy in 1918.
   Jean, wearing a sailor suit, is seated in the centre.

2. Brussels, 1930.

3. In the Second Lancers, 1932.

From Scourmont to Shantivanam

1.

2.

3.

1. Jean with his parents on an
   autumn Sunday visit

2. At Caldey Abbey (Wales) just
   before leaving for India, 1955.

3. With the abbé Jules Monchanin,
   1956

KURISUMALA

1.

2.

3.

1. The monastery site in 1965, seen from the Mountain of the Cross. The reservoir and its retraining wall, the terraces and woods can be seen surrounding the monastery buildings.

2. Kurisumala in September 1959. To the left are the monks' quarters, to the right the church and the guesthouse. The first vegetable garden can be seen in the foreground.

3. Fathers Francis and Bede Griffiths with the young community in 1960.

INCULTURATION

1. An Indian Mass (Bharatyia Puja) in
   Mumbai (1968). From left to right: Fr
   Deleury, Fr Aroojio, Fr Amaldass, Fr Henri
   Le Saux, Father Francis Acharya.

2. Indian Mass at Kurisumala. Since 1972
   there has been a daily celebration at 6 am.

3. Francis Acharya with Thomas Merton
   at the first Asian Monastic Congress in
   Bangkok, 1968.

DAILY LIFE AT KURISUMALA

1.

2.

3.

1. Five monk-priests, seated during the procession during the Qurbana and the reading of the Epistle.

2. The community in the refectory.

3. The dairy cooperative (1994).

Contacts With the Cistercian Order

1.

2.

1. The first visit of Dom Bernardo
   Olivera, Abbot General of the Order
   of Cistercians of the Strict Observance,
   1994.

2. Fr Francis at Albano (Rome) during the
   Cistercian Chapter General in 1996.

INCORPORATION INTO THE CISTERCIAN ORDER

1.

2.

1. The ceremony incorporating Kurisumala into the Cistercian Order of the Strict Observance, 9 July 1999. Seated at the right are Dom David Tomlins, abbot of Tarrawarra Abbey in Australia and Father Immediate of Kurisumala, and Mar Timotheos, bishop of Tiruvalla.

2. The abbatial consecration of Dom Francis, 14 October 1999. At the far right is Fr Mariananda.

Everything is a blessing…

No doubt it is time for us also to look at the other facet of their life, consecrated to prayer, liturgy, the formation of novices, the building of a community of those who seek God.

THE LITURGICAL PROJECT

The land is meant to bear fruit, and man is created
to have the joy of singing the praise of his Creator.
(F. Acharya, *Prayer with the Harp of the Spirit*, p. viii)

Like Athos or Sinai, Kurisumala is a mountain from which rises incessant prayer: prayer of praise, supplication, repentance, or a song of marvel at God's action in the history of the world. This prayer unfolds in three ways: daily Eucharist, the monastic office, and silent meditation. It occupies the monks for about six hours every day, of which four hours are between three and seven o'clock in the morning.

The Wakers rejoice today
for the Wakeful One has come to wake us up:
on this night who shall sleep
    when all creation is awake?
Because Adam introduced into the world
the sleep of death in sins,
the Wakeful One came down to wake us up
from being submerged in sin.[11]

During the first ten years, from 1958 to 1968, Francis and Bede reproduced and taught the novices the liturgy they had learned and practiced at Pushpagiri with the Syro–Malankar priest. *Qurbana* was sung in Syriac each morning. These two hours were heavy in the daily schedule, very full of work of all kinds. The monastic office according to the *1*, the weekly parish breviary, was also sung in Syriac. Each day, which has its proper prayers, celebrates an event in the history of salvation.

On Sundays it's the resurrection of Jesus, the 'heritage that nothing can destroy or harm', Mondays the kingdom of God, its announcing by

---

[11] Brock, *The Luminous Eye*, p. 140.

John the Baptist who called to repentance and justice. Tuesdays the Church, Wednesdays the incarnation, Thursdays the Eucharist—'the body and blood are a furnace in which the Spirit is the fire'—on Friday the cross, suffering, and death transformed into source of life with 'the martyrs for whom the Holy Spirit braids wreaths and in whose bones he dwells.' Saturday it's the parousia, the return of Christ in glory at the end of time, with the resurrection of the bodies which brings us back to Sunday.

The whole liturgical cycle, although here reduced to the seven days of the week, was a miniature crown of the complete yearly cycle; it made them relive and reactivate in some measure the history of salvation with creation, promise, incarnation, passion and resurrection, the Church, and finally, the parousia. They celebrated sacred events, they relived them, and they were nourished by them. No dogmas or particular devotions such as the Sacred Heart or Christ the King, but the main events of this long love story between God and his creature where all of creation— plants, animals, stars, rivers, and angels—is involved. Francis explained one day: 'Here we celebrate the Conception, with the irruption of the Holy Spirit and Mary's trusting answer.' He added 'Immaculate?' with a pout that meant 'Maybe, but that adjective is not ours.'

Even though during the 1960s they recited only the invariable weekly office and that of Sundays, and despite their very limited knowledge of the liturgical language, Francis was convinced he had introduced his young community to another spiritual world, a much more beautiful one, that of Saint Ephrem and the syriac tradition. A tradition that, as Sebastian Brock underlined, 'is likely to be very interesting to all those who in Asia, Africa and elsewhere, are presently seeking a Christianity that is not burdened by the cultural and intellectual inheritance of Europe' (*Prayer with the Harp of the Spirit*).

> I was surprised that children
> Cry when they leave the womb
> Cry, because they abandon
> The darkness for light
> And leave a stifling place
> To arrive in the universe!
> Death also for man is
> A sort of birth
> Where nevertheless those who die cry

When they leave this universe
Which is the mother of sorrows
To be born into the gardens of glory
(Saint Ephrem, 'Hymns on Paradise')

Under the hymns' apparent simplicity, under their often paradoxical structure, more analogical than logical, the dialogues, stories, and images (the mother's womb, the chick, oil, the robe of glory, the eye of light) rather than abstract concepts promote a profound and powerful theological vision. It is a narrative theology that forces its reader to go beyond the exterior words towards their inner meaning and the truth to which they point without restricting it. 'Whereas western Christianity excels in clarity of expression, conciseness, and precise dogmatic definitions, the East—including the christian East—prefers the language of poetry in which parable, symbol, and even myth make the mystery accessible to believers and often carry them closer to the spiritual realities' (*Prayer with the Harp of the Spirit*).

The two founders had learned enough Syriac to taste the particular sweetness of the texts. Already knowing some Hebrew, they easily began to learn this other semitic language. This was not the case for the indian novices: they learned everything by heart—it was relatively easy because the same texts recurred every week—but understood only a few words. This left Francis unsatisfied. All the more so, since he started to decipher the *Penqitho*, where he discovered a great richness of hymns and prayers for all the liturgical feasts that succeed one another throughout the seasons like a luminous colored halo. He would like to enrich the prayer, vary it—as it was chanted in the syrian[12] monasteries of the first centuries—and especially make its beauty accessible to his young monks.

Theoretically, there were several options available. The first, used during the first years, consisted in teaching everyone Syriac. The results were slow and discouraging. There was already so much to teach these young people, the teachers were few and overloaded with many tasks, certain candidates' education level was elementary, and at that time the study periods were often drowned by work for survival. Vatican II's openness allowed them to envision a different approach: translating into

---

[12] The word *syrian* here covers a territory much larger than Syria: the sphere of influence of the Syrian Church of the first centuries went from the Mediterranean to Mongolia.

the vernacular. But neither Bede nor Francis had mastered Malayalam. Besides, this choice would limit the texts' dissemination to the boundaries of Kerala and would not facilitate comprehension of the offices by foreign guests, who came to the ashram in ever greater numbers. Little by little the idea grew of undertaking a true restoration of the original syriac liturgy in its complete version and annual cycle, from the *S'himo* and *Penqitho*, rounded out by a volume of biblical readings appropriate to the calendar of the eastern saints. Such a text did not exist, and the only 'common' language in which the founders were capable of accomplishing such a reconstruction was English. Towards the middle of the 1960s, experimentation with a liturgy proper to Kurisumala began, translated into English and reorganized little by little. In 1959, Bede Griffith undertook the translation of the *S'himo*, which would be published in 1965 under the title *The Book of Common Prayer*. Bede did not have Francis' physical strength and did not hide that he preferred to make himself useful by translating or giving courses in the library near the stove rather than planting trees or carrying manure on windy fields.[13] His rather literal translation into prose was not usable for prayer as it was, but it saved Francis considerable time when in 1968 he undertook a complete revision of the weekly monastic office, a considerable work that would lead to the 1980 publication of the first volume of *Prayer with the Harp of the Spirit. The Prayer of Asian Churches*. The title, *The Harp of the Holy Spirit*, is an allusion to Saint Ephrem, a composer and deacon in Nisibis in the fourth century. The subtitle, added to the second edition in 1983, underlined the eastern origin of the texts, and the plural *Churches* witnesses to their ecumenical concern.

Besides an eighteen–page introduction, the first volume contained three major offices: the evening, night, and morning prayers for the seven days of the week. The 'little hours' of Sext, None, and Compline continued to be celebrated in Malayalam. The *Harp of the Spirit*, however, was more than a simple translation: it was a complete reorganization of the breviary, which became a weekly celebration of the mysteries of salvation. The texts were composed in rhymed stanzas that favored alternating recitation. Francis inserted an extract from the sacred writings of Hinduism into each office, entitled 'seed of the Word', an innovation uncommon at that time. Certain strophes were mixtures, modeled on the jewish *midrash*, which wove

---

[13] *The Human Search: Bede Griffith Reflects on his Life*, ed. John Swindells.

biblical quotations with hindu verses, sometimes with commentaries from contemporary indian sages. This was not an academic work for exegetes but a practical tool for the community's prayer, a church service.

Praise to You, Gentle Son of the Mighty Father, who of Your own will came to the river Jordan and stood naked in its waters to hallow them for the remission of our sins in baptism.

Praise to You, Heavenly Bridegroom, who call all peoples to Your marriage feast where You Yourself are immolated and given to them as the food of immortality.

Praise to You, Apostle of the Father, who sent Your Holy Spirit to Your Church, and He descended on the disciples in the form of flames of fire.

Praise to You, Word of the silent Father, who entrusted Your Word to Your Holy Church, and she enshrined it in Your Gospel, and she gives it to us to be born anew and to draw life from it, as we meditate on it at this evening hour.

(Tuesday Vespers [recited on Monday night], p. 77)

Forgive us, Lord, Your unworthy servants.
In the company of the saints we have not profited.
We have not learned their ways,
We have become strangers to the life they taught us.

(Night Vigil on Tuesday, Third Watch, p. 87)

Our Lord, be gracious to us on this passing morning.
And on that morning which does not pass away
Make us to stand at Your right hand.
In the morning the creatures come
and knock at Your door, O Compassionate One.
Give them from Your treasure–house
graciousness, compassion, and forgiveness.
The messenger of the morning has come
with the harp of praise in his hand.
He strikes upon it and rouses those who sleep:
Rise and give praise for the light has come.
As the dove returned to the side of Noah the Just,
bearing a branch of olive,

May our petitions return
and bring us compassion and graciousness.

(Morning Prayer, pp. 97–98)

During the 1960s, this work, like their cultivation of the land, was in its experimental phase. They tried, adjusted, and modified the prayers' texts constantly. They wove and sewed green capes bordered with red and encrusted with a silver dove. They perfected the setup and decoration of the church: an apse was added to the choir, where the tabernacle was surmounted by the silver cross ordered in Jerusalem and surrounded by six small oil lamps. They progressively acquired a collection of icons, framed there by the carpenter–monk. The gestures accompanying prayer became more precise: vigorous incensing, repeated prostrations or inclinations, and elevation of the hands. The Council would accelerate this movement, opening spaces of liberty that had been unthinkable and allowing the open practice of daring ideas that until then had only been expressed in confidential circles.

Meanwhile, the six copies of *Penqitho* that Francis had bought in Mosul had great difficulty in reaching their destination. Msgr Benni told them he would not send anything before receiving money! Dom Guerric, always magnanimous, sent a check. The volumes were then packed in a wooden–studded box and transported by truck through the Iraq desert to Basra on the Red Sea. They were forgotten there for some time, but a lazy cargo ship finally deposited them at the Bombay harbor. There, they had to clear customs. The letter sent to Kurisumala for this purpose got lost in the mountains. After several months, a cryptic card announced to Francis that in the absence of customs declaration, the contents of the box would be sold at auction the following week. A priest friend was sent there immediately. At the last moment the precious in–folio were saved from dispersion and sent by train to Cochin, where their owner came to take delivery of them himself.

The work of restoration of the syrian monastic liturgical heritage would become a long–term project, intimately linked to the monastery. Francis would give himself lovingly, fervently, and without measure to this project for more than thirty years, at the beginning devoting most of his nights to it and until old age remodeling, improving, and constantly refining with small touch–ups each of the four volumes that would comprise the complete work.

'After Compline', he would recount, 'I went to my cell and began to translate. I would read, translate, seeking the most appropriate word, and the texts spoke to my soul so that it was a true meditation that unfolded like a prayer. I would lose all sense of time. Suddenly, I would jump at the sound of the metal jugs being loaded onto the dairy truck. One o'clock in the morning already! I would lie down to sleep a few hours before *Lilio.*'

At this pace, he broke down from time to time, on average once a year. The bishop required him to go rest, sometimes with the Ingle family, sometimes in a convent where the sisters would care for him maternally, preparing fortifying meals for him, with sweet desserts.

MONASTIC VESTURE

The curriculum of the monk–candidate at Kurisumala followed the three traditional stages, to which the names used in the ashrams of India were given: the postulant was admitted after one or two retreats and a few talks. He wore a white *dhoti* with an ordinary white shirt. After a time of probation, he was received as *sadhaka* or novice, during a short admission ceremony that took place at the evening chapter. Then for two years he wore the white cotton smock with the *dhoti*. The *brahmachari* are the equivalent of temporary professed. They wore a white shawl. The confirmed monks wore the *khavi* [saffron colored] habit reserved for the *sannyasis*, those who commit themselves forever to renunciation. For three years, Francis and Bede were the only ones to wear the *khavi*, which had been solemnly given to them by Mar Athanasios the day before their departure for the mountain.

In July 1961, three novices were judged ready for solemn profession: Sylvester and Vargheese, companions from the very first days, and Andrew, whose jesuit formation and maturity allowed him to advance more quickly. The date for the ceremony was set for 14 September, the Feast of the Glorious Cross. It was the day set for admissions to Scourmont. It was also the third anniversary of the consecration of the church of Kurisumala. Here was new ground for liturgical experimentation: what ritual to use for these first solemn professions? One night after Compline, when Bede, who suffered more and more stomach problems, had gone to bed in his small room behind the library, Francis discussed this question at length with

Edouard Hambye, who, to his great delight, had returned to spend six months at the ashram as 'extraordinary professor' of eastern patrology.

> Don't you think that it is time to finalize this ceremony? We are
> an eastern monastery of cistercian inspiration, integrated with
> indian culture . . . and we are the first of the kind! We do not
> have a model. The syrian Catholics in India have not had
> monks for several hundred years. How will this profession
> ceremony be conducted?
> Your daily Syro–Malankar liturgy is that of Antioch, as our jacobite
> brothers use. Why not start from the text we found at the syrian
> patriarchate of Sharfeh during our recent trip, remember?

Francis searched in the books lined up on the ground along the walls of his cell.

> Here it is! *Toulbasho D'Dairoye* [The Ritual of the Clothing of
> Monks]. Could we use it as is? Without integrating the
> benedictine vows into it?
> Why not? The vows have a juridical character proper to the
> West. The investiture ceremony is more symbolic, more
> poetic also. It is a *rozo*, that is, a mystery, a sacrament, closer
> to the hindu *sannyasa*.
> If you are not too tired, we could reread this text together tonight
> and see a little how we will organize this for the very first
> time in India?
> Yes, yes, I am very excited about it!

The two men whose friendship was strengthened during their trip to the Near East spent half the night on the syriac text, interrupting each other to imagine, with supporting gestures, as a play's producers might, the different stages of what seemed to them to be a sacred drama with several characters.

'What strikes me', concluded Francis as he closed the book, 'is the structural analogy between this antiochian ceremony and the rite of consecration of the *sannyasi* in the hindu ashrams. Everything is there: long readings from the holy scriptures, marking with the divine seal, tonsure, abandoning the old garments, purifying bath and finally clothing with the monastic habits.' 'That is correct' agreed Hambye. 'On both sides, it seems to me that the deep meaning of the ritual is to elevate the one being initiated from the profane level to a sacred level.' Francis nodded his affirmation: 'That reinforces the idea that the monastic life is the ideal place for inter–religious dialogue.'

In the weeks that followed, Francis still spent a lot of time choosing readings, translating certain dialogues into English, preparing the clothing and accessories, and practicing with the community. He wrote Msgr Khouri in Paris to ask for clarifications. Every day also, in the silence of his meditation, he entrusted the three future monks to his Lord, and asked for a special grace for the celebration.

Wearing his embroidered cape, he now stood on the choir step. He was the *Rish Dairo*, the superior of the community. At his side were Bede, Hambye, and several Syro–Malankar priests who had come from Tiruvalla. On a table on the north side, the saffron clothing, scissors, cross, and basin of water were waiting. Facing this, on the ledge of the open window, the great censer was ready, a burning fire that consumes the old desires and transforms them into a perfumed offering. The young community—about twelve of them—stood in the nave. At the back, the candidates' families stood together, the men to the left, the women and children on the right. The three young men were lying down in the center, side by side, face down on the ground. Francis' voice broke the silence and pronounced the introductory prayer:

> O Holy One,
> and Lover of the holy ones,
> who take delight in the holy ones,
> God Holy above all,
> receive This Your servant set apart for You in holiness.

At the end, the community answered, with a malayali accent: *Aamiin!* The candidates rose and intoned an antiphoned psalmody that ended with the Magnificat: 'The Lord has done wonders for us.'

A series of readings followed from the Old and New Testament, interspersed with prayers and acclamations, incensing and hymns. Then the voice of the *Rish Dairo* lifted his voice again, for the admonition:

Beloved, behold before whom you are standing! You are offering
your vows and promises not before mortal and perishable people,
but in the presence of Christ God who searches the minds and
hearts! . . . All that happens to be suffered, it is appropriate and
right for you to sustain. When you remember as it is written on
the table of your heart, the holy word of the great sage, Ben Sira,
which has just been read: My son, if you come forward to serve
God, prepare yourself for temptations and trials. Cling to Him.
Do not leave Him, because you will learn through your way of
life (2:1–2). Keep His way and He will lift you up to inherit the
fertile land, while you apply yourself to humility, patience,
gentleness, obedience, kindliness, good hope and with and above
these, true love which is the perfection of the Law and the
Prophets.

(Acharaya, *The Ritual of the Clothing of Monks*, p. 34)

Then began the mystery itself, the rite of initiation to the monastic
charism. Their forehead marked with the seal of the Lamb, a cross–
shaped tonsure in their hair, the candidates were undressed, clothed with
the *khavi*, their loins were girt, their head and shoulders covered with a
shawl, and their sandals were laced. At that moment, the ministers and
candidates went into the sanctuary where the mysteries are accomplished. On their feet water, which purifies but also gives life, the gift of
the Holy Spirit, was poured. At every stage the ritual words were pronounced, 'May the Lord clothe you in the robe of glory, by the power of
the Holy Spirit' (*Ritual*, p. 40). 'May the Lord give you strength from on
high, that you may tread on snakes and scorpions and all the power of the
Enemy for ever and ever' (*Ritual*, p. 42). And every time, the community
cried out, '*Barek Mor*! Blessing upon us.'

The new monks prostrated four times in the direction of the four horizons of the earth, imploring the community to accept them: '*Barek Mor*!
My brothers, receive me!' And the community answered, 'May the Lord
receive you in His mercy!' A wooden cross was placed on their shoulders,
and they exchanged the kiss of peace with each of the brothers. The *Rish
Dairo* concluded the ceremony with this last supplication: 'Strengthen,
Lord God, with the strength which comes from You, Your servant who has
received the habit of humility that he may be able to quench all the fiery

arrows of the Evil One, and that Your Holy Name may be praised because of him, now and always and for ever' (*Ritual* p. 46).

This ceremony marked a new stage in Francis' spiritual quest. He consecrated his first monks and also renewed in a way his own commitment to an eastern, original, and universal monastic order. In preparing this ritual, he felt the discoveries confirmed where the practice of the *S'him*, reading Saint Ephrem, and the *Penqitho* had led him: the central place that the 'economy of salvation' occupied in syriac Christianity and the monk's particular role in this 'economy'.

At the age of twenty–eight, Jean Mahieu had committed himself definitively to the Cistercian Order just as he would have committed himself to the army, scouting, or some great enterprise. He placed himself in God's service, he signed his contract, he gave his word in the chivalrous spirit of Saint Bernard, with all his generosity and enthusiasm. At the age of forty–nine, he found a new charism in the Antiochian Church, a more interior, more cosmic, and more mystical vision of his monastic choice. The ritual for the investiture of the monk actualizes and reactivates symbolically the huge movement of creation towards its creator. At each stage that the candidate monk reaches during the initiation ceremony, he reproduces humanity's journey towards the parousia.

Made of dust, like Adam, he was destined for paradise. But seduced by the serpent, he sank in the swamp of sin. Like the chosen people of the old covenant, he was chosen, called by God to follow him through the desert, towards 'fertile land'. He lives—or he will live—the passion of Jesus, his trials and temptations. He will accede to resurrection, the joy of the divine life that triumphs over death. He was called, as the Church's spear point, to prepare, to anticipate the kingdom of God on the earth, to keep company with the angels who stand near God and sing the praise of his name night and day.

To answer this call, to realize this privileged alliance with God, the monk must renounce sin, abandon the 'old man' (his hair is cut, his clothing strewn on the ground), purify himself (the bath), separate himself from the world (the consecrated garment, different clothing), accept deprivation and suffering (the cross), and, especially, implore God's help and the support of the community to 'hold firm', to cling to Jesus's garment and not let go.

In the commentary on the ceremony of investiture that Francis would write over the years and publish in 1999 at the Saint Ephrem Ecumenical

Research Institute in Kottayam, Kerala, he noted that one could think of it as a sacred mystery with four characters: God, though invisible, is the main character, often evoked and invoked under various forms—unique, absolute, most holy, creator, father, incarnate word, Jesus Christ, Trinity and especially Holy Spirit, who like oil penetrates the densest matter and gives it the strength of Love. The *Rish Dairo*, the master of ceremonies as well as the superior of the monastery, never speaks in his own name: he is the voice of God, his representative here below. One single time, however, he says 'I', to remind the candidate of absolute obedience to the pope, the bishop, and 'to me, poor monk responsible for this monastery'. The candidate, a humble sinner and glorious elect, ceaselessly implores God to make him able to respond to his call, and the community, which represents the Church and the whole people of God, surrounds and welcomes the consecrated brother. Secondary characters intervene at times: Satan, the evil one, the tempter, but also Mary, model of response to the call, the angels, companions of the monks, the prophets, and the fathers who show the way to follow.

His trip to the Near East reinforced Francis' adherence to eastern monasticism and had no doubt helped him grieve the loss of his affiliation with the Cistercian Order, obstinately claimed and desired for a long time. The first 'investitures' in the Antiochian rite consecrated his choice of a *sui juris* monastery rooted in the tradition of the eastern church. Piece by piece, often painfully, he tore off the pieces of his formal and juridical attachment to the Order of Cîteaux. In July 1961, he still hesitated to forego vows and a signed schedule. By 1962, these questions were past. But he kept and fostered in his novices the cistercian spirit: discipline, obedience, silence, alternation of manual work and study, complete detachment from the world, and night prayer—all practices that harmonized perfectly with those of hindu monasticism. Through the reading of the texts, the daily repetition of the office, and the work of translation, he steeped himself and the community in eastern spirituality that returned to the source common to the spirituality of Saint Bernard and Saint Benedict, and from a time even earlier than those founders. The visitors who, despite the unfamiliar indian customs, recognized in Kurisumala from the very first hours of their stay this atmosphere of silent fervor, benevolent austerity, and attentive discretion proper to cistercian abbeys, were not mistaken.

VISITORS AND EARLY FRIENDS

Their spirit of thanksgiving in the midst of trials evoked the spirit of the Beatitudes and the Pascal Mystery with its suffering and joy. This spirit found its daily food in the liturgy, the living theology of this community which although it grew up in a wild region on a high mountain, offered a remarkable witness to all those who from near or from very far, came to participate in their offices or share their life for a time.[14]

Despite its geographical isolation, from its first years Kurisumala attracted a large number of visitors. The first, as we have seen, were people from nearby: young boys on school breaks who were looking for work, peasants asking for agricultural help, the wounded or sick seeking medicine, or simply the curious come to see more closely what the *swamis* were doing in this forsaken place. Christians from neighboring villages came to Mass on Sunday and on the great liturgical feasts, and they enhanced the ceremonies with dances and drumrolls. At times of famine, for example during the summer of 1964, lines of villagers formed on the narrow mountain paths and converged towards the monastery where they all waited, squatting on their heels, for the distribution of rice.

Of course there were Francis' old friends: Edouard Hambye, who was almost part of the community; Arthur Ingle, precious as architect in the permanent construction site; Jacques Cuttat, who loved the eastern liturgy and initiated the Indo–Swiss development project; and Suzanne Siauve, who now works in the french Institute of Indianism in Pondicherry. There were the belgian neighbors: Jacques Tombeur, the former cub scout now missionary in Tamil Nadu; Clarie Vellut, who continued her fight against leprosy in Pollambakkam; and Simone Liégeois, nurse in Pollambakkam. All of these people came to the ashram seeking a beneficial pause, a spiritual recharging of their batteries.

Very early, warned by word of mouth information circulating in ecclesiastical circles, bishops, priests, and religious of every order and denomination—indian or europeans living in India—came to spend a few days of retreat and went back home with their soul reaffirmed and appeased, with the feeling that they had discovered a unique place, witness to

---

[14] E. R. Hambye, SJ, 'Early Sowings', in *Vidya Jyoti* (1965).

the spirit of the beatitudes. A few daring people came from Europe as well. They had heard of the ashram from the 'chronicles' typed by Francis' nieces in Belgium, stenciled and disseminated to a hundred friends, or through articles, such as 'The Chatterings of a Kurisumala Novice', written by Andrew the Jesuit and published unsigned in 1962 in *Église vivante* and in *L'Orient Syrien*. In 1958, the alumni publication from Sainte Marie College in Brussels had published a letter from Francis describing the foundation's heroic beginnings.

These guests arrived in a rented car, whose driver became a porter for the last kilometers. Often, they were escorted by someone familiar to the ashram, who introduced them: Edouard Duperray, Father Monchanin's faithful friend arrived in 1961, brought by the Ingle family. Canon Edouard Beauduin, founder in Belgium of 'L'Œuvre d'Orient' visited Kurisumala as early as November 1960, invited by Hambye. Others who came included Pierre Baranger, the religious artist from Paris; René Voillaume, disciple of Charles de Foucauld and founder of the Brothers of Jesus; and Dom Jean Leclercq, a french benedictine specialist in monastic history. He was invited to speak to the monks and to explain to them the new orientations of the Second Vatican Council, adding that here, they were ahead of the council fathers' recommendations, which evidently pleased Francis.

During Christmas 1963, they had to serve the meals in two shifts and did not have enough room to lodge the guests. The conference tour Bede Griffiths gave in the United States a few months earlier had publicized Kurisumala in America. In the veranda at mealtime, sitting cross–legged along the wall and eating side by side were the german bishop of Essen, two american hippies, priests from New Zealand, a japanese monk, a french couple, and several protestant missionaries from New Mexico, not counting the numerous indian guests. Among them were many religious, a few hindu swamis, young men, several of whom asked to join the community. The best were selected and the others were sent back into the world.

In a few years the ashram became a place for international meetings and exchanges, without its contemplative character suffering. Besides direct conversations, Francis knew only one way of communication: mail. It was by a letter, sent to Kurisumala and which caught up to him in Beirut, that he learned in March 1961 of the death of his father. By letters, he shared his family's grief and left his inheritance to his brothers and sisters, suggesting only an offering for Masses *ad perpetuum* for all the deceased of the family. Kurisumala was certainly the Vagamon post office's largest customer, and the post office was its main channel for information. Not only letters from friends and more and more numerous correspondents but also books ordered and periodicals, both indian and european, sometimes very specialized, to which they subscribed, thanks to the help of Father Maur in Scourmont or Marie-Thérèse in Brussels. They ranged from *Clergy Monthly* to *Informations Catholiques* to *Irénikon* published by the abbey of Chevetogne, and we must not forget *Cistercian Studies* or the *Revue Saint-Jean-Baptiste*, edited in Paris by Jean Daniélou's team. Complete collections were shelved in the library, beside volumes of eastern patrology, sacred texts from India, and technical works on agriculture or husbandry. There was no radio, no telephone, and no daily newspaper. However, the monks were very well informed about the world's problems, through articles in monthly periodicals that extracted the essential without the futile gossip that comments on the news day by day.

Correspondence was an important occupation for Francis: he spent his rare free time in it and often despaired of keeping up. He insisted on answering the innumerable letters and cards he received at Christmas himself, using a pen. Later he would have illustrated sheets printed, with an appropriate text, but on each one he always added a short message by hand.

The growing reputation of the monastery and its founders brought them more and more invitations to come preach retreats or give conferences. Bede rarely refused. Francis tried to maintain a balance among the many tasks that required his presence there and the desire to answer the requests for spiritual assistance. In January 1961, he preached a retreat to the benedictine nuns of Bangalore. It was the first time that he was away for about ten days, in the thirty–four months he had been on the mountain, and for him it was an opportunity for a little rest as well as a pleasing public recognition, because the Benedictines spoiled him. One year later, he was invited to preach to the Carmelites. He found that more difficult. At the beginning, he was ill at ease speaking to invisible figures completely veiled in black. In 1965, with a great deal of happiness he preached a retreat of several days to a hundred and twenty young men from the Jacobite (Orthodox) Church of the diocese.

Returning from one of those retreats in Nagpur, in central India, after several days of travel by bus and train, interrupted by long waits, Francis came home to a community in trouble.

GROWTH CRISIS

Around the mid–sixties, the community consisted of about fifteen men, of whom five were professed. Survival on the mountain required from each one a serious dose of manual work and great frugality. Daily life had fallen into a rhythm, and the dairy assured their self–sufficiency in food. Until that time, their energies had been taken up by struggle against the elements, work for subsistence, and adaptation to a new and difficult world. In such circumstances, groups are happy to have an energetic leader who takes responsibility and shows his authority. When the largest problems are resolved, when direct threats are averted, disputes or discords often resurface, and the rank and file demands a greater share of power. This is what happened at Kurisumala between 1964 and 1967. We have few details about these difficulties: the official accounts do not speak about them. Bede Griffiths, who gave many interviews about his own history after his departure in 1968, showed himself discreet and reserved about these episodes during which the divergence of views between the founders crystallized the problems in the young community. A few allusions in Francis' correspondence, notes in his personal journal, a confidence gathered long afterward: from these we can attempt to reconstitute what happened.

While the prior was preaching a retreat in Nagpur (on the theme of how the silence of the intellect allows us to listen to our heart), the monks were sharing their dissatisfaction with the sub–prior, who listened to them with his customary benevolence. He promised to communicate the sentiments to the prior on his return. A few weeks earlier, Father Hambye, apprehending the conflict, had written Francis a long letter in which he developed 'a friendly and critical opinion' on the working of the community: was it not time to draw up specific constitutions for Kurisumala? Would they not have to develop a more formalized course of formation, with marked stages? Institute further more systematic studies in languages, philosophy, theology? Was it good for the superior to be the confessor for the whole community? He concluded his letter by putting his friend on guard against his tendency to want to do everything himself, and encouraged him to delegate a certain number of tasks so that he could spend more time forming the young. He suggested to him also not to accept so many guests, who distracted from classes and caused more work. The community's demands were in line with some of those questions, especially the necessity of drawing up constitutions, or, in other words, guidelines for interior order.

What did Bede think of this? What was his role in this crisis? During Francis' absence, did he encourage the expression and formalizing of the demands? His attitude was perhaps tied to his recent decision to remain permanently in India. Until then, he rather had counted on returning to England after a few years of eastern experience, to write more books. At the end of 1963, invited by the Catholic Art Association, he gave a conference tour in the United States, where he received a prize for his first book *The Golden String*. It would seem that it was this american experience that brought him to decide to remain in India, as if it had reflected to him the image of the indian guru he had become, and had given him the desire to remain one. As soon as he returned, he asked the abbey of Prinknash to allow him to change his stability to Kurisumala. Since Francis had done the same from Scourmont, the two were now heading towards the future in the same boat. Two natural leaders on the same adventure foreshadows problems. Bede was more permissive, more tolerant, less ascetic than Francis. He could not get used to night prayer—he fell asleep often—or to the absence of chairs or spoons. He had entered the Benedictines, not the Trappists. At the same time, he had willingly left the exclusive direction of the construction, finances, dairy, soil improvement, liturgy, and spiritual guidance to Francis; his tasks of teaching and hospitality were congenial to him and amply sufficient. But he was starting to find his partner too authoritarian, and the monks who were asking for constitutions and a monthly consultative meeting about the monastery's business found in him an attentive ear. He had been enthusiastic about the United States. His letters of the time witness to this fact. There he met the vanguard of the libertarian spirit that was developing during the mid–sixties in the universities and intellectual milieu of California. He brought back democratic ideas, the desire for assemblies where each one could express himself, and the dream of a freer monastic life.

Francis implemented a charismatic and patriarchal model that corresponded with his temperament, his project, and also his familial image and that of the eastern monasteries that inspired him. He was the *abba*, the father who guided the flock and took upon himself all the responsibility, made all the sacrifices, and whom it was appropriate to obey without discussion. Renunciation, gift of self, spirit of service without counting the cost were at the heart of this undertaking. Power was neither analyzed nor shared.

When Bede brought him all the community's complaints, the day after his return, the superior listened to him, frowning. When the Englishman had finished his report, he asked, 'Is that all?' 'Well, I believe I transmitted to you all they are asking', Bede responded. 'Perfect. I will answer them tomorrow. You can tell them that'. Francis prepared his answer to the dissenters in writing. 'Either all of this is a misunderstanding, and we will clarify this, or this is a real discord between the community and me, and then I can only present my resignation.' In fact, as early as 1964, Francis had proposed that Bede replace him and take charge of the ashram. But he had declined the offer. It was too early, and he did not feel ready to take up this charge. The prior, bent over his wooden plank, wrote his answers in one session.

At chapter the next evening, he dealt one by one with the contested points. Constitutions? They have constitutions: the eastern canon is sufficient to give a legal framework at the stage the community is in. The length of the novitiate? That requires reflection, perhaps the curriculum should be revised. The rules of daily life? The cistercian customs are perfectly adequate. He recalled in passing that in all the East, the monastic vocation took precedence over the priesthood and did not necessarily imply it. He praised manual work, especially the humblest kinds: 'It protects from acedia, balances the soul, develops personal discipline.' (No doubt these two points also had been the object of more or less clearly expressed wishes: why do we have to work so hard, instead of going to a seminary to study for the priesthood? The question would resurface several times.)

How was this first stage of the crisis resolved? What did Francis answer about studies and confession? We do not know. The dissent died down for some time, or so it appeared. Francis negotiated nothing, yielded nothing. Faced with his threat of resigning, the dissenters were silent. Bede probably had told them that he was not a candidate for prior. The monks, however, understood that the sub–prior was disposed to allow them permissions that the prior refused. The unity of the community was weakened.

Francis wrote to Dom Guerric: 'The most difficult thing here is to build a spirit of community. There is not yet a monastic tradition in the local religious life. The individualistic character of the Malayalis, their taste for intrigue, their clan spirit, do not make things easier.' To his sister, he confided, 'I feel my personal insufficiency, the lack of framework, my need for divine grace since the monastery is progressing and the community is growing.'

The community's complaints did not lead him to question his goals, his methods of formation, or his leadership model. Two unexpected defections would touch him more: two brothers, both professed monks, left the community within a few weeks. Andrew the Jesuit had left his teaching position in Ranchi to become a Syro–Malankar monk. Vargheese, the companion from the early days, had held fast through the hard first years but then departed. For Francis, their departure was a hard blow. For a few months, Vargheese had been exhibiting worrisome signs of mental disorder. Suffering from great nervousness, he would hide when he saw Jacobites arrive, persuaded that they were coming to kidnap him. After a violent scene in the chapel, they had to resolve to entrust him to a care facility, then to exclaustrate him. Andrew's voluntary departure, returning to Ranchi to rejoin his students and thus depriving the community of one of its rare teachers, was even more difficult to accept. Francis discovered, appalled, that Andrew had been careful to maintain his place in the Society of Jesus canonically open, thus providing an escape route. He realized that in his haste to form a community, he himself lacked discernment by admitting the first novices to solemn profession too quickly. The canonical visitation by Father Placide Podipara, an indian carmelite and consultant to the oriental congregation in Rome happened at this point to urge him to reflect on the formation curriculum. They decided to prolong the time of probation and set up four stages in the monastic commitment: after the three years of novitiate, or *sadhaka*, and they set up a temporary profession of six years—*bramacharia* or monk of the white habit. Only after that, the solemn investiture with the saffron habit, or *sannyasa*, and fifteen or twenty years later, the great habit symbolized by the wooden cross on the saffron habit. Podipara was benevolent, intelligent, cultured. He remained in Kurisumala for more than a week. 'His presence is a great comfort for us', Francis wrote.

Soon promising new arrivals came to make up for the departures: Jeshudas and Ichananda would become leading figures in the community. Always optimistic, Francis cheered up and wrote, 'Time for pruning. . . . the more lukewarm are going, that's a good thing.' But the tension between the two founders remained. Those young monks who balked at Francis' demands went to complain to Bede, who agreed with them. Bede himself, without losing his kindness or civility, showed his 'difference' more and more, in a humorous or diverting way. This difference would cause a new 'Pentecost crisis' during the summer of 1967.

On 3 May, Francis returned from Bangalore, where he had gone at the request of the benedictine abbot of Saint-André in Belgium, to visit the foundation of Asirvanam.[15] In the plain, the heat was heavy and he experienced a great well–being on feeling the wind in his beard as he happily went up the road to the monastery. He was always seized with a sort of jubilation when he returned to his horizon, his growing trees, his walls that undulated around the pastures. With the point of his umbrella, he picked up a paper that was littering the ground and stuffed it in the hole between two rocks. 'Look', he said to himself, 'there is Bede coming to meet me. I hope nothing bad has happened.' The two men conversed:

Hello, Father Francis, did you have a good trip?
Excellent, thanks. I am happy that I have returned in time for the
    community retreat.
How are they in Bangalore?
Not too bad. They have new recruits but also many problems.
    And here?
Hmmm. No new recruits, but problems, yes. . .
What kind of problems?
Well, I would like to see you this evening to speak to you about
    it privately.
Come after *Sutoro* (Compline), we will examine this together.

While Francis was in Bangalore, Sylvester and another brother named Paul had met with Bede several times to discuss what they considered abuses of power. Strengthened by the sub–prior's support, they decided to try again and demand changes from their superior. They supported their requests by arguments based on eastern canon law—that they stud-ied at length—and met Mar Athanasios in order to obtain his support. What was this about? Always the constitutions. After ten years in exis-tence, they thought it was high time to establish constitutions, to place

---

[15] The benedictine foundation begun at Siluvaigiri, near Salem, was transferred to Asirvanam, near Bangalore in 1966.

clear limits on the superior's arbitrary decisions. They also wanted to share the financial control, what in the Church is called 'temporal affairs'. Since there no longer exists a trace of the document drawn up by the dissenters, we do not know its tone or exact formulations. It is through Francis' answers, the talk he gave the community (of which the drafts have been kept) that we can reconstitute the list of grievances.

When he learned what had happened during his absence, and listened to Bede's report on the supposed 'canonical irregularities' in the community, he became angry. He had the impression of hearing again the voice of Father Colomban, Scourmont's canonist, whose pet peeve Francis had been. In his own community, built from nothing in these far hills of Kerala, he had the experience of coming up against the ideas that led him to leave Europe and western monastic life to build something different in India, something closer to the origins. He did not try to understand his monks, to know what led them to this, to meet them where they were. Angry, he wrote several pages of a very hard talk, pierced through with disappointment and anger:

Personally, I have a solid aversion for monastic life dominated by canon law, counsels and chapters. Discussing the rights and duties of each one, developing the juridical aspect of the life more often than not leads us away from spiritual realities. Worse, it generally ends in making us deaf to the call of the Holy Spirit who dwells in us. . . . Yes, I perceive that canon law as it is taught and used presently in the Church of Rome, the dioceses, religious communities, seminaries, is one of the main causes of mediocrity, one of the main factors of this spiritual impotence so evident in the life of the Church, especially in this country, where, despite remarkable achievements in teaching, good works and territorial administration, the spiritual impact on the hindu population is nil. This incurable legalism was the sin of the Pharisees. Even the cistercian rules of discipline, in my view, rather than favoring conversion of manners, are rather an obstacle to *metanoia*, abandonment to God and his Holy Spirit. I have suffered a great deal from all of that, for a long time. I find it impossible to share the juridical bent of certain brothers. It is obvious to me that these monthly council meetings and chapters every three months, far from leading us closer to God, would give us a sort of false good conscience. What we need are meetings where we take in hand our work of conversion, by divesting ourselves of our jealousy, our anger, our envy, our desire of prevailing over others. . . .

He put away his notebook and kept silence for a week. He reflected, prayed, calmed himself, and decided to go see the only authority he recognized: Mar Athanasios, his bishop. The feelings, arguments, possible decisions followed one another in his head while he descended towards Tiruvalla, his shawl rolled around him, squeezed against the rusted window of the bus, along this narrow road he knew by heart. The legalistic requests of his monks disappointed him. Had he not explained to them clearly what he wanted to build? Had he not given them the example of a radical monasticism, detached from worldly goods, rights, and privileges? In any case, he would not give it up for himself. If they do not want to follow him that far, if they want something more 'canonical', more 'soft', he will leave. Let them stay with Bede, let them draw up their constitutions with him. He was tired of dragging them along, of carrying everything himself. He remembered his trip north the previous September. Some sisters in Mussoorie, at the foot of the Himalayas, had invited him to preach a retreat. He crossed all of India by bus or train, sleeping in convents or train stations, sometimes under the stars. He ate at the side of the road, what people gave him or what he bought for a few rupees from the walking vendors: cookies, doughnuts, a portion of spiced rice rolled in a banana leaf. He took advantage of the trip to visit a hindu ashram. He felt a great desire to return there for a few months, to take a kind of sabbatical to renew his spirit and to experience hindu monasticism more deeply. It would be good too to return to Shantivanam, to go back to his original hut with Monchanin, to find himself alone. . . . But would Le Saux want to receive him? And what would become of Kurisumala? Are they capable of facing the work without him, of managing the farm and dairy, and especially of maintaining the monastic spirit?

At the bishop's residence, in his office cooled by a large fan, Mar Athanasios listened to him at length. When Francis spoke of a sabbatical, he feared for a moment that he wanted to return to Belgium and showed reticence. But when he understood that on the contrary his plan was to go deeper into the heart of India, he approved without reservation and even suggested that he take a whole year. They then spoke about temporal affairs. Thanks to the dairy, the monastery was now autonomous insofar as daily life was concerned. There were no urgent works to be started and, for the first time, there was even a small reserve of money. Reassured about the finances, the bishop turned the discussion towards the future of Kurisumala. 'We need to work with the existing personnel', he said, 'even if it is not perfect.'

In fact, Bede and Sylvester had come to see him two weeks earlier, and told him of their frustrations with what they considered their prior's excessive authoritarianism. We do not know what the bishop thought of this, or what he answered. What is certain was that he wanted Kurisumala to continue. In his function as well as his character, he was more diplomatic, more inclined to negotiate than Francis. He feared the community's division. And no doubt he knew his prior well enough to know that he would not yield. And thus he encouraged him in his project of a sabbatical year. In a year, he said, the spirits will have calmed, the constitutions will be written. If Bede was able to make the present recruits work together and draw up satisfactory constitutions, and manage the temporal affairs, so much the better. Then Francis could start a new foundation, presented from the very beginning as being more eremetical, more radical. Or, another possibility, Bede would not succeed very well, and the community would be relieved to see their leader return, all bitterness forgotten.

During the long return trip, Francis had leisure to examine these suggestions. 'After all', he thought, 'since Father Bede took the side of the rebels, let's let him direct them. Often the best way of testing—or confounding—the opposition leader is to give him power. This could become a trap, but it can also be the opportunity to give his full measure. The same for the others. My departure will avoid a confrontation which can only be harmful to the work. And thus, I am going to the limit of what I am defending: I renounce everything. I can no longer preach detachment and at the same time hang on to my dominant position. They would soon reproach me for this, and they would be right.'

When he returned, he rewrote his talk. The convictions remained the same but the tone was more moderate and the arguments were supported by multiple references. It was on Trinity Sunday, more than two weeks after his return from Bangalore, that he gathered the community and spoke to them for more than an hour.

During these last two weeks, I have reflected a great deal, and it is time to share my thoughts with you. I ask you to listen to them calmly, with confidence in God and an unshakeable resolve to follow His will. . . .

Some of you, with the support of Father sub–prior, have insisted on drawing up a new constitution and have even begun the work by compiling the Code of Canon Law for the eastern churches. Even though I am favorable to the idea of progressively building a constitution for our monastery, I feel very little enthusiasm for this work as it is presently being done and want to tell you my reasons: some regard the community and some are personal. Regarding the community: good laws are a codification of customs. Laws should not precede life but consolidate it, make it faithful to the chosen orientation. The particular circumstances of our life here, as well as the profound change of spirit manifested by the Second Vatican Council should encourage us to extreme prudence in establishing a written constitution.

There followed a long demonstration, with conciliar references to support it, of canon law's discredit as an uncontested guide to behavior in the Church, who from now on wishes to be guided by the 'spirit of Pentecost'. This diatribe ends with a passage still tinged with bitterness:

The congregations and religious orders now have three years to revise their legislation with the new orientation. We ourselves, here in Kurisumala, have often been regarded as precursors of the council's spirit, and this is the time you choose to imprison us in this eastern canon law that was published fifteen years ago, and severely criticized ever since, by the Melkite Church among others! Patriarch Maximos wrote that it was roman law disguised in eastern clothing, a 'wolf in sheep's clothing'.

All that is way out of date and completely inappropriate to lead us in the way of new foundations, characterized by simplicity, a real poverty (not only 'in spirit!'), a life of renunciation of the world's views and of high social status, a true conversion (*metanoia*) to God. This regressive attitude could lead us in a short time to the level of the ordinary christian congregations of Kerala. If our goal was to arrive there, we need not have given ourselves so much trouble establishing a monastery in this wild place. . . . Did not Our Lord himself put us on guard against the danger of keeping new wine in old skins? (. . .) Personally, I feel attracted, more deeply than ever, towards a more charismatic monastic life in which the juridical element is very much in the background. And this is not only by a very old personal attraction but also because the renewal of Vatican II orients all religious life towards a 'de–institutionalization' very necessary in India if we desire christian monasticism to meet the monasticism of India. I do not have a plan but I would like to use the sabbatical year that Mar Athanasios offered me to meditate, pray, reflect on all this and at the same time recharge my batteries. Maybe at Shantivanam, and then a pilgrimage to the Himalayas.

The perspective of seeing Francis away for a year worried the community, who asked the bishop to reduce the time to three months, without success. A few days later, Francis gathered a few books—the Bible and the Gita—an iron goblet, a change of clothing, his old pen, and a notebook in a saffron cloth bag. He gave his last recommendations to Father Bede. Both of them agreed on one thing at least: in a year, one of the two would leave. The community's evolution, the people Francis would meet along his pilgrimage and, who knows, perhaps some providential sign, would indicate which one was to remain at Kurisumala.

On the road to Shantivanam, what feelings did he experience? Even if some worries or some remaining disappointment overshadowed him still, let us bet that the dominant feeling was a sort of relief, liberation, happiness to be going again as a light pilgrim on the roads, and joy at returning to the banks of the Kaveri where he had been so happy with Monchanin, marveling at his indian beginnings. He was fifty–five years old.

FOURTH PART

KURISUMALA ASHRAM, ITS INFLUENCE
(1968–1988)

KURISUMALA ASHRAM, ITS INFLUENCE

AN INTERRUPTED SABBATICAL YEAR

O N THE SANDY ROAD that leads to the Kaveri, Francis asked himself how he would be received at Shantivanam. His first meeting with Father Le Saux, twelve years earlier when he had arrived in Bombay, had not been successful. We remember the misunderstanding at Elephanta. Later, after the death of Monchanin, the monastic charisms of his two disciples had led them to different paths. Francis had been immersed in caring for his own foundation. Le Saux–Abhishiktananda, fascinated by the advaitic mysticism of non–duality, had led the life of a wandering *sannyasi*, divided, and sometimes torn, between the heritage of Shantivanam and the hermitage he built himself at Uttarkashi, in the himalayan foothills, amid the saddhus covered with ashes. His radicalness distanced him more and more from 'normal monastic life', and he found Father Mahieu too integrated in the Church of Kerala for his taste. With irony and some condescendence, he wrote to his friend Father Joseph Lemarié in 1959: 'The syriac liturgy is far from having the "formative" value of the Latin rite. Or one should study it completely and use its possibilities for development. This was Father Mahieu's dream: his archeologizing and abrupt attitudes caused him a lot of trouble.' To the same correspondent, he wrote in 1960: 'As for Father Mahieu, his monastery has become—would you believe—a center for the artificial insemination of cattle, with government support. I do not know the details, but this at least is astonishing.' In 1961 however, during a trip to the South, he stayed at his cistercian confrère's monastery, and his tone changed:

> I spent four days at Father Mahieu's ashram at the end of July. A marvelous solitude, as I have experienced only in the Himalayas. But what a climate! Rain, wind, fog, cold. The inhabitant of the happy tamil plains had to flee very soon. An austere life of silence and work in the cistercian manner, even though Father Mahieu is changing and becoming more and more 'eastern'. The work is succeeding thanks to his enthusiasm. If he can keep going long enough for it to penetrate deeply in his brothers, it will have a future. In any case, it is the only monastic foundation here that is succeeding.[1]

He continued by criticizing the Syriac rite, but one senses that this brief stay changed the image he had of Kurisumala.

Several times between 1962 and 1967, the two men found themselves in Bombay or Delhi in the pioneering groups around such persons as J.-A. Cuttat or R. Panikkar, which prepared the renewal of the church in India in the light of the Spirit of the Council. Protestants participated in these, led by Reverend Murray Rogers, living in Bareilly in the north with his family, where the ashram of Jyotiniketan (House of the Light) was a model of simple life at the service of the poor, in Gandhi's tradition. It was also a center for meeting of religions. The Bible and the *Upanishads* were read during seminars in which the two monks participated together.

Despite these connections, Francis was not sure that he was welcome in Shantivanam. It was, however, what he desired most at the moment: to return to those places where he had drawn such strong inspiration in 1955–56 beside Monchanin. But he was not unaware of Le Saux's reticence towards him and expected a reserved welcome.

The opposite happened. At day's end, the sun played through the mango leaves and made spots of light on the roof of the little church

---

[1] Le Saux, *Lettres d'un sannyasi chrétien à Joseph Lemarié.*

where the hermit was cementing cracks. When he saw Francis arriving alone, on foot, covered with dust with his small bundle, he put down his trowel, came down from his scaffolding and, opening his arms, embraced his brother in silence. He led him to his ancient hut, which was unchanged. 'It was with deep emotion', Francis would say, 'that I returned to the oratory and the little cabin where I had known so many happy days and luminous nights, like a novitiate for my monastic life in India. Especially I found there Swami Abhishiktananda, and that was a true meeting.'[2] The hermit was busy, talkative, and attentive, and the two men carried on a lively conversation:

> Of course you may stay here as long as you want. I plan to go back up to Uttarkashi in August but that does not change anything, Father Dominique would be thrilled to have you keep him company.
>
> He is still here?
>
> Since January. He obtained permission to leave Asirvanam. He is not in good health. He stays all day in his hermitage at the far end of the garden and finds it difficult to remain alone when I go away. But you must be tired. Put your things down, make yourself at home, go sit on the bank of the Kaveri while I prepare supper. We have rice, lentils, fresh mango. We will eat together, the three of us. Heaven has sent you. I have so many problems here, I will tell you about them, but not today.

Free from all responsibility, Francis let himself be led. He obeyed Le Saux and went to sit on a flat rock still warm from the sun. His eyes followed the white birds perched on the branches that the brownish silt of the sacred river carried along. Great serenity engulfed him and praise of the Lord rose from his heart following the rhythm of his breathing.

June and July passed in this way, as a prolonged happy stop in the quiet oasis of the plain. His time was divided between prayer in common, silent meditation, light domestic work, and long conversations under the trees. He would later write of this time:

---

[2] Francis Acharya, *Chronique des douze années*.

In this meeting with the Swami after eleven years, I felt an unexpected joy at discovering how close we were at the deepest level. From day to day this joy was renewed and strengthened, as we continued a wonderful dialogue. Our constant subject was the need for an incarnation of the Church in the current of life in India as well as in her cultural and religious heritage, a desire so dear to Father Monchanin.

At the time, our meeting made us aware very vividly and globally of the major changes that had taken place in a short time. Pope John XXIII had marked these years by opening wide the windows of the Church. Vatican II had confirmed his main intuitions, organized them, and had drawn a well–defined line of conduct for the universal Church. In the 1950s, the indigenization of the life of the Church, meeting with Hinduism and adoption of indian customs were done by only a handful of men, generally considered as poor losers and even mavericks even by the most enlightened. Now, all these problems were taken on officially by the indian hierarchy. We could scarcely believe it. When the Conference of Bishops met in Delhi in November 1966, examining the possibility of adopting indian forms of prayer, they voted favorably to study the question, despite a few opposed. This work had been entrusted to a pan–indian liturgical commission, on which we had both been asked to collaborate actively.[3]

At that time, in India as in Europe, changes were rapid, causing Cardinal Suenens to say that Vatican II was like the French Revolution of 1789 in the Church. Some were frightened or scandalized by it, but for our two friends, it was a godsend. Soon, Le Saux confided in Francis that being in charge of the two hermitages was becoming too heavy a burden for him.

> Financially especially, it is becoming untenable. But there is also
> the fatigue of these trips across all of India several times a year.
> In fact, I am realizing that I do not have the charism of a
> founder, and I no longer believe in the project of a monastic
> community in Shantivanam. I am attracted by the eremitical

---

[3] *Ibid.*

life in the hindu manner, and the banks of the Ganges suit me more than the banks of the Kaveri, even if I am finding it hard to leave all this.

If you move north for good, what will become of Shantivanam? We can't just abandon it!

You are right, I don't feel that I have the right to give it up to just anyone or even to give it back to the bishop. The solution, I am thinking more and more since you arrived, is this: why don't you take it up yourself? It could be a sort of foundation of Kurisumala. You have enough personnel to take two or three young people here with you and start the monastic life again with the help of Father Dominique. What do you think about that?

It is perfectly imaginable. That might be a providential solution to the problems my community is experiencing right now. Shantivanam would be a more eremitical place, still more detached from the world than Kurisumala, a sort of lavra, a semi–anchoretic skete, as in the Fathers of the Desert. We would begin with a small kernel of volunteers.

Really, you would accept? If you only knew how relieved I would be. I could retire to Uttarkashi with a tranquil conscience, certain that Monchanin's work is in good hands.

Obviously, my community has to agree. I have to return to Kurisumala in September for the investiture of three novices. I will gather the chapter and transmit your proposal to them. I would be very surprised if there were any problem.

At the end of August, Abhishiktananda went back up to the Himalayas, and Francis returned to Kerala, stopping on his way at Saint Paul's Seminary in Trichy to speak to the students about the contemplative life. 'The openness to the world advocated by Vatican II', he told them, 'cannot be conceived without a counterweight of interior life that bears witness to our call to share the very life of God'.[4]

The prior stayed at Kurisumala only a week. He gathered the elders of the community, who approved the return to Shantivanam. Abhishiktananda had insisted that Francis himself take charge of the new foundation,

---

[4] Diaries 1967 and 1968, Francis Mahieu.

and he, in the sabbatical and eremitical dispositions in which he found himself, inclined in that direction. But he wanted to reflect on this some more, and at the community meeting was careful not to be specific about the names of those who would go down from the 'Mountain of the Cross' to revivify the 'Wood of Peace'. On 14 September, they celebrated with their habitual solemnity the investiture of the three novices: Augustine, a young priest; Joseph, a young man from the neighborhood; and Yesudas, a student. The very next day, Francis left again, going to Goa this time, where he preached in several colleges and religious institutes in favor of the contemplative life. He sailed from Goa to Bombay, a two–day mini–cruise that allowed him to meet several interesting persons and add a series of useful addresses in his notebook. In October he visited most of the seminaries of the Bombay–Poona region. Everywhere he was invited to speak. The conferences often were followed by informal exchanges with a few students particularly interested by the subject or, rather, by the person of this atypical monk/swami. Francis recalled:

My meeting with the personnel from these institutions and their students, to whom I was invariably asked to speak, was very revealing. No doubt the measure of their zeal for the Church's aggiornamento and for the indianizing movements was very variable—often related to the particular christian communities to which the students belonged, related to the missionaries who were in charge of their clerical formation. But on the whole, consensus in favor of the new leanings was irresistible. Ten or twelve years earlier, the saffron robe of the *sannyasi* was often regarded with disdain and suspicion. Sometimes even, for this reason, I was asked not to stay in such a seminary or such a religious house unless I wore a white habit. Today, the most cordial welcome is granted me everywhere, at least from the younger generation.

In all these seminaries, meetings were organized quickly, and often were held indian style: everyone crouching on the floor, in the joyous light of oil lamps and the sweet perfume of incense sticks, with the chant of sanskrit mantras. Indian music was becoming more and more popular both in the seminaries and in the faraway missions. This was not always without resistance from the more westernized groups, as is still the case for the indianization of forms of prayer. At the Bombay seminary, for example, the students had started an orchestra of indian musical instruments. Their first public performance had been organized for a feast day. When, shortly before the beginning of the performance, the musicians went to their rooms to get their instruments, they found the membranes of the *tablas* [tambourines] cut with a knife. It was the work of their more orthodox colleagues to prevent the performance.

In many places, attempts were made to use readings from hindu scriptures at prayer services, as a point of departure for a meditation on these sacred texts. My visit to Poona coincided with the feast of Roberto de Nobili. Organized by a group of students fully committed to indianization, it was celebrated in the best indian style. The order was that of a *satsang*, daily practice in hindu ashrams. There was a christian *bhajan* accompanied by the *tabla* and *veena*. The scriptural readings started with the *Upanishads* and ended with the Gospel according to Saint John, interwoven with chants. I had the privilege of presiding over this service and of giving the homily. I demonstrated how the upanishadic text prefigured and was fulfilled in the Gospel.

All this filled my heart with joy, and my hopes for the indigenization of the forms of prayer grew stronger and stronger. Evidently, this was not just a fad for the younger generation. Everywhere, even in the Delhi circles, which were very western in mentality, I could meet people who were convinced of the necessity for a deeper integration of the Church and the religious heritage of India.[5]

At the de Nobili college, where he stayed a week, Francis took the measure of the change of mentality which was occurring in the Church of India and of which the young indian Jesuits were the pioneers. Notably, he met Father Anthony De Mello, who at age 37 was already known beyond his congregation as a spiritual director. He renewed the popularity of the '30 day retreat' dear to Saint Ignatius, and directed several every year with growing success, welcoming priests, religious women, and lay people in the same group. A native of Bombay, educated in the United States in the Carl Rogers psycho–therapeutic school, and gifted with

---

[5] Francis Acharya, *Chronique des douze années*.

great talent in communication, he defined himself as an 'eastern Christian'. His teaching, called *sadhana* (a sanskrit word meaning 'way of spiritual realization') joined the best of jesuit theological formation, hindu spiritual tradition, and non–directive american psychology.[6]

Francis and he were not drinking from exactly the same sources or exercising their talents in the same fields, but they harmonized very well on their mission's essential point: the catholic clergy was fossilized, paralyzed by formalism, taboos, 'hairsplitting', whereas announcing the Good News required of its witnesses a joyous freedom, detached from this world's goods, a tender and merciful love for all men, a humble and stubborn seeking for the Ultimate Reality through silent prayer where man abandons himself to the love of God. De Mello promised himself to come to Kurisumala as soon as possible, and Francis made note of the references to Carl Rogers, Harvey Cox,[7] and Msgr Robinson, an anglican bishop whose book *Honest to God* was having great success at the time and arousing many controversies.

The traveler was preparing to continue towards the north when a letter from his sub–prior urged him to return to Kurisumala: negotiations with the government about restarting the veterinary center were turning sour, the agricultural cooperative society[8] was blocked by dissensions between farmers, and Bede himself was more and more ill.

At his arrival, Francis found out exactly what was going on. At Sylvester's initiative, they had built another story above the kitchen. This large room would be used for yoga practice, classes, and chant practice. So far, so good. The drawing up of the constitutions was the subject of many meetings, but no text came out of them. The prior refrained from commenting, but no doubt he was secretly rejoicing at the lack of result. The big problem was the dairy cooperative. Bede let himself be named president, not realizing that from that point he bore the ultimate financial responsibility for that enterprise. The secretary and assistant revealed themselves to be crooks. The public was threatening lawsuits. Francis

---

[6] De Mello, *Sadhana, A Way to God.*

[7] These authors' books are still in Kurisumala's library.

[8] Kurisumala Milk Suppliers Cooperative Society: This organization, encouraged by the government, aimed to replace the old feudal system of landowners (or *zamindars*) by an association of small farmers who would assume together the responsibilities of the larger owner: loans, help in case of natural disaster, common equipment, etc. The associates expected guaranties for their protection but did not want to assume the risks.

was annoyed, to say the least, and harshly reproached Father Bede's naiveté. But his anger turned to worry when he realized that his sub–prior was very ill: he had lost weight again and could not tolerate any food. He could scarcely drink milk. At the beginning of November, he had to be hospitalized. A serious stomach ulcer was diagnosed. Week by week, Francis delayed continuing his interrupted pilgrimage and finally resigned himself to waiting until spring. He took business into his hands again, led endless negotiations with the farmers belonging to the cooperative, but could not avoid a trial and contrary judgment.

Bede left the hospital at the beginning of December, and they spent Christmas 'as a family' in a more peaceful ambiance. The sub–prior remained weakened, and even though he made it a point of honor to participate in all the offices, his state still required a lot of rest. It was in this context that the practical details of the return to Shantivanam were discussed. Swami Mariadas, a deacon, was presented to Le Saux as a candidate to take over the permanent charge of Saccidananda ashram and had been received with enthusiasm. 'He was born a monk!' the hermit had exclaimed. But meanwhile, a second foundation was taking shape, requested by Father Jacques (James) Tombeur at Cape Comorin. Mariadas would be more useful there. The bishop wished Francis to stay as Kurisumala's superior, and the community, when consulted, agreed with this opinion. They believed that the administration of the monastery in full expansion and managing the farm, which was more and more involved in the enterprise of regional agricultural development, seemed tasks too heavy for the sub–prior's shoulders. The latter was thinking more and more about returning to England. Francis spent a whole afternoon convincing him, during a long walk. It was finally while they were walking along the reservoir's barrier that he found the last arguments that made Bede decide to return to the hermitage of Tamil Nadu, but for a trial of one year, at the end of which they agreed that he would make his definitive decision. He was granted permission to take along two monks of his choosing. They gave themselves a few months to establish a 'foundation charter' and decide on practical details. They agreed, despite Father Le Saux's impatience, that they would return in August. The hermit did not hide his disappointment: he had been hoping that Francis himself would return to Shantivanam. It was no secret to anyone that he had no sympathy for 'the Englishman'. 'I can't stand him', he confided to a european visitor. 'It's the Thames fog that came to India.' Was this the stubbornness of a man from Brittany? Incompatibility of character? A rivalry between writers? Or between Benedictines? One could have expected that Bede Griffiths would seem, on the contrary, to be the right choice, as the man who had all the qualities necessary to develop the heritage of this pioneering foundation: he was an intellectual, passionate about the meeting of Hinduism and Christianity, and a free thinker, already internationally renowned. We will see what came of it.

TO THE HIMALAYAS

At the beginning of March, Francis continued the route of his pilgrimage to the Himalayas. In his bag, he had put the large saffron woolen pullover his sister knitted and went to Delhi by train. After a few visits/conferences to the seminaries, in April finally he went to Rishikesh, the great hindu monastic city. During the slow trip, he experienced the spontaneous devotion of the Indians of every religion towards men of God. This was no longer the excited wonder of discovery that it had been in 1955, but a deeper communion with the population. What he was now discovering was how much he himself had become half Indian. His saffron robe, his beard, his light baggage, his staff, and his iron cup afforded him many moving meetings. He spoke about a few of them; let us listen to him:

> A few hours after my arrival in Delhi, I was looking for a bus to take me to my destination for the night. A man about forty years old approached me visibly to help me, and we began a conversation. He asked me questions: who I was, where I was from, when and why had I embraced the life of a *sannyasi*? I explained briefly that I am a christian *sannyasi*, that I started an ashram in the south, and that for ten years I had been leading a life of prayer and work there in the company of about twenty Indians, a life very close to the one Gandhi loved. He was moved by these words. He presented himself as a journalist and friend of the Bharat Sannyasa Samaj, the official association of the *sannyasi* of India, established in Delhi. He asked me several times to come that very evening to visit the president of that association and share with him and a few other friends my experience of the life in an ashram. I deeply regretted that I had to decline his invitation.

The place I had to get to for the night was still unknown to me and very far. Besides, the bus I had to take had arrived and stopped beside us. I said goodbye to my companion, but as I took my place in the bus I saw him run across the wide street to a fruit shop. He quickly purchased a few bananas, oranges, and grapes and came back still running, not afraid to jump into the bus that was starting to move. He placed his gift on my knees, his face radiant, with fervent compliments, then quickly jumped back into the street, leaving me stunned but delighted and touched by this affectionate and respectful gesture that was unexpected, performed with so much grace despite the impromptu setting. . . .

Later, I was leaving Delhi to go to Bareilly by the night train. When I arrived at the platform, the train was full. The travelers, as is the custom here, were hanging on to the outside of the doors of all the third class compartments. In the hope of finding some access to the train, I cleared a path to the sleeping wagon. The train conductor was there checking reservations. I asked him for a bed for the night. He answered that there was not a single one available and besides, there were a good number of names on his waiting list. Despite these prohibitive words, not seeing another way to take the train, I threaded my way in the hallway and sat there on my bag. As usual, when the train started to move, conversation started with my travel companions sitting on the seats. They were taking an evident interest in this christian *sannyasi* who had come from such a distance to become a monk in India. I was not at all certain of the sentiments behind their questions. Travelers from the south are not always well regarded in the north of India, and foreign missionaries are regarded suspiciously by a large part of the population. Our conversation took a favorable turn, however, when they realized that I had studied the languages, religion, and culture of India. One of them took a copy of the *Bhagavad Gita* from his pocket and handed it to me, inviting me to read it. As soon as they had verified that I could read and explain the text, their mistrust and indiscreet curiosity that I had perceived melted, and I was adopted as one of them. It was at that moment that the train conductor, continuing his inspections, became aware of my presence in the hallway. Indignantly, he asked me how I had dared to go into his wagon despite his warnings! I had nothing to answer and prepared to endure with patience the consequences of his just anger. But my embarrassment did not last. One of my new friends cried out, 'He is a great saint! You should give him a bed!' And to my great relief, the conductor did so right away. . . .

Often, in sanctuaries or on pilgrimage routes, the greatest marks of reverence were given to me: people who bowed profoundly or touched my feet with their right hand, or even prostrated full length on the ground. This happened at Ellora, when a whole group of indian tourists left their guide long enough to give this spectacular homage to the *sannyasi* who was passing by. There again, while I was sitting in contemplation in a buddhist cave in front of a series of rock sculptures marvelously describing the different stages of meditation, pilgrims, after prostrating themselves, began to place their alms before me, as they were accustomed to doing in holy places for their saddhus sitting immobile, completely absorbed in *samadhi*.[9] In a few minutes, I had enough money to buy my food for the next day! I am sure that if I had moved there, they would very quickly have completely taken charge of me.[10]

In the high valley of the Ganges, the Divine Life Society ashram had several hundred monks and since 1936 had welcomed pilgrims from the whole world. The influence of its founder, Swami Sivananda, extended far beyond the borders of India. The buildings, functional and without style, rose in tiers on the slope that separated the road from the river, which one approached by large flat steps: *ghats*, as at Benares. On the bank, two small white temples shelter the daily ritual celebration of *puja*. Across from this, the sight of the high mountains is enthralling. This is the *Sri Himalaya darshan*, the vision of the Lord Himalaya, abode of the gods, symbol of the Ultimate Reality. Monkeys spring in the evergreens, birds flit among the rhododendrons, children run after each other laughing on the stairs and jump into the water. When Francis arrived, for several days he felt that he was discovering a lax monasticism with little structure: no one paid attention to him, no obligation was imposed on him, and there was apparently no official superior authority. He tried to

---

[9] *Samadhi*: state of perfect concentration.
[10] Francis Acharya, *Chronique des douze années*.

participate in a maximum of activities and meetings, and little by little realized that there was an authentic life of prayer and work, a general atmosphere of fervor—some spoke here of 'spiritual vibration'—which led the newcomer to participate more and more deeply in *tapyasa* [asceticism], *bhakti* [adoration], *yoga* [meditation], and *karma* [service and action]. He fit in very quickly, all the more since the ideal of Sivananda ashram was very similar to that of Kurisumala: prayer, work, and hospitality. Different from other hindu ashrams that were exclusively devoted to personal ascesis (and which criticized Sivananda ashram as deviating from this), here they practiced manual work and service of others, made concrete by a small hospital and a factory of ayurvedic pharmaceutical products. It was also a center for the spread of 'spiritual knowledge', helped by a modern print shop that sent periodicals, books, and brochures everywhere in the world. Yoga and music, both vocal and instrumental, were practiced and taught at a high level.

The daily schedule—Francis copied it into his notebook—was almost identical to that of the Cistercians:

4:00 AM	Rise
4:30 AM	Prayer and meditation in the *bhajan* (music) room
5:30 AM	Yoga
6:30 AM	A cup of tea is brought to the cell for those who hold out their cup
7:00 AM	Teaching of religious chants and instrumental music
8:00 AM	Work in the various departments
11:00 AM	Meal, with recitation of the eleventh chapter of the *Bhagavad Gita* and chant
3:00 PM	Tea, work until around 5 PM
4:00 PM	(three times a week) Spiritual conference
5:00 PM	Supper
5:30 PM	*Satsang* (meeting with holy men)

These two months of immersion in hindu monasticism allowed Francis to improve his practice of yoga and his knowledge of the holy scriptures of India. His admiration for the eastern spiritual approach was strengthened. He discovered more and more convergences between the hindu understanding of the *sannyasa* and the practice of the first christian monastic establishments of Egypt or Syria, which gave rise to the Syro–Malankar

Church that had welcomed him in Kerala. The search for awakening, attention, and concentration on the essential was of first importance. The yogi was attentive. The monk—according to Saint Ephram—is 'an eye of light open to the heart of the world'. In all the syriac literature, angels are called 'watchers', those who do not sleep, the Awakened ones:

> Happy the one who has acquired
> A luminous eye through which he sees
> How the Watchers stand
> Before You in adoration'[11]

This stay led Francis to ask himself questions about the governing of a community and the education of a monk. Informal permeation under the guidance of a master characterized the eastern approach, whereas a formalized curriculum was proper to western novitiates, with an accent on conventual discipline and respect for rules, the fruit of the roman juridical spirit. This was an inexhaustible subject for reflection.

At the end of April, the pilgrim continued on his way. He visited several other ashrams, sometimes very different from Sivananda, and took detailed notes about each of them. At Svarga, he found Abhishiktananda–Le Saux, and a few days later they were joined by Dr Bettina Baumer, an austrian orientalist, and two belgian Jesuits from Calcutta. The five friends, all interested in the meeting of Hinduism and Christianity, met one morning in the grove of mango trees near the ashram for a meditated reading of the *Kena Upanishad.* There a meeting that Francis called 'astounding' occurred, a sort of direct contact with someone modest and unknown, who just came out of nowhere, and who had reached that contact with the 'real' of which the text spoke. This experience, manifestly difficult to describe, can only be glimpsed from the account he gave of it:

> As we were considering and searching together for the meaning
> of the series of questions posed by the Seer and leading his
> disciple to awareness of the ultimate reality beyond everything, a
> saddhu of very ordinary appearance who had quietly approached

---

[11] Saint Ephrem, *Hymns on Faith*, 3:5. Translator's note: The four lines are my translation of the french version. However, Brock translates it differently: 'Blessed is the person who has acquired a luminous eye with which he will see how much the angels stand in awe of You, Lord, and how audacious is man' (*The Luminous Eye*, p. 73).

us asked us suddenly: 'Do you understand what you are reading?' Some of us worried about his intentions and were afraid of being chased away from the mango grove. But the exchanges that followed revealed our interlocutor's good dispositions. This meeting was for us a sort of revelation of hindu 'realization' with all that it entails of detachment, abandonment, illuminated by a vivid experience of the divine, conferring a deep discernment between the real and the unreal. We had extremely enlightening exchanges on this subject until our *saddhu* gave us a new surprise by inviting us with insistence to share his noon meal. We followed him, like children facing a man of God. He led us to his hut where, all six of us, crouching, some of us outside for lack of space, shared the chapatis, vegetables, and fruits that seemed to multiply like heavenly food. When we separated, one of us evoked Moses's mysterious meal on the mountain with the notable men of Israel, 'who were able to gaze on God and ate and drank'.[12]

Before returning to Kurisumala at the end of May, Francis spent a few days with Reverend Murray Rogers at Jyotiniketan, described in his diaries later as follows.

Arrival at Bareilly Station at 5 AM. A cyclo–rickshaw brought me to the oratory. From afar, I heard the Vande Saccidanandam sung. Silent meditation, Eucharist in the Indian rite. Great fervor. The birds shared in the praise, and two beautiful peacocks danced under the flowering trees. Later it was the sun that showed its ardor, and we sought the shady corners refreshed by a light breeze. The site is enchanting. The buildings were built by Laurie Baker. No servants: the ashramites do all the work including the dispensary. There are families and children here. Panikkar and Le Saux are great friends and come regularly. At noon, they pray for them. The food is vegetarian, partly grown here on a few acres of garden. Water is drawn from the reservoir by a great paddle wheel moved by two white water buffaloes, strong and peaceful, who on occasion are harnessed to the plow or the harvester in the wheat field. Murray

---

[12] Francis Acharya, *Chronique des douze années*.

divided his time between manual work, Bible classes, retreats, visits in the neighborhood, and ecumenical meetings.'[13]

The two men spent several evenings organizing the meeting to pre-pare the All India Seminar planned for 1969, which would elaborate on the implications of Vatican II for the local church, especially the integra-tion of the cultural and spiritual heritage of India. This preparatory meet-ing was planned for the following July in Bombay, at the jesuit novitiate of the province, where Father De Mello was master of novices.

Francis returned to Kurisumala at the end of May, his heart happy and full of the fruit of those many meetings. His hindu pilgrimage completely fulfilled his expectations: to have closer contact with hindu ashrams and *sannyasis*; to develop dialogue, share ideals, and create spiritual emulation. The repercussions on Kurisumala were not long in coming.

FIRST FOUNDATION: SHANTIVANAM

On 27 August 1968, at dawn, eight monks squeezed into a rented jeep and went up the Peryar Lake road to Shantivanam, on the other side of the mountains that form a natural border with Tamil Nadu. Fog was yielding to the rising sun when they arrived in the dry plain, so different from the gardens of Kerala that were always green. At noon, they stopped at the Rosarians' in Manaparai. Three more hours of travel in the heat of the afternoon to cover the hundred kilometers separating them from Kulitalai. The young ones fell asleep, their heads leaning on the shoulders of the more hardened elders.

'Look!' shouted Francis. 'It's the Kaveri. We are getting close.' Ajit, one of the two novices designated by Bede, craned his neck. He was happy about this adventure, this novelty, and a little worried also. The day was declining when the small band got out in front of the hermit-age's portico and walked around the small buildings. 'Nothing has changed here in twelve years', Bede remarked quietly. 'We will have to make a few changes to make this place livable.' The young people were seduced by the calm and beauty of the place. Francis was disappointed that Abhishiktananda was not there. He had left that morning without

---

[13] Diaries 1967 and 1968, Francis Mahieu.

waiting for them, more moved than he had thought by his definitive departure from this symbolic place that had been his home for almost twenty years. He felt unable to face the handing over of powers and the goodbyes. He would never return to Shantivanam, and would even abstain from traveling in the south to avoid going there.

Father Dominique who had been left alone since September, returned to Asirvanam. So Swamiji had asked that Anugrah, the oldest of Bede's companions, be sent a week earlier to facilitate the transfer. It was with joy that the *brahmachari* welcomed his Kurisumala brothers. He gave Francis the keys and the act of donation in his name that Father Le Saux, always scrupulous, had insisted on drawing up in due form, authenticated by the local civil authority. Introductions were made: Visuvasai, the guardian/caretaker/gardener; Stephen, a familiar of the ashram since Father Monchanin's time, devoted but of a difficult character; and a few neighbors, artisans or farmers who had come to greet the newcomers.

After an office celebrated under the indian style *mandapam*, they ate in the straw hut that served as a refectory and spent the night under the guests' *pandal*. The next day, they paid a courtesy call on the bishop James Mendonça, who evoked his memories of the origins of Shantivanam and the already legendary figure of Father Monchanin at length to them. Francis held back a smile when he heard the elderly prelate profess unconditional faith in the principles of indigenization: he seemed not to remember the patience the two hermits had to exhibit to obtain the necessary permissions from him twenty years before.

Towards the evening, they crossed the Kaveri and continued to Srirangam to visit the temple of Shiva with its multiple surrounding walls. The monks were as excited as children at this unusual nocturnal trip. The youngest especially were impressed: in Kerala, the temples were closed to non–Hindus, and it was the first time they saw the interior of one. The terraces and sanctuaries were crawling with people. Everywhere the flames of the oil lamps caused copper reflections to quiver in the darkness. They breathed odors of incense, cut jasmine, and melted butter. Along the portico, with its thousand columns, they answered the salutations of the Hindus who welcomed them by joining their hands and bowing their head. Near a side chapel, they stopped to listen to a *bhakti* [devotee] sitting in the lotus position on the tiles, eyes closed, singing with all his heart, as the ancient *alvars*[14] used to, without pausing. The modulated chant echoed in the vast granite building. The eight monks stayed there a long time listening. Later, they watched the preparations for a wedding that gathered hundreds of guests. It was dark when the group returned to the hermitage. Everyone kept silence, remembering those joyous and intense meetings that made concrete in an uncommon and almost sensual way the hindu–christian communion for which they prayed every day in their church.

The 'foundation charter' of Shantivanam by Kurisumala specified that the ashram would keep the name given it by Father Monchanin—Saccidananda[15]—and would remain a small colony of two to six monks, a sort of skete[16] that would develop its own charism following the impulsions of the Holy Spirit. However, it would remain dependent on Kurisumala for the formation of its novices. It would use the Latin rite, because of the diocese to which it belongs. Kurisumala intended to work not only toward the renaissance of the monastic traditions of the eastern Church but also to favor the impregnation in the Catholic Church of monastic institutions and schools of spiritual development that were part of the cultural heritage of India. This would be the particular mission of Saccidananda ashram, in continuity with its founders, Fathers Monchanin and Le Saux.

Sat–Cit–Ananda [Being, Thought, Beatitude] is the title of a hymn written at the beginning of the twentieth century by Brahmabandhab Upadyay, a converted Bengali thinker who had vowed himself—at the cost of his life—to the hinduization of Christianity.[17] Monchanin had heard about him in 1936 at Lyon, and this had been a dazzling revelation for him. He declared himself in his heart of hearts to be the disciple of such a man and from that day on recited this hymn in his prayer for India. In 1950, he made it the dedication of his ashram. Francis had fallen in love with this chant during his first stay at Shantivanam. At Kurisumala, he had

---

[14] The *alvars* or 'deep ones' were tamil poets between the sixth and ninth centuries. They went from temple to temple singing hymns they composed. Their conviction was that liberation consists for man in abandonment full of love for the unique and eternal God who in his mercy shows himself here below under the likeness of an avatara without renouncing his infinite nature. Their poetry is sung or read in the sanctuaries or in families still to this day.

[15] *Saccidananda*: From the Sanskrit *sat* (being), *cit* (thought), and *ananda* (beatitude).

[16] *Skete*: monastic establishment widespread in the deserts of Egypt from the fourth century and composed of several hermitages grouped around a spiritual father called Abba.

[17] Lipner, *Brahmabandhab Upadyay*.

transcribed it in large Sanskrit characters and placed it in his cell, under the icon of the Transfiguration. It was often sung at the *satsang*.

> Vande Saccidananda. . .
> Adoration to the one who is Being, Knowledge, and perfect Joy
> The highest goal, the one for whom the ascetics sigh
> But the world rejects.

Great undertakings often begin in a shared dream. Monchanin had been seduced by the dream that Upadyay described lyrically:

> In this hermitage, the words of the eternal Word will be sung on eastern melodies. On the banks of the sacred river, catholic piety will be dressed in hindu garb and the wisdom of the Vedas assimilated with christian truth. There, in solitude and silence, true yogis will practice, for whom contemplation of the *Saccidananda*, One and Triune, will be food and drink. They will possess nothing in order to possess everything, they will want to know nothing in order to know everything, they will take joy in nothing in order to take joy in the All. We will not rest until we have seen the religion of Christ lived by hindu monks, the Gospel preached in the language of the Vedas, the liturgy celebrated according to the spirit of India, religious poverty practiced according to the norms of hindu ascesis, so that we may finally contemplate the beauty of the catholic faith in its eastern garb.[18]

In what way could this return to Shantivanam, unforeseeable when Francis left it in 1956, realize Upadyay's dream? Only time will tell. Today, leaving the small band there, the prior can only trust in God.

He returned to his rainy, stormy mountain with relief. He would always prefer the roughness of the wind to the heavy heat of the plains. During his evening walk on the path along the western pastures, his thoughts turned to the new foundation:

> I hope Bede can hold fast. But if the worst happened and he persists in wanting to go back to Prinknash, by then we could

---

[18] Quoted in Monchanin and Le Saux, *Ermites du Saccidânanda*, p. 182.

have formed someone who could take over from him. Meanwhile, let us allow our small group to find its way. I don't want a daughterhouse of Kurisumala, a carbon copy of the motherhouse; no. In the East, and especially in India, it is best to be flexible and let each foundation find its own identity, respecting the fundamental objectives of contemplative life. We can count on Father Bede's imagination as much as on his true vocation as a monk. I am only a little worried about the material questions: sometimes he has so little common sense! He moves in the stratosphere of ideas. . . . It is a good thing that Anugrah is with him. If he is given clear directions, he can be very effective.

He stopped at the very tip of the plateau, at the edge of the precipice and sat on the large black rock where it was his custom to go meditate, his legs crossed, back straight, hands open. The rain had stopped. His worried thoughts left him, he entrusted himself to the Holy Spirit and contemplated the red sky, the wavy line of blue mountains, until the gong for Vespers.

ENCOUNTER WITH HINDUISM

> Your continent is rich with a very ancient civilization. It is the cradle of several great religions, the homeland of a people who sought God with a constant desire, in profound meditation, in silence, in fervent hymns. This burning desire for God has rarely been expressed so well, in words so full of the spirit of Advent, as in your sacred books, many centuries before the coming of Christ: 'From the unreal, lead me to the real, from darkness lead me to the light, from death, lead me to immortality.' This is a prayer that is equally appropriate in our times. This should arise from every human heart.
>
> > (Talk of Paul VI to representatives of the
> > religions of India meeting at the Bombay
> > Eucharistic Congress, December 1964)

From its very beginning, Kurisumala was part of the local life–style. Inspired by Monchanin, Lebbe, and de Nobili, and limited by the real poverty of his resources, Francis organized the life of his monastery according to rural indian standards: buildings, furniture (or, rather, its absence), food, clothing; everything was made according to local patterns and with the most ordinary materials. He held firm despite the opposition, skepticism, and even pity met in certain circles in the Church, where many in charge remained convinced that they could not live and recruit young people here except by following the western model and resources, despite talks favoring indianization, aroused by Vatican II.

Over fifteen years, he had opened their eyes to the true India. These bishops, who flattered him when he arrived and whose 'seduction' he underwent, saw in him a providential Cistercian, an anchor who would allow them to be joined to the powerful western networks. What would his project have become if, duly sent by Scourmont, he had answered the invitations of a Msgr Feuga of Mysore? Providence was watching over him. 'In the end, even the oppositions contributed to a deepening of my ideal as much as to the strengthening of Kurisumala', he wrote to his family in 1970. The dazzling meeting with the Syriac rite was the decisive turning point in 1955, joining his research in the spirituality and liturgy of an eastern Church rooted in India for many centuries.

His trip to the Himalayas, various stays in hindu ashrams, and even dialogue finally established with Abhishiktananda led to a rapprochement with hindu practices during the 1970s. Contrary to what was happening in other institutions, where the indianization of christian worship was a fashion and a veneer on a westernized life, the introduction of hindu rites and monastic practices at Kurisumala was a prolongation, the refining of the ordinary where, except for the typewriter and pullovers, all the material was 'made in India'.

Naturalization, 6 August 1968

In spite of his choice and his will, Francis was still, administratively, a belgian citizen residing in India. He was waiting for the results of the inquiry that would allow him to become an authentic indian citizen. The good news reached him a few weeks after his return from Rishikesh. He went to Kottayam at once to swear an oath of fidelity to the indian constitution during a protocol where the local press was invited. On the photo we can see Francis, his head shaved but with a full beard, signing the certificate of naturalization that he put—in all modesty (!) in the

name of *Acharya*. This was done under the aegis of the communist authorities, because the last elections brought this party to power in Kerala.
The document was dated 6 August, the day on which Catholics and Orthodox celebrate the Transfiguration of Jesus on Mount Tabor. 'If this
was not a transfiguration', wrote Francis, 'this can at least be considered
a new birth, in the sense that it gives me a new identity. I have now been
adopted by my second homeland, which accepted me as a christian *sannyasi*, a full member of this young nation.'[19]

Dhyana *(Meditation)*

Every Monday, Francis hung a sign 'Day of silence' on the door of his
cell and retired to a small hermitage a few meters square at the edge of
the jungle. He spent the day there in silence. He felt the necessity of
keeping this interior peace, this quest for the presence of God that he
pursued as a priority during his sabbatical year and that risked being nibbled away by the worries of his responsibility and the constant demands
of more and more numerous visitors. At this time, for his personal meditation, he returned to the sermons of Saint Bernard on the Song of Songs
that had enchanted him during his novitiate. He also spent a great deal of
time, during those blessed days, taking up again the sacred scriptures of
India, choosing texts that harmonized with the Bible, from which the
prayer of the syriac churches was woven. This is an example of the 'Seed
of the Word', which evokes many accents of the biblical theology of the
Holy Spirit, from Genesis to the cosmic Psalms, culminating in Saint
John. Francis saw in it 'the seminal perceptions of the seer of the Atharva
Veda, who evoked the mysteries of Providence and the participation of
man in the divine life.'

> Adoration to You, when You come, when You go,
> when standing still or when You come to rest.
> O Breath of Life, You take care of all living creatures
> as a father takes care of his beloved son.
> You are supreme, all things revere You, Lord of all
> Lord of whatever breathes and of whatever breathes not.

---

[19] *Kurisumala, A Symposium of Ashram Life.* Edited by Francis Acharya.

O Breath of Life, You rule all life, all moving things.
You stay awake when others sleep and never fall down prone.
Turn not Your back on me.
None other than, I, shall You be.
As an embryo in the waters bursts into life,
so I, within myself, bind You, that I may live.

He preceded these vedic strophes with a few lines from Genesis and from the Book of Wisdom:

The Spirit of God hovered over the waters . . .
From the dust God formed Adam into a living creature,
breathing into his nostrils the breath of life.

(Gn 1:1 and 2:7)

God's Spirit fills the universe and holds all things together.

(Ws 1:7)

Francis translated these texts into English to include them in the *Prayer with the Harp of the Spirit*, of which he was preparing the second volume of the monastic offices for Sundays and feasts.

To those who protested this interreligious dialogue through Scripture, he opposed the encyclical of Paul VI on the missions, promulgated eleven years after his visit to Bombay: 'The non–christian religions of India have a literary history on the search for God that goes back thousands of years. They possess a heritage of profoundly religious texts that have taught many generations how to pray. These texts steeped in "Seeds of the Word" can be an authentic preparation to the Gospel. In the Lord's intention, the Church is universal. But when it takes root in different cultural milieus, the Church adopts different expressions.'

Satsang

Without *satsang*, no salvation.
And without the grace of God, no *satsang*
Satsang is the root of all good and source of all joy
The true fruit of all the spiritual exercises
          (*Valmiki*, vernacular version by Ramayana, 16th century)

Another innovation was the establishment of the *satsang*. Francis experienced this practice at Sivananda ashram and decided to include it in the daily life of Kurisumala. It was a very old custom of the hindu ashrams. The word meant in Sanskrit 'company of good men'. It is a public meeting, in a hall or outside, that gathered the community and guests for about an hour at the end of the day.

AUM![20]
Let the whole world be in joy!
Shanti, shanti, shanti [Peace, peace, peace]

These *mantras* (sacred formulas) repeated three times in Sanskrit, began the evening, followed by *bhajan* [religious songs] accompanied with the music of harmonium, *tabla*, and cymbals. The meeting continued with instruction by the presider or by talks about spiritual subjects or news events, given by *sannyasis* or visitors. Readings completed them.

In May 1969, they inaugurated the new *satsang* hall, which could hold fifty people and had been built across from the church. It was surrounded by guest rooms and sometimes served as a dormitory when there were many guests. At Kurisumala, the *satsang* began at 8 PM after Vespers and supper and was very much appreciated by the guests and young monks. Each one could exercise his talents as a musician or singer. The guests were sometimes invited to speak. For example, one could hear a palestinian monk talk about his life in a small byzantine monastery near Jerusalem, illustrated by slides. Another time, a belgian Dominican, professor of eastern languages at the University of Louvain, exhorted the novices to a deep study of Syriac. But interventions also could be about news or social experiences: a german man who found balance during a prolonged stay at Kurisumala a few years previously returned to visit and spoke one evening about the international school of Kodaïkanal (Tamil Nadu) where he was now professor, and who gave himself the mission of teaching these young people from the whole world to live in peace and respect their cultural and religious diversity.

---

[20] *AUM* is the essential mantra that contains all the others. It is the sacred syllable, made up of the three sounds A, U, M, ending with a nasal resonance. It is the Word, the audible and pronounceable symbol of the human word in its ascension to the absolute.

The prior's talk was always simple, usually improvised. He let his heart speak, often about the day's readings. He sometimes gave news of friends or faraway monasteries that the mail brought him that morning. When the bishop made one of his frequent visits, he presided over the *satsang* (he had the right to sit in the only armchair, which they went to fetch from the narthex) and delivered the messages from the Church of India or the news of the diocese.

The *satsang* was a joyous meeting, framed by certain rituals (oil lamps, incense, chants, invocations in Sanskrit, set places), but it left an impression of conviviality, spontaneity, and warm exchanges. After the final chant, the novices and women put the mats away, extinguished the lamps, and joined the monks in church for the last prayer, Compline. Then each member of the community, in order of seniority, beginning with the Acharya, went up to the lectern where the Bible was, gave it a reverential kiss and went to the icon of the day to get the *arati*. This is a gesture of the palms, which are exposed briefly to the light of the oil lamp before placing them on one's eyes, thus absorbing the divine light for one's soul before confronting the darkness of the night.

Bharatyia Puja[21] *(Indian–rite Mass)*

The 'Indian–style' Mass was the subject of a few confidential conferences and almost clandestine experimentation between 1964 and 1967. Father Le Saux practiced it in his own way, alone in the narrow garret of his himalayan hermitage, or out in the open, with his friend Panikkar, at the sources of the Ganges.[22] After Vatican II had authorized and even encouraged the adaptation of the liturgy to local culture, the Conference of Indian Bishops (CBCI) gave the green light to research, and then they worked openly: a national seminar organized in May 1969 in Bangalore gathered Le Saux, Panikkar, Francis, and a few Jesuits such as Tony De Mello and Jacques Scheuer, among pioneers of inculturation from all over India. They celebrated several Eucharists, integrating authentic forms of indian worship and art: decoration, costumes, seated position on the ground, low altar, flowers, and gestures but also hymns, prayers, music,

---

[21] *Puja* comes from the Sanskrit root *puj*: to venerate, adore. It is more linked to *bhakti*, affective devotional worship, than to the vedic worship. In the tamil region, *puja* is the common name for Mass.

[22] Le Saux, *Une messe aux sources du Gange*.

and even dances borrowed from indian culture. At Kurisumala, all that was put into practice on various occasions, and they continued to refine it numerous times. Certain excesses were abandoned, and it was only in 1972 that the Indian–rite Mass found its fixed form and was practiced every weekday at 6 AM, with the syriac *Qurbana* reserved for Sundays and feast days. The prayers, readings, and chants of the *bharatiya puja* were pronounced in the vernacular language, Malayalam. A booklet containing the english translation is available for foreign guests. But even without understanding the words, a sort of charm is at work through very tangible symbols (aspersion with water, offering of flowers, incense, music) and the contemplation of the carpets of multicolored flowers surrounding the *nilavilakku*, the large polished copper oil lamp surmounted by the Saint-Thomas cross of Christians and placed on the woven carpet. Three, sometimes four or five, priests concelebrate, assisted by two deacons, all seated on the floor, a simple stole over their ordinary saffron or white clothing. The ceremony lasts only half an hour and requires less preparation and putting away than *Qurbana*, which was fine with everyone because there was no lack of work.

The bishop was not enthusiastic. He would prefer an abridged *Qurbana*, which Francis considered a distortion and flatly refused: the entire grandiose *Qurbana* or nothing! For a long time, the indian catholic hierarchy, while letting them do this type of eucharistic celebration, reserved its official opinion on it. Only in 1988 did Francis publish and distribute, with prudence, in the form of a duplicated limited edition brochure, a complete description, abundantly annotated, of the indian Mass as it was practiced daily at Kurisumala and which was in the tradition of the anaphora of Saint James, the most eastern and the most venerated. The introduction of this text, based on conciliar references, was entitled *Bharatiya Puja. A Plea for the Approval of an Indian Rite Eucharist*. (This had not yet been achieved!):

> It is a completely indian and completely christian celebration which, by its unpretentious style is appropriate for a contemplative community on work days. . . . Rooted in the Bible and apostolic tradition, it adopts the richness of indian tradition and dons its garment. Water, light, incense, fire, flowers are signs of homage in the whole world. They are not only decorations. It is the language

of Creation, dear to the Indians for whom the cosmic dimension is preponderant. . . . We do not want to suggest that the *Bharatya Puja* be introduced into parishes, especially in Kerala. It will not be a question of this for a very long time. But in the ashrams where the simple lifestyle of India has been adopted, resisting the globalization that affects the Third World so negatively, it is in a place of honor.[23]

The Indian rite would be practiced little by little in all of India, first in the ashrams—notably at Shantivanam daily—but especially in the Latin–rite religious communities and the jesuit milieus. The parishes and places of popular pilgrimage remained attached to more 'missionary' traditions, and the eastern Churches to their own liturgy.

Dharmananda, The Hindu Swami

Francis had been friendly with Dharmananda right away, at their first meeting in Tiruvalla in 1956. 'We had a heart to heart conversation and started to get to know one another by the light of religion and spirituality.'[24] This was not surprising: both men were from the same generation and had a fairly similar youth. Dharmananda, born in Kerala to a fairly well–to–do family of hindu merchants, pursued his college studies and in the 1920s was employed by an english firm in Bombay, where he worked for a few years. He was a little more than twenty years old when he was called to the *sannyasa* and left his employers to join the 'novitiate of the indian roads' and the company of wandering saddhus, stopping in sanctuaries and places of pilgrimage. 'I chose', he said, 'the insecurity of the anonymous *sannyasi* rather than the constraints of a monastic congregation.' Later, after one of the masters he met conferred the saffron habit on him ritually at Vrindaban, a place traditionally associated with the birth of Lord Krishna, he returned to Kerala and joined the Ramakrishna mission of Tiruvalla. He became a sort of monk/preacher, sent here and there to explain the Vedanta and the doctrine of hindu dharma. He was a quiet, smiling, deeply benevolent man. He had a deep knowledge

---

[23] *Bharatiya Puja*: booklet published by Kurisumala Ashram.
[24] *Kurisumala, A Symposium of Ashram Life*. Edited by Francis Acharya.

of the sacred scriptures of India and interpreted them in a very open manner. Like Francis and his friends, he thought that religions were made to meet and to dialogue, not to be rivals or to fight.

Twelve years had passed since Francis and Bede had gone to see him when they were at Pushpagiri. Dharmananda heard the Tiruvalla gossip and thus followed from a distance the adventures of his christian friends on the mountain. In June 1968, he decided to visit them. He came unannounced, during the monsoon. He discovered Kurisumala, and it was a great joy, a revelation of the life he was dreaming about. He wrote, 'I arrived as a stranger, and they welcomed me as one of their own. This ashram is a response to a crying need in our present world. The dignity of work is associated with the grandeur of the spiritual quest.'[25] He stayed only forty–eight hours. He spoke to the community at *satsang*, and the very next day he returned to the plain where his commitments kept him another year. The following year, it was Francis who went to pester him. But the swami was on a conference tour. At his return, he found a letter that invited him to join the ashram. He decided quickly: a week later he moved there, in July 1969. He was enthusiastically admitted as an associate member of the community, which thus fulfilled one of its dearest goals: to establish a living daily dialogue with the hindu world.

Swamiji, as everyone called him at Kurisumala, fit in easily to the monastery's life. Promoted to assistant guestmaster, he attended to the guests' well–being with sensitivity. This was his portion of work. He participated in all the offices, without experiencing a need to change religions: he adapted to and was nourished by the readings, meditations, all the worship praising the Creator God, the Spirit of love who breathes on the world, his incarnation Jesus Christ.

Francis asked him to give courses on the Rig Veda, which he did with pleasure and competence: that was his profession. With his long white beard, his snowy white hair, and his brown eyes that reflected goodness, he exerted a great influence on all who came to the ashram.

When he felt his strength decline in 1976, he said goodbye to his adopted community and explained that he would finish his life as a hermit, at the foot of the Himalayas, on the banks of the Ganga–our–mother, as every good Hindu desired. He went on foot, without baggage. He

---

[25] *Ibid.*

would not reach Rishikesh. At Bhopal, in the middle of India, in a temple where he had stopped to pray, he died of cardiac arrest.

For Francis–Acharya, such an experience of total, concrete sharing was more important than the conferences and seminars on the meeting of religions. The inhibitions, prejudices, and worries that each one had towards the other's religion dissolved in the personal relationship, in the friendship of daily company.

India Idealized

Francis saw in Dharmananda the personification, the accomplishment of those values of eastern spirituality that he so admired. In his enthusiasm, he tended to oppose them in a sometimes caricatured way to the 'rigid and heavy formalism of the West',[26] forgetting that he was himself a product of it, no doubt a deviant and fringe product, but formed all the same by this constraining monastic discipline to which he remained attached for his own novices. He did not willingly allow them to run around the roads of India or to have just anyone give them the saffron robe on the banks of a river, even a holy river. And he no doubt had good reason because, if Dharmananda and many of his confrères were true seekers of God, there also existed among begging saddhus—Le Saux, who lived with them closely agreed on this point—drifters and imposters. Here we touch one of the contradictions that we find with all the pioneers of inculturation: following the example of Monchanin, who while giving himself to India without reserve called himself a 'Greek' to the end and was always wanting french literature, Francis, while criticizing the West, remained a Cistercian and a Fleming, concerned about effectiveness and discipline.

During the 1970s, his talk on the rejection of the hierarchical and canonical system of the Catholic Church would be the harshest, leaning on this alternative model of the 'free and non–institutionalized spirituality of the hindu *sannyasi*'. We cannot fail to see in this a convergence with the large movement of questioning authority that followed May 1968 and Vatican II. At Kurisumala also, Martin Buber, Karl Rahner, and Hans Küng were read. At the same time in the West, the hippie movement caused an extraordinary infatuation with India. Many young people went

---

[26] *Ibid.*

on 'the road to Katmandu' and found themselves in Goa or Benares smoking marijuana. However, this attraction for an India of their dreams, this new avatar of the *Drang nach Osten* led some of them to an authentic spiritual seeking.

These years were when Achille, formerly a ward of the Public Assistance in Paris, landed in Kurisumala completely 'crazy'. He moved there and in time, a true monastic charism appeared in him. After an episode of wandering, he returned to his studies and became the director of the Alliance Française in Bombay.

Two young Belgians arrived one December evening in a Citroën '*deux-chevaux*'. They had crossed Europe, Turkey, and Afghanistan to reach India through the Khyber Pass, intending to cross it from north to south.

American hippies were welcomed, sometimes for stays of several months. One of them would later enter a cistercian monastery in the United States. But many others were content to 'reject the system', to advocate the soft ideology of peace and love where emotions are above reason: 'Make love, not war; enjoy without hindrance', including in artificial paradises. Psychedelic music, fringed clothing, astrology, yoga, and a varnish of mixed eastern religions are the main brushstrokes of this picture. At Kurisumala, the monks were led to moderate certain excesses and even to exclude certain guests. At Shantivanam they found this type of pilgrim in great numbers at that time.

Francis, who became indianized in a more austere and studious manner, outside all fashion, earned an ambiguous popularity among Europeans and Americans. As he used to say, success can be more dangerous for the soul than trials.

CONGRESS IN BANGKOK

We come here, not to civilize, not to conquer, not to convert but to live. We hope to discover more deeply what we are, and grow more deeply in our monasticism by contacts that we will make here with representatives of a tradition different from our own.
(Dom Rembert Weakland, Abbot Primate of the Benedictines
Bangkok Congress, Opening talk)

The conference room was well–lit, cooled by fans, equipped with movable blinds and a modern and discreet sound system. Monks and nuns were clothed in white or black cotton robes, against which the bishops' purple cinctures stood out, as well as the saffron shawls of Bede Griffiths and Francis, who was beside Thomas Merton, the american Trappist and already a well–known author[27] who wore the strict cistercian habit: black scapular and leather belt. Suddenly everyone stood up to mark the solemnity of the event and show respect to the eminent visitor who had just entered: the supreme patriarch of thai Buddhists. Accompanied by three of his monks, he took his place on the little throne set up for him. It was with emotion that the Primate of the christian monks of the West, Dom Rembert Weakland, greeted him with the words usually reserved for the roman pontiff: 'Your Holiness.' The patriarch, an elderly ascetic, smiled as he accepted the parchment and books brought to him by two abbots, an Australian and a Vietnamese. He answered in Thai with a message of gratitude and expressed the desire to see all the religions collaborate in service of peace, rightness of thought, and perseverance in good. Francis' and his neighbor's attentive and serious glances betrayed a deep joy, that of seeing the Catholic Church recognize the value of asiatic religions and non–christian monasticism in a public and official way.

The monastic congress of Bangkok, the first of its kind, was conceived by AIM at the request of the asian superiors. After the enthusiastic echoes of the pan–african meeting held at Bouake in 1965, they had wanted to have a similar colloquium organized for their 'region'. A Red Cross estate thirty kilometers from Bangkok was chosen. The place was full of charm: bamboo groves, water ponds, individual bungalows to lodge those attending the congress, and a large modern building, in 1950s style for the conferences, working meetings, and meals. About sixty monks and nuns met, from every corner of the continent: China, Japan, Korea, Vietnam, India, Indonesia, and Australia. A few experts on oriental cultures, including several Jesuits, were invited, westerners representing founding houses, and, of course, all of AIM's french personnel.

---

[27] Thomas Merton had known celebrity from his first autobiographical work that recounted his turbulent youth and conversion (*The Seven Storey Mountain*). He entered the trappist abbey of Gethsemani in the U.S.A. and published several books on the contemplative life. One of his last works, *Zen and the Birds of Appetite* (1968), followed by *The Asian Journal* (pub. 1973), gave an account of his trip to Japan, Tibet, and India just before he died.

Most of them had never met the others, but they knew of the existence of the monasteries and the names of their superiors through periodicals, information bulletins, and General Chapter reports. When Sister
Pia Valeri, secretary of the AIM, was introduced to Father Odo Haas,
german superior of the benedictine abbey of Waekwan in Korea, she
found a young man barely thirty–five years old, with an angelic face lit
up by light blue eyes, and she cried out with her customary spontaneity:
'Oh, Father, I imagined you old, with a long white beard!'

'Bangkok 68' was a daring enterprise in many respects. It was not
yet in monastic customs at that time to ignite free speech, critical exchanges on daily life, recruitment, formation, and the meaning of the
contemplative vocation in the modern world. Neither was it customary to
gather men and women, religious of different orders in open dialogue in
a 'neutral' place that was not a catholic house. The post–conciliar context, with the winds of change and the unanimous sentiment that everything could be reexamined, favored the impression of renewal, or even
revolution. A joyous excitement filled the exchanges, even more so
when, after returning from a walk, a group recounted that they had been
welcomed in the neighboring pagoda where there lived a community of
buddhist monks. Each day, a few would go there, thrilled to see how
much their thai brothers' lives resembled their own. They came back
with their arms full of flowers and cakes. For some it was a discovery
that outside Christianity there was an ancient, serious, numerous and organized monasticism.

They also experienced moments of tension, because those attending
the congress did not necessarily have the same vision of their mission. A
rift appeared between proponents of a monastic life based on the western
model and partisans of small foundations very integrated in the local culture, the approach defended by Dom Leclercq, the Jesuits, and, needless
to say, Mahieu and Griffiths. Some japanese nuns were shocked by the
way their many–storied brick houses and neo–gothic cathedrals were
caricatured. For Europeans who, after having benefited from a good education and a powerful motherhouse, left everything to go to the East and
its mystery, it was difficult to understand that the young asiatic recruits
saw the christian religious life as a social promotion and saw access to
western education as 'progress' compared to their culture of origin. All
the more so because, until 1965, those who came from non–christian milieus—and they were more numerous in the Far East than in India—were

told that their parents' religion and culture was pagan, diabolical, to be resolutely rejected in order to remain faithful to their baptism. As one of the participants quoted Dom André Louf: 'We can't reproach someone for being rich. Poverty is essentially a grace. To choose poverty is the act of a rich person.'

During a boat ride on the Chao Phraya river, Francis found himself at the back of the boat with Sister Pia, who questioned him on his presence in India and the route that had led him to Kerala. She herself had returned from Africa a short time before. They were both fifty–seven years old and for the last thirty years had lived many joyful and painful experiences. Right away this drew them to listen to each other sympathetically. Francis confided in his benedictine sister: 'For a long time, I was seeking something; I did not know exactly what, but it was something I was not finding in Europe. When I arrived in India, very quickly it was like a certitude: I was where I had to go, I had found my way, my vocation.'

Thomas Merton was no doubt the star of the Congress. The television cameras always converged towards him. In an unforeseen way, he would amplify considerably the media's repercussion of this gathering. The second day, he gave a talk on 'Marxism and monastic life', clarifying that he was not talking about the Marxism in the USSR or China, but the Marxism he knew well and which was growing on American campuses, inspired by Herbert Marcuse. His talk detained the congress attendees, but looking at his watch, he delayed the questions to the evening session and ended with these words: 'It is time for me to disappear.' After lunch, he retired to his bungalow, telling his neighbor he intended to take a siesta. He was found around 3 PM lying on the bathroom tiles, a fan still plugged in lying across his body, evidently electrocuted.

The emotion was great. A funeral wake was improvised, the monks recited psalms and the rosary in different languages, while in the bungalow where this had happened, the thai personnel made a hole in the ceiling to let the demons escape. The civil authorities were alerted. In the middle of the night an american army helicopter came to take away the body. The next day, after a requiem Mass, the conferences continued according to the schedule. This brutal departure left an impression of mystery, of sign, even of grace, some said. Dom Marie de Floris observed, 'They continued and finished their work with redoubled fervor and in a charity that was a sign for them that the Lord had passed by.'

The six Trappists present for the congress wrote a collective letter to the abbot of Gethsemani in the U.S.A., telling him about the exact circumstances of his death and expressing their admiration for the departed and their certitude that he had reached his ultimate goal. Francis signed it: 'Dom Marie-Francis Acharya OCSO, India.'

Francis was one of the twelve persons who were asked to give a talk. His was on monastic formation in an asian context. From the beginning he spoke about Vatican II and the 'adapted renovation' of life and formation that must flow from it, enlightened by hindu monastic traditions. His talk revealed the partisan state of mind, still very polemical, that was his in 1968: all that is eastern, monastically speaking, is better than what is western. Hindu monasticism must not only be recognized as valid, it also should serve as our model. In India, each christian monk should visit a hindu ashram, have a meditative knowledge of the *Upanishads* and the Gita. We can see there a sort of precursor's excessive zeal that would be transformed later. Singling out canon law in passing, he insisted—and this was the high point of his talk—on spiritual realization, what is called *metanoia* in Greek. This theme was dear to him, and he would rework it during his whole life: spiritual conversion, a call to every Christian but a requirement for the monk, which implies a constant struggle against his nature, his instincts, his selfishness, his pride; a never–completed abandoning of the 'diabolical' or simply animal part of himself. A sort of *kenosis* like Christ's: as he came down to us by renouncing his divine privileges, we can go to him by abandoning the 'old man' in us. *Admirabile commercium!*[28] Francis concluded.

Sister Pia and Dom Marie de Floris, accompanied by Father Tholens from Holland, missed his talk to go to the neighboring pagoda. It was their only time!—they excused themselves. But he was very disappointed and reproached them strongly when he saw them at lunch. Did he want his ideas and success to be relayed to Belgium, to Scourmont?

The Bangkok meeting opened a dialogue on thorny and crucial questions: inculturation, poverty, and relationships with other religions. For Francis, it was the official consecration of the way he opened ten years earlier, in spite of the skepticism or hostility of the religious authorities

---

[28] *Admirabile commercium!* [wonderful exchange!] is an exclamation attributed to Saint Thomas Aquinas about the mystery of the incarnation. It is used in the Christmas liturgy of the Roman Church.

of the time. The message of encouragement from the pope, received the first day, the beginning of fraternization with the buddhist patriarch, and, of course, Thomas Merton's accidental death would be relayed by the televisions of the whole world. It was a turning point that marked for christian monasticism in Asia the beginning of a policy of openness to other religions. For Francis, it was international recognition that would lead to invitations, articles in the media, and conference tours in Europe and America. But he returned to Kurisumala disappointed. Many talks, but few concrete projects; little real will to abandon the material comfort and intellectual habits of the West.

THE COMMUNITY AT THE BEGINNING OF THE 1970S

The monks of Kurisumala with their long beards leave an impression of deep peace that is reflected on their faces. I was able to speak with several of them, whom I admired. Their main preoccupation is to maintain awareness of the presence of the Holy Trinity as much as possible.

(Dom Jean Leclercq OSB, 1967)

After the hard years of moving in, Francis began a phase of consolidation and also exporting a work that had proven itself and appeared to be more and more a good example of what was expected from post–conciliar monasticism in so–called 'mission lands'. The difficulty would be to balance the internal demands (formation of young people, government and spiritual leadership of the community, hospitality towards ever more numerous guests) and the external requests (participating in congresses and seminars, giving retreats, conferences and other workshops which grew in popularity in christian circles even in India).

It was a good thing that in 1969 the farm was doing well. Under the direction of Sylvester, helped by Ishananda, it was working to capacity, filling not only the monastery's daily needs but also those of the hired agricultural workers and about a hundred associated families. Their small houses, flanked by a wooden barn, were scattered on the once–deserted neighboring hillsides. Despite persistent epidemics that would continue to decimate the herd and tornadoes that would uproot many trees, the ashram would overcome these trials by its own strength—with God's help—and would continue to assist its neighbors in more precarious situations.

The community also experienced storms. It had passed the heroic times where the struggle for survival in an often hostile nature absorbed all its energy. It was growing, had structured itself, the elders became more assured, and the new postulants were more demanding. The waves that caused a great movement of protest and 'liberation' in America and Europe were felt all the way to Asia.

The candidates came in great numbers, but many had to be refused and others left of their own accord after a trial period, sometimes after several years. These departures, especially when they were gifted, generous young people, on whom Francis founded his hope—'a novice after my own heart' he wrote about one of them—caused him real pain. At the same time, the installation of Bede Griffiths in Shantivanam relaxed the atmosphere. 'The community is experiencing a new springtime. There is more harmony, more cooperation,' Francis wrote to his sister.

The perfecting of the 'Indian rite' for the Mass (*Bharatyia Puja*), instituted in an almost clandestine way because of the opposition of the syrian bishops, was a creative research project in which the whole community participated. The year 1969 was a year of grace, of euphoria: there were seven novices, individual cells were built for the *brahmacharis*, the *satsang* and the new guesthouse were inaugurated, and the hindu *swami* joined the community.

In April, Amy Henn came to visit her childhood friend. She had never traveled except in Belgium, to go visit Francis in Scourmont or visit the Mahieu family in Brussels. An unexpected inheritance allowed her to purchase a plane ticket from London to Bombay to Cochin. 'Little John' went to meet her at the airport. 'Great joy at this visit! I had often invited her but I didn't believe she would come. It's very brave of her!' Unfortunately, after a few days, Amy, frightened when a nocturnal animal burst into her room—she was staying in the house of Dr Sina, near the hospital—panicked and shortened her stay. For a city dweller over sixty years old, the night is very dark in Kurisumala, and the jackals could be heard. Amy took risks to see 'John' again, the great man in her life, and she had a nervous breakdown.

But tensions reappeared in the community. At the beginning of Lent, Francis wrote to Bede. His letter expressed a voluntarist resolution for reconciliation but especially revealed his irritation.

Forgive me my lack of follow–up since the foundation of Shantivanam. This was due to two reasons: I did not want to interfere but let you find your own way, your own identity as an ashram. The second reason is that I do not feel that I am a very good teammate for you right now. It has been so for several years, and this is not without its lot of frustrations. I had hoped that the foundation of Shantivanam would release this tension and would permit me to find serenity again. This is not the case. In fact, wherever I go, to Bangkok, Delhi, Bombay, Calcutta and of course Kottayam or Tiruvalla, I am forced to listen to people who seem to know everything about the foundation of Shantivanam. A toned–down version of its history appeared in the *Examiner*.[29] I should not worry about all this and, in fact, I really don't have time to spend on this kind of rumination. But it dries up my inspiration about Shantivanam. And so, while asking your forgiveness if I have hurt you, I ask you also to acknowledge your part in these problems. . . . Time will no doubt smooth out the road.

Later, Brother Paul– the one who in 1967 had opposed Francis and sought Bede's alliance to establish constitutions—protested the decision to admit Ishananda to investiture, alleging that procedure had not been respected. The bishop was called in to arbitrate, and finally Brother Paul, disowned and furious, went to Shantivanam without saying goodbye. After a few months he would be excluded from Shantivanam as a troublemaker.

The *brahmacharya diksha* [investiture with the white habit] of Ishananda—a solid vocation, tireless worker, very educated—gathered everyone in joy and fervor. The new monk's large family was present, and more than a hundred meals were served. Sylvester and Philipose were the first to be admitted to the priesthood, after a completely local formation. Their ordination on 19 February 1970, was also the occasion of a colorful ceremony and one of those large family gatherings dear to the Indians.

Tensions remained however, and concerned the sharing of power, as they often do. Should a community be governed 'democratically'? A big question. At Kurisumala, the structures of consultation and decision were quite light. There was a government body, a sort of board presided over

---

[29] The *Examiner*: one of Bombay's main daily newspapers, to which Bede Griffiths regularly sent articles.

by the prior, with the elders as members: Sylvester its secretary, Philipose the treasurer, and Mariadas a member. A *synaxis* or community assembly was called four or five times a year, according to need. Each summer the financial situation was communicated to the community assembly. During Francis' absence, when he went on sabbatical, Bede had gathered the chapter more often. Was it his natural permissiveness that caused him to yield to demands? Or did he enjoy these meetings, soon transformed into chats? Francis considered them rather as a waste of time, a source of squabbles or discussions that cause more division than unity. Unity in prayer and work, dissensions in meetings to discuss. That was his deep conviction. Negotiation and compromise were not his strong points. He reflected, prayed, decided, and 'let those who love me follow me!'

Meanwhile, the situation in Shantivanam deteriorated. The two novices chosen by Bede returned to Kurisumala, where Anugrah returned to his service of secretary/typist with pleasure. Ajit, drifting, left the monastic life to marry. Bede remained alone with Stephen, a sort of unpredictable associate who, after having praised Bede to the skies, turned against him and spread malicious insinuations that would make their way to the local bishop. Bede was very depressed. 'The Shantivanam experience seems to be still–born', he wrote to his friends who had invited him to come to England to rest, an invitation that he accepted with relief. However, he returned to India after a few months. He loved the banks of the Kaveri and had not lost all hope of living there.

At Kurisumala, one of the young professed, Amaldas, a yoga expert, asked to experience the free and solitary eremetical life. How could what was given as an example by the syrian Fathers be refused? So Francis permitted the young monk to live alone in the nearby forest. After a month, he returned: it was too hard. But he balked at bending to common life and schedules; he asked for liberties: participate in work and Mass in the morning and then be alone to meditate until the next day. There, the prior refused. There was no way each one would make his own individual schedule, even if it was to meditate! Common prayer was the essence, the strength of the cenobitical life. Christudas, another young man, had a hard time accepting that he had been refused access to the priesthood and had been asked to wait a year for his profession. The two dissatisfied men packed their bags and went to join Bede, who conferred the *sannyasa* on Christudas immediately and sent him to the seminary to prepare for ordination. With those two men, Bede would revive Shantivanam.

Alina, the italian collaborator of Hilde Sina, politically tending to follow Gramsci,[30] met Francis on the road. As he told her about the two young people running away to Shantivanam, a little grieved, she answered, 'Soon, there will be no one left here! They will all go to Bede. Deep down, you're an authoritarian patriarch, a real land owner.'

These events, we may be sure, did not facilitate reconciliation between Francis and Bede. We will see later what came of them. The evolution of Kurisumala, however, did not depend only on this difference, which was minor. Formation was a large problem. It was Bede's most useful function. In his very pure English he taught philosophy and theology. Francis had always reserved specifically monastic formation for himself: the syrian Fathers, the Rule of Saint Benedict, Saint Bernard, and spirituality. For the rest, from this time on, he called upon external professors, mainly Jesuits: Father Lobo, Father Cherian, Father De Smet, and always his old friend Hambye. They came from Poona or Kurseong, in turn, to give forty–hour course modules at the rate of three hours per day for two weeks. A precious recruit joined the community: Father Varkey, a forty–year–old indian Jesuit who became a monk and was immediately put in charge of the english course. The hindu swami taught the exegesis of the Bhagavat–Gita. The bishop approved this system for monastic formation, but he was reticent when it was a question of ordaining someone to the priesthood, for which he judged that a stay at the seminary was required. Francis accepted once, and the novice did not return, sucked up by the pastoral company and the world. The prior no longer let them go. He would obtain four ordinations: Sylvester and Philipose in 1970, Yeshudas and Ishananda in 1972, which would be sufficient for the sacramental and liturgical service to the community. In the spirit of eastern monasticism, Francis wanted to dissociate the monastic commitment from the priesthood: they are two different vocations. The best monk is not necessarily one who is a priest. He had to struggle against the prestige and social promotion associated with the priesthood in the culture of Kerala, which made renunciation of it very difficult to accept.

---

[30] Antonio Gramsci (1891–1937) was an italian revolutionary, co–founder of the communist party in that country. Arrested in 1926, he continued his work of marxist political theory in prison, where he died.

The Kurisumala community grew, revitalized and unified by Francis' energy, authority, and faith. Crises troubled it, when the purely human passions surfaced again, sweeping the Spirit's light breath.

At the beginning, we feel that we are the protagonists and agents of our history. We know what we want and we try to realize it.

But little by little our *logismoi*, our demons, our passionate thoughts spring up again. The hidden tensions manifest themselves, we try to impose our own opinion, the desire for power causes rivalries. Small jealousies deform the truth, impatience wants everything right away, suspicion prevents us from facing each other. Some, unconscious of or on the fringe of this agitation, pray, praise and give thanks and ask the Lord of history for help.

And their prayer is heard. The omnipresent Spirit manifests his action in many ways. He speaks to us daily and in the liturgy nourishes us with the body and blood of the Risen One. We succeed in what we thought was lost. Forgiveness heals wounds, hope illumines hearts, a sense of humor allows us to put problems into perspective. We recognize that we are brothers and sisters with one common Father. And to tell the truth, this does not just happen to us: the Holy Spirit works and we perspire.'

(Extracts from the homily by Dom Bernardo Olivera,
Abbot General of the Cistercians, at the closing Mass
of the Lourdes General Chapter, 1999)

A SECOND FOUNDATION: THIRUMALAI

June 1971. Francis left the ashram, alone, before dawn. His black umbrella did not protect him much from the torrential rain as he made his way down to the bus stop, barefoot in the muddy water that streamed in places across the potholed road. He took the first bus to Kottayam and went to visit the syrian Carmelites. They exclaimed, 'Father Acharya, you are soaking wet! Would you like a little coffee?' 'Yes, thank you,' he replied. They brought him a cup of the sweet coffee with milk that they drank in Kerala, with a banana and an assortment of homemade cookies. 'Would you like us to drive you to town in the jeep?' the sisters asked. Francis explained, 'Thank you, you are very kind, but I am only passing by. I am going to Cape Comorin, to see Father James. It is time, the bus leaves at eight thirty. See you soon!'

The bus followed the coast road bordered with coconut trees reflected in the lagoons. The rain had stopped, the clouds parted and the square–sailed dugout canoes glided like shadows on the pink horizon. Francis gave thanks for the beauty of Creation. But his thoughts turned back to worries. The monastery's farm had been in a state of permanent alert for three months. Dozens of cows and heifers had died. The epidemic of foot–and–mouth disease continued its ravages, despite all their efforts. The men were exhausted, the resources were diminishing. Every day, each animal's tongue and feet were disinfected. They built a sanitary barn in haste, eight hundred meters from the other buildings, to isolate the infected animals. Nothing helped. A catastrophe. And that was the time Jacques Tombeur chose to tell him that Msgr Arokyassanny, the bishop of Kottar, offered Kurisumala a second mountain: Thirumalai. Less spectacular than the first, more modest, it is rather a rocky hill in the middle of rice paddies. The bishop and Father James had the firm hope of seeing a group of monks move there. Francis hesitated. The community had twenty–two members, of whom some were still in their time of probation. As for the finances, if this epidemic continued, it would soon mean ruin. And Shantivanam still needed to be supported. Was this the right time to accept an additional burden?

The bus stopped in the country, at a crossroad congested with carts pulled by cattle with humps. Jacques was there, making a sign to him. At some distance, the bishop's chauffeur, leaning on the hood of an old white Ambassador took a last drag on his cigarette before throwing it away. Francis got down the bus steps, almost tripped, and repressed a grimace of pain. Jacques grabbed him by the elbow. The two men embraced. 'Are you all right, Francis? Did you hurt yourself?' 'No, no, it's nothing.' Francis replied. 'My right leg plays tricks on me sometimes. These ten hours on the bus stiffen it. Where are you taking me in this magnificent limousine? To see the property?' Jacques explained, 'I'm afraid that it's too late to do that today: darkness is falling. Let us return his car to the bishop and visit him. Then I will take you to Parakunnu where you can freshen up and rest. Tomorrow morning after Mass, we will go to see Thirumala. I won't tell you any more. It's a surprise!' 'Very well,' said Francis; 'I am following you.'

Jacques Tombeur—whom we call Father James here—was an old acquaintance. He spent his youth in Brussels in the same neighborhood, the same college, the same scout troop as Francis and even was one of his cubs. He went to India as a Samist in 1950—the second after Monchanin —and he was in close communication with the hermits of Saccidananda ashram. It was he who brought them in contact with Father Mahieu in 1953. Faithful to his congregation's ideal, he placed himself at the service of a local bishop, the bishop of Kottar, at the very southern point of India, in tamil land. He served several parishes, traveling from one village to the other by motorcycle, and developed social services: dispensaries, schools, and cooperatives.[31] In his small rectory after supper, he spoke to Francis about his hopes, his project of collaboration:

> The Christians in this region are very poor. They belong to the poorest classes: they climb coconut trees, they fish. It would be very good to have a small monastery in the diocese. The priests, religious, teachers, and social workers need a spiritual center to catch their breath, to find the breath of the Spirit again. And this could be a place for interreligious dialogue: the protestant Salvationists are very active here, and the Hindus from the Ramakrishna mission are quite open. Finally, the parishes' social work would be completed by a center for agricultural development where the experience acquired at Kurisumala could be shared. What do you think?

Francis was non–committal. 'I think like you, my dear friend, but I do not know if we are ready. We need to see the property, consult the community, reflect, pray.'

The next morning, the two men walked around the sixty–five acres that the bishop, very interested in the project, proposed to Francis. They left the rickshaw near a small chapel painted in bright colors, a short distance from the main road. Father James pointed: 'It's Holy Cross chapel.' 'The cross above the door is unusual: a cross with a double bar,' Francis observed. 'Yes, it is characteristic of the old latin churches here. It must be from the sixteenth century!'

---

[31] Tombeur, *Led by God's Hand.*

Following their road in silence, they arrived at the rocky hill where a packed earth road wound. 'It goes up, one would think we are in Kurisumala!' Francis murmured, trying to master his slight limp. 'In fact,' noted Father James, 'this hill is the very southern point of the western Ghats. It is the last high place before Cape Comorin.' How far away is the Cape?' Francis queried. 'About twenty miles. But in the west, the Arabian Sea is only five miles away.'

On the side of the hill, they stopped in front of a large, dilapidated brick building. 'It's an old farm, abandoned for many years. The walls are solid, the roof and the interior need to be repaired and perhaps a few windows added', James explained. 'This would not be a very large investment. There are local workers. You could make the plans to suit you, obviously. With a few acres of coconut trees and a vegetable garden, a small community's subsistence can be ensured'. He paused before continuing. 'The only problem is water. To tell you the truth, that is why we could purchase all this for a very small price.' 'What do you mean?' asked Francis. 'I can see nothing but water all around!' 'That is irrigation water for the paddies.' James explained. 'It is not drinking water. The well is dry. It would need to be dug deeper.'

Before entering the old farm building, Francis turned around. In the west, the mountain rose gradually with its brown and purple slopes, covered with jungle in places. At their feet the light green of rice paddies spread, and in the east a long row of tall coconut trees were reflected in the water. A light and constant breeze cooled the air, clouds moved rapidly in the pale sky. He later recorded in his diary, 'The site is so beautiful, the offer so pressing, they are leaving us very free. It would be a shame not to accept. However, we are overwhelmed by the immensity of the task. We are not ready to make this new seed grow. Only the Lord can do this' (Diary 1971).

When Francis left Father James at noon, he had decided to convince the community to 'accept in faith', beginning by sending two experienced brothers, Mariadas and Yeshudas, for example. That year, he would travel there six times. In July, he brought Mariadas along, with the mission of directing the construction work. On 6 August of the following year, the Feast of the Transfiguration, the whole community, augmented by Father Cherian sj, temporary professor of Holy Scripture, piled into a rented van for the foundation ceremony. Mariadas organized everything there. Father James received the foundation cross from Francis and in return he placed a garland of jasmine around his neck. The new monastery was placed under the sign of the Transfiguration of Jesus on Mount Tabor. Thirumalai means Holy Mountain. After Mass, a meal was given to the poor, according to the hindu custom of prasad. Then the community ate in silence in the hastily renovated buildings. They visited the site: a small chapel, six cells, of which two were in the former rice straw storeroom—and a kitchen had been built in the main building. The walls had been given a fresh coat of paint and windows added so that each cell opened to the sky. Yeshudas would stay to be a team with Mariadas, whom Francis planned to have ordained priest by the very obliging local latin bishop. That afternoon, the whole group went on a 'pilgrimage'—the monks' excursions were always called by this name—to Cape Comorin, where Gandhi's statue covered with flowers and surrounded by souvenir shops dominated the three seas. After ten hours in the van during the night: it was the time for Vigils when the monks got out in Kurisumala, 'exhausted but happy', according to a formula dear to their superior.

When Francis returned in October to encourage his monks, he noted, 'My visits to Thirumalai give me great joy. The joy that arises naturally from being able to set down the daily burden for a few days, but especially this joy of new beginnings, as we knew them during the first years in Kurisumala, in simplicity, poverty, absolute confidence in Divine Providence. The old building took on a new appearance and a new interior structure. As for the well, it is not yet deep enough. During the dry season, we will have to bring a motor drill. There is much to be done for the spiritual life also. It is heartening to see the two brothers say together, faithfully, the prayers of the hours in the english breviary adopted after the Council. As for the liturgy, the bishop would like the ashram to be a center of experimentation in the Indian rite. We have to start by learning Tamil! And by building a real community, not just between the brothers but with the neighbors who are so poor' (Diary, 1971).

A few months later, a postulant came: he was sent to Kurisumala for his novitiate before joining the group in Thirumalai. At the end of 1972, Mariadas was ordained a priest in Latin by the bishop of Kottar, without having passed the seminary exams as the syrian bishop required. This 'subversion' was not appreciated at Tiruvalla and fueled the controversy on the formation of monk/priests.

The confidence Francis placed in Divine Providence to finance the foundations he started was upheld several times by unexpected gifts.

Without mentioning Scourmont, his family, and his personal friends, from whom he naturally hoped for help in times of destitution, a few mysterious donors appeared at the right time, as if sent by french itself. The most extraordinary was no doubt this one: when the farm was experiencing difficulties and the Thirumalai building had more than emptied the coffers, an official document from a notary arrived from England. Francis discovered, intrigued, that he was designated by a certain Frank Finn Collar—of whom he had never heard—as the heir of half his fortune, the other half going to a 'Cheshire Home'.[32] He examined the papers, reread them several times, and counted the zeros to be sure that he was not dreaming. No, this was not a joke. Soon his account received the promised 30,000 sterling pounds. Amy, charged with making discreet enquiries in Norfolk, could not elucidate the mystery. Francis never would know why Frank Finn Collar chose him. A few years later, a second inheritance fell from the sky. This time it was not a stranger: Miss Emmeline Stuart, a pious single lady, had made retreats at Caldey in 1953, when Jean had been master of novices there, and had corresponded with him since his departure for India. She had a particular affection for the Trappists, because she divided her goods between Kurisumala and a monastery of english Trappistines.

In January 1972, the community celebrated its prior's sixtieth birthday with flowers and song: in India, it is a particularly important birthday that marks maturity, the summit of life. For this occasion, Francis published a collection of articles in English illustrated with photos, which gave a fairly complete picture of Kurisumala's history and activities.[33] Of course he sent a copy to Scourmont and had the pleasure of finding a review of it a few months later in the Collectanea Cisterciensia, from the pen of his old colleague Maur Standaert:

> In this album, with many photos, there are almost fifty short contributions: from Cardinal Pignedoli, Monsignor Fernandez, Father Hambye SJ, Dom Leclercq OSB, R. Panikkar, Dom Bede Griffiths, co–founder of the ashram, Swami Darmananda, a hindu monk residing at Kurisumala for several years, and others.

---

[32] 'Cheshire Home' was a foundation by Captain Cheshire, an english observer in the american plane that launched the atomic bomb on Hiroshima. Converted to Catholicism, he spent the rest of his life caring for physically handicapped people.

[33] *Kurisumala, a symposium of ashram life*, ed. Francis Acharya.

The most numerous and certainly the most interesting pages are by Father Francis Acharya himself: his itinerary from Scourmont until his arrival in India at Father Monchanin's then Kurisumala, his contacts with the western 'spiritual seekers' in India, as well as a reflection on contemplation, the incarnation, vedic meditation, the Jesus prayer, the monastic experience at Kurisumala. . . . It goes without saying that such an album is of the 'homage and praise' literary genre. But they did not go overboard. The fact is that the work accomplished is remarkable and this ashram seems to be on the right path to an authentic monastic, christian and indian realization, with its successful integration in the Syro–Malankar rite.

GHEETA BHAVAN

The little girl appeared in the frame of the open door, as she did every morning. She wore an electric blue dress, with a black and white flounce. Her long hair was braided in the back. She stood there saying nothing, watching the christian swami sitting on his bed, his legs stretched out, writing on a sort of stand placed on the mattress. When Francis noticed her presence, he put his pen down and said hello—*Namaste!*—his hands joined and head bent. The little girl's black eyes shone, she smiled and greeted him in turn, gravely, then ran away.

She was the eldest of the five children of the Ayur–Veda doctor by whom Francis was being treated since November 1974 in his house called *Gheeta Bhavan* [the house of the *Bhagavad Gita*] in Kottayam.

The doctor was a Hindu, formerly a pharmacist who turned towards traditional medicine in which he acquired a great reputation and large clientele. In his thirties, tall, jovial, a bit boastful, he developed a friendship with this christian *sannyasi* who trusted him.

How do you feel this morning, Swami Francis?
Well, very well. Your generous hospitality is giving me a complete
    rest. But this leg still refuses to serve. One would think it had
    died.
And the pain?
It's still there. Sometimes it is very bad, sometimes it lessens.

Turn on your side. . . . (the doctor opened his scented vials and poured the oil on his large brown hands.) I told you, it will not be fast. The joint is inflamed and the tissues have degenerated. I am afraid you asked too much of your body. Moderation, Swami.

While talking, he slowly massaged the sick joints.

When do you think I will be able to walk again, Doctor?
Hard to say. Two months, three months? You will walk again, I promise.
But I have to be back at the ashram for Christmas! And I have to give talks in Poona in January.
We will see, we will see. The important thing is to rest and not interrupt the daily massages. Are you not happy here? he added with a malicious smile.

Francis' smile turned into a grimace when he turned to resume his position for reading. At the end of the morning, he heard quick footsteps on the gravel in the garden.

Father Hambye! It has been a long time since we last saw each other. Sit down, there, near me, tell me the news of Kurseong.
It is rather your turn to tell me news. You are paralyzed! What happened to you?
Let us say that it came on little by little. This leg caused me pain for months. Last winter I traveled a lot. To Bangalore in October for the second AIM congress. Then I went to Sri Lanka to give a course in spirituality. I made several trips to Thirumalai and gave retreats in many convents in Kerala and Tamil Nadu.
And obviously you went everywhere by bus or walking, as usual. You could have taken a rented car, it's more comfortable. Your community now has the means.
My dear, you know well that it's a question of principle. The religious of this country strut around in large automobiles much too often. Monks should live like the poor of the country.
Still, with your osteoarthritis. . . . You forget that you are sixty–two.

Almost sixty–three. In June I went to Poona, invited by Tony De Mello to give a *sadhana*, a retreat week to a group of Jesuits. Very interesting, very prayerful. And Tony is still full of humor.

Yes, his charism and success sometimes cause others in the Company to be jealous. But in all this you were still very vigorous? What happened?

On my return, I stopped at Calicut, where they have a large center for Ayur–Veda medicine.

You really believe in it?

Of course. It is a holistic, non–violent medicine that has proven itself for centuries. Close to chinese medicine as I understand. Doctor Sina from our hospital just gave me painkillers, telling me that it was not a cure. I was taking more and more but it is not a solution.

And at Calicut, what did they say?

They diagnosed osteoarthritis and a muscular weakness on the right side. They prescribed potions and massages. I went to the herbalist and returned to Kurisumala with a package of leaves, powders, and oils. Thankfully we had a brother who knew all about Ayur–Veda care, Brother George. He prepared them and gave me the massages.

From what I can see, it did not have much result!

In fact, Brother George left, I no longer had anyone competent up there, and at the beginning of this month, I had a severe attack. The pain was sharp, day and night. My leg gave way, did not hold me up any more. I had someone drive me here, Calicut is too far. The doctor proposed to shelter me and take care of me himself, for free. He is a very good man, even though a bit boastful.

No doubt he hopes that you will be good publicity for him.

I hope especially that he will help me walk again.

But, tell me, was Bangalore good?

Oh, it was less euphoric than Bangkok, maybe more realistic. We especially shared about questions and preoccupations.

For example?

Well, can yoga as a method of meditation be dissociated from the doctrine from which it came? Or: does the concept of guru have its place in christian monasticism? What about poverty in countries of extreme destitution? And the perpetual question: after so many declarations, after Bangkok, why is the western model practically the only model in Asia, when we have eastern monastic models in our own christian tradition?

It is true that Kurisumala is practically the only actualization. With Shantivanam, maybe, in the hindu style.[34]

Yes, maybe. Except that there are practically only young american and german guests. Bede was at the congress. He is always in his element in that kind of international meeting.

Did Le Saux come?

No. He had been invited, but he sent AIM a furious letter, like 'How dare you pose as christian monks in a country like India! You should hide yourselves.'

Wow. He is really unpredictable.

There were some remarkable interventions. A canadian Trappist, Father Armand Veilleux, whom I appreciated very much.[35] He came to spend a few days in Kurisumala after the congress. Another Trappist, a young Australian, also made a very good impression on me. Casey, Michael Casey if I remember correctly. The two tibetan lamas were magnificent with serenity, kindness, and competence in their talks.

So you came home content?

---

[34] Dom Jean Leclercq, in his Introduction to the *Acts of the Bangalore Congress*, observed, 'Except at Kurisumala and its foundations [christian monasticism in India still] owes nothing, or practically nothing, to Eastern monasticism" (*Cistercian Studies Quarterly* 9 [1974], 85).

[35] Father Armand Veilleux, who in 1998 became Dom Armand Veilleux, abbot of Scourmont, had argued for a 'globalization' of the preoccupations of monasticism, reacting against a narrowness of view that he called 'provincialism': 'This provincialism showed itself at Bangalore and the Abbot Primate of the Benedictines deplored it in his closing speech. The easterners seem inclined to consider the western forms of monastic life with a certain condescendence and the westerners, even if they are now experiencing an infatuation with eastern prayer techniques, exploit them with a spirit similar to exploiting opium from Asia or the Middle East's oil wells. This provincialism urges both to consider the behavior and ideologies inherited from their own cultural traditions as essential and immutable monastic values. This marginalization not only prevents a monk from the role of prophetic critic that should be his in the church, but also has negative effects on monasticism itself. It causes in monks a certain candor which can easily change into naivety, which makes them so much the more vulnerable to the influences of the surrounding society the more they believe that they are strangers to it' (see Leclercq, *Nouvelle page d'histoire monastique.*

Hmm. It did not advance anything, but the right questions were
asked. And it was pleasant to see old friends: Suzanne Siauve,
Panikkar and Nicole Shanta, John Moffit, Sister Pia Valeri,
Dom de Floris.

And what are you doing here all day? Are you bored?

Not at all. I am trying to consider this trial as a sort of second
sabbatical. I am not saying that this is the form I would have
chosen. But it's a retreat, a time of solitude, which is also a
benefit. I pray a lot, I meditate, I take advantage of the opportunity to advance in my translation of the *Penqitho*.

Where are you in this?

I am finishing a text of prayers of the hours for the weekday
ordinary. The literal prose translation that Father Bede had
published is helping me a great deal. I am recomposing it in
stanzas, with a rhythm of alternating recitation and
especially I intersperse texts from the Vedas, *Upanishads*, or
the *Bhagavad-Gita*. The difficulty is choosing them and having
them resonate with biblical texts that will be printed in italics.

These hindu texts are what you call 'Seeds of the Word'?

That's right. It's coming along well. At the same time, I am translating the volumes of the *Penqitho* that I brought back from
Mosul. Brother Vincent is a precious collaborator. He reads
the Syriac and identifies the words with the help of the dictionary. I then translate, select the hymns, and rewrite them in
verses in good English. But he saves me time. Brother
Anugrah types as we go along. He comes here twice a week.
We correct his work, and he takes back the next section.

I would be happy to see all that.

You'll have to wait a little longer. It's not yet presentable.

After his friend's departure, in the silence that had returned, Francis fell
asleep. At the slightest movement, pain woke him. He tamed it, tried to
free his spirit of it. That afternoon Sylvester came for a brief visit, to
bring him the mail, clean clothing, a few presents from the guests or the
brothers for his host and volunteer doctor.

What news is there, Sylvester?

Everything is going well, Acharya. There are many guests.

What kind?

All kinds, even hippies. They are curious, ask lots of questions, want to learn yoga. We had to be firm with those who smoked, I think they have now accepted that it's a rule in our house. They are sometimes undisciplined but their fervor is real. Some stay several hours a day in meditation on the rocks or in the church.

Welcome them. God is surely waiting for them somewhere.

There arc also sisters. The two groups don't always get along together.

And the farm?

Right now, it's doing well. Another calf was born yesterday. The milk production has almost returned to its pre–epidemic level.

And for your scholarship, have you heard any news?

I wanted to talk to you about that. There is a letter from Germany in the mail. It might be the answer from Misereor?

Let's see. . . . Yes, that is it. They agreed. I am happy for you, Sylvester. You can take that spirituality course and travel a little in Europe. I will write a letter of recommendation for you to my sister in Belgium and AIM in Paris.

Acharya, I would like to go to your monastery, the one where you were a novice, of which you spoke to us so often.

That will surely be possible. One of my nieces can drive you there.

I thank you very much for allowing me to take this course, Acharya.

He knelt down. Acharya placed both his hands on his head. Then the tall monk went away, after bowing silently. Francis watched him go. He had hesitated about this trip. But Sylvester had given very much. He was the first of the two companions, who used to pick up wood in the jungle to dry the hut and cook, in the terrible monsoon of summer 1958. He was twenty–five years old at that time, now he was over forty. He was a *sannyasi* and a priest. He had matured a great deal.

Night had fallen. Francis was able to stand and, using his two canes, went to the garden where he stretched out on a stone bench. Between the immobile palm trees, he could see the sky and the constellations of stars.

Everything was peaceful. He stayed there a long time and an ineffable joy filled him, like a foretaste of heaven, giving him profound freedom, despite his suffering.

AROUND THE WORLD

July 1975. Francis, sitting on the ground in his cell, was sorting the mail that had accumulated during his absence. He went home to the ashram at Easter, half cured: he still walked with difficulty and had to contort himself in order to sit down and get up again. The pain stabilized 'at a bearable level'. A french friend, Pierre Baranger, sent him some oil of his own composition with the instructions: three drops in the morning on some bread, rub the leg every evening. Francis followed this prescription to the letter and practiced the yoga exercises that his joints permitted.

He attacked the hundred letters that awaited. Many were thanks and congratulations for his pamphlet *Chronique des douze années: 1958–1970*, privately printed and distributed by AIM in Europe and elsewhere. Doctor Ferrière, whom he had consulted about his leg, urged him to have an operation in Belgium as soon as possible. Father Jacob Mitterhöffer, from the Austrian Pontifical Missions, who had visited Kurisumala the previous year, invited him to come and give yoga and meditation seminars in several cities of his country. The costs of the trip would be completely paid.

This proposal became a reality in 1977. Francis left Kurisumala 27 February and took the bus for Trivandrum, where an Air India flight took him to Bombay. He was stuck there for a week waiting for his indian passport and austrian visa. Visa problems had followed him all his life! Finally he took a Lufthansa flight which, after stops in Rome and Frankfort, reached Vienna 6 March. When he disembarked, Father Mitterhöffer took charge of him and took him by car to the Saint Gabriel convent in Mölding, across hills covered with wineries. Father Mitterhöffer spoke about the seminar series:

> You see, Father Acharya, the viennese youth seems more and
> more seduced by eastern religions. Many *gurus* give seminars
> on hindu or buddhist meditation every year, accompanied by
> yoga exercises. They draw crowds and many youth abandon

our christian churches to follow them. Our bishop believes
that we should listen to this request instead of criticizing it
and to show the young people that what they are seeking
already exists in our religion. He thinks you are the right
person to present this synthesis and lead a christian yoga
seminar: *Yoga für Christen.*

This is what I had a premonition about from your letters. It is an
interesting project, and I will do my best. Concretely, how
will we work?

The seminar lasts three or four days. You give the conferences
and meditation. Helga, a yoga teacher, will do the exercises.
We have arranged for simultaneous translation.

Where will it be held?

We thought of several courses, in six different places: the Regina
Laudes convent, a few kilometers from here, the University of
Vienna, St Pölten at the foot of the Alps, in Salzburg, Linz, and
Klagenfurt. You see, we are exploiting you to the maximum.
We will drive you to Regina Laudes tomorrow. The superior,
Mother Mercedes, an energetic person, will introduce Helga to
you. You can decide together how you will collaborate.

In preparation for these courses, Francis had reread several works on
indian spirituality and its sacred writings, the works of R. Pannikar,
among others. In the plane, he had summarized and formalized his ideas
on the points of convergence between Hinduism and Christianity, on the
hidden presence of Christ in the *Upanishads.* With Helga, he cut the subject up into modules, alternating talks and exercises: a total of twelve
meditations on texts from the Bible and the *Upanishads.* The sessions
gathered from one to two hundred persons. Francis expected to see
mainly young people, but there were doctors, judges, and lawyers, many
with their families. In the University's Great Hall, five hundred persons
came to hear the second seminar's introductory lecture.

For Francis, these three weeks were recreation and consecration. Everywhere, people questioned him about Kurisumala. The slides and audio-
tapes he brought were a great success. He organized *indische liturgien*
[indian liturgies], he was brought to visit old abbeys set in the depths of
forests, he was given envelopes full of shillings collected 'for India', and

female students gave him flowers after classes. His German returned to him very quickly, and he was booked for the following year.[36]

On 29 March, Francis was in Rome, where he met Father Ivan Zuzek SJ, secretary for the commission for the revision of the eastern code and others in charge of the eastern churches. It was an opportunity to speak with specialists at the highest level of the hierarchy. Father Zuzek had already come to Kurisumala and considered the ashram with benevolent interest. Everyone accepted the idea that Francis' foundation had its own vocation, and that it was not useful for it to belong to a religious congregation. He was invited to concelebrate in Saint Peter's basilica the next morning with thirty–five cardinals, which he did not refuse! And then he was brought to Tre Fontane, a very old cistercian abbey in Latium.

A terrace in the April sun. A monk in sandals, dressed in saffron cotton, pulled a pen and a small address book out of his bag made of the same cloth. He wrote a series of postcards beside his plate, from which the last crumbs of pizza had been meticulously cleaned. From time to time, he stopped, drank a sip of *cafè latte* and, sighing deeply, contemplated Assisi below, the cypresses, the hills. Francis permitted himself a getaway, a vacation day consecrated to the Poverello, the hero of his youth. He left very early that morning from Rome and took the rapid train to Bologna. There, by Foligne, he arrived in Assisi just in time for the pilgrims' Mass in the chapel. Memories of his first visit came back to him, forty years earlier, with Guerric, Maur, and Théodore. They had stopped here on their way to the Gregorian University.

A young man sitting at the next table watched him for a while and then began a conversation. He introduced himself as Anki Romme. He proposed to take the monk to visit the surroundings in his car, and there they were, both of them in Anki's minuscule Baby Fiat 500, on a complete tour: Santa Chiara—emotion of looking at the Christ who spoke to Saint Francis—Eremo dei Carceri, San Damiano, the cell in the mountain above the abyss, and the Portiuncula, the garden of the Canticle of the Sun. Francis took the last train back to Rome. In his diary he wrote, 'This

---

[36] These sessions were revived in an album illustrated by very beautiful photos by Andréas Hoffmann: Francis Acharya, *Yoga, ein Weg zu Gott* [*Yoga, A Way to God*]. Two brochures authored by Francis Acharya were published by the Austrian Pontifical Missions and distributed in the classes: *Yoga/Meditation für Christen*, and *Die Kunst des Lebens*.

whole day was like a dream, unforgettable.' And beside it: *Anki Romme, via dell'Anfiteatro Romano, 16, Assisi.*

A short stop in Paris. Dom de Floris and Sister Pia came to get him at Orly. At the AIM secretariate, they conversed the whole afternoon. That evening, they took the subway and went up to Montmartre, illuminated in the darkness. Francis hummed an old Maurice Chevalier song: *Paris, reine du monde* [*Paris, Queen of the world*]. Happy memories awaited him here at each street corner: with Antoinette in 1935; with Dom Anselme and Father Théodore, after the war; a happy stop on the road to Brittany where they used to go get provisions at the Le Bail family farm; and later, Sanskrit and Hinduism courses with Olivier Lacombe.

He went to his friend to renew his supply of Baranger oil, visited Edouard Duperray, and made a short stop at the benedictine abbey of Ligugé, where he spoke to the community about indian monasticism. On the way back, he stopped in Poitiers to visit Marie Baranger's workshop and order four icons for Kurisumala.

The next day he got off at the Hirson station. Who had come to greet him? He scanned for his former comrades. A woman in a fur coat walked toward him, but he did not recognize her, despite all the questions she was posing. Finally she introduced herself: Mme Manfroid, the widow of Doctor Manfroid from Chimay, a classmate of Albert Derzelle and a friend of the monastery. She had been sent by Scourmont to bring the prodigal son back to the house. No welcoming committee was on the platform.

His heart beat faster when he saw Scourmont's pointed belltower from afar. The previous day, it had snowed all day, and Francis recorded, 'Beauty of the pastures all white, with black trees underlined with ribbons of snow. But the cold! I had forgotten that it could be so cold here.' The first contact with the community was quite cold as well. Is this exotic bearded Acharya in his orange shawl still one of us? Do we recognize in him our brother Francis Mahieu? They approached him with prudence. Father Godefroid Leveugle proposed to give him a tour of the house. Francis later toured it alone, noting all the changes that had happened since he had left twenty–two years earlier. After supper, Father Corneille came to ask him about India.

Holy Thursday. Stricken with a cold, Francis spent the morning writing letters in his cell and the afternoon in bed. On Friday, he found the office 'sparkling in its melodies and exuberant in its words, even on Good Friday'. On Saturday, it snowed all day. He prepared the homily that he had been asked to give at the pascal vigil. He spoke at length with Father Bernard de Give, a Jesuit who had become a Cistercian and who was interested in eastern religions. That afternoon, Father Hambye, on vacation in Belgium, came to see him with his brother and niece and took him to Chevetogne, where he bought more icons. That evening, he attended the Easter vigil. He discovered the western post–conciliar liturgy: the fire outside enchanted him, each one lit his candle before going in procession into the church.

After Easter, the ice was broken, grace touched everyone: many brothers came to speak with Francis and asked him at length about his life in India, his foundation. He was given a typewriter, and they took him to the oculist who prescribed new glasses. Dom Guerric went to Chimay with him to buy them. Father Jacques Blanpain took him on a tour of the farms. He was asked to speak to the community two evenings in a row. He told them what he had experienced, in a personal and concrete way. The first talk was devoted to the monastic experience in India: the himalayan ashrams and Swami Dharmananda. The second was about the history of Kurisumala. Before leaving, he obtained two favors from Guerric: to say Mass in the chapel of the infirmary where Dom Anselme had lived his last years, and to take with him the copper crucifix from the small altar.

In Brussels, he stayed with his sister Marie-Thérèse. He toured the city by car with his nieces, to revisit the places from his youth: François De Greef Street; de Haecht Street with Sainte-Marie college; the barracks of Général Jacques Boulevard; and the Cambre woods. Everyone wanted to see him, invite him. But first he went to consult Doctor Ferrière in Ottignies. His brother Charles drove him there. Cinette, the doctor's wife, welcomed him with great joy. She was an activist, slightly fanatic, very active in the anti–establishment christian circles that flourished after the Council. Late into the night, they stayed in the living room, telling each other about their respective journeys during the past twenty–five years. The next day she brought him to the brand new campus of Louvain-la-Neuve, which was still being built. Groups to help the Third World countries and Christians 'seeking' met in the attic of one of the old farm buildings. They were reorganizing the world, playing the guitar. In the evening, in the large house in Ottignies, awaiting the doctor's return, Cinette played records of byzantine liturgy and Jacques Brel's latest hits for her friend to listen to. Francis jotted in his notebook: 'Brel, Flemish. *Ne me quitte pas* [Do not leave me]. Very beautiful.' The next day at breakfast, they spoke about old friends, Louis Evely who left the priesthood, married, and went to the Drome region where he also welcomed people who were seeking. Before Charles arrived to take his brother back to Brussels, André Ferrière examined Francis and asked him about his health. He advised him to have x–rays taken, and before leaving to purchase warm 'Damart–Thermodactyl' undergarments.

For several days, Uncle Jean went from one party to the next: his sister, then each of his three brothers invited in turn all their descendants and organized a dinner in his honor. He participated in all these familial feasts, and leaving aside the vegetarian dishes that had been prepared for him, tasted the red wine, the pâtés, and the cheeses with a pleasure that gave joy to his hosts. He baptized the last of his grandnieces, went to Ypres to visit his godmother who slipped him a check, and made a quick visit to Eastbourne to see Amy and Ida. He walked at Beachy Head as he used to, swam in the sea, and took the tea in the garden, out of lovely Wedgwood cups. The two sisters were happy and moved, honored to be associated with the morning meditation on a text of Rabindranath Tagore. A few books purchased in London, then a return to Brussels. He persuaded his niece Janine to drive him to Recklinghausen in Germany, where he stocked up on icon reproductions at Bongers. In a café where they stopped for lunch, Francis picked up a newspaper and started to read it out loud. Janine was a little embarrassed. Her companion's saffron clothing was already attracting attention. 'It's to keep up my German', he explained.

Before returning to Kerala, he had a complete check up of his joints at the clinic of the Two Alices in Uccle. His spinal column was judged satisfactory, but his right hip was in a sorry state. 'And you can walk with that?' Asked the physician examining the x–ray photographs with a dismayed expression. 'You should have hip replacement surgery soon.'

Francis postponed the idea until later. He gathered his bags, said goodbye to Marie-Thérèse, and went to Amsterdam by car with his nieces. His return flight left from Schipol. He took advantage of this to go have lunch with Father Cornélius Tholens in the indian ashram that he set up in the heart of the amsterdam beguine convent after his stay at Shantivanam. There they ate rice and vegetables, sitting on the ground amid the odor of incense, to which sometimes the scent of hashish was added in the evening. This ensured success with the many hippies living in the city, and also with many intellectuals seeking eastern spirituality.

On 4 May, the traveler got off at Cochin. Sylvester was waiting for him with the jeep. The winding road in the dark, with the small lights of the little houses in the mountain, the scent of cardamom: they were approaching. They arrived at Kurisumala at 9 PM. The whole community was waiting, silent and smiling. Mariabhakta, one of the eldest, came forward and spoke the words of welcome and gratitude. A prayer of thanksgiving in the church, blessing. Acharya had returned. They were reassured, they were happy, and so was he.

One year later, he left again for a long trip that this time would lead him to the New World. After a second series of courses in Austria—this time he had read in German the book by Bettina Baumer, *Die Upanishaden als Meditationweg* [*The Upanishads as a Way of Meditation*]—he flew to New York. Hema, an american woman who had lived in Kurisumala for several months and considered herself an 'associate' of the ashram, welcomed him at the airport in a *brahmachari*'s clothing. He promised to go to her house on his return because he was going to Boston that very day. He had been invited to participate in a religious symposium organized in Vina, California, on the theme of the spiritual father: Abba. But first he would cross the United States from west to east by plane, car, and train, visiting fourteen monasteries along the way. Everywhere he was welcomed as a brother, invited to speak about his experience, and to celebrate in the 'Indian rite'. The first notes he wrote at Genesee, a trappist monastery near Lake Ontario, where he spent several days, revealed the commercial engineer and agricultural manager: 'It's a very large property, 2,200 acres of fertile land. They use tractors and large machines to do all the work. At present, they cultivate only corn and soy. In a single day, they can plough 60 acres and seed 140. In fact, agriculture does not interest them as much now. Their principal revenue comes from a bakery where twenty–five monks work. That is a manner of speaking, because all the work, kneading, baking, wrapping, and even pre–slicing is done by machines.' The indian citizen was scared by the richness and a certain ease: 'Here, as at Spencer, there are a dozen cars. The monks who take a day of silence, borrow a car to go to the hermitage.' But soon, it was as prior that he wrote, 'A few years ago, the community still had fifty monks, but now they are only thirty–five, with five novices. They are nevertheless preparing to found a house in Brazil.' And as a traveler, always ready to head off: 'They invited me to go there.'

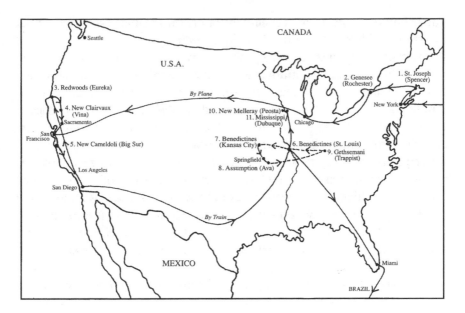

Figure 3. A map of the U.S.A., showing Acharya's visits to Cistercian/Trappist monasteries.

The American 'way of life' that had entered the convents here aroused his surprise: 'The meals are self–service, the church is triangular, they play violin and guitar during the offices, the nuns drive cars, and everyone hugs each other, even the monks and nuns!' (letter to his community, 9 June 1978).

At Redwoods, near San Francisco, he found the 'nuns very anti–establishment'. But he appreciated the car trip across the Sierra in Sister Diane's company to the abbey of New Clairvaux in Vina. The Sacramento valley was burning, wild, grand. In the evening they dined in the garden. The symposium lasted a week. Three approaches of the theme 'Abba' were examined: the western tradition, the contemporary cistercian practice, and a comparative study of the western and eastern traditions. In fact, the East was the star. Each speaker had a partner to assist and question him. Francis' talk was entitled 'The Guru, Spiritual Father in the Hindu Tradition' and his partner was none other than Raimundo Panikkar, who was very eager to start the debate on the subject. The speaker insisted on the deep knowledge of the sacred scriptures that the

guru showed, his role as teacher, initiator, on the master–disciple relationship.[37]

During free time, he evoked his native country with Dom André
Louf, abbot of Mont des Cats, and when his work had ended, he let Father Basil Pennington bring him to Big Sur, where the italian Camaldolese had a house. He wrote, 'The full moon reflected by the ocean
illuminated my whole room at night.' He went to Chicago by rapid train,
in a sleeping wagon. He was amazed by its comfort. At the beginning of
the trip, the railroad tracks went along the west coast in a countryside
that evoked the creation of the world, 'an opportunity for meditation on
the cosmic Alliance.' He also observed that the 'women wear pants or
shorts'; he conversed with his travel companions; and he found the food
insipid. In Kansas, he visited Sister Pascaline, who had lived in India for
a year in Shantivanam, and made a two–week retreat at Kurisumala. She
now lived, with her bishop's permission, in a hermitage in the woods in
Ohio: Osage Monastery (OM!). 'Good talks, indian Mass', Francis recorded. Sister Rachel, novice mistress, brought Francis by car to the
benedictine nuns of St Louis, Missouri, the last and very happy stage of
this tour of the United States. Long conversations with Mother Tharsilla,
the superior, and evenings with the novices to whom he talked about his
monastic youth and his indian vocation: the meeting with Gandhi, love
for Francis of Assisi, the visa, and his arrival where Father Monchanin
lived. For these young American women who grew up during the 'golden
sixties', it was like a historical novel told by the hero himself. In the
plane that took him to Miami, he wrote an almost lyrical page about his
wonderful memories of his stay in St Louis that he was taking with him:

> Without ceasing, my thoughts bring me back to Sister Tharsilla,
> towards the novices and their novice mistress. This rekindles my
> memories of the Sermons on the Song of Songs. *Osculum oris
> sui.* An authentic meeting does not consist in exchanging polite
> formulas without meaning. In these times where we see a search
> for meaning permeate the liturgy as well as life, a true meeting
> consists in transmitting the living flame of our love, our prayer,
> our life. The words that we exchange are always too poor, often

---

[37] The Acts of the Vina Symposium were published in 1982; see *Abba*, ed. John
Sommerfeldt.

clumsy. Even well chosen, they hide the mystery, which reveals itself only by symbols and gestures.

He wrote to Sister Tharsilla to thank her and added a note for Sister Rachel, where he spoke about his cistercian novitiate: 'Through the Sermons of Saint Bernard on the Song of Songs, I had a revelation of the love of God in terms of flesh and blood. That moved me deeply and then I was able to sublimate all that in pure love. What we usually call monastic discipline became a *schola caritatis*, a school of love and a school of service of Christ.'

In America, spontaneity, the absence of formalism, and the freedom that permeated the relations between brothers and sisters delighted him. He admired the communities' dynamism but was disappointed by the cultural poverty and a certain materialism brought about by wealth and too much comfort.

His sister Antoinette had sent him a plane ticket so that he could come to visit her in Sao Paulo before returning to India. He spent two weeks in Brazil and met his brother–in–law and nephews. The youngest, Jo, about thirty years old, immediately showed him admiring and demonstrative affection. When it was time to say goodbye, at the airport, he took the silver chain bracelet bearing his name off his wrist and thrust it into Francis' hands.

Back in Kurisumala, Francis decided that every Monday, during his day of silence, he would once again meditate on Saint Bernard, and that he would make a new translation from Latin to English. He started with the Sermons on the Song of Songs. But the pain in his leg now tormented him day and night, transforming the slightest movement into agony. Despite his desire to master it by his spirit, he finally yielded to the arguments of the doctors he had consulted in Europe and the friends in which he confided: he had to face a hip operation.

THE OPERATION

After three months of dry season, Francis was still suffering as much. He finally went to Kottayam to ask his orthopedist for a medical certificate that should facilitate obtaining a passport. In a letter to his sister dated 22 February, he wrote, 'It's always a problem for an indian citizen to leave the country. The Pontifical Aid to the Missions, which invited me to Austria every year, offered to pay for the trip. That will be welcome. I contacted Scourmont in December. They offered to pay for the hip operation, as long as it is done at Lobbes, near the abbey. Write me what you think of this.'

Everything was falling into place and after going to Rome and Assisi again, Francis arrived in Scourmont the day before Pentecost. This time, the welcome was fraternal. Everything had been arranged for the orthopedic surgery, and on Tuesday, Father Corneille brought his former novice to the Lobbes clinic.

12 June. Saint Joseph Clinic, room 33
Dear Father Abbot and all my Scourmont brothers
Here I am at the end of my first day of hospitalization, and I am happy to tell you that everything is going well and inspires confidence for the four weeks I am to stay here. The atmosphere is very good, orderly, clean but also a family spirit. I have a very good private room with all the comfort a sick person could desire, even a radio, that I have not yet turned on. Let us await the time when I feel despondent.

Last night, after I was admitted, accompanied by Father Corneille, we met the chaplain. He told us that it was he who had taught my dear Father Paul to read! Then we walked along the Sambre—almost romantic. After that, we separated with regret.

16 June. A little groggy. And this leg for which I came here in order to give it new youth is an inert block. It feels like a beam of reinforced concrete weighing heavily on my right side. Father Abbot spent the two first nights at my bedside. (Diary 1979)

24 June. Francis was still immobilized on his bed. A metal wire went through his knee, attached to a system of pulleys and counterweights. He craned his neck to observe the Sambre, where the barges glided slowly. On the shore, the fishermen teased the roaches (european freshwater food fish that have a greenish back), and from time to time one could be seen wiggling at the end of the fishing line. On his table, his syriac breviary, an old edition of *The Brothers Karamazov*, and a few bars of the Côte d'Or chocolate he had loved since childhood. His whole family brought him some!

One of his nieces cautiously opened the door. He turned his head and placed a finger on his lips, making a sign for her to look towards the window. Some birds were pecking at the crumbs of his meal. He remained in silence a moment. 'I find pleasure in watching them', he said smiling. 'As I used to on François Degreef Street. But you brought me food again! You are spoiling me.' 'These are fruits, Uncle Jean, vitamins to give you strength,' she protested. 'But I am doing very well! Tomorrow they will take out the wire, and I can start to walk again. This anemia is only a memory. I tried to explain to good Doctor Loodvoet that in India, we live with less blood than in the West, just like we use less gas, but I was unsuccessful. They transfused five units of blood into me.'

His niece changed course. 'When will you be able to leave the clinic?' 'In fifteen days, the doctor promised. If all goes well, I will return to Scourmont on 15 July. The physiotherapist, Mr Mouchet, will come there one or two times a week to finish the rehabilitation. He advised me to pedal on a stationary bike, but I don't think they have that kind of machine at the abbey. Do you think you could get me one?' 'I wonder if my father might have one at home', she responded; 'I will talk to him.'

In fact, it seems that Francis' hip was in such a bad state that the prosthesis had to be placed deeply in the femur, and his recovery was quite difficult. It took him four days to be able to sit, and at the end of June he was allowed to walk a few steps in his room, leaning on two canes or crutches.

Francis continued his convalescence at Scourmont, in the quiet of a very beautiful summer. Father Charles Dumont had returned from Caldey and questioned his former novice master about the indian adventure. Curious about the state of the collaboration with Bede Griffiths—'How is your Benedictine?'—he received only this answer, a little cynical: 'Didn't you know? He left me.'

On 15 August, all Marie-Thérèse's children and grandchildren—more than thirty persons in all—gathered in her garden of Rhode-Saint-Genèse. Francis had arrived the previous day. Early in the morning, he had said Mass at Regina Mundi church nearby. He still limped and leaned on a cane to walk. While his nieces were busy preparing the meal, he found an old bicycle in the garage, leaned his cane against the wall and went by bicycle for an hour in the Soignes woods, on the sly, with pure pleasure. The Sunday morning strollers took a second look at this

bearded cyclist in orange undershirt, but he didn't care. He returned just
in time to begin the meal, very satisfied with his escapade.

A few days later, his niece Marthe, Charles' daughter, drove him to
the airport of Zaventhem. His cloth bag on one side, his cane on the
other, only with difficulty could Francis carry his fairly large suitcase.
He wanted Marthe to accompany him into the plane, but the inspectors
refused: 'it's impossible', they declared. He insisted. 'Go ask the airport's police officer', said the gatekeeper. 'Only he can give you permission'. So the limping monk and the young woman carrying his bag
wandered in the halls and elevators up to the fifth floor, looking for the
office in question. The boss had them sit down. Francis made his request,
while the policeman examined him suspiciously. 'Show me your papers',
he grumbled grouchily, with a strong Flemish accent. Francis searched in
his cloth bag, and gave them to him. 'You were really born in Ypres (he
said Ieper)?' The civil servant's face lit up. Francis started up in flemish
at once and briefly told his history and how he had become an indian
citizen. Nothing more was necessary. 'I am from Roulers', said the officer, handing him the permission.

As soon as he returned to the ashram, the traveler wrote to his sister
to tell her this anecdote and reassure her that he had safely arrived.

> After a five hour wait at Fiumicino—I ate a piece of pie with a
> glass of white wine, that's all I could buy with the three dollars I
> had on me—I got on the jumbo jet. There were very few
> passengers. I was able to stretch out on three unoccupied seats. At
> Bombay, I stayed with the Jesuits. The next day they drove me to
> Santa Cruz airport. There, the waiting line for the small plane to
> Cochin that has only forty seats was crowded, but by a real
> miracle, I obtained the last empty seat. When we landed, I got off
> the plane first and quickly recognized the group of monks who
> were waiting for me. They were accompanied by an austrian film
> maker who had come to make a film about India, which will
> include a sequence on Kurisumala, notably our indian Mass. This
> took me all day yesterday. Today, the governor of the province
> with his wife and two children are visiting for twenty–four hours.
> So my time is very occupied. But at all cost I want to continue my
> exercises. For this I have reserved the morning hours from four to
> seven. I think that my walking will continue to improve.

For several years, Francis would regain a health and dynamism that he had not known since his first attacks of arthritis in 1974. This would lead him to abuse his strength sometimes, and to forget that he was almost seventy years old. But, in the meantime, that winter, he lived in the gratitude and euphoria of newly regained mobility, as he states in this text, distributed to his friends as a Christmas letter.

A thanksgiving pilgrimage to the 'Mountain of the Cross'
Christmas Chronicle, December 1979

When I had a hip operation last June, I had vowed to make a pilgrimage to the top of our mountain when I returned. Since I came back at the end of August, I have been waiting impatiently for the right time to keep this promise. Today, on 5 December, we had a luminous morning. Brother Sun was shining in all his glory. But in the afternoon the clouds made their appearance and invaded the blue sky. Soon Brother Wind started to blow with strength: it was a tonic, an inspiration. This led me into the spirit of advent: like a need to purify oneself by *tapas*; penance, repentance, with an ardent thirst to seek the Lord, to go to meet him.

I must say that this day was particularly quiet because of a *bandh*, a kind of total stop to all commercial activity practiced in Kerala to protest a government decision. There were no buses, no jeeps to bring us visitors. At 3:30 in the afternoon I felt impelled to accomplish my vow. The sun was still playing hide and seek with the clouds that were becoming more dense and darker, as if a downpour or storm was brewing. This was perfectly in accord with my state of mind. I borrowed a work shirt from one of my brothers and, wearing this light coverall, I set off, barefoot, my rosary in my hand. I had decided to suffer no interruption to my prayer, and I experienced a great desire to keep complete silence. The first test was waiting for me on the road: I ran into Doctor Hilde Sina, who was going down towards the hospital. I smiled kindly and made her a sign that I was going up, looking at the mountain. She smiled at me in turn and for a moment we walked side by side, in silence, in a deep peace. Later down, a neighboring farmer came straight to me with a large smile that left no doubt as to his intention of asking me some favor. I was successful in returning a similarly wide smile and again showing him the mountain with my eyes, made him understand where I was going, while with my hand I encouraged him to go to the ashram.

Soon, after passing the hospital, I started along the path that crosses the tea plantations. Thanks to my daily physiotherapy exercises, combined with the practice of hatha–yoga, I had made great progress since my return. Week after week, I found increasing pleasure in walking, especially during my many visits to Kottayam, where for years I had had to take a rickshaw for the slightest trip. Now, when I came home in the afternoon, once again I blithely went up the road from the bus stop to the ashram. Recently, I had been able to sit cross–legged or on my heels again. I had even taken the risk of running a little. So I trusted myself to reach the summit. Of course I had some apprehension: would this steep ascent revive Sister Arthritis's redoubtable pain? I was walking prudently, carefully choosing the rocks where I put my feet. I prayed without ceasing, very seriously. The profound silence and solitude revived my desire to see the Lord.

At the bottom of the valley, I crossed the little river, refreshing my feet in the running water. Now I was climbing the rocky path, which at one time had been a road suitable for motor vehicles for the bishop's visit but today is only the pebbly bed of a stream. I sat on a rock overlooking the valley already clothed with this mysterious splendor of our Sahya mountains at nightfall. I continued, still more recollected in prayer. Suddenly, I discovered at my feet all the Kerala plain, to the horizon where the backwaters and the arabian sea were shining with purple hue by the light of the setting sun. Marveling, as if seized by a respectful fear, I realized that I was already on the south slope and that I had gone past the path that went up to the sanctuary. I retraced my steps, seeking the little chapel of Saint Thomas that marks the beginning of the way of the cross, but I had become completely lost. I was starting to worry when a little girl, carrying her little brother on her hip, suddenly appeared in this desert place and put me back on the right path. At each cross, I stopped in silent adoration. I could not formulate any prayer. My heart was praying with too deep a desire and love for words.

At the eighth station, I emerged from the rocks and weeds onto a rocky platform. The view expanded on the northern part of the valley. I could see our ashram with its lands stretching at my feet. The buildings disappeared under the trees, but I could clearly make out the terraced plantings all around, like a large pale green Japanese garden, with the reservoir that reflected the clouds.

I felt myself full of strength and joy, marvel was bursting into praise, as if I were full to overflowing. However, I continued to ascend, because I was in a hurry to complete my expedition before allowing myself some rest. When I reached the fourteenth station, I fell to the ground and prostrated, in the manner of the *shastanga namaskar*, my body and face against the rock at the foot of the cross. I did the same at the chapel door and at the foot of the large Christ. Each time I pressed my forehead against the soil in adoration, I kissed the rock with a long kiss of devotion and love. I felt one with our Mother Earth, with all of Creation through this surface of black rock, as large as an elephant's back, still warm with the day's warmth, like living flesh. My heart was overflowing with joy, I walked back and forth on this rocky platform without thinking of resting. I had forgotten both hip replacement and arthritis. My eyes plunged into the deep valleys all around. I could recognize Adivaram, Peringulam, and Velli-kulam with their white churches emerging from the vegetation. I felt as if immersed in this infinite beauty. Instead of the pain I had feared, I discovered a sort of euphoria, a kind of ecstasy. The idea of spending the night up there came to me. It was the week of full moon, it would have been splendid. But I felt that I should join the community for the night prayer and at once I went back down. I had already tried to run to retrain my leg muscles, but there I can say that I was hurrying down the slope as if I were dancing. I felt so light, as if filled with the Spirit, so living so conscious of his presence, with my heart overflowing with grati-tude and love for each rock, each flower, each blade of grass.

When I arrived in the valley, everything was calm. The rare persons I met were returning home after the day's occupations. They made me aware of the freedom I had experienced by the joyous and peaceful friendship I spontaneously felt for everyone. I went back up the road at a good pace, as if I had gone for only a short walk.

Night had fallen when I reached the gate of the ashram. It was time for the night prayer. *Brahmachari* Mathai, my most faithful guardian, had just gone out to look for me, fearing that I had had some accident. But as soon as he saw me, he perceived my joy and was reassured. The community had been waiting in the church for a few minutes. I went in immediately and led the prayer with a sentiment of joy and gratitude, conscious of the fact that I had been carried by grace all along my pilgrimage. I had climbed the mountain to pray and thank God but, as was often the case with Him, I had received more than I had given. I had gone up there to praise the Lord of illness and of health, the Lord of life and death, to pray for peace in the world and healing of all suffering, and I had experienced salvation. I had lifted my eyes to the mountain of the Lord and I had felt his hand touch me, his presence completing my healing, filling my being and all of creation. There had been neither rain nor storm, only a shower of graces.

SHANTIVANAM EMANCIPATED

Bede Griffiths' revival of Shantivanam has been retold in several books about the english Benedictine who was the focus of media attention.[38] Here we will attempt to give an account of these events from Kurisumala's point of view, since that is the purpose of our work.

When in 1968 Le Saux proposed that Francis take charge of Shantivanam, he was very happy about it. It was a gift with a very high symbolic value: the legacy from Monchanin, whom he considered his spiritual father in India. Had he not himself caused the seed planted by his elder on the then–sterile banks of the Kaveri to germinate and fructify in syriac soil? To see Shantivanam officially return to his hands concretized this filiation in some way. But he could not take over the material and spiritual direction of two monasteries, many hundreds of kilometers apart, in different churches and states, no matter how much energy he had. For a short time, he thought of leaving Kurisumala for Shantivanam. But the worried community clearly

---

[38] Among the many works about Father Bede Griffiths, we have particularly appreciated his biography by Shirley Du Boulay (*Beyond the Darkness*) for its objectivity and the richness of its documentation.

manifested its desire to see him keep the reins. In the end, it was his choice also: he dreaded the stifling climate of the plains.

Sending Father Bede to take charge of this first foundation presented the great advantage of appeasing the tensions that the two leaders' diverging views had been causing in the community for the past few years. There was one risk, however: of seeing this prestigious place, so full of memories, the place of his initiation to India, his moving meeting with Monchanin escape from Francis.

In several articles, he had already written about the freedom foundations enjoyed in eastern monasticism.[39] He denied wanting to create 'daughterhouses' or 'carbon copies' of Kurisumala, and desired to let the communities founded by his monks follow their own path, 'attentive to the breath of the Spirit'. He established Shantivanam with the status of *skete*, that is, in the eastern custom, a small group of monks living an ascetic and eremitical life under the direction of a spiritual father but dependent on a larger monastery for the formation of novices or the more important decisions. All of this had been recorded in a 'charter of foundation', which specified that Shantivanam's main mission was to continue the work of the first founders, Monchanin and Le Saux, 'favoring the integration of India's spiritual heritage into the Church, especially its monastic traditions and its schools of spiritual seeking.'

The beginnings were shaky. For four years, from 1968 to 1972, the ashram vegetated. No true community life took shape. Modernizing was accomplished thanks to the inheritance Dr Mary Allan, one of his english friends, opportunely left Father Bede. Running water, lavatories, electricity, furniture—Bede, with his long legs, had never really got used to sitting on the ground—library, and guest rooms. The mango trees were leveled: some thought they were charming, others that they were infested with serpents and scorpions. A plantation of coconut trees irrigated by a motorized pump now replaced them. But the young monks from Kurisumala did not stay, and those who came to try left again after a few months.

As for Bede, he felt at home in Shantivanam right away. The warm plain, the sand, the peaceful river were more suitable for him than the abrupt rocks beaten by the wind. When in 1971 he found himself alone, ill, plagued

---

[39] In eastern monasticism 'the monastic vocation is more independent from the priesthood than in the west, while the grouping of monasteries is more fluid: in general they are federations, allowing for considerable diversity' (Francis Acharya, *Chronique des douze années*, p. 28).

by Stephen's prosecution,[40] and the bishop of Trichy's mistrust, he went back to England to recuperate, rest, see his friends, and distance himself a bit. But after a few months, he returned to India, haunted by the desire to resurrect Saccidananda ashram. No doubt he was aware of the *guru* he had become and the expectations of the young people of the seventies, who had turned to the East seeking masters to teach them to think.

During these years of trial and error, Francis stayed away. He was overworked by the second foundation of Thirumalai, by the guests who were more and more numerous, by the retreats he preached to the indian communities of the region, without mentioning the epidemic of foot–and–mouth disease that was again decimating the herd. He would let Bede find his way, he said. In fact, there was already discord between them. Besides his disappointed hope of seeing this foundation with its prestigious renown bear little fruit, Francis was still tense with anger at the way in which Bede, at the end of 1968, had published several articles in the Bombay press in which he presented himself as the heir of Father Le Saux–Abishiktananda, without mentioning the link to Kurisumala. For a long time, Francis would reproach Bede for having created the *fait accompli*, spreading a version that would prevail in many publications from that time forth.[41] 'In the context, such as you presented it, any intervention from me concerning Shantivanam can only appear authoritarian and abusive', he would write to Bede in 1975.

Amaldas and Christudas running away in 1972 did not help. These two young monks went to Bede to seek what Francis had refused: a freer life and access to the priesthood. Amaldas was a young man with a confident bearing, intelligent, and especially gifted for yoga. He acquired a reputation as a master yogi, and his courses were esteemed by Shantivanam's guests. Christudas was a solid man, a pragmatist. His devotion to his *guru* was complete. He would be faithful through trials and illness, to the end. These two men would relieve Bede of the material tasks and allow him to devote himself completely to reading, preparation of his books, welcoming and giving spiritual guidance to guests, to whom he gave without counting of attentive and benevolent listening. With the help of the two tamil novices who joined them a few years later, they took over being on duty at the

---

[40] Stephen had been a familiar of the ashram since the time of Monchanin. After having praised Griffiths to the heavens, he turned against him, hounded him, and caused him to have an appalling reputation, especially with the bishop.

[41] *Bulletin de l'AIM,* 68 (2000).

ashram when their superior traveled more and more. His conference tours in America, Europe, and Australia saw enormous success and caused a flood of visitors to Shantivanam beginning in 1976.

The way in which Bede developed his ashram caused disappointments and frustrations in Kurisumala. He suppressed night prayer, relaxed the rule about clothing, wrote the sacred syllable 'OM' on the cross in the church, and accentuated personal meditation rather than communal liturgy. In fact all these changes put into practice the monastic tradition of India as the charter of foundation prescribed. But this 'hindu' and permissive style irritated many, both Christians and Hindus themselves. The threat of syncretism that part of the local catholic clergy experienced met the indignation of certain brahmans who saw in it a profanation of their own religious symbols. The echo of these rumors reached Kurisumala, angering Francis. The correspondence he exchanged with Bede between 1975 and 1980 revealed growing irritation and discord, but also a patient, opinionated will on both sides to explain themselves and to establish mutual gratitude and appeasement. However, the misunderstandings became more serious. Bede resolved to write to Mar Athanasios, the syriac bishop of Tiruvalla and the only person who had authority over Francis, to ask him to liberate Shantivanam of all supervision and grant it autonomous status. 'No one here desires to depend on the authority of Kurisumala in any way any more.'[42] That was clear. But the bishop was ill and died a few weeks later without resolving the matter.

What was the problem, especially? Here we are dealing with a limit to the indianization of christian monasticism, in that the guru's total autonomy, as it is practiced in the hindu ashrams, is not possible within the Catholic Church. Every christian ashram must place itself in a canonical structure, depend upon a superior, give an account, under penalty of being excluded and not be able to receive novices, or celebrate the liturgy. This is a constraint that pioneers sometimes found difficult to assume, but it is also a security against abuses. Francis insured his insertion in the church as early as 1957, with the approval of the roman congregation for the eastern churches, while enjoying the great freedom given him by the *sui juris* status. Bede did not obtain the same support from Francis for the innovations that his superior judged to be inopportune and eccentric. He

---

[42] Letter of 1–7–77. Kurisumala Archives.

was seeking to escape this supervision, but had to find another—a less onerous one—and this was not easy.

Between Kurisumala and its eldest daughterhouse, we can speak about misunderstanding to the degree where each protagonist defended the same cause—the development of a completely indian christian monasticism—in his own way, but where the two leaders' personal history, style, character, talents, and methods were very different. However, they collaborated harmoniously for more than ten years: the strict monastic discipline of the one joined with the kind courtesy of the other permitted this temporary partnership in a shared project.

Francis was a christian monk, formed in the austere school of the Trappists. He was a leader of men, turned towards action and concrete enterprise at the same time as an ardent mystic. Bede was an intellectual, formed in Oxford, a speculative and poetic spirit gifted with an uncommon talent for oratory and relations. Both were authentic seekers of God, faithful lovers of India, spiritual masters. According to Catherine Cornille's typology,43 we could see Bede rather among the 'healers' and Francis among the 'teachers'. Francis was a man of fire, enthusiastic and intransigent. Bede was quiet, flexible, and tolerant. Francis found his path in 1957–58 in Kurisumala, where he started his own project. Bede accompanied him but was still searching for himself. It was at Shantivanam, ten years later, when he was already fifty–eight years old, that he unfolded his own dream, as crazy and improbable at the beginning as Francis' had been, but of a completely different style.

The root of the difference that opposed them was the issue of recognition. Bede did not recognize Shantivanam's filial relationship to Kurisumala. He 'ignored' the fact that Le Saux gave a gift to Francis and he never accepted the supervision a motherhouse exercises towards its foundation. Shantivanam quickly became his own project. He forever was acting freely and accomplishing his ideas without worrying or even noticing perhaps that they hurt Francis and frustrated his exercise of paternity. This initial lack of recognition blocked the relationship. Not recognized, Francis had difficulty in recognizing.

Shantivanam had had a double heritage from its beginning: that of Monchanin, ecclesial and theological, and that of Le Saux, based on the religious experience in relationship with Hinduism. Francis claimed to

---

43 Cornille, *The Guru in Indian Catholicism.*

represent the first and Bede the second. In addition, since Bede did not belong to the same original congregation as Francis, he considered himself his associate, his partner, not a member of his community. Separating himself from Francis, he found it normal not to depend on him any longer. Nonetheless, his long presence in the Kurisumala community permitted Francis to consider him as one of his monks, under his jurisdiction, which the charter of foundation specified.

For ten years, from 1972 to 1982, Bede pursued in various directions his search for an ecclesial statute that would support him canonically while leaving him a maximum of liberty, seeking in vain for Francis' approval. For a time he imagined a *pia unio* in the form of an open community that would gather religious, laymen and laywomen, and even married couples, with the goal of spiritual seeking. That was not to Francis' taste.

Bede needed to consolidate the stable core of his small community. When, to this end, he granted solemn profession to Christudas and Amaldas and oriented them towards the priesthood by sending them to the seminary to study, Francis judged that he was breaking the foundation pact: in the monastic spirit of the East, the priesthood is a service decided by the community based on its needs, not the project of an individual. Francis struggled a great deal to dissociate the monastic vocation from clerical aspirations, often associated with social promotion, and for these reasons had been opposed to the request of these two young men when they were at Kurisumala.

When Bede, for whom the spirit transcended the rite, conferred the *sannyasi* the saffron habit of renunciants during a sacred ceremony preceded by immersion in the Kaveri, to western disciples, some of whom had stayed in the ashram only a few weeks, the neighboring brahmans exclaimed this a sacrilege and Francis was consternated. He reproached Bede with devoting his very indianized ashram to the initiation of his european and american disciples, neglecting the project of insertion into the local church and the neighboring village communities. Bede protested this accusation. He reproached Francis with not understanding him and imposing his own ideas on him authoritatively, contrary to his own declarations on the freedom given to his foundations.[44]

The outcome of the crisis in 1982 sanctioned separation in fact. Bede Griffiths, to get out of the canonical ambiguity in which he was struggling,

---

[44] Correspondence between Father Francis and Father Bede, Kurisumala Archives.

was admitted by the camaldolese Benedictines who had given him a warm welcome in Rome and first at Big Sur, California, where they were in close contact with the many 'liberation movements' starting there at that time. He obtained the guarantee to be able to maintain his ashram's life-style and its indian style of prayer and hospitality. So that things were clear, he constituted with several friends a 'civil society'[45] and made it owner of the site, of which most of the buildings had been built by his efforts. There, Francis was indignant. He considered that as a real misap-propriation of goods, since in 1968 Le Saux had given the ashram to him personally. The minimum, he said, would have been that he himself or a monk of his community be a member of the new juridical structure. Francis experienced these events to be a double dispossession, a material one and a spiritual one. Everything was slipping away from him. He was asked to give his agreement in principle to Bede joining the Camal-dolese. He gave it reluctantly, but he considered this solution to be an abandonment of the initial project. Bede went to Kurisumala with Amal-das to have Francis sign the papers. Francis kept an unpleasant memory of this interview, because of Amaldas' aggressive attitude.

The two ashrams would continue their journey independently, and tensions would lessen with time. There would even be moments of grace, as at Kandy (Sri Lanka) at the asian monastic Congress, when Acharya would go get Amaldas to help him improvise Mass in Indian rite that he had been asked for the next day, and Bede would come congratulate him after the ceremony. In 1984, Bede would write a review praising *Prayer with the Harp of the Spirit*, which Francis had just published.

In August 1992, after the unexpected death of Amaldas, an aging Bede—he was eighty–six years old—wrote a friendly letter to Francis and proposed coming to visit him. Francis answered him with joy: 'Come whenever you like, but it might be better to wait until December? You never liked the raging monsoon on the ghats!' In December, a stroke made of Bede a diminished man. He would never return to Kurisumala and died on 13 May 1993 at Shantivanam.

---

[45] Like the ASBL in Belgium or an *Association-loi-1901* in France.

PRAYER WITH THE HARP OF THE SPIRIT

The Restoration of an Asiatic Monastic Liturgy

'Our mouth is too small to sing Your praise.'

Praise, thanksgiving, glory, honour and exaltation continually and without ceasing, at all times may we be worthy to offer to the Mighty and Strong who alone is good, who bestows His gifts freely. When He shows anger it is that we may repent, for He Himself is not subject to passions. To Him belongs glory, honour and adoration, at this time of evening, and at all times and seasons and hours and moments of the days of our life for ever. Amen.

(Sedro, Eucharistic Prayer, *Prayer with the Harp of the Spirit*, Evening Prayer on Monday, p. 49)

A 'seed of the Word':
'God's all pervading presence'

All this that we see in this great universe
is enveloped and permeated by God.
Renounce it that you may enjoy whatever is given by Him.
Harbour not any greed in your heart,
for the wealth of this world is not your own.

(*Prayer with the Harp of the Spirit*, vol. 1, p. 45,
Evening Prayer on Monday
Extract from *Isha Upanishad*, I)

From the beginnings in the clay and straw hut, the perfecting of the divine office in the Syriac rite was a patient work, untiringly elaborated, perfected, corrected, and enriched. The Syrian Churches of India, both Jacobites (Orthodox) and Catholics, besides the text of the Mass (*Qurbana*) had only a book of daily prayers for parish usage, a sort of breviary limited to the weekly office.[46] The search for the *Penqitho* through the Near East and its discovery in Mosul in 1961 allowed Francis to have a complete text of the prayers and hymns from the entire liturgical cycle,

---

[46] Shehimtho or Breviary of Pampakuda.

what is called the 'crown of the year', at his disposal. But the large in–folio volumes, printed in Syriac in the nineteenth century by the Domini-cans in the old, once Persian, diocese of Mosul were not usable as is. The texts had to be adapted, pruned, reorganized, and, above all, translated into English so that everyone—monks, guests, novices, visitors from In-dia and elsewhere—could profit from them.

This was an enormous work: the seven syriac volumes totaled four thousand pages. Translated into English this came to four volumes and almost three thousand pages. For twenty–five years, Francis spent on this task a good part of his nights, reducing his time for sleep to three or four hours. He loved this work very much, he admitted. First he read the text in Syriac, choosing one passage instead of another, recollected himself and prayed over those words. Then he translated, seizing the exact meaning, the semitic nuance, the poetic metaphor. Then he wrote it in the form of stanzas appropriate for alternating recitation. Finally, he attached an ex-tract from the sacred scriptures of India, of which thankfully good english translations existed, to the beginning of daily Vespers. For the syriac texts, however, except for the poems of Saint Ephrem—called 'The Harp of the Spirit'—translated by Sebastian Brock in Oxford and a few highly special-ized works done in Leyden or Cambridge, Francis had only the 'Book of Common Prayer', Bede Griffiths' translation of the 'Breviary of Pampa-kuda', which covered the ordinary of the week and corresponded to the first of the four volumes in the *Prayer with the Harp of the Spirit* series.

His courage, he often confided, 'came from the joy [he felt] working on this carefully woven meditation on the divine work of creation and redemption and man's response through the economy of salvation. It was in this magnificent liturgy of the great feasts of the years that the depth of syrian theology and contemplative tradition was revealed. It showed a mysticism centered on the Holy Spirit, different from that of the Greek Fathers who put their emphasis on the restoration of the divine image in man by Christ.'[47]

At the beginning of the 1980s, the work was sufficiently advanced to envision publication. This presupposed revising everything, carefully craft-ing the layout, titles, and writing an introduction and footnotes. Francis wrote by hand in pen, on the back of recycled paper. The books invaded his cell, lined up along the walls, piled on the ground or on the window

---

[47] 'Kurisumala ashram after twenty–five years', *Bulletin de l'AIM* 36 (1984).

ledge, protected by pieces of patched cloth. Anugrah, the copyist monk, kept up with him, typing on a ribbon typewriter with a metal shell pitted by the humidity. On onionskin paper, he was able to make eight copies at a time. The corrections were labor–intensive: Tip–Ex and carefully glued patches yielded a real patchwork that was brought to CMS Press, one of the largest printers in Kottayam, run by Protestants since 1848.

At the beginning of the 1980s, Francis went several times each week—the return trip was four hours in the bus—to correct the proofs. On the corner of a table, he made his annotations in red ink, concentrated on the text, indifferent to the din of the huge printing machine, which had to date from before the war, operating in the next room and to the movements of the many employees coming and going. In the afternoon, the heat was intense. The sweat running down from his arm stained the paper. Someone brought him a glass of water. He paused, took off his glasses, wiped them, rubbed his eyes and took his father's old pocket watch, protected by an orange crocheted cover, from his pocket. 'Three o'clock already. It's time to return if I want to be back in the ashram for Vespers.' He returned to the workshop to give his instructions to the compositor, sitting in front of his enormous case of type where the latin, hindi, and malayali characters in various sizes were lined up. 'OK, OK Father, I'll do my best', the man repeated. Francis insisted. He didn't let anything slip by. He checked each comma, despaired at the slowness of the work and at the many errors that persisted despite his instructions. Finally, night was falling when he went out. He would miss Vespers. Too bad.

The first volume was published in March 1981. Francis' joy was great when he finally held in his hands the bound book, covered in dark red cloth with a saffron jacket. He himself designed the cover illustration, representing a dove over a harp resting on a lotus flower and framed by a granite arch with a Persian inscription.[48] We recognize here the symbols of the Holy Spirit, India, and the syriac Church. A few weeks later, he received a letter from Cardinal Rubin, who was the secretary of the Pontifical Congregation for the Eastern Churches. A subsidy of five thousand dollars was allotted to him for the publication of *Prayer with the Harp of the Spirit*. This money came at the right time to finance the

---

[48] This arch represented the one that can be see in Madras, in the church of Mount Saint Thomas, on a seventh–century christian stele.

printing of the following volumes, and especially it was the sign that Rome supported the work, in spite of the insertion of hindu texts.

In 1983, a second edition of the first volume was printed, with a few improvements. The three other volumes followed, covering all the night offices (*lilio*) and evening offices (*ramsho*) for all the feasts of the year. From that time on, it was from these books that monks and guests of Kurisumala prayed the hours every day. Some visitors brought a series home with them, as a resource for their personal prayer. From various foreign countries, from South Africa to the Solomon Isles, universities and religious institutes ordered some. In India, groups of syrian Christians, both Catholics and Jacobites used them. Francis' dream was to see these texts used by a growing number of asiatic communities. As a subtitle on the cover he wrote, *The Prayer of the Asian Churches*. In fact, even though many indian and roman catholic periodicals noticed them with enthusiasm, the hierarchy remained reserved. He would have to wait until 1996 for the conference of bishops of India, gathered in Trivandrum, to give them homage and use them as support for public prayer during plenary meetings. In the meantime, specialists like Robert Taft SJ in the United States or André de Halleux in Louvain[49] published very positive reviews:

The fourth and last volume, which crowns the restoration of this treasure of theological and spiritual riches reveals, even better than the preceding volumes, the semitic structure of the yearly cycle into seven periods of seven weeks, partially disfigured by the wear and tear of centuries and which Father Francis tried to restore. . . . It is especially in the choice of feasts that he had to make the greatest choice and adaptation. He wanted to return to what had been the practice of the churches of India before the latinization of the synod of Diamper, of disastrous memory, while eliminating those ancient feasts whose meaning no longer speaks to us today. But he also introduced some new feasts. No one would object no doubt to that of the Poverello of Assisi, the most ecumenical of saints, whose veneration goes beyond the christian world. To compose his office, Father Francis was inspired by the 'Canticle

---

[49] André de Halleux, professor of Syriac at the University of Louvain, had stayed at Kurisumala in 1981. 'He installed himself in our modest library," remembered Francis, 'and immersed himself in the fairly rare works of the syrian fathers there'.

of Creatures' and also by 'The perfect joy of Saint Francis' by Félix Timmermans! Another novelty, more meaningful still: the introduction of a liturgical office for the great festival of Kerala, Thiru Onam, celebrated during the full moon in the month of Chingam (September). The legend of King Mohabeli, who sacrificed himself for the coming of universal compassion was joined to the memory of Thomas the apostle, the evangelizer who came to sow in India the 'seed of the Logos' by establishing the Church. Here we find concern for the indian and hindu inculturation of the christian ashram of Kurisumala. May its book of prayer nourish the hearts and spirit of the venerable Indian Churches in the syro–antiochian tradition for many generations.'

(André de Halleux, *Revue Théologique de Louvain*
[1989], no. 4, pp. 495–96)

. . . one can only applaud the prudent flexibility with Acharya of Kurisumala in adapting the ancient Syrian offices to the concrete needs of a living, vibrant, monastic life in the mountains of India's lush southwest coast.'

(Robert Taft SJ, in *The Liturgy of the Hours in East and West*
[Collegeville, 1985], p. 246)

Bede Griffiths wrote about the second volume in an indian catholic journal:

It is a book of great erudition, which presents a corpus of liturgical texts never before translated into English. By making known some of the treasures inherited from its rich past, it serves the whole church. This is also a work of great importance for the Church of India. Everyone is in agreement to say that if we have a liturgy proper to India, the Syrian tradition was largely responsible for its development.[50]

---

[50] Quoted in *Bulletin de l'AIM*, 36 (1984), p. 58.

SILVER JUBILEE

If we consider these last twenty–five years, we would want to
share our joy with our friends near and far. Our hearts overflow
with gratitude for God and for all those with whom we live or who
have come to us, as simple visitors or committed partners.[51]

The year of Kurisumala's silver jubilee (1958–1983) was a year of grace.
Francis, at seventy–one years of age, found energy and health he had not
known for ten years. He was freed from the constant pain that the advanced osteoarthritis in his hip caused him and threw himself joyfully
into intensive work.

This jubilee year was conceived as a celebration of life and a permanent thanksgiving rather than a set of formal festivities. The Lord himself
began it by calling suddenly to himself, on the evening before the Ascension, Father Varkey, a priest and *sannyasi*, who had left the Company of
Jesus at the age of forty to become monk in Kurisumala. 'The firstborn
of our community into eternal life!' said Acharya. The brothers were
visibly shaken and were shattered by this first death, so sudden: Father
Varkey had participated with the others in the night vigil. A few instants
later, he stretched out on his cot for a short rest, when cardiac arrest surprised him and he drew his last breath. Preparing his body to be waked in
the church, the monks tried to accept this event with serenity and gratitude. The bishop, Mar Youhanon, who succeeded Mar Athanasios, came
for Ascension the next day. The body was in the choir, uncovered and
surrounded by flowers, according to the indian custom. During the night,
a place for burial had to be decided and a grave dug. The place chosen
was the highest point of the property, the closest to heaven in the East,
and they named it the Garden of the Resurrection. The family and friends
of the deceased, who came to the ashram, participated in the ceremony of
farewell in the Malankar rite, and it was a reverential procession that led
Father Varkey, along a steep path, to his last resting place exposed to the
wind, facing the rising sun.

A few months later, on 14 September, they celebrated the great feast
of the jubilee. That very evening, Francis wrote to Dom Guerric:

---

[51] 'Kurisumala after twenty–five years' published by F. Acharya in *Indian Theological Studies* 21/2 (June 1984) and quoted in *Bulletin de l'AIM*, 36 (1984).

We celebrated the 25th anniversary of the dedication of our church today, consecrated by Mar Athanasios on the same date in 1958. The Exaltation of the Cross (as we continue to call it here) has been our annual feast since then. This year it was blessed on every level: reception of three postulants, investiture of one novice, investiture of a *brahmachari* (simple profession) and two *sannyasis* (professed monks). It was a very beautiful day. Night vigil as usual at 4 AM, Lauds at 6 AM, concelebrated Mass at 10 AM. The investitures took place before the Offertory. . . . It was a feast, with a congregation of more than two hundred persons. The meal unfolded in three sessions of about fifty persons. On this festive occasion, the food was served on banana leaves. It was very colorful, rice with vegetables arranged around it as well as spices for seasoning. I presided at the first service, for the ladies. There was music as well. All that was very joyous. In the afternoon, the guests dispersed to return home. Those who had come from the greatest distance are staying with us overnight. . . . The community now counts twenty–one members, of whom eleven are novices. I would not want to give you the impression that everything is marvelous. No, our joy is steeped entirely in faith, with its darkness and trials in the temporal order as in the spiritual order. One of our *brahmacharis*, the most gifted, who was to have become *sannyasi* today, asked for a time of reflection. He became very uncertain and only prayer can give him the light that is now lacking.

A twenty–page article, illustrated with photographs and summarizing the ashram's activities for the past twenty–five years was sent to various publications and religious houses. The AIM bulletin published it in 1984.[52] Other original publications were edited under the impulsion of Kurisumala, among them was a Malayalam translation of the 'Philokalia or Prayer of the Heart'. It was the fruit of an ecumenical collaboration: the translation was done by a Hindu from the Ramakrishna mission, the preface was written by a jacobite (orthodox) bishop and printing by an anglican ashram.

The 1960s were marked by setting up pioneer facilities and struggle for survival, the seventies by consolidation and expansion. With joy,

---

[52] In Diary 1983, Kurisumala Archives.

Francis saw his most ancient *sannyasis* founding new ashrams, which often joined a social vocation to the work of prayer and meditation. He visited them several times per year. After Thirumalai, directed by Mariadas, Chayalpadi ashram was founded by Philipose in 1972, near Trivandrum 'in a dense forest, crossed by rivers, inhabited by elephants, not far from the ruins of an ancient church, witness to a Saint-Thomas community that disappeared centuries ago'.[53] Dhyana ashram, near Bathery, was started by Sylvester in 1980. Others went much further north to Benares, or in the Andra Pradesh, one of the driest and poorest states of the indian union. In the immediate neighborhood also, the agricultural development was consolidated and spread: twenty–eight family farms had been built so far, and the jubilee year alone would see twenty–five others begin. This was a true cooperation, giving responsibility to the beneficiary families: the ashram offered the land, and furnished cement, roofing, door, and windows. The farmer had to find the stones there, gather them and participate in the work.

The eighties were especially marked by the enormous work that the publication of liturgical prayer in English represented and by the widespread recognition that followed the dissemination of these works. The welcome shown in various parts of the world to *Prayer with the Harp of the Spirit*, recognition by Rome, and the interest aroused in India were for Francis sources of great satisfaction. But perhaps the deepest joy came in 1983 in a letter from Scourmont. After thirty years of silence, Father Albert, his former novice master, wrote to him:

Very dear Father Francis,

On my visit to Scourmont, I saw the beautiful photos of the Jubilee of Kurisumala. I allow myself to share your joy. I congratulate you and I am even proud. . . . For me, after twenty–five years in Africa, I returned to Scourmont at Easter and I will return to Mokoto in May to care for the young people and the novices, as well as the young nuns from la Clarté-Dieu[54] and the Bernardines of Goma. Then, evidently, to die. I will be seventy–seven years old on 19 July. I believe that your work is more solid in India

---

[53] *Ibid.*

[54] Mokoto: cistercian monastery founded by Our Lady of Scourmont in 1954 in the Congo (then the Belgian Congo). The cistercian nuns had founded the monastery of Clarté-Dieu in the same area.

than in Africa. Dom Anselme saw clearly, as always, when he preferred India. After twenty–nine years, Mokoto is still a 'foundation'. Our sisters are further ahead.

A Dieu, my very dear Father. I would gladly call you 'venerable' father because of your handsome beard. May the Lord continue to bless your works and your sufferings. With affection and congratulations from your old brother,

Albert

Francis, very moved by this letter he no longer expected, answered at once, and it was the beginning of an affectionate correspondence that would continue until Father Albert's death in 1992.

The alacrity and physical energy that Francis regained after his hip operation allowed him at the beginning of the 1980s to take up again a rhythm of intense work and sports activities that some would judge excessive: swimming in the Peryar river—'an hour without stopping!' he wrote to his sister, Hatha–Yoga (he tore his knee joint forcing a posture), frequent climbing the mountain of the Cross, an eventful trip to Poona on foot, in a truck, and on train and bus. He wore out his eyes translating the *Penqitho* at night and went back and forth to Kottayam to correct the proofs—he often went down with the milk truck at 2:30 in the morning. In 1981, he worked feverishly with Ishananda to conquer a mysterious epidemic of spontaneous abortions in the herd. A couple of young swiss agronomists, the Stampfli, called to the rescue, suspected brucellosis. The epidemic stopped as suddenly as it had started, without anyone knowing why.

From time to time, from 1984, severe crises of arthritis in his left leg exhausted Francis. In 1985, bronchitis and sore throat dragged on for several months. Anugrah asked to retire to the Himalayas. They hired a young woman, Achamma, as secretary/documentarian and librarian. She would show herself a discreet collaborator, devoted, intelligent, and faithful, carrying out with unchanging patience Francis' never–ending reworking of turns of phrase and layout for the *Harp of the Spirit* and the other works he would publish during the 1990s.

In 1986, a second brother, Benjamin, died suddenly in the same way and almost at the same date as Father Varkey. Now there were two graves in the Garden of the Resurrection, where each first Sunday of the month, after Mass, they went up in procession with censers to pray 'for the brothers who have gone before us into the kingdom'.

The arthritis attacks intensified, aggravated by severe pain in his legs. Francis asked himself whether he should consider a second operation in Lobbes. Dom Guerric agreed to host him again. In the meantime, the neurologist he consulted in Kottayam prescribed a corset that improved the situation. Francis now added a knee brace and woolen underwear to relieve his permanent joint pain, but he did not reduce his activities: leading the liturgy, teaching the novices, daily overseeing of the monastery, welcoming the guests, presiding over the *satsang* every evening, not to mention the retreats preached in other communities and the conferences or various interventions in religious congresses or symposia, sometimes far from Kerala. He wanted to continue to serve, lead, control. He continued his 'Monday of silence' in the hermitage, through it all, to practice personal solitary meditation . . . and to keep up with his correspondence. Conscious of his impetuous temperament, sometimes excessively so, still he neglected to listen to the warnings his body had been giving him for several years.

He wrote to Amy: 'Pray for me that I may obtain moderation and self–control!'

FIFTH PART

FULFILLMENT
(1988–2001)

FULFILLMENT

O CTOBER 16, 1988, was a Monday, a day of silence for Francis. He retired to his hermitage as usual. A growing vague faintness prevented him from concentrating on his reading or correspondence. He felt a great fatigue and went to bed around 8 PM but could not sleep. Around two o'clock in the morning, he went to wake up Father Ishananda in his cell and made him a sign to follow him. He was the brother who had the most medical knowledge. Ishananda got up at once and followed Francis to his cell–office.

I don't feel well at all, can you help me?
How do you feel?
I can't sleep—that happens to me very rarely—I have a pain in
    my left side and a kind of oppression.
Exactly where is the pain?
There, all the way to my arm.

Acharya was very pale, his features drawn. A little sweat beaded on his forehead. Ishananda was worried; he had an opinion but did not risk a diagnosis.

I think you should go to Marian Medical Center for a consultation. The wagon is ready to go to deliver milk there.

Oh no, it's not worth it. In the morning, I will go to our hospital
to consult Dr Sina.

As you wish. Until then, rest. Stay lying down.

Good. I won't go to Vigils. You can preside for it.

Would you like me to stay?

No, go back to sleep. I am feeling better already!

Ishananda went out, closed the door quietly and sat in the hall, attentive
to the slightest call, until the time for Vigils.

Around 8 o'clock, Francis got dressed and walked to the hospital. The
pain was still there. When Doctor Hilde saw him coming, she interrupted
her conversation with a nurse and had him go into her office. He told her
about the night's events. She listened and watched him while she prepared
her blood pressure meter. It did not take her long to realize he was having
a heart attack, and she did not hide her astonishment and dismay:

And you walked here? You're crazy. You must go to a well–
equipped hospital right away. The nearest one is Marygiri in
Palai.

What is wrong?

It's your heart, Father Francis. I am not equipped to take care of
you here. There is no time to lose. Let's see, what's the
fastest way to get you to Palai?

The dairy truck will be coming back soon.

Yes, that is the best. They will bring you back down right away.

I will write a letter to my colleague right now.

Acharya slipped the letter in his pocket and started to go back to the ashram to wait for the truck. Doctor Hilde stopped him short: 'You are not
going back up! Stay here. Lie down on this bench. As soon as the truck
comes, we will intercept it and it will turn around with you.' She used
her tone of medical authority, and, for once, Francis obeyed. He objected
only that he would like one of his monks to accompany him, Yeshudas
for example. 'I will send someone to get him', Doctor Hilde promised.
'You, do not move!'

The yellow truck came at the same time as Yeshudas. A short discussion with the driver. They went to get Francis, who climbed into the cabin and sat near the open window. He was barely breathing. Two hours of twisting road to Palai. In places, the monsoon had dug ravines in the road. They slowed down, going carefully. It was starting to get hot. 'Stop!' Francis cried out. He had the impression of suffocating, dying. He got up, wanted to get out and breathe. It was an illusion. There was no more air outside than in the truck. It was his chest that no longer pumped enough air. He gasped, 'Let's go. Fast.' He was suffocating now and holding his chest with both hands. His companion watched him, more and more worried. He was gritting his teeth, concentrating his will, clutching his letter. 'Hold on. Get to the hospital. Give the letter.'

He was shaken. The pain was now sharp. The driver went faster and faster. He went past Teekoy, and the road widened. He honked at every turn, braked abruptly for a cyclist, a rickshaw passing on the other side. It was noon when he stopped in the parking lot of Marygiri Hospital, in front of the emergency entrance. Yeshudas quickly got out from behind the driver and went around the truck. Leaning on his brother, Francis got out and walked to the door. He sat on a bench. His head was spinning. He saw a doctor come running. He got up, held out his letter, and only then fell to the ground unconscious. Before going under he heard echo, as if in a dream, the four words shouted by the doctor: 'Stretcher . . . Oxygen . . . Intensive Care'!

SLOW APPRENTICESHIP OF REST

A few hours later Francis regained consciousness. A mask covered his nose and mouth, plastic tubes of various colors ran along his torso and arms, he was lying on fresh sheets, and a fan turned above his head with a slight purr. Reassured, he let go and sank into a deep unconsciousness for forty–eight hours, watched over by his old companion, Brother Mariabhakta, who prayed immobile at his bedside. All his senses disconnected, his body's strength was concentrated on mending the tear in his heart.

He came to on Thursday, asking the silent smiling nurses who cared for him their names: Annie, Victoria, Sheeba. He repeated their names, smiled in return, but did not have the strength to talk. After a week, the crisis was past. He received visitors and was impatient to be able to return home. The cardiologist who took charge of him was an orthodox Christian, Dr George Jacob. He was clean–shaven, with a fair complexion and attentive brown eyes that were always smiling behind his glasses. He had already talked with Dr Hilde Sina, her blond hair pulled back in a small bun behind her head, so thin in her blue–grey sari the same color as her eyes. She had come several times to see 'her' patient. The two doctors agreed that this seventy–seven year old man had exceptional stamina.

On November first, Francis was allowed to leave the hospital, on condition of observing complete rest. Doctor Hilde brought him back to the ashram in a rented car. Achamma had cleaned his cell and brought flowers. Ishananda and Yeshudas took care of the management of the monastery and led the liturgy, but Francis wanted to continue to teach the novices and receive visitors. The first check–up visit took place 15 November in the hospital. Dr Jacob remained prudent and insisted on the necessity for rest. The next day, Mar Timotheos, the new bishop of Tiruvalla, went up to Kurisumala to use his authority to oblige Francis to renounce all responsibility during the coming months: 'I saw Dr Jacob, Father Francis. I have great confidence in him; he is also my physician for heart disease. You have to organize yourself in such a way that you unload everything. Delegate, let others do it. Your life depends on it and we need you!'

Until Easter 1989, Acharya remained very tired. He had frequent headaches and tried to rein in his tendency to take back the management of affairs. He let the community take care of the retreatants and the visitors, very numerous as usual in the dry season, and kept only what was dearest to him: the novices' classes and a few hours of work at his table in the morning. Dr Jacob, whom he went to see twice a month, grew in friendship with this energetic patient. Since there was no way to keep him quiet, he had to support his weakened heart. He tried several medications, and in February had perfected a cocktail that seemed to work. At the end of March, Francis returned to regular life with the night office and the great *Qurbana* on Sundays. Every afternoon he walked for several kilometers, which brought him the ever–renewed joy of contemplating the mountains, trees, and flowers.

James, a novice with a shining face and gifted with a great natural gentleness, had been taught medical care by Ishananda. Already before he had entered the ashram, he had been interested in Ayur–Vedic medicine and had acquired some knowledge of it. Since Sylvester had left to found his own ashram, Ishananda was in charge of the farm and dairy, helped by Christudas, a young monk with an athletic build. James progressively took over the infirmary. He prepared Acharya's medications and brought them to him at fixed times. During attacks of osteoarthritis, he massaged the painful hip with aromatic oils. He would make his profession as *sannyasi* in 1994 with the name of Mariananda [Joy of Mary], which suited him very well.

In July, great hurricanes fell on the region, uprooting trees, tearing off the barn roof that fell on the road, but thankfully not causing any injuries. At the end of the month, Francis agreed to give a conference to SEERI[1] in Kottayam, during a seminar on syriac spirituality. In September, on several occasions he went to CMS Press alone by bus. But every time, he came home exhausted and needed several days of rest to recuperate. In October, one year after his cardiac accident, he wrote:

I have the impression that I am beginning to recover. My life remains intense, but it's a more interior life. My bodily infrastructure is definitively weakened from head to foot, especially my skeleton and vital parts: knees, hip, spinal column and of course, my heart. The least imprudence brutally confronts me with my physical limitations: I am called back to order by pain, sometimes blinding pain. I constantly have to hold back, use that moderation that is a fruit of the Holy Spirit. At the same time, I experience a new joy, a sort of more intense communion with others, felt through my suffering body.

The process of healing is slow, much slower than I had imagined at the moment where I returned to earth after having been sent brutally towards the 'other shore'. Now I am obliged to slow everything down, it is contrary to my desires and to my nature. I am diminished in what we customarily call 'vitality' but at the same time it seems to me that I understand better what I am reading, that I enter better into what I am learning, that I am more

---

[1] SEERI: Saint Ephrem Ecumenical Research Institute. Founded at Kottayam, Kerala, in 1987, by the dynamic Dr Jacob Thekeparampil, a Syro–Malankar priest, the institute's objective is to facilitate meetings between those who have inherited the syriac culture (ten million in India), whatever their church, at the local and international level, and to gather documents, texts, and works that can help the study of this ancient patrimony. It also offers complete formation programs.

sensitive to others: I listen more attentively to them, I accept their limitations better. I am learning to see myself no longer as being someone who 'does' but rather as someone who simply 'is'.[2]

The first months of 1990 were calm and sunny. Francis renounced his long night watches for study—from now on he went to bed at 9 PM— but during his morning hours of work, he started new enterprises. He prepared a course on the Psalms, read the Acts of Thomas, the books of McVey on Ephrem, and the second volume of the monumental work by Vööbus on syrian monasticism. On Dom Guerric's advice, he had the work of Tresmontant on biblical metaphysics sent to him and adapted it to give a course to the novices. He corresponded with Sebastian Brock, who sent him his latest work on holy women in the syriac Church and talked with him about Candida and Aphraate the Sage.[3] He also asked his advice about certain points of translation in *Harp of the Spirit*. What he loved above all was the retranslation of the Odes of Solomon that he began. He had the syriac text. An irish friend, Father Eoin, sent him an english translation by J. H. Charlesworth, but this did not satisfy him. The poetry and spiritual power of the Odes gave him enthusiasm and he poured his personal prayer into it.

The Spiritual Wedding

I put on the love of the Lord
The members of his body are there
He embraces me, He loves me passionately.

I would not know how to love the Lord
If he himself had not loved me constantly
Who can discern love
Except the one who is loved?

---

[2] Diary, 1989, Francis Mahieu. The apparition of introspective notes in Father Francis' diary is in itself a novelty, revealing the reversal of 1989. Before, his notes contained, in addition to brief mention of objective events, only notes from reading, preparations for courses or talks, references, accounts, and addresses; in short, work tools.

[3] Candida: young Christian martyred by the sassanid emperor Vahran II in the third century. Aphraate the Persian sage: instructor of a pre–monastic community, beloved contemporary of Saint Ephrem.

I love the Beloved passionately, yes, I love Him,
And where He takes his rest, I am with Him.
I will no longer be a stranger,
Because there is no resentment in the Lord
The Most High, the All–Loving.

I am mingled with him, because the lover has found the
    Beloved.
Because I love the Son, I become a son.
Yes, the one who adheres to the Immortal
Becomes himself immortal.

The one who finds his joy in Life becomes himself life
It is the Spirit of the Lord in whom dwells no deceit
Who teaches men to know his ways
Be wise! Understand! Stay awake!
Alleluia!

This is the first meditative song of Solomon, on the love of his Lord and his response to Him.

The poem recalls the themes of the Song of Songs, but uses the vocabulary and mysticism of the johannine writings: 'That day, you will understand that I am in my Father, and you in me and I in you' (Jn 14:20). 'The one who loves me will be loved by my Father and I will love him and will show myself to him' (Jn 14:21). 'It is not you who chose me, it is I who chose you' (Jn 15:16). 'We love, because He first loved us' (1 Jn 4:19).

This song is probably from the beginning of the second century, the first bud of what would become judeo–christian theology, which reached maturity with Saint Ephrem and flourished until the thirteenth century in monasteries, despite the islamic regime that dominated Mesopotamia and Persia very early. The sixth Ode of Solomon opens on a similar theme:

As the hand runs over the zither
And makes the strings sing

Thus sings in my members the Spirit of the Lord
And I sing in his Love[4]

The year 1990 did not end as quietly as it had begun. Let us allow
Francis himself to tell us the rest of the story:

8 August 1990

As usual we had many retreatants in April–May, and besides
that the monsoon arrived early: since May 20 our mountain has
been drowning under the rain, swallowed up in the fog and beaten
by furious winds. The last batch was a group of ten theology
students from Hyderabad, in the center of India, come for ten
days of 'ashram experience'. There was no way to take any walks.
We had to organize all their activities inside. On 3 June, we
celebrated Pentecost with them, a grandiose liturgy. That night,
my heart started to beat irregularly. The Monday of rest allowed
me to recuperate. However, at the next check–up, the cardiologist
sent me to intensive care, under monitoring for a week. He freed
me reluctantly, making me promise to take a complete month of
rest. I went up toward our mountain very happy.

But a few days later, June 18, I had a bad fall, from a height
of only three feet, on the stone steps that form the threshold of
my room. I was in great pain. They drove me to Marygiri Hospital
where an x–ray revealed a fracture of the pelvic bone. I was put
to bed immediately, and ordered to stay on my back. My right
leg was put in traction. After three weeks, the traction was removed but I still had to remain lying down.

Even though there were no lack of visits—our bishop himself
came to see me three times—I still had a lot of free time to be
quiet. I was fortunate to have a large room with two beds, all to
myself. A large window opened on to the garden, a sort of grassy
hill crowned by a majestic coconut tree. This view invariably
plunged me into meditation. The tree was often completely

---

[4] French translation (from the Syriac) and commentary written by Francis in January
2001 for the present work. The text ('En Juxta', Syriac–English), was sent by Father Eoin
and edited by J. H. Charlesworth.

motionless. Not one of its palms swayed, even when a downpour
of rain flooded it. It was an image of silent prayer.

I was very well cared for: two physicians came every day,
one a heart specialist, the other a bone specialist. There was a
multitude of nurses, some were students at the nearby school of
nursing. And Swami Mariabhakta, the senior of our community,
faithfully took care of all my personal needs, going so far as to
feed me when I was immobilized flat on my back in bed. There
was the daily visit of our dairy's truck that brought the milk to
the hospital, and which always brought some package for me, so
that I lacked nothing.

After six weeks, I was allowed to test whether I was able to
stand up on my legs without pain. I took a few steps, leaning on a
stand: the test was a success, I was able to return here very happy.
But I still had to stay lying down on my back for six more weeks
in my cell. However, I was allowed to stand up to go to the bathroom, or to sit at my little table to eat. At the beginning of August
I was able to walk prudently to the church for Vespers and there
sit on a chair (except of course for the prayers I had to recite
standing). We were celebrating the Feast of the Transfiguration!

Despite my temporary incapacity, the community is still very
much alive. There are several aspirants in their period of probation. Four *sadhakas* are finishing their second year of novitiate.
As for the classes that I used to give them, I had them take a
correspondence course on the New Testament, which is a part of
their program. The other classes are continuing as before, with
Father Lobo and Father Cherian.

For my part, I rejoice that I have long periods of silence and
that I am able to read. This is obviously a new stage in my life,
the last in my pilgrimage on this planet. I am concerned about
leaving my community a *typicon* [constitution] to help them find
their way in the future. When I am healed, I will take three
months of retreat to finish this work, or else it will never be
done. But I am putting my hope in the grace of God. It was He
who caused this community to exist, literally from nothing. Let
us pray that He will remain at work here, and make his presence

felt in the joys and difficulties, in the trials and blessings, for all of us: monks, guests, visitors.[5]

On 18 October, exactly two years after the first, Francis had a second heart attack. He awoke at dawn with the chest pain that he recognized right away. This time, he went to Caritas Hospital by jeep, where Doctor Jacob admitted him immediately to intensive care. Twelve days later, before releasing him, the physician tried one more time to reason with him: 'Father Francis, this second accident was due to your lack of prudence. You really have to rest, stop working as you have before. If you want to survive, you have to definitively change your rhythm of life, accept your limitations.'

This time, the warning was heard. The second warning brought about a deep change. For several months, Francis stayed in his room, cared for by those near to him, his brothers and sons. He renounced attending the communal liturgy. He greeted guests on their arrival and departure, but avoided conversations; they exhausted him, especially conversations accompanied by emotions. In the afternoon, if the weather was mild, he went for a short solitary walk, on level ground, with frequent pauses, leaning on his walking stick. For an hour or two in the morning, he started to write a new book: *Saints and Sages of Asia*, a sort of menology that gathered together asian saints of various religions and different times. Achamma, who attached herself to him as to a second father, helped him to the maximum for transcriptions and correspondence, while protecting his rest against inopportune visitors. From her place in the library where she worked all day long, she watched over access to the cell of her Acharya.

The return of Mariadas made things easier. The Thirumalai ashram, after twenty years of development, had been returned to the diocese of Kottar. Mariadas had given himself completely to it. The fruits were remarkable on the social level: the ashram, with its sanitary–education teams and professional formation teams, spread its influence over 126 villages, with a total of 35,000 families.[6] On the spiritual level, however, the fruit was slim. The only local monastic recruit had left after several years. But Mariadas had held firm, sharpening his spiritual substance in a difficult solitude, preaching retreats to all the religious and social workers of the

---

[5] Diary 1990, Francis Mahieu (draft of a letter, without mention of recipient).
[6] Cornille, *The Guru in Indian Catholicism*, p. 138.

region. Now, however, he was getting older. He was exhausted and gratefully welcomed the invitation to return to Kurisumala to act as prior as long as would be needed. He would personally take care of the novices' formation, in collaboration with the 'invited' professors, and would take care of groups of retreatants.

Acharya, always optimistic, judged that this second heart attack was, all in all, a blessing: it gave him more time to write and offered Mariadas a well–earned promotion, at the same time as an honorable way to leave Thirumalai. He recorded in his diary: 'The Lord desires to associate me more closely with his kenosis, self–emptying. The physical kenosis is only the sign of the interior kenosis that must be accomplished. This is my present preoccupation.'[7]

CISTERCIAN APPROACHES

On 11 August 1992, Acharya gathered the *sannyasis* of the community for a synaxis, a meeting of the solemnly professed. 'This year I reached the age of eighty and I had a few health issues', he told them. 'It might be time to think about electing a new superior. I would not be hurt by this. Tell me sincerely what you think.'

The brothers refused unanimously: 'You are our Acharya, we want you to remain so as long as possible'. 'Very well', Acharya replied. 'I accept your decision. But we must think about the future anyway. Some day I will cross over to the other bank of the river. What will happen to the community?' After a silence, Yeshudas started to speak, 'We do not wish to continue by ourselves, with our strength alone. We want to remain a contemplative monastery, a community of prayer and manual work. We are afraid that we will be absorbed in pastoral work, as were the Fathers of Bethany. We would like to be attached to an existing monastic order.' Everyone agreed silently. Acharya guessed that they had already spoken about this among themselves. He responded, 'I understand you. This can only be found in the West, and personally this is not my desire. But now, we are speaking about you. I respect your request. I will think about it and speak to our bishop Mar Timotheos about it. Does anyone wish to add something?' Ishananda spoke in turn: 'I believe that we are all attached to

---

[7] Diary, 1990, Francis Mahieu.

our Syro–Malankar liturgy and our indian lifestyle. Affiliation to a western monastic order would have to allow us to keep these.' Acharya's face lit up. He was happy to hear these words and responded, 'What you say is so true, Ishananda. I think we have to do all we can to preserve our identity, our specificity. I should perhaps buckle down and draw up a *typicon*, to put in writing what characterizes Kurisumala.'

The dialogue continued. Ishananda asked, 'Acharya, your former cistercian monastery in Belgium, could they not take us under their protection?' Francis responded truthfully: 'I don't know. Scourmont does not have much dynamism right now. But they have a new abbot, a young man 38 years old. There is hope. I will begin the dialogue and I will keep you informed.'

One week later, after reporting to Mar Timotheos and receiving his green light, Francis wrote to the new abbot of Scourmont, telling him the community's desire. He did not receive an answer, but in September, a letter from Africa reached him, as a sign. Elderly and ill, Father Albert had to leave the priory of Mokoto to become chaplain to the cistercian nuns of la Clarté–Dieu, in the region of the Great Lakes.

> My very dear Father Francis,
>
> I have just concelebrated the Mass of the Glorious Cross. It was for you, for all your intentions that I wanted to offer it to the Lord. For the last time, no doubt, because I have been confined to bed twenty–two hours out of every twenty–four since February 1991, trying to abandon myself to the Lord, maternally cared for by the sisters. It should be near you, with you, that I finish my life. The Lord disposed otherwise. I want to believe that dear Dom Anselme forgives me. You at least have accomplished his great dream. God be blessed.
>
> With my poor prayers and all my affection. I embrace you,
>
> Your old brother
> Albert

This letter let loose a flood of gratitude and deep joy in Francis' heart. It reestablished an old bond in all its strength and cleared up an old misunderstanding. After forty years, it was the long–awaited blessing from his former master.

Five months later, at the end of February, Dom Gérard Van Gheluwe's answer arrived, handwritten in large deliberate characters. His tone was direct, almost colloquial: 'I met you at Scourmont during your visit in 1978. We conversed. Do you remember? I saw photos of Kurisumala, read the brochures you sent to Scourmont. Although I was in Rome for a few years, do not be afraid of me. You know that our sisters of Soleilmont have had a foundation at Makkyiad, in Kerala, since 1988. I plan to go visit them at the end of the year. I will take that opportunity to spend a few days at Kurisumala.'[8]

Francis informed the community and remained circumspect. 'Let us wait to see what will happen', he told himself. However, he suspended his dear personal work on the *Odes of Solomon* to draw up a *typicon* as soon as possible. He wanted Kurisumala's specificity to be clearly defined in a text, in order to offer solid resistance to future 'all–encompassing powers'. He recorded in his diary: 'Cistercian affiliation risks implying a sort of renouncing of our past and no one here can accept that'.[9] But soon he had to leave the *typicon* in suspense, to go to the hospital.

A little before Easter, despite his fatigue, for a whole afternoon, he entertained a group of twenty–two religious women who had come to ask his advice for a contemplative foundation. He was aware that he could no longer hear very well, and he had to make a constant effort to follow the conversation, especially in such a large group. The next day, a new cardiac alarm sentenced him to two weeks of intensive care. A state of generalized weakness was diagnosed, vitamins and a month of rest were prescribed. Unwillingly he had to accept having to spend Holy Week far from his brothers. He gave his instructions in writing to Mariadas for the liturgical offices. 'Doctor Jacob is perplexed about my case, but he is caring for me as a brother, and Brother Mariananda is my guardian angel,' he wrote to a friend.

On his return from the hospital, his larynx refused to work. Was it a ruse of the Lord to prevent him from returning to presiding over the liturgy and tiring discussions? On his door, they put up a sign: 'Voice at Rest'. Mariananda prepared Ayurvedic syrups for him.

---

[8] Soleilmont: a belgian cistercian abbey going back to the thirteenth century, motherhouse of the first cistercian women's foundation in India: Makkyiad, Kerala, in 1988.

[9] Diary, 1995, Francis Mahieu.

In October, his state improved. He returned to community prayer, celebration of the Sunday *Qurbana*—a two–hour–long solemn Mass!— and presided over the *satsang* in the evening, where he had the pleasure of announcing to the community that Kurisumala took four prizes at the Munnar cattle show!

On 11 November, in the evening, Dom Gérard arrived in a jeep, brought by Sister Paule-Marie and Sister Isabel of Makkyiad. The monks virtuously tempered their excitement. Everywhere the murmur was heard: 'It's the abbot of Scourmont, you know, Acharya's former monastery!' All the next morning, the two men discussed together in the prior's cell. Discussed what? In which language? Let us bet that Francis could not resist the temptation of exchanging a few words in Flemish with Gérard, who, like him, was originally from West Flanders. No trace remains of what was said in that private conversation. After supper, the Cistercian presided over the *satsang* and spoke to the community in English. The next day, he walked up to the Cross with Mariabhakta and Nirmalananda. That evening, Francis explained the purpose of the abbot's visit: to see if and how Kurisumala could be associated with Scourmont. The next day, Monday, Francis respected his vow of silence. Dom Gérard walked around, visited all the property, and spoke with the monks. Before his departure, a first community vote revealed that seventeen of the eighteen members were favorable to an association with the Cistercian Order. There had been one abstention.

During the winter, the news circulated in the Order. The prior of Caldey wrote, 'We hope with all our heart that these contacts will bear fruit!' The prior of Bolton Abbey in Ireland deliberately anticipated: with the veterinary surgical instruments he sent to Kurisumala, he sent a card saying 'Welcome to the OCSO!'[10] Dom Bernardo Olivera, the Order's Abbot General, was more prudent: 'I am in close contact with Dom Gérard. I will do all I can so that God's will in this circumstance will be accomplished.' The young abbot of Scourmont was enthusiastic:

> Thank you for your card from Kurisumala, our future daughter-house! Thank you especially for having welcomed me so kindly, as a monk and a brother. Here in Scourmont, we have spoken a great deal about your request. We will soon vote. It is almost

---

[10] OCSO: Order of Cistercians of the Strict Observance.

certain to be positive. India has won over my heart and my soul. I think I will come back in April. The dedication of the church of Makkyiad will be held on 30 April. The Abbot General will come. That would be the opportunity to come together to see you.

Francis was preoccupied by the Abbot General's visit. He wondered how this high dignitary should be received. In the past at Scourmont, when the Abbot General announced that he would visit, they got out the large cruets and the starched tablecloths; a main dish was added to the menu. The abbot celebrated Mass with his mitre. How to preserve Kurisumala's simplicity while welcoming this distinguished guest with all the respect due his rank? When Dom Bernardo got out of the jeep in May 1994 under a torrential downpour, lifting the hem of his muddy white robe, a limpid smile lighting up his ascetic face, Francis relaxed. Mother Marie-Paul, abbess of Soleilmont, with her sisters from Makkyiad, Dom Gérard of Scourmont, and the Abbot General's secretary escorted him. They were all soaked. The monks got busy settling them in. The secretary did not have a change of clothing. Someone ran to get him a saffron robe while his was washed. When he came back, admiring and amused murmurs welcomed him. The sisters laughed as they took photos: inculturation is making great strides when the Romans from the Generalate[11] put on the *sannyasi*'s robe! The tone was set. Francis discovered that the time of the extremely restrictive rules and customs that he had known in the Order had passed: since Vatican II, Cistercians had adopted new constitutions and swarmed into the whole world, adopting the customs and cultures of the regions where they settled. A sign of the times was that the Abbot General was argentinian—the first non–European to hold that office. Francis took Mother Marie-Paul aside and confided, 'I thought that he would be a great gentleman to whom we had to bow and give all kinds of privileges. In reality, I discovered him to be very simply a brother.'

The abbot stayed only three days. When it was time for farewells, Dom Bernardo took his host in his arms for a fraternal embrace. He then took a step backwards and removed his pectoral cross, his abbot's cross. In front of the group that stood immobile, intrigued, he placed it without

---

[11] Generalate: the headquarters of the worldwide Cistercian Order in Rome, where the Abbot General and his team reside.

a word around the neck of Francis, who was left speechless with surprise and emotion.

25 May 1994

Very dear and revered Father General,

You will not be surprised to learn that we have very moving memories of the few days you spent with us at the beginning of this month. Your openness to our form of prayer and lifestyle strengthened our hope of being received into the cistercian family, when the time comes. Your gesture of offering me your pectoral cross in the presence of the whole community will remain unforgettable for me.

I am waiting for the end of retreat season to give the community a first teaching about cistercian life. We are also preparing a group for temporary profession and I would be happy to receive the ritual presently used in the Order.

In the meantime, I ask for your prayers and your blessing on all of us.

Affectionately, in the love of Jesus,
Francis Acharya

Dom Bernardo's visit reduced the apprehensions that Francis still had towards cistercian affiliation. The Generalate's circular letters and publications now arrived regularly in Kurisumala. Francis read them with interest and posted the essential ones in the veranda. Loyal towards the community, he continued the process that had been voted. But to a few close friends, he admitted that he remained personally reticent.

First, he had kept the ideal of a monastery integrated into the local church, independent, with indigenous recruitment. This is what had motivated him to join Father Monchanin in 1954: the french samist, a brilliant intellectual, had placed himself under the authority of an indian bishop. 'But we have to recognize that we did not succeed in recruiting candidates in our own Malankar Church,' he acknowledged; 'almost all have come from the Syro–Malabar Church. This is perhaps a sign.'

In addition, he was afraid that joining the Order might lead Kurisumala into a richer, more westernized lifestyle, and into a large organization planned in Rome, which would remove part of its initiative and originality. He continued:

It remains that even if we have here a remarkable community, we can see no one here at this time who might be capable of taking leadership. There is also the problem of formation. We lack teachers not only for monastic formation but especially for priestly formation. Our bishop refuses to ordain candidates who have not followed the complete seminary course. This is a subject of tension between us. The young people I accepted to send to the seminary a few years ago did not return. I am negotiating an agreement: professors from the malankar seminary would come here to give forty hour course modules: Sacramental and pastoral theology, Canon law. These subjects had not been taught previously.[12]

To provide for these two functions in the future—leadership and formation—Francis agreed to follow his community in seeking cistercian patronage.

In June 1995, the Order's central commission met at Orval in Belgium to prepare the General Chapter to be held in Rome the following year. They voted unanimously that Kurisumala's affiliation be put on the agenda and that Father Francis (or his delegate) be invited to come personally to present his request. When this commission's report reached Francis, he was moved when he read that 'the wearing of the cistercian habit should not be an obstacle' and that, while the community may keep the Syriac rite, it should 'follow the OCSO constitutions for all the rest'. The saffron habit of the *sannyasis* had considerable symbolic importance for him. He was not ready to make the slightest concession on this. Unfortunately, at the same time a dissension arose with the Makkyiad nuns about young syrian Christians who, desiring to enter monastic life, had been oriented by the sisters towards a cistercian house of the Latin rite in Canada. Scourmont had previously agreed to take one or the other into the novitiate. Francis was scandalized by what he considered a hijacking of vocation and a new sign of the latin imperialism over eastern churches. Angry, he requested a moratorium, but he was also prudent in proposing a simple association, a partnership before canonical affiliation.

An exchange of letters clarified the question of the habit—it was a misunderstanding: there was no question of requiring the indian monks to wear the black and white habit—and reassured Francis about respect for

---

[12] Draft of a letter to a friend, Diary, 1994.

Kurisumala's own specific identity. Now it was a question of who would go to Rome in October 1996. Francis hesitated to undertake such a trip. 'I get around with difficulty', he wrote to Dom Bernardo. 'Our bishop assures me that we can obtain a very small car in airports. But would you accept me at the Chapter in this state?' In February, the community insisted that someone go. Ishananda volunteered. Mar Timotheos offered to accompany the delegation. Finally Francis, overcoming his reticence and apprehension, decided to go himself with Mariananda, his faithful nurse. The bishop took care of the reservations and practical details.

In March 1996, Dom Gérard resigned, Scourmont was without an abbot, and the community there was in serious crisis. There were worries in Kurisumala: wasn't the affiliation compromised? Until now, everything had led them to believe that Scourmont would become their motherhouse. Uncertainty remained. In May, the whole Order was upset by the assassination of seven of its members in Tibhirine, in Algeria. Kurisumala joined in the emotions, mourning, and prayer of all the brothers throughout the world.

Meanwhile, Francis continued to write the *typicon* and improve *Prayer with the Harp of the Spirit* for the new edition. The prior general of the Camaldolese, accompanied by Christudas from Shantivanam, visited Francis and gave him a copy of Bede Griffiths' latest book. Francis took advantage of this to ask him for a copy of the camaldolese constitutions, to inspire him. He learned with deep sadness about the premature death of Father De Halleux from Louvain. 'He was for me one of those persons that one meets for only a few instants in one's life and with whom we feel united in a deep and lasting way', he wrote. 'I will never forget his joy full of surprise when he found a few of his books on the shelves of our small library.'[13]

As September 1996 approached, the monsoon abated, Francis' osteoarthritis was less painful, and the trip to Rome was approaching. The official invitations came: the General Chapter was meeting at Rocca di Papa, not far from Albano and Castel Gandolfo, in the roman countryside. Francis was expected for a week beginning October 10. After a complete exam, the cardiologist gave his green light for the trip, together with the now traditional warnings to be prudent. Francis concentrated his strength and entrusted once more his future and that of his community to

---

[13] Francis, in a letter to his niece.

Providence. Mariananda prepared the bags, medicine, and the rare patched woolens available in the ashram. At dawn on October 9, a jeep drove the three travelers to the airport at Cochin, and the next day, after stops in Bombay and Zurich, a taxi transported them to Rocca di Papa. Francis looked out the window, silent, happy that the trip had gone well, and happy to see the light of Italy again, its cypresses, its yellow stone houses. Now that he had arrived, he gave himself completely to the event and felt only joy at the meetings to which he was journeying, through the hills and vineyards of Frascati.

ALBANO

He said, 'It is I, Joseph, your brother.' (Gn 45:4)

The General Chapter of the Cistercians had been held since 4 October, about thirty kilometers from Rome in a congress center called *Per un Mondo Migliore* [For a Better World]. Ninety–four abbots and sixty–five abbesses from around the world were working there for three weeks. The schedule was full: Mass, monastic offices in four languages, two plenary conferences, and two or three meetings of small commissions occupied the capitulants all day long. The building enjoyed the most modern technologies: photocopy machines, fax, e–mail, Internet, word processors, and electronic voting system. During the breaks, the lines overheated in all the languages. About thirty interpreters, 'facilitators', secretaries, and typists took care of communications and reports. On a long table were photo albums like those which people exchange in family reunions.

From the central hall, a long staircase led to the conference room. A banner there read in large red letters: *Schola Caritatis* [The School of Love].[14] It was the theme of the meeting.

Africans or Asians, Europeans or Americans from north or south, monks and nuns wore a white woolen robe, black scapular and leather belt. One exception: the two sisters from Makkiyad (India), who represented the women of the ASPAC (Asia–Pacific) region were in saffron saris.

---

[14] This expression is from Saint Bernard: the cistercian community should be a *schola caritatis*. In the nineteenth century, this was translated 'school of charity'. The present tendency is to translate *caritas* as love.

Our three guests got out of their taxi at the beginning of the morning's second plenary assembly. Their entrance in the auditorium did not
pass unnoticed. Mar Timotheos was majestic, with his hood embroidered
with silver crosses and his purple belt. Francis, small, with lively eyes,
draped in his saffron shawl, and leaning on his two canes looked like a
kind of bearded Gandhi. And young Brother Mariananda, also in saffron,
appeared modest and radiant.

From the stage where he presided over the debates, surrounded by
his counselors and interpreters, the Abbot General introduced those arriving. After a brief hesitation, the applause began. Francis remained dumb-
founded for a moment. He finally let his canes drop and lifting his arms,
he joined both hands above his head, as a victorious boxer greeting his
audience. This time, the 160 abbots and abbesses stood up, and it was a
standing ovation that greeted the brother returning to the fold.

At the break, he was surrounded, congratulated, and affectionately
asked about his trip and his health. He held by the sleeve Brother Gabriel,
who represented Scourmont—still without a superior—to ask news of his
former colleagues. Mother Paul of Soleilmont brought him a cup of tea. He
relaxed, contemplating these joyous and studious people going up and
down the large staircase as in a heavenly vision. In a few instants, beyond
words and time, he found again the great fraternity that he had lived
intensely during the twenty years of his cistercian youth. The misgivings
he still had towards the Order dissolved in the warmth of that welcome.

After the break, Mar Timotheos was invited to speak. After introducing
himself, he praised the monastic life and made his request with simplicity:

> Kurisumala ashram has brought a great deal to the population of
> Kerala, not only to the Catholics but also to the Orthodox and
> Hindus. They all go there for retreats and spiritual counseling.
> The monks have adopted an indian lifestyle, the saffron habit,
> vegetarian diet, but in their heart they are Cistercians. When
> Father Francis is no more, who will be in charge? We need the
> help of the Order, of someone who will be in charge of the
> ashram. We ask to become a monastery of the Cistercian Order.[15]

---

[15] Minutes of the sessions of the 70th General Chapter of the Order of Cistercians of
the Strict Observance, Rocca di Papa, Italy, 4–21 October 1996.

Francis was invited to speak. Giving an abbreviated history of his journey in India, he was careful to make the canonical distinctions that such an audience would want. However, what came through his speech was his stubbornness that sustained a project led by the Spirit and transformed it into reality:

> My bishop introduced me as one of your brothers. I was happy to hear that, but at the same time I feel like a prodigal son or brother. My departure from Scourmont took place under painful circumstances. I wanted to go to India but Scourmont had decided to make a foundation in Africa (Mokoto). There were tensions. When I was asked why I wanted to go to India, I had a hard time answering. It was a dream that was born when I heard that Dom Anselme Le Bail planned to make a foundation in India. . . . I remember the twenty years I spent in Scourmont as a benediction. In Bombay, Paul VI sang this vedic hymn:
> From the unreal to the real
> From darkness to light
> From death to immortality
> Well, in Scourmont, I went from the unreal to the real. . . . For forty years in the Malankar Church I have been experiencing the same joy. As a husband would say of his wife that she is the best in the world, I would say that the malankar liturgy is the best in the world. . . . In 1992, I wrote to the abbot of Scourmont to ask him to integrate us into the Order. Dom Gérard and Dom Bernardo came to visit us. When we learned about Dom Gérard's resignation, we were very worried. . . . I am here to find a new mother-house.[16]

That afternoon, a small commission questioned Father Francis about life at Kurisumala, the cursus of formation of the novices, the resources, liturgy, and observances. It also questioned Dom Bernardo, who had visited the ashram, and Dom David Tomlins, whose abbey of Tarrawarra in Australia was approached to be the motherhouse. This commission's report, approved unanimously by its nine members, would be presented a few days later. It proposed a four–stage process:

---

[16] *Ibid.*

1. incorporation would be prepared during the present chapter;
2. a monk from the Order would go live at Kurisumala for six to twelve months to teach monastic doctrine and the new constitutions and statutes;
3. two abbots, including the future Father Immediate,[17] would then go visit the ashram and make a report; and
4. the Abbot General and his council could, following this report, approve the incorporation before the next chapter in 1999.

The report added, 'This accelerated process seems appropriate to the situation, given Father Francis' age and state of health'.[18] In other words: they were afraid he would no longer be in this world in 1999.

In the meantime, his mission finished, Francis took a few days of roman holidays before attending the assembly that would vote on the report. His niece came to visit him. He asked, 'Do you have a car? I would like to see the surrounding area'. With that they were off on the road to the Castelli Romani, between lakes and hills, crossing charming villages gilded by the autumn sun. Francis was curious about everything, tried to read the signs with an italian accent, and observed the agriculture with a knowledgeable eye. In Albano, he found a watchmaker's shop. He asked his niece, 'Do you think they could repair my watch? The glass is broken and the hands catch on each other. In India, they were not able to repair it.' He took a silver engraved pocket watch, wrapped in an orange crocheted cover, out of his deep pocket. It had been given to him for his first communion in 1922. The two pieces of glass were fixed with yellow tape, the hands were twisted. 'Do you want to go buy a new one?' his niece asked. 'Look, they have some similar'. 'I would prefer to have this one repaired', Francis interjected. 'I like it very much.'

The watchmaker asked Francis to sit down—*Prego!*—examined the watch, and searched in a drawer full of glass pieces of all kinds. After a few fruitless attempts, he found one that fit perfectly. With his magnifying glass held in his eye, he then straightened the watch hands. Meanwhile, his wife stole glances at this unusual customer. Considering his old habit and his beard, no doubt she was comparing him to Seneca or Socrates. She murmured to herself: *C'è un filosofo!* [He is a philosopher!].

---

[17] The Father Immediate is the abbot of the motherhouse.

[18] Minutes of the sessions of the 70th General Chapter of the Order of Cistercians of the Strict Observance, Rocca di Papa, Italy, 4–21 October 1996.

Mar Timotheos left for Rome to take care of some business. He would meet his traveling companion at the airport. Francis was invited to participate freely in the morning's conferences. When Dom Amandus, from Tegelen in the Netherlands, gave a very beautiful talk on forgiveness, a capitulant from South America suggested during the exchanges that followed: 'Bringing the subject closer to us, we might apply it to Father Francis. The Order could ask his forgiveness for having left him alone during these forty years.' Applause. As they went out, Francis asked Mother Paule: 'Someone spoke about me, but I did not hear very well. What did he say?'

On Sunday, a bus brought about fifty participants to Tre Fontane, a venerable abbey where a solemn service was celebrated to the memory of the seven martyrs of Tibhirine. Mariananda was part of that trip. He came back that evening, thrilled and laden with small souvenirs that he gave his superior to dispose of at his discretion.

On October 16, the process of incorporation proposed by the committee was approved by the assembly of abbots by a vote of ninety out of ninety two. Dom David Tomlins, abbot of Tarrawarra, agreed to 'follow with pastoral solicitude the community of Kurisumala with the goal of becoming its Father Immediate'.[19]

The next morning, Francis and Mariananda said goodbye to the assembly. The Abbot General spoke of his joy and gratitude for their presence, as well as his hope of seeing the incorporation. Francis as his goodbye exclaimed, 'When, this morning, someone asked me if I was satisfied, I answered him: "No! I am enthusiastic!" I am leaving with my heart full of joy and gratitude.' Then the abbot of Cîteaux read a message composed by his predecessor, Dom Loys, who had become a member of the Abbot General's council:

Kurisumala is a gift the Lord is preparing for the Order
Before it is a favor the Order does for Kurisumala
It is for us to receive this gift
Not to conquer it
To serve it
Not to enslave it

---

[19] *Ibid.*

It is not a question of imprisoning the spirit in law, in the Order
But of enriching the Order with the spirit that lives in Kurisumala

The cistercian charism must be able to express itself
In all the cultures
In each culture

It is not a question of imposing western expression on all the
 cultures
But of favoring the proper cultural expression
Of the original charism of our founders

We have perhaps more to receive
Than to give
In welcoming Kurisumala

INCORPORATION INTO THE CISTERCIAN ORDER

Francis did not wait for the official instructors' arrival to begin initiating his community in the history of Cîteaux and the life of the founding Fathers; he began this himself, as soon as he returned from Rocca di Papa. He wanted the community to make a good impression in the first exchanges. Dom David Tomlins went to meet his new daughter in February 1997. The Australian abbot was welcomed with enthusiasm and deference. His teachings were followed attentively by the whole community. Francis attended all the lessons and took notes. For him, it was an updating: many things had changed since the time he used to instruct the novices in Scourmont and Caldey. The monks asked many questions. They were curious to know how other monasteries were run, about the daily life of Cistercians in their smallest details. Dom David listened and explained without getting tired. He himself took his role as future Father Immediate of a Syriac–rite indian ashram very seriously. He wanted to learn about India, its religions, and its culture and went away with a list of works recommended by Francis: Naipaul, Panikkar, Gandhi's autobiography, Griffiths, Le Saux, Monchanin . . . and Saint Ephrem!

In July–August, it was the prior of Tarrawarra, Michael Casey, who came to give six weeks of courses on the constitutions[20] for two hours every day. Every evening at *satsang*, he spoke about the spiritual foundations of the Rule of Saint Benedict, emphasizing humility. He would return twice before the end of the year. He discovered how much the community of Kurisumala was permeated by the spirit of Cîteaux in its life of prayer and work, even if it did not always have the vocabulary or the doctrine. It was judged unnecessary to send other instructors: the six months of courses were reduced to six weeks!

The following year, they went on to the third step: official inspection before admission. The 'visiting' abbots, Dom David and Dom Filomeno from Our Lady of the Philippines, arrived February 26, 1998, and remained one week. The monks were a little stressed. Antiphonal recitation in the choir was not always harmonious. Some went too fast. They practiced, however, and they were on their best behavior. All day, it was as if they were writing an exam. Francis oversaw everything, rectifying situations with a gesture or a frown that would be immediately noticed by the attentive brothers. As usage required, the abbots spoke to each of the monks separately, to allow them to express themselves in all freedom. The secret vote revealed the *sannyasis'* unanimous agreement. This time, there was not a single abstention. The two visitors also met Mar Timotheos in Tiruvalla and, of course, spoke at length with Francis. Every evening, one or the other spoke to the community for almost an hour. At their departure, they did not hide their satisfaction: the community had passed the exam, and the visiting abbots hoped to see Kurisumala incorporated before the end of the year.

During the following weeks, during the noon meal, the reading of the life of Saint Bernard followed that of Evagrius Ponticus. Francis wrote special offices for the feasts of Saint Benedict, Saint Bernard, and the founding fathers of Cîteaux: Robert of Molesmes, Stephen Harding, and Alberic, who would be added to the syriac calendar as well as the new edition of the *Harp of the Spirit*, which he was revising.

On May 23, 1998, the Order's central commission met at Latroun in Israel. Abbot General Dom Bernardo, with his counselors and the thirty

---

[20] The Second Vatican Council called all religious orders to return to their original charism while adapting to the present situation and local culture. The present cistercian constitutions, published in 1990, are the fruit of this long work begun twenty years earlier.

abbots and abbesses representing 'the four quarters of the earth'—as the *Penqitho* says—voted unanimously for the incorporation of Kurisumala ashram into the cistercian family. They voted to give the ashram the rank of abbey, whereas it had asked to be received only as a simple priory. It is true that the new daughter was already over forty years old, had more than twenty members, and had already formed several generations of novices.

The official news was announced that very day. By electronic mail, many houses were told instantaneously, and from around the world, congratulatory messages poured into Kurisumala, where they had just installed a telephone—but only at the farm! Several of those messages alluded to the parable of the prodigal son. But Scourmont—was this a discreet allusion to Dom Anselme?—used another parable, the one about the talents: 'Have you not multiplied the share of inheritance the Father entrusted to you? Your return home is that of a good and faithful servant.'

The official public ceremony of incorporation was set for July 9, 1998. The guest list was drawn up. They were busy setting up less spartan guest rooms for the VIP abbesses and abbots. With Dom David's approval, Francis prepared the ritual for the celebration: everything had to be invented! An intense correspondence was exchanged to settle the practical details. Mother Marie-Paul sent a tape of the *Salve Regina* in English and also sent a hi–fi tape recorder for the chant rehearsals. The abundance and complexity of documents received from the generalate perplexed Francis. 'A good part of all that goes above our heads', he wrote. 'The adaptation to the present state of Cîteaux can only be done gradually.'[21]

Dom Bernardo reassured him again: 'Kurisumala was accepted as it is' (he underlined this).[22] In the same letter, he told him that he had been urgently and suddenly sent to Japan by the pope for an apostolic mission, and thus he greatly regretted that he could not preside at the incorporation ceremony. He delegated his powers to Dom David.

It was obvious that the Abbot General wanted to let Kurisumala keep its indian lifestyle and eastern liturgy: he was careful that the structures of the Order consolidate the new abbey without changing its nature. With his characteristic sense of humor, was he not publicly saying at Albano in 1996: 'If Father Francis asked my permission to give up the saffron shawl for the black scapular, I would refuse!'

---

[21] Letter to Father Godefroid of Scourmont, 7 February 1998.
[22] Letter from Dom Bernardo Olivera to Francis, 16 June 1998.

On 9 July, the little church was full to bursting. The solemn *Qurbana*, presided over by the bishop and concelebrated by nine priests, opened the ceremony. The homily in Malayalam was short, personal, and vibrant. The bishop entrusted this mission to Father James Vadakel, a syro–malabar priest and old friend of the community, for whom he regularly held sessions of biblical meditation.[23]

After this solemn and colorful liturgy full of mystery and perhaps slightly long for those who were not accustomed to it, the guests spread out on the veranda for a refreshment break. It was a happy effusion of fraternal embraces, congratulations, and emotional reunions, with a glass of tea or water and cakes in hand. During this break, a few monks put away the liturgical material and moved the church furniture around. Four chairs, simple wooden chairs with plastic caning such as were found everywhere in Kerala, were lined up in front of the altar and awaited the dignitaries: Dom David, Mar Timotheos, Mother Marie-Paul, and Father Michael Casey. After the Trisagion dear to the Malankars—Holy are you, O God!—everyone sat down. Francis took his place on a low stool, near his community sitting on the ground in rank of seniority, almost at the foot of the abbots. The visitors overflowed onto the porch, even into the confessional: religious superiors were side by side. The Fathers and Sisters of Bethany—the only Malankar Order—Camaldolese, Vallombrosans, Sylvestrines, and Cistercians represented the great benedictine family. There were also Jesuits, associate professors, parish priests, friends, doctors, nurses, neighbors, farmers from the cooperative, and farm workers with their families.

Francis opened the session with a word of welcome and thanks for all those who had made incorporation possible. He retraced its history since 1992: four years of postulancy, two years of novitiate! He ended by expressing his gratitude, particularly to Dom David, and his joy at welcoming him as Father Immediate.

In his talk, Dom David first evoked what he described as the three great joys of the Order in this nine hundredth anniversary of Cîteaux: the large gathering organized in March on the very place of its origins, the beatification of Father Cyprien Tansi, the first african Cistercian, and . . .

---

[23] Francis had met Father Vadakel in 1969, in a very unacademic way. When he was sleeping on the ground in the Palai station, where he had spent the night, the priest, seeing the first bus arrive, woke him up and started a conversation that was the beginning of a long friendship.

the incorporation of Kurisumala, the first cistercian abbey in India. 'Today, the Order tells you, through those of us who represent it from Makkiyad, Soleilmont, Tarrawarra: you are our brothers. We are your brothers and sisters. Welcome to the family.' He specified what Kurisumala brought to the Order and what the Order offered to Kurisumala.

> You bring us enrichment, through your monasticism deeply rooted in the eastern indian culture: a new branch on the old benedictine–cistercian trunk, a branch which itself transmits the vigor of the very ancient traditions of indian and syriac spirituality. What the Order offers you: first its structures full of wisdom, created in the twelfth century in the Charter of Charity. Filiation, for example, that created a permanent and reciprocal relationship with a motherhouse and implies regular visits. These structures strengthened our communities and maintained them in life for nine hundred years. There is also the corpus of monastic teaching and doctrine accumulated by the Order: a treasury of texts, meditation on which favors the conversion of manners in each of us.

Father Casey, in his function as notary, then proceeded to read the Acts of the Central Commission of Latroun, which were the juridical foundation for the incorporation. The monks of Kurisumala stood up, the blue book printed for the occasion was given to each of them, and in the total silence that had fallen, Dom David asked the ritual question: 'Brothers, what do you ask?' He received the ritual response: 'The grace of God and of the Order', and responded in turn: 'Then pronounce the collective renewal of your monastic vows.'

They read together the formula of commitment. Then each in turn, Francis first, they went one by one to sign the common schedule and symbolically receive from Dom David's hands a carefully folded cistercian cowl.[24] Francis could not help but think for a brief moment about the cowl he had had to remove during his farewell visit to Scourmont, without participating in Vespers for Pentecost 1955. It was returned to him solemnly with joy, forty–three years later, when he was in his eighty–seventh year.

---

[24] In fact, only two cowls were brought, but Mother Marie–Paul discreetly had a sister keep bringing them back in turn for reissue.

With a single voice, the community then intoned with great energy a sort of martial scouting song with appropriate words:

We are happy seekers all united in the Lord
    We belong to one family
Jesus Christ has chosen us to carry on His life
    over every land and sea
From the north and from the south
    and from the east and west
He has called us all together

And we are delighted that we are united
    into God's own family. (twice)

Mar Timotheos concluded with a word of thanksgiving. He thanked the Order for having agreed that the new abbey keep the Syro–Malankar rite. He thanked Dom David and his community of Tarrawarra, who would henceforth watch over Kurisumala's future. He told them of the personal affection he had for this house and his desire to retire there some day. At the end, turning towards the cross and addressing the Lord directly, he offered him praise and gratitude for the graces he showered on Kurisumala in this fortieth year of its existence.

The *Salve Regina*, the ancient hymn in honor of Mary, then arose, sung slowly in the somewhat rocky English of the Malayalis, by the assembly who turned towards the brand new icon of the Queen of Cîteaux. On it we see [the founders] Robert, Alberic, and Stephen under the cloak of the Theotokos.[25]

That evening at the *satsang*, Francis succeeded in having Mother Marie-Paul speak. He took her by surprise. She told the story that her abbey, Soleilmont, was doubly Kurisumala's sister, because it also had been founded outside the Order, in the twelfth century, and incorporated later.

At the end of July, during the monsoon, an american Cistercian, Sister Kathleen O'Neill of Mississippi Abbey, came to give a course on John

---

[25] *Theotokos* in Greek signifies 'she who bears God'. The name of a byzantine icon representing Mary bearing Jesus in a medallion in the center of her body.

Cassian.[26] She went home delighted. Francis was just as delighted: 'It was a deep spiritual communion', he wrote. Sister O'Neill would mention her stay a few months later in an article of *Cistercian Studies Quarterly*:[27]

> Night was falling when my jeep started on the road that zigzags up the mountain. It started the rain and we drove into thick fog before reaching the heights where the ashram is. Thus my first impression of this new cistercian monastery was truly mystical. During the two weeks I spent there, I was swept away by the monks' enthusiasm and by the joy they felt at having become members of our Order.

Francis' main concern was to answer the innumerable messages of congratulations he received, especially from all the cistercian monasteries of the world. He thought of writing and printing an illustrated brochure to recount the ceremony of incorporation and present Kurisumala to its new brothers and sisters. At the beginning, he envisioned a pamphlet of about twelve pages with a few photos. But he wanted to share everything, tell everything, to make their liturgy known, reproduce the talks and the chants extensively. And there were the photos. How could they choose? All of them reflected the spirit and atmosphere of the house, as much as the texts. The 'little brochure' grew by the day. Francis wrote, added, and interspersed; the docile Achamma calmly typed, cut, and pasted. It became a real book of 158 pages! Meanwhile, Francis was revising volume 2 of *Prayer with the Harp of the Spirit* for the second edition. His physician told him not to work more than two hours a day, a prescription he obviously did not obey. Finally, shortly before Christmas, the dummy of the souvenir book was entrusted to the Capuchins of Bharanganam who have a well–equipped print shop.

Printing techniques had progressed a great deal in India in the past few years: the glossy white paper and excellent quality of colored photos would make this book an album Francis could be proud of in Europe and in the United States. Francis did not allow anyone else to correct the

---

[26] John Cassian: monk and author of works on the monastic spirituality of Egypt and Palestine, fourth century. His *Conferences* were daily reading in many monasteries and he is considered a saint by the eastern churches.

[27] Sr Kathleen O'Neill, Review of [Francis Acharya], *Kurisumala Ashram: A Cistercian Abbey in India*, *Cistercian Studies Quarterly* 35:4 (2000) 557–58.

proofs, especially for this mirror of Kurisumala that would be sent to the whole Order. He himself went to Bharangaram to give orders to the head of the workshop. When he returned to check the first printing, he returned very displeased: the references were not well positioned, there were errors everywhere. He was irritated and wrote detailed notes, which he had John, the faithful 'associate', bring.

In January 1999, everything was finally ready, and Francis was exhausted. Such stress was not good for him. A serious cardiac alarm—a Sunday at 2 o'clock in the morning—brought him back to Caritas Hospital. Once again, Dr Jacob settled him in intensive care. After a few days, he could move to an ordinary room and have visitors. One morning, the cardiologist entered, closed the door, pulled a chair close to the bed, and looking his patient in the eye, gathered his arguments to convince him:

Father, your heart has been damaged since the heart attack of 1988. In fact, it is only working at two–thirds of its capacity. In addition, the arteries that supply it are in bad shape, partly blocked. Ideally, you should have a bypass, but practically, the fragility of the tissues does not allow it. It would be too risky.

Francis asked, 'But then what can you do?' The doctor replied, 'Not much more, unfortunately. It is you who must avoid all effort, all fatigue, live at a slower pace.' He continued, 'In short, do what you have never done: pace yourself. Have you not celebrated your eighty–seventh birthday?'

Francis was relieved to leave the hospital on 17 February, armed with all sorts of prescriptions and orders for complete rest for two months. On the way home they stopped at a pharmacy where Mariananda watched over the preparations.

As at each alarm, the community had been worried, orphaned. This morning, they watched for the abba's return. When the car stopped in front of the door, they ran to it, forming a silent and joyous circle. Francis took his canes, extracted himself from his seat and glanced all around, looking at each one with a smile. Then, without a word, he went into the church and put his canes against the door frame. The brothers who followed him stopped instinctively, like friends stay at a distance when two persons who love each other meet again and embrace after a long absence. With his head bare, barefoot, bare–handed, small in the middle of his empty church, in threadbare cotton jacket and pants, Acharya returned to visit his Lord.

LOURDES: DOM FRANCIS MAHIEU ACHARYA

The General Chapter was held every three years. The next one took place in October 1999 in Lourdes. This time, Francis did not hesitate long: he insisted on consecrating his community's belonging to the Order by attending the General Chapter as an abbot among abbots. Mariananda would accompany him. As early as July the formalities were started: reserving plane tickets, passports, visas. The closest french consulate was in Pondicherry, five hundred kilometers away. Francis sent his request by mail. The consul informed him that he could grant him a visa only if a french citizen residing in the place he was staying would 'take charge of him' and if he had health insurance: the Republic was not risking having to take care of an elderly indian citizen at its expense.

After intensive exchange of mail and faxes with various persons able to resolve these problems, both in the Order and in the family, Dom Jean-Marie, abbot of Our Lady of the Desert, obtained the necessary formulas for the 'taking charge' of Francis, and asked the dominican sisters living in Lourdes to fill out the forms in their name and have them stamped at the city hall. The Mahieu family, nieces and nephews, went looking for health insurance. But there they failed completely. No company was willing to insure a traveler more than eighty years old. Finally the whole family joined together and made the situation known to the consul, joining to the letter a list of all the family members living in Belgium or in France and presenting guarantees of creditworthiness.

The consul was still not satisfied. He required diplomatic support from the Vatican and wanted to see the requester in person to question him! Certainly, Francis would always have problems with visas. His physician strongly discouraged a road trip of a thousand kilometers. Finally, Mariananda was sent as his ambassador, armed with one of the beautifully illustrated books about Kurisumala. After having waited two hours in the waiting room, he was admitted and endured detailed questioning. He was successful in 'placing' his album so that the consul started to leaf through, visibly interested. 'Very well,' he muttered. 'Wait outside. I will reexamine the whole file. Someone will call you.'

After two more hours of waiting, Mariananda was readmitted to his office and had to answer a series of questions of a different kind: Could the consul come to Kurisumala? How does one get there? Can one stay overnight? 'This time, it's going well' Mariananda thought to himself.

He was not wrong. Soon, with the two visas in his pocket, he hurried to a yellow and blue 'call center' to telephone the good news to the ashram before taking the bus back.

There was one problem left before the departure: the abbatial ordination. Francis wanted to do things according to the rules of the art, and the liturgy was for him the art of arts. Since Kurisumala had been elevated to the rank of abbey a year previously, he had been searching for the text of this blessing in the Syrian rite. In the Malankar Church, there is a ritual of monastic ordination conferred on the *remban* [solitary monks] and performed before episcopal ordination. But since there were no longer monasteries or monastic communities, they abandoned the prayer concerning the *Rish Dairo* (the superior of the community, literally: 'head of the flock'). Francis inquired from his usual sources: the seminary of Sharfeh in Lebanon and the patriarch of Damascus. He was sent the ritual for the ordination of the *Cor–episcopa*, originally an auxiliary to the bishop for the country parishes, now an honorary title conferred on a priest for eminent services to the local church. It was only after laborious research in this thick document in Syriac that Francis finally found what he was looking for: the ordination of the *Rish Dairo* was a relatively short prayer, common to the *Cor–episcopa* and the *Rish Dairo*. It was a simple addition to the prayer of consecration that took place before communion during a Mass celebrated by the bishop, as for other ordinations. Francis judged that, in the context of their recent incorporation, the presence of the Father Immediate was necessary. All this research took time—it was already September. They agreed that Dom Tomlins would travel by Kurisumala on his way to Lourdes, which would permit them to organize the abbatial blessing and then to travel together the rest of the way.

On 14 October 1999, during a morning Eucharist celebrated by Mar Timotheos, Francis in his eighty–eighth year was officially consecrated first abbot of Kurisumala, the first cistercian abbey in India.

Lord, dispenser of all graces and all duties
Come to the aid of your servant
And give him goodness, solicitude, vigilance, discernment
And sufficient strength for this ministry entrusted to him.
Be at his side so that he conducts himself in an irreproachable
    and disinterested way
Grant him the intelligence necessary to lead with wisdom

To instruct and correct those who err while compelling them
with goodness.[28]

The assembly's acclamations marking its consent rang in the church,
while Francis received from the bishop's hands the insignia of the *Rish
Dairo*: the black head–covering adorned with twelve silver crosses, and
the pectoral cross—the very same one that Dom Bernardo, just before his
departure three years previously had put around his neck without saying
anything, in a prophetic gesture.

The ceremony was simple, moving, but tiring: Francis had the habit
of returning to sleep after the night vigil, and at that hour he felt twinges
of pain in his heart during long periods standing. 'I will choose another
day to go ask Dr Jacob for a certificate', he joked. When he arrived in
Lourdes a few days later, Dom Bernardo introduced him teasingly: 'This
is the youngest of our abbots!'

Saint-Pierre City's bungalows were built on several levels in the side
of the hill overlooking Lourdes, facing the Pic du Jer. The view was superb and recalled Francis' escapade along the rails of the funicular with
his brother in 1920. Practically, it was not easy for him. It was impossible for him to walk, even with his canes, on this uneven terrain. The
spanish, belgian, and french abbots who had come by car took turns driving him from his room to the morning Eucharist, the conference rooms,
and the refectory at the very top. Soon, someone got a little cart that allowed him to circulate in the afternoon along the paths around his building, to observe the birds—he searched his memory for their french
names—the mountains, and the peaceful pond suitable for meditation.

Francis was greeted warmly by all the participants, including those
whose language he did not understand: Chinese, Korean, and Japanese.
He found old friends from Asia and Belgium: Dom Filomeno of the Philippines; Dom Frans and Mother Martha from Indonesia; Dom Armand
Veilleux, recently elected abbot of Scourmont; Mother Marie-Paul; and
those from Westmalle, Achel, and Orval. He was particularly pampered
by the women, as his advanced age shielded him from ambiguities: the
japanese sisters held his hand and had their photo taken with him at the
marian grotto; others put affectionate notes, flowers, and candy at his

---

[28] Extract from the prayer of consecration of the *Rish Dairo*, translated and communicated by Father Francis in a letter of March 14, 2001.

place. 'One day, I found a treasury bond for 10,000 francs slipped under my door! I gave it to the abbot of the Desert.' The abbess of Chimay, his former neighbor, had her community embroider liturgical linens with indian motifs on the occasion of Kurisumala's incorporation. The superior of Klaarland, in belgian Limbourg, gave him a small rare work in honor of his mother tongue: an edition of the *Seven Manieren van Minne* [*The Seven Ways of Loving*] by Beatrice of Nazareth, a nun and mystic from the thirteenth century. The text was in ancient Flemish and present–day Dutch, the dedication in Flemish.

At dawn, while the other participants prayed the hours by language groups, the two Indians recited the syriac office from the *Harp of the Spirit* in their room. Mass was celebrated in common, every day in a different language. And in the evening, just before supper, everyone went towards the esplanade and gathered in silence around the immense lit statue of Mary. A voice intoned *Salve Regina* in gregorian chant, and from two hundred fifty voices, from more than fifty nations, the ancient cistercian hymn arose in unison in the darkened valley.

The problems raised in plenary assembly—a sort of parliament for the Order—were new for Francis and held his interest. For example, should one allow the young monks who expressed the desire to move to Tibhirine in Algeria to replace their assassinated brothers? What should be the status of priestly ordination for monks? Should one maintain strict enclosure for the nuns? Francis listened, learned the Order's news, but intervened very little: he was too 'new'! Only once, he pleaded in favor of the incorporation of a small autonomous community in Denmark, similar to his own in certain respects. On another subject, he gathered general support when he gave his opinion about priesthood: 'if the priesthood should not be the subject of personal ambition, refusing ordination seems to me to be inverse vanity. If the community needs a priest as it needs a gardener or novice master, the abbot will ask this service and send this monk to study. This is a question of obedience!'

Thanks to the headphones transmitting simultaneous interpretations—French, English, Spanish, or Japanese—Francis heard clearly and understood all that was said. 'The interventions are always courteous, but sometimes stubborn!' he remarked about the plenary sessions. But he also came away with a positive impression: 'The debates are well conducted. There are tenors who speak frequently, others who are never heard. The women speak less but some have had remarkable interventions.'

During the free day, two bus excursions were organized. Francis would have loved to go to Spain—it would have been his first time! But he thought it was his duty to go thank the abbot of Our Lady of the Desert who had gone to such trouble to negotiate his 'affidavit' and obtain his visa. He also went to thank the dominican nuns of Lourdes, who invited him and Mariananda to a festive lunch with their entire community. They had done all the formalities at city hall. He returned very impressed by the mixture of strength and gentleness he perceived in Mother Marie-Isabelle Lopez, the superior of a community of about twenty contemplative nuns.

Leaving Lourdes on 12 November, he had only one regret: not having been able to meet everyone he wanted to greet personally or thank for their gifts, because he lacked the time and perhaps the mobility. Still accompanied by Dom David and Mariananda, he went to London via Paris by plane from the airport of Tarbes. Francis was tired; his legs were painful. He was happy to stop with the bernardine sisters in Slough before getting on the plane to Bombay the next day at dawn. But a visitor had arrived: the brother of a belgian Jesuit who had recently died after having spent his life in India. He absolutely wanted to meet Francis and had come to Slough just for that reason. His affection was overwhelming and dire: he stayed more than five hours talking and making the old monk, who wanted a little rest, talk. The following night, heart congestion seized him. He was suffocating. Mariananda woke Dom Tomlins. They were very worried. Should they interrupt the trip? Drive the patient to the hospital? The attack diminished, and they went to the airport just the same. Francis was in a state of great weakness. He felt oppressed; he was unsteady. Mariananda feared for his life and prayed without ceasing during the flight, which passed without incident. But they had scarcely returned to Kurisumala than new heart troubles arrived. No doubt the happiness Francis felt in Lourdes, the joy of the many warm meetings, had hidden the fatigue that the inherent tension of daily work sessions on unfamiliar subjects had on his weakened heart, without counting the stress of the long trip. The inopportune friend in London had been the 'drop that caused the vessel to overflow'. In December 1999, he underwent, in his own words, an 'irrepressible physical decline'. His entourage feared the worst. No one dared to hope that he would begin the new millennium, except Francis himself.

AT THE GATES OF SHEOL

At his return from London, Francis insisted on meeting the community that very afternoon, to tell them about his experience of the General Chapter. He participated in all the offices, but felt extremely tired. At the end of two days he went to Caritas Hospital for a cardiological exam. Dr Jacob recommended a week of complete rest in the hospital, but Francis refused to consider that. 'Doctor, I have just been away for three weeks! I have to be at the ashram as soon as possible! Can't you give me an injection, or medicine?' 'In your case,' the doctor explained, 'the medicine has its effect only accompanied by rest. Here, you are forced to rest.' Francis pleaded, 'Listen, it is really not possible right now. Let me go home, I will rest there.' And the doctor acquiesced, 'As you wish. I can't keep you against your will!'

As we could expect, once back at the ashram, Francis did not really rest: the mail had accumulated in his absence, and there were problems to solve on the farm. And he had such pleasure in returning to the offices, the novices! And this article on the liturgy of the Passion he promised Dom Armand. . . . As we could also fear, the cardiac congestion manifested itself again in full force. After a particularly difficult night, he was resigned to return to the hospital. But this time, neither bed rest nor medicine nor attentive care had any effect. The painful congestions constrained his thorax day and night and left him exhausted. Dr Jacob no longer knew what to do. He suggested a consultation in a hospital better equipped with medical imaging equipment, with experts. The nearest was Madras. Mar Timotheos took charge of this, reserved the plane tickets, and made the appointment. He also wanted to make the trip, but, prevented by a meeting over which he had to preside, he finally sent his secretary to watch over Francis and his personal car to drive him to the airport with Ishananda and Mariananda.

On 13 December, the more exhaustive exams at Madras Medical Mission were analyzed by three renowned cardiologists. Their conclusion: two of the heart valves were completely obstructed and no longer working. A third was almost blocked and let only a small amount of blood through. A bypass was not possible because of the patient's age and the general state of his arteries. They could only try new medicine, attempt to dissolve the blockages and make the blood thinner by chemical means.

After a few days, Francis was brought back by airplane to Caritas Hospital, where they experimented with the treatment proposed in Madras. He was still suffering very much. In addition, he had difficulty accepting the conclusions of the Madras doctors. 'They rejected me because of my age!' he confided to a friend, offended. Little by little, the pain diminished and he was able to return to the community just before Christmas. A lull at the beginning of January allowed him to write his article on the paschal liturgy and fittingly welcome Dom Armand Veilleux and Mother Marie-Paul, who took advantage of a regular visitation to Makkiyad to come visit him. Dom Armand taught the juniors and spoke to the community about the formation of a monk, 'a process that lasts the whole life long and leads us to be transformed into images of Christ'. An Australian friend, Peter Abotomey, a retired teacher, came to live at the ashram for a few months. Francis asked him to put order in his last writings, to prepare *Saints and Sages of Asia*, an attempt at interreligious hagiography, for publication.

During the night of 20 January, a severe attack brought Francis 'to the gates of Sheol'.[29] He felt his heart suffocate, his brain paralyze. He felt he was sinking, going away. Ishananda telephoned Dr Jacob, who answered that he had reached the end of his resources: if the medicine prescribed at Madras had no effect, he could do nothing further. 'He is a monk, he has to accept his lot with patience!' As a last resort, they phoned Dr Hilde Sina, who came at 6 o'clock in the morning and gave him an intravenous injection. Towards 8 o'clock, Francis got up and had some breakfast. It was Sunday. He concelebrated the *Qurbana*, but sitting down most of the time. That evening, he wanted to attend the *satsang* and conduct at least the prayer of Compline, the last prayer of the day. But his voice failed him, and when he returned to his cell, another heart congestion struck him down. After a few hours of complete immobility, calm returned to his chest little by little, but he remained without strength and could not sleep.

'Continuing like this is impossible,' he thought. 'This is awful. If I have to reduce my participation in the offices to a passive attendance, or even stay here in bed without doing anything, I prefer to die. I would so like to

---

[29] This was Francis' expression. In the Old Testament, 'Sheol' is the place of the dead; it designates the spiritual condition where all the souls find themselves after death: a dark abyss where humanity lies in darkness and the shadow of death.

continue to serve the community.' Dr Jacob admitted he could do nothing. 'He minimizes these congestions. Accept my lot with patience!' Francis fumed. 'I would like to see him do that! But let's stay calm. Let's not get excited or irritated or my heart acts up. Who can help me?' he prayed, 'O God, come to my assistance, Lord, make haste to help me!' (Ps 80).

Meanwhile, the seniors got together. They had an idea. 'Acharya', they suggested, 'you could perhaps try natural medicine. A center of macro-biotic medicine recently moved to Panikkappalam, twenty–five kilometers away. They heal the sick with plants, massages, diet, without chemical medicines. It is said that they obtain surprising results'. Francis told himself he had nothing to lose. At the end of January he met Doctor David, a Hindu member of the Macrobiotic Society of India. Mariadas and Mariabhakta, both in their seventies and suffering from various ills, accompanied him, as well as Mariananda in his role of nurse, partisan to this therapeutic approach. The doctor spent about an hour listening to each of the patients: he had them describe their symptoms and tell him about their medical history, he questioned them about their occupations, habits, and nutrition. He concluded, 'I will study your case and determine an appropriate regimen for each of you. You will receive the prescriptions in a few days. You will have to apply these in a rigorous way, without any deviation. We will see you again in a month.' 'For you', he added, addressing Francis, 'I think we will be able to make these chest pains disappear and have you return to normal activity. But it will take time.' Francis was ready for any sacrifice as long as a hope remained of continuing to be useful: teach the novices, celebrate liturgy, read and write, welcome visitors, and share a 'word of life' at the *satsang*. He asked for nothing more, but for the present he was incapable of that.

Dr David's prescription came on January 25th. Francis communicated it to the community and his bishop right away, and by fax to his Father Immediate, Dom David, in Australia. It was severe and consisted of four points:

1. A draconian diet: whole grain rice and certain vegetables, boiled without salt or sugar. As drink: water, rice water and herbal teas. Fruits, milk, bread, cookies (and chocolate!) were forbidden;
2. Vegetable compresses (potato, mustard seed, ginger) on the chest and back twice a week for several hours;
3. Steam baths in a fiberglass cube where only his head protruded, to cause abundant sweat; and

4.   Complete silence for three months.

It was the last prescription that at first glance seemed hardest for Francis. It presupposed canceling his appointments, disappointing guests and visitors, and reducing his exchanges with the seniors and the community to the exchange of notes, without mentioning the liturgy.

The first week was difficult. The meals seemed insipid to him, the long sessions with the compresses put his patience to the test (he endured them thanks to the *nama japa*, the repetition of a short invocation). The absence of verbal exchange was a real penance. He slept very badly. His skin was irritated by the compresses. However, there were some positives: the congestions were lighter and the chest pains, although still frequent, now calmed after fifteen minutes of immobility. Thankfully, reading and writing were still allowed.

The community put great hope in this new attempt and tried to sustain its abbot by daily attentions: they showed him that the tasks he had to entrust to others were accomplished with zeal. They slipped notes of affection and encouragement into his mailbox, they put flowers on his work table, and especially, they prayed for him unceasingly day and night. Western friends and family were more skeptical and even frankly worried. Won't this more than ascetic regimen take away his last strength? Is all this not part of dangerous eastern ideas? Dr Jacob, the cardiologist of Kottayam, informed by letter of the new treatment his patient was following, answered ironically:

> I am sorry to learn of the tortures that your naturopathic doctor is inflicting on you. Having spent your life in a monastery, you are probably capable of enduring these persecutions, as the first Christians did at the beginning of our era. But how can the material hard as rock that clogs the blood vessels feeding your heart be dissolved by a diet and enforced silence, when even the powerful laser is incapable of doing this? I pray that God will give you the courage to confront this strange situation.

One month later, in March, the pain had almost disappeared, his sleep improved, but this was at the price of a state of general weakness and even a sort of intellectual numbness. Francis wrote to his niece:

I am going through a 'night of the senses', to use the expression of Saint John of the Cross. The difficulties, I would dare to say the trials, that the macrobiotic treatment brings me weigh on me, sometimes even overburden me. Despite this (or maybe because of this), I am being very careful not to compromise it. The doctor is now considering prolonging it one month, which would be after Easter. . . . I remain confident that my constitution of Flemish peasant stock will hold up and, certainly with patience, with this treatment will see a marked improvement to my heart condition.[30]

Mariananda tried to make the treatment less difficult. He made a little cotton corset lined with plastic, which allowed Francis to work at his table during the sessions with the compresses. He went to the kitchen himself to try to prepare tastier vegetable dishes and supervised an organic garden where they grew the vegetables recommended by the doctor, including yams.

Lent passed under the sign of Saint Benedict. Francis wrote his communications to the community every day and had one of the monks read them. He still tired easily, the least slightly rapid movement, even to dress, caused pain and heart troubles.

One Sunday night, he decided to test his strength and went to the *satsang*:

The short distance from my room to the hall with its three steps down and three steps up immediately made my heart protest. The hall was full, with several people behind the windows of the façade. When I sat down, facing this crowd, I felt myself completely paralyzed. Thankfully, the *satsang* starts with mantras and chants, this allowed me to catch my breath and I spoke for a quarter of an hour. But back in the church for the two psalms, I had to sit down. In spite of this, I went up to the altar for the last blessing, the night blessing. I very visibly made the triple gesture, but my voice remained inaudible. It seems that I am paying a great price to be delivered from severe congestions. On the other hand, I want to continue the treatment scrupulously because I have no

---

[30] Letter to his niece, March 12, 2000.

other option to return to my abbatial ministry: community prayer and teaching.[31]

However, slowly, his sleep improved, his writing became firmer, and he laboriously finished his Christmas correspondence.

The departure of Anthony, a young monk and university graduate whom Francis had tried as *socius* caused him sadness and relapse. The boy wanted to found his own malankar ashram outside the Cistercian Order, arguing that he was not able to use his talents here. They sent him to discuss with Philipose, who was encountering the greatest difficulties in a similar project, then with the bishop who tried to reason with him, but he persisted in his idea. Francis finally summoned the seniors for a meeting after Vigils, at 5 AM, in his room. Tense, he listened to them pinpoint the problem, then communicated through his notebook: 'I don't have the strength to discuss with him. Go speak with him and if he does not change his mind, let him go!' But the irritation and nervous tension tied to these events brought a new attack of congestions.

Every month, Dr David saw his patient, listened to him, and slightly modified the diet. Finally the palpable improvement hoped for was seen at the end of May. Francis no longer took any medicine, his strength returned, and the pain had almost completely disappeared, as long as he made every movement slowly and avoided all excitement. He started to get around again, and his first visit was to his two old companions: Jacob, weaker and weaker, and Mariabhakta, suffering from cancer, both were dying in the hospital. On the same occasion, Francis went to see Dr Jacob. He had written to him in a spirit of conciliation, and maybe also to show him that he was victoriously undergoing the 'persecutions and tortures worthy of the first Christians'. The cardiologist, a good loser, examined him and admitted that he was impressed by his good condition. Francis later explained:

> The treatment I followed for the last four months freed me from the heart congestions that overburdened me all during the two preceding months. I am not pretending that my arteries are free from the deposits clogging them. My heart remains mutilated, extremely sensitive to any physical or emotional stress. I am well

---

[31] Letter to his niece, March 17, 2000.

aware that I need to treat it gently. I will soon be 89 years old. I am learning the art of living free of internal or external stress and of remaining calm in all circumstances. This seems appropriate for this last stage of my life.[32]

Mariabhakta died on 22 May. They brought his body back that afternoon in an open coffin strewn with flowers and placed him in the church, surrounded by lit candles and aromatic sticks of incense. Two monks watched with him. His sister arrived that evening and stayed all night, sitting on the ground, reciting psalms with the community. The deceased's friends and large family, alerted by an announcement in the morning newspaper, arrived in great numbers on the next day to lead the eldest of the monks to the 'resurrection garden'. He had joined the ashram in 1960.

A few days later, after four months of silence and severe diet, Francis was allowed to break the silence and broaden his regime a bit. He joined the community again for the offices of noon and evening and led the *satsang* on Sundays and feast days. In August, he took up the novices' classes three times a week, and in October he resumed night vigil, daily *satsang*, and, to his great joy, walks to the great reservoir facing the mountains. Leading the liturgy was now shared: in the cistercian manner, one 'hebdomadary' priest led it in turn, and for the offices, the prayers to be recited alone were shared among the seniors, which created a very harmonious alternation of voices while sparing the abbot's breath. The steam baths, compresses, and diet were maintained on the advice of Dr David, in whom Francis now put all his confidence. One small addition, however: a belgian chocolate bar, 'Côte d'Or' brand, on Sundays and feast days . . . and there are many feasts in the syriac calendar! Francis was overwhelmed with gratitude:

I thank the Lord who seems to renew my strength to persevere in the service of this monastery I love, while putting me on guard against the impetuosity that characterized me for a long time. I just also have more attention for the community so that it can gradually find its own form, its own rhythm and this can happen only with much patience, delicacy and even tenderness on my

---

[32] Letter to Dr G. Jacob, May 17, 2000.

part. . . . The macrobiotic treatment bailed me out when my boat seemed to be drifting.

During this jubilee year, Francis completed a sort of very intimate inculturation, experiencing in his own body the alliance of western voluntarism with the empirical and patient wisdom of the East. Before Christmas, he had the joy of seeing two more good vocations arrive, bringing the group of novices to four and, with the students, his class size to nine. For them, he worked again on the one-hundred-thirty page syllabus he wrote to lead them on the ways of 'Monastic Spirituality' and the 'Cistercian tradition'.

ALL IS BLESSING

Kurisumala, Wednesday, January 17, 2001

3:30 AM. The stars are beginning to pale. Acharya's window is lit up. He sits on his bed and waits a moment for his heart to stop pinching, as it always does when he wakes up. He dresses deliberately, with slow movements, rolling a corner of his shawl over his head, careful to keep his good ear uncovered. Another pause and he starts down the hall. All the monks are already in the church, where oil lamps were burning. He takes his place, to the left, near the window and speaks,

It is good to rise early to pray to You, our Creator
And with the angels, to make a joyful noise
Singing thrice the acclamation: Holy, Holy, Holy are you, O God
In your tenderness, be good to us, O You the Merciful One.[33]

5:55 AM. It is still night. The full white moon has ended its course at mountain level and now projects long shadows on the road. Small groups of neighbors, of nuns, climb toward the church.
6:00 AM. Three priests in saffron shawls sit on the choir mats, around the low altar covered with yellow, pink, and red dahlias. The Indian–rite Mass is about to begin. Nirmalananda, in charge of the liturgy this week,

---

[33] *Prayer with the Harp of the Spirit*, vol. 2, 'Night Vigil for January 17', p. 567.

officiates in the middle, Yeshudas at his right and Acharya at his left. Usually, Acharya said his private Mass after Vigils and was resting in his cell at this hour. Would this be a special day? The congregation seemed large for a weekday.

6:45 AM. The priests withdrew, the faithful sat waiting in the church for the signal for breakfast. But an unusual coming and going, whisperings in the hallway, packages hidden under the saris hint that something is being prepared.

7:00 AM. When the gong sounds, instead of going to sit in silence along the wall, the assembly walks in procession towards Acharya, singing together 'Happy birthday to you'. A little girl dressed in white organdy is pushed towards him with a bouquet. Each person in turn approaches Acharya to give him a flower, a colored card, a message. A square cream cake is brought to him, with pink sugar letters spelling out 'Acharya 90th'. In India, as in China, birthdays are celebrated at the beginning of the year, not at the end of the completed year. Acharya today begins the 90th year of his existence, and the community affectionately joins in the festivities organized by his friends from the neighborhood, an agape limited to this morning interlude. Photos are taken, a recording of traditional indian music is played. Christudas comes out of the kitchen armed with an enormous knife, cuts the cake into small squares, and distributes them. Acharya does not eat any, because of his macrobiotic diet. His joy is in the messages he received.

8:00 AM. Brother Anand, the old gardener, stands at the edge of the new flowerbed, in front of the guesthouse built last year with a VIP wing: an abbot's room and a bishop's room. He leans on the wooden barrier and watches his assistant work. A guest stops, asks about his health, and then congratulates him on the beautiful garden. He smiles and points to the young *brahmachari* watering the beds. 'It's his work', he says.

8:30 AM. The herd invades the road, one hundred animals urged towards the pastures by two young boys armed with sticks. Father Ishananda watches them, examining each dairy cow with an expert eye. But his inspection is interrupted by one of the workers: someone from Cochin is calling him on the telephone. The director of the travel agency tells him he will arrive the next day to organize a return trip to Pusan, Korea, where the cistercian chapter of the Asia–Pacific region would be held in May. He, Ishananda, member of the Council of Elders, will represent Kurisumala. Dom David will accompany him.

10:00 AM. Acharya, in his cell, reads his mail and writes several
letters. When he finishes, he takes up again and rereads the letter that
gave him the most pleasure. It is signed 'Dom Emmanuele Bargellini,
Prior General of the Camaldolese' and had been given to him personally
by its author, who had come yesterday from Shantivanam for a brief
visit, accompanied by Father Christudas, the disciple of Bede Griffiths,
and Father Georges, the present prior of Saccidananda ashram:

> In Shantivanam, as you know, we are presently celebrating the
> fiftieth anniversary of its foundation. This golden jubilee is for
> us a reason for joy and gratitude, first to God, the origin of every
> gift that comes from above. But we also wish to express our
> gratitude and filial homage to those who, with prophetic sight
> and by their sacrifices, allowed this work of God to be born and
> take form, to become a precious spiritual inheritance, given and
> entrusted to our generation. We know, Father, how much you
> contributed to the birth of ashrams in the Church in India, in
> particular Kurisumala but also Shantivanam, where difficulties
> and suffering were not lacking. We express our thanks to you
> with all our heart for this service you have rendered to the
> Church and for having permitted the incorporation of the ashram
> in the congregation of the Camaldolese of the Benedictine Order
> in 1981.
> 　　Today, with a single glance of love and marvel, we contem-
> plate the light of God that revealed itself to us—in a manifold
> way—in the face of those we venerate as the 'fathers' of
> Saccidananda Ashram. We accept this communion in diversity,
> taking it as a guide for our sincere commitment to keep and
> develop the spiritual inheritance entrusted to us.'

There is also a card from the hospital's doctor, Hilde Sina, which
Acharya takes up again from the pile of envelopes:

> The psalmist sees the span of our life as seventy years, eighty for
> those who are strong. I suppose ninety for those who are 'still
> stronger'? On this celebration of your life, I would like to thank
> God for your presence here, on this mountain. We have been
> neighbors for thirty years, with tensions at times but also a growing

nearness, understanding and friendship. Father, I want to thank you. I am grateful to you for your openness, your wisdom, your tolerance and your attention to people and events. Thank you for your affection, for your love.

Acharya turns his gaze towards the window and ponders a moment. Yes, there were tensions, disappointments, and sufferings—with Shantivanam and with the hospital. Memories come back: Alina the nurse who had called him a capitalist and had predicted in 1972 the rapid end of Kurisumala; the painful separation with Shantivanam; Dom Albert Derzelle's long silence. For the past several years, reconciliations and gratitude had come to him from every direction, bringing him happiness and peace in this last stage of his earthly pilgrimage. Yes, he thinks, everything is blessing: the trials because they purify us; the joys because they are grace and gift.

10:45 AM. Brother Augustine, the most advanced of the students, knocks on the door. Class time began very soon, and he had come to get instructions: will Acharya teach class or should he himself practice the office for the day? No, no, despite the morning's change in schedule, Acharya is not tired, he will give the class. Augustine bends down for Acharya to touch his forehead with the back of his hand then goes out to get the others.

11:00 AM. Nine young men dressed in white, arms full of books, sit in a circle in the cell. Acharya, with measured movements, turns his chair towards them, places a blackboard against the shelves, and prepares texts to read. Today is the feast of Saint Anthony, hermit of Egypt, father of all the monks, an exemplary figure to exhort the juniors to renunciation and vigilance.

These classes are a moment of happiness for the old master. The bearded faces, serene and attentive, listen to his words with gravity. He has the feeling of passing the torch, preparing the future. 'This class is of great quality', he thinks as he watches them leave. Among the recently admitted novices, there is a musician, an iconographer, a carpenter, an engineer, and an economist. 'They are more educated than the elders were when they arrived', Acharya muses, 'yet just as fervent'.

12 noon. Midday prayer. In the church, there are now four seats for the oldest. Many *sannyasis* have recently been ordained deacons. The community, like a family, comprises three generations: the elders who transmit

their wisdom and experience; the men in the prime of life, assuming responsibility for daily tasks; and the young people who learn and practice.

12:30 PM. Dinner. There are more than sixty persons to serve.
Brother Sunny is busy trying to understand the signs Father Nirmalananda
made him. When he picks up the metal plates, he lets one fall. Din, food
dropped on the ground, the master frowned, embarrassment. No one
moves. The Japanese woman in front of whom the incident took place
picks it all up with her fingers. Sunny runs back with a cloth, and in a
few minutes there is no more trace of his clumsiness. The reader never
interrupted his reading.

3:15 PM. Three monks read in the library. Two more are cleaning the
bakery where this morning they baked about fifty loaves of bread.
Brother Christudas prepares the doses of vaccine for the calves in the
room beside the farm office. Brother Amaland keeps the cooperative's
books. Brother Joseph cares for his tomato plants. Achamma, the secretary, makes brochures by sewing bundles of typed sheets of paper with a
needle full of thick thread. In the *satsang* hall, Father Mariadas preaches
a retreat to a group of sisters. What story is he telling them in Malayalam, for their laughter to be heard through the open window?

5:00 PM. The sun tints the sky pink behind the casuarinas trees.
Acharya, leaning on his canes, descends the stone steps and crosses the
lawn. He approaches the wall surrounding the clump of trees, forming a
bench where he likes to sit at the end of the day, on the still–warm stones.
He contemplates the bougainvillea flowers, hears the birds, makes out the
brown mountains in the distance, behind the new tea plantation.

Yes, truly, everything is blessing.

EPILOGUE

At the end of November 2001, I had left Acharya sitting on the wall facing his window. He was happy at the imminent publication of 'our book'
as he called it and rejoiced to show it to his community. The serenity that
pervaded the atmosphere did not let us guess that events would happen
quickly. But the nuns of Makkiad who visited him in January sent alarm-
ing news to Belgium. At once I sent him a message telling him of my
concern. He answered by fax:

Kurisumala ashram, Wednesday January 30, 5 PM

My very dear Marthe,

Your message found me sitting at my table reading *Communio* after a long nap until 4 PM, such as I take each day.

Last Saturday, during my breakfast I suddenly experienced a heart congestion similar to those at Caritas Hospital which led me to the gates of Sheol. Mariananda reached Dr David by telephone. He prescribed new compresses that freed me. The congestion progressively diminished during the afternoon, but I get out of breath when I speak or make some physical effort. They bought a wheelchair for me, like the one at Lourdes. This week I will not use it because I am on bed rest.

But I will be ready to greet the family group Saturday. It will be a peaceful visit. Nature is beautiful and will offer its contribution. Please inform Ghislaine of her welcome.

With all my affection
Uncle Jean Acharya

Tiruvalla Bishop's House, Thursday, 31 January 2002

10:30 AM. Mar Timotheos is in Delhi. His assistant, Thomas Mar Kurilos receives the news from Kurisumala by telephone: Acharya has succumbed to another cardiac congestion this morning at 8:30. At once an email is sent to the family and all the close friends:

He was taking his breakfast when suddenly he felt ill. Dr Sina was called. She got dressed quickly, gave the order to bring the oxygen equipment up by jeep and she arrived running. But he was already leaving. After fifteen minutes he lost consciousness and his face became peaceful: he was no longer suffering, he had fallen asleep in the Lord. He was a great *sannyasi*.

The next day, while I am trying to get a plane ticket, the bishop calls me to tell me that the funeral will be held Monday, 4 February.

Pushpagiri Hospital, Friday, 1 February 2002

Acharya rests in a glass coffin surrounded by flowers. They brought him to Pushpagiri, where he had established his first eastern monastic community in 1957 under the aegis of Mar Athanasios. The services of the malankar diocese are still mobilizing their resources to organize a funeral worthy of 'their' father abbot, in this syriac liturgy he loved so much.

All weekend, hundreds of persons from all walks of life file by to leave a last offering: a flower, an image, a message, simply their silent presence, a touch of their hand on the glass. For three days and three nights, they keep vigil with him in the cold room. Two monks are in a room looking over the funeral parlor and take turns reciting the office and greeting the guests. They pray, they chant, and groups of nuns remain as for eternity.

In the church at Kurisumala they set up a catafalque of stretched saffron cotton cloth, on which Acharya's portrait is placed amid pink and yellow dahlias from the garden. When night falls, they light an oil lamp, and in its flickering light, the portrait's eyes seem to move. All around, people sitting on the ground pray. It is as if time were suspended. The offices break this meditation: at the regular hours, monks and novices line up in the choir and everything seems as it used to be, except for this strange oil painting that seems to watch you.

Monday, 4 February 2002

Very early this morning, Acharya is prepared for his last ceremony. Joshua Mar Ignathios, the auxiliary bishop of Trivandrum, dresses the deceased in his most beautiful sacerdotal garments: chasuble, embroidered stole, green cope with silver braid, and pectoral cross. Only the ochre hood from his old discolored shawl recalls that this priest was first a monk. In his hands they place a chalice covered with a satin corporal. They set up his body on a canvas stretched over the coffin, so that everyone can see him. Or perhaps, since they put his glasses on him, so that he himself should not miss any part of the event? He is not only going to be buried by his friends and family, he will also attend his own funeral with his face uncovered, participate in it so to speak.

They slide the body into the ambulance. The monks and a few nuns sit around him. A large photo is attached to the hood, and more ribbons and garlands of flowers. Behind, those from Tiruvalla who are going up to the ashram climb into the available jeeps and taxis. A whole caravan sets off through the villages, then into the heart of the mountains, on those winding roads that Francis crossed so often. The people who recognize him—'It's Kurisumala's Acharya'—line up along the route and stand still a few minutes to greet the cortege.

When they arrive at the monastery at around eleven, the back doors are opened, and the monks carry the body into the little church. Emotions are high. For the group of his nephews and nieces, several of whom have not seen him since his trip to Belgium in 1978, it is a shock. Achamma sobs.

At the invitation of the master of ceremonies, the community, the family, and close friends file past to kiss him, or touch his hands. He looks asleep, or even to be looking through his closed eyelids to make sure everything is going as it should. But under our lips, the coldness of his forehead dissipates that illusion.

After the opening prayers and songs, Acharya is transported under the blue plastic dais set up in the garden, where a few hundred of the faithful have been waiting since morning. The parish of Vagamon provided volunteers with badges to channel the crowd. More than three thousand persons will file past that afternoon to touch his body, or kiss it, leaving a souvenir. People hold up children to kiss Acharya. Some women take an object—a handkerchief, a rosary—from their shopping bag and touch it against his body for an instant before putting it back in their pocket furtively, like a talisman they have stolen. Later they distribute pictures with, on the reverse, the text of the blessing the old monk used to offer—with personalized variations—to visitors who knelt at his side when they were about to leave:

> May Jesus grow more in you, and you be filled with the love of Jesus so that you can give Jesus to one another and to those with whom you live and come in contact. Love one another as Jesus loves you.

The solemn *Qurbana* concelebrated by twelve priests and presided over by Sylvester, the eldest of his companions, does not interrupt the parade. The heat that rises is attenuated by a slight breeze. An elderly nun stands near Acharya and perfumes him at regular intervals with a small vaporizer that she pulls from her pocket. Then she wipes his fore-head with a large white handkerchief, and a smile brightens her wrinkled face, where tenderness and veneration mingle.

Towards two o'clock, Mar Timotheos arrives, his face drawn. He came directly from the airport. With archbishop Cyril Mar Baselios and two other bishops, he will now lead the funeral ceremony proper.

After the traditional prayers are recited in unison with the congrega-tion, a sort of theater performance about the separation begins, amplified by the microphone that the protagonists pass from one to the other in turn. One plays the part of the deceased and the other the part of his stricken friends come to say goodbye and encourage him in his last trial. In the silence that overtakes the crowd, one can hear a few muffled sobs.

My friends, why do you stay far from me? Come here, say farewell to me, pray for me and pity me. Because today death has dragged me for good to the gates of Sheol. Truly, my friends, I am afflicted, terror seizes me and my spirit is troubled. Christ, the liberator of the world, seized me and is sending me to the other shore and I leave you with great sadness.

'*Barek Mor*! [Bless us, Lord]', said the deacon.

The voice of the deceased continues:

'Farewell, world and its inhabitants, because none of these per-ishable things to which we cling can be taken with us over there. You see: I am dragged far from you and I will give an account of my actions before the Supreme Judge, who uncovers all hidden things.'

'Friend', answers the other voice, 'as the lilies of the field receive a garment that has not been woven by human hands, may the Great Accountant thus clothe you with the tunic the Holy Spirit weaves for the children of Adam'.

'Farewell, my brothers, pray for me, for I have sinned towards all of you.'

'May the Father in his mercy forgive you all your faults. May the
   voice of the Son, who made Lazarus walk out of the tomb,
   pluck you also from the earth and send you to Paradise'.

The alternating litany continues for almost an hour, passing progressively from pain and distress to light and peace. The community moves
closer to the body, close enough to touch it. Christudas wipes the tears
that flow down into his black beard with a corner of his shawl. Six
monks take the coffin and carry it on their shoulders back into the little
church. Mariananda enters last and holds the head with his hand.

Only the close friends, family, and community are allowed in. They
stand along the walls. A slow chant rises on three notes, as if arising
from the depths of the ages, sung by a chorus of young priests whom the
celebrant answered. Twelve times the monks lift his body as far as their
arms can reach above their heads, three times towards each of the four
cardinal points of the heavens.

At each elevation, the solemn chant arises: 'Oh, oh, oh, you may
leave now, go, go in peace.' Through the voice of the bishop, the one
who is now leaving on his final voyage returns to the whole universe the
wishes for peace addressed to him:

Farewell, church and its altar, remain in peace.
   Oh, oh, oh, go in peace, head of our flock.
   Peace upon you, ascetics of the whole world, heads of all the
monasteries.
   Oh, oh, oh, go in peace, heir of Paradise.
   Peace upon you, cities, villages and all their inhabitants.
   Oh, oh, oh, may the Father welcome you in the nuptial
chamber of joy.

This hieratic choreography, these words of peace, this melody sweet as a
lullaby a father would sing, brings peace to the assembly's hearts. A procession now forms in the failing light and leads Acharya towards the little sanctuary set up along the road, where a small cave has been dug in
the cement floor. At that very spot stood the clay and straw hut where the
founder of Kurisumala lived with his three first companions in spring
1958. A last rite awaits him there before burial. The bishop pours the

contents of a flask of consecrated oil on his body: a little on his face, a little on his chest, the rest on his knees, saying:

> Lord, you have taken your servant from this earthly life.
> Now send your angels to get him
> And may this oil that I pour on him make him slippery and hard to hold
> So he may escape the hostile forces and the claws of the enemies
> Who in the heavens watch the souls of men to snatch them.
> Lead him safely into the heavenly dwellings in company of the saints.
> May he sing your praise and give you thanks forever, for the ages of ages.
> *Barek Mor*! Amen.[34]

Tuesday, 5 February 2002, 4 PM

The muffled murmur of the past few days has died down. Any agitation has disappeared. Calm has returned, placing a peaceful silence on the site of Kurisumala.

From the flower–covered tomb, we can see casuarinas, the tall trees with light leaves that Acharya himself planted forty years before. He loved trees so much that he had stubbornly insisted on making them grow in this poor and thankless soil.

The wind moves the branches softly without troubling the meditation of this woman, sitting on the cement floor, her back leaning on the chapel wall. She waits there without moving. What is she doing in this peace that had returned? She thinks, she prays, she cries. She is not disturbed by the villagers who stop here after bringing their milk to the farm. They came to throw a flower on the grave and went without saying anything.

---

[34] Johannes Madley, 'Tekso D'ufoyo D'annide'. Free translation from *Die Ordnung der Bestattung Verstorbener nach dem Ritus der Syro–Antiochenischen Kirche SEERI—Kottayam* (Paderborn: Verlag Ostkirchendienst, 1995). With the help of Father Jacob Thekeparampil of SEERI (Kerala) and Ms Andréa Schmidt from the Catholic University of Louvain (Belgium).

At the other end of the buildings reserved for the monks, Acharya's room is closed. Someone locked the door and took away the key. Nothing moves in this room, where everything stayed in place: the old pocket watch on the table, the open book, the sheaf of correspondence, the documents unsteadily piled up in boxes. But in the air there is nothing but emptiness and absence. Through the window we can see, folded up against the wall, the wheelchair that was never used.

March 2002

Every morning since the funeral, the community has celebrated a solemn *Qurbana*. Today, Monday, 11 March, the 'fortieth day' marks the end of the mourning. Four hundred persons come from the whole region to attend the ceremony led by the bishop. The cistercian abbots are there: Dom Armand Veilleux from Scourmont in Belgium; Dom David Tomlins, from Tarrawarra in Australia. It is they who will now help Kurisumala continue its journey.

As always, in times of important decisions, they begin by recollecting themselves and praying: a week of retreat during which the monks ask the Holy Spirit to enlighten them with his wisdom. Monday, March 18, the community elects Father Yeshudas as second abbot of Kurisumala. The next day, Dom David proceeds to his 'installation', and on March 20, the bishop comes to give him the abbatial blessing. He touches his forehead with his large golden cross and puts around his neck a cross given and blessed by the pope. All the monks, one by one, come to promise him obedience and he then blesses the assembly. 'Father Yeshudas seemed as if larger, illuminated by grace', wrote a witness. 'Dom David smiled, visibly happy, everyone embraced.'[35]

The next day, they resume the indian Mass for ordinary days.

Yes, the work continues, it's a new stage that begins.
Barek Mor! *Aum Shanti.* . . .

---

[35] Letter from Dr Hilde Sina, September 5, 2002.

CHRONOLOGY

January 17, 1912	Birth in Ypres
April 1915	Exodus to Normandy
1921	Return to Belgium; settled in Schaerbeek
1922–28	Studied humanities at the Collège Sainte Marie, Brussels and the Collège de Melle
1929–31	Work at the Union Factory; evening courses in Business at the Institute Saint-Louis
1931	Polytechnic School in London
1932–33	Military Service in the Second Lancers
1934	Associate in the Union Factory (Cruise to the Near East)
September 14, 1935	Entered la Trappe Our Lady of Scourmont in Chimay
1938–40	Theological studies in Rome
October 12, 1941	Priestly ordination
1941–44	German occupation, move to Momignies
1946	Novice master in Scourmont
September 1949	Operation on his spinal column
1950–51	Convalescence, stay in Aiguebelle
1952–53	Return to Scourmont; eastern studies in Paris one day a week
July 1953	Novice master in Caldey, Wales
June 24, 1955	Departure for India on a ship from Southampton

September 1955   Hermit at Shantivanam with Fathers Le Saux and
                    Monchanin

November 1956   Established a small community at Pushpagiri (Kerala) with
                    Father Griffiths, under the aegis of Mar Athanasios; study
                    of the Syriac rite

March 1958   Move to Kurisumala

September 14, 1958 Dedication of the church

1960   Indo–Swiss project for agricultural development

March 1961   Trip to the Near East with Father Hambye, seeking the
                    Penqitho

1967–68   Stay at Shantivanam with Father Le Saux and in the ash-
                    rams of the Himalayas

August 6, 1968   Indian naturalization

August 27, 1968   Took over Shantivanam again, entrusted to Father Bede
                    Griffiths

1971   Foundation of Thirumalai, Tamil Nadu, entrusted to Father
                    Mariadas

1974   Osteoarthritis attack. Hospitalization at Gheeta Bhavan

1977   First mission in Austria; visits to Scourmont and the family

1978   Second mission in Austria; long trip through the United
                    States and Brazil

1979   Hip operation in Lobbes; convalescence at Scourmont

1980   Publication of the first volume of *Prayer with the Harp of
                    the Spirit*

1983   Kurisumala's twenty–five year jubilee

October 18, 1988   Heart attack, reanimation, hospitalization, long convales-
                    cence

April 1989   Return to regular life

1990   Fall, fracture, second heart attack

November 1993   Visit of the abbot of Scourmont, in view of a future affilia-
                    tion with the Order

April 1994	Visit of Dom Bernardo, Abbot General of the Cistercian Order
October 1996	Participation, as a guest, in the General Chapter of the Order at Albano
July 9, 1998	Ceremony of affiliation with the Cistercian Order
October 1999	Abbatial blessing by Mar Timotheos, in the presence of Dom David; participation as abbot in the General Chapter of the Order in Lourdes
2000	Macrobiotic treatment, improved health
31 January 2002	Francis Acharya falls asleep in the Lord

BIBLIOGRAPHY

The sources mentioned below fall into four categories:

5. 'books', available in bookstores or libraries;
6. 'periodicals', some of which have now ceased publication but complete collections of which can be found in libraries;
7. 'documents' copied and distributed in a limited circle (commemorative brochures, reports, minutes of meetings, acts of colloquia); and
8. 'unpublished' manuscripts or typescripts (correspondence, note books, agendas, monastic chronicles).

The 'documents' generally come from religious congregations and generally may be consulted by contacting the superiors.

The 'unpublished' items are gathered as 'Archives of Father Francis Mahieu–Acharya', at Our Lady of Scourmont Abbey, 6464 Forges, Belgium.

BOOKS

Acharya, Francis. 1974. *Kurisumala, A Symposium on Ashram Life*. Kerala, India: Kurisumala Ashram.

———. 1978. *Die Kunst des Lebens*. [S.l.]: Kurs & Vortrag.

———. 1982–1985. *Prayer with the Harp of the Spirit: The Prayer of Asian Churches*. 4 vols. Kerala, India: Kurisumala Ashram.

384 Bibliography

————, Andreas Hoffmann, and Martin Kämpchen. 1992. *Yoga, ein Weg zu Gott*. Munich: Kösel.

————. 1999. *Kurisumala Ashram: A Cistercian Abbey in India*. Kerala, India: Kurisumala Ashram.

————. 1999. *The Ritual of the Clothing of Monks*. Trans. from Syriac, SEERI, Baker Hill. Kottayam 686001. Kerala, India: St Ephrem Ecumenical Research Institute.

Åmell, Katrin. 1998. *Contemplation and dialogue: quelques exemples de dialogue entre spiritualités après le concile Vatican II*. Uppsala: Swedish Institute of Missionary Research.

Bernard of Clairvaux. *Sermons sur le Cantique*. 1996. 4 vols. Latin text by J. Leclercq, H. Rochais, and Ch.-H. Talbot; intro., trans., and notes by P. Verdeyen and R. Fassetta. Paris: Cerf. English trans. by Kilian Walsh OCSO and Irene Edmonds. Spencer and Kalamazoo: Cistercian Publications, 1971–1980.

Bhagavad-Gita. 1992. Trans. from Sanskrit by Alain Porte. Paris: Arléa.

Bossuet, Jacques-Bénigne. 1999. *Bernard, que prétends-tu dans le monde: Panégyrique de saint Bernard*. Paris: Allia.

Brock, Sebastian, trans. 1983. *Harp of the Spirit: Eighteen Poems of Saint Ephrem*. Oxford: Fellowship of SS Alban and Sergius.

————. 1992. *The Luminous Eye: The Spiritual World Vision of Saint Ephrem*. Kalamazoo: Cistercian Publications.

Charlesworth, James. H. 1978 [c. 1977]. *The Odes of Solomon: The Syriac Texts*. Missoula, MT: Scholars Press.

Cornille, Catherine. 1991. *The Guru in Indian Catholicism: Ambiguity or Opportunity of Inculturation?* Leuven: Peeters.

Cuttat, Jacques-Albert. 1967. *Expérience chrétienne et spiritualité orientale*. Paris: Desclée, De Brouwer.

————. 1960. *The Encounter of Religions: A Dialogue between the West and the Orient, with an Essay on the Prayer of Jesus*. Trans. Pierre de Fontnouvelle with Evis McGrew. Foreword by Dietrich von Hildebrand. New York: Desclée.

Daniélou, Jean. 1962. *Unité des chrétiens et conversion du monde: Thèmes de réflexion et de prière*. Paris: Éditions du Centurion.

De Mello, Anthony. 1984. *Sadhana, A Way to God: Christian Exercises in Eastern Form*. New York: Seabury Press.

Demariaux, Jean-Christophe. 1990. *Pour comprendre l'hindouisme*. Paris: Cerf.

Desjardins, Arnaud. 1982. *Ashrams*. Grands maîtres de l'Inde, coll. Spiritualités vivantes. Paris: Albin Michel.

Du Boulay, Shirley. 1998. *Beyond the Darkness: A Biography of Bede Griffiths*. New York: Doubleday.

Evagrius Ponticus, 'Treatise on the Eight Capital Vices.' 2006 [2003]. In Robert E. Sinkewicz, *Evagrius Ponticus: The Greek Ascetic Corpus*. Oxford and New York: Oxford University Press.

————. *Chapters on Prayer*. 1981. In John Eudes Bamberger, *Evagrius Ponticus: Praktikos and Chapters on Prayer*. Kalamazoo: Cistercian Publications.

Griffiths, Bede. 1954. *The Golden String*. New York: Kenedy.

————. 1982. *The Marriage of East and West*. London: Harper Collins.

Jaffrelot, Christophe. 1996. *L'Inde contemporaine de 1950 à nos jours*. Paris: Fayard.

Lanza del Vasto, Joseph Jean. 1945. *Le Pèlerinage aux sources*. Paris: Denoël.

Le Bail, Anselme. 1932. *L'ordre de Cîteaux, 'La Trappe'*. Paris: Letouzey et Ané.

Le Coz, Raymond. 1992. 'Histoire de l'Eglise d'Orient' [*L'Eglise d'Orient: chrétiens d'Irak, d'Iran et de Turquie*, 1995]. Paris: Cerf.

Le Saux, Henri (Swami Abhishiktananda). 1967. *Une messe aux sources du Gange* Paris: Seuil.

————. 1986. *La montée au fond du cœur: Le journal intime du moine chrétien–hindou, 1948–1973*. Intro. and notes by Raymond Panikkar. Paris: O.E.I.L.

————. 1999. *Lettres d'un sannyasi chrétien à Joseph Lemarié*. Presented and annotated by Joseph Lemarié and Françoise Jacquin. Paris: Cerf.

Leclercq, Jean. 1986. *Nouvelle page d'histoire monastique: History de l'AIM, 1960–1985*. Vanves, France: Aide inter-monastères.

Lettere di dom Jean Leclercq (1911–1993). 2000. Collected by Valerio Cattana, Claudia Galli, and Henri Rochais. Cesena: Badia de Santa Maria del Monte.

Lipner, Julius J. 1999. *Brahmabandhab Upadhyay: The Life and Thought of a Revolutionary*. New York and Delhi: Oxford University Press.

Merton, Thomas. 1948. *The Seven Storey Mountain*. New York: Harcourt Brace.

————. 1967. *Mystics and Zen Masters*. New York: Farrar, Strauss and Giroux.

————. 1968. *Zen and the Birds of Appetite*. New York: New Directions.

————. 1973. *The Asian Journal of Thomas Merton*. Ed. from his original note-books by Naomi Burton, Patrick Hart, and James Laughlin; consulting ed. Amiya Chakravarty. New York: New Directions.

Moffit, John, ed. 1970. *A New Charter for Monasticism: Proceedings*. Intro. by John Moffitt; foreword by George N. Shuster. Meeting of the Monastic Superiors in the Far East, 1st, Bangkok, Thailand, 1968. Notre Dame: University of Notre Dame Press.

Monchanin, J., and H. Le Saux. 1951. *An Indian Benedictine Ashram*. Trichy, India: St. Joseph Industrial School Press.

————. 1956. *Ermites du Saccidânanda; un essai d'intégration chrétienne de la tradition monastique de l'Inde*. Tournai: Casterman.

Monchanin, Jules, and Françoise Jacquin. 1989. *Lettres à sa mère (1913–1957)*. Collection 'Textes'. Paris: Cerf.

Monchanin, Jules. 1995. *Lettres au père Le Saux, 1947–1957*. Collected and annotated by Françoise Jacquin; preface by Jacques Gadille. Paris: Cerf.

Panikkar, Raimundo [Raymond]. 1972. *Le Christ et l'Hindouisme: Une présence cachée*. Paris: Centurion.

Pressouyre, Léon. 1990. *Le rêve cistercien*. Paris: Gallimard.

Selis, Claude. 1988. *Les Syriens orthodoxes et catholiques*. Fils d'Abraham. Liège: Editions Brepols.

Simonet, André. 1963. *L'Orient Chrétien au seuil de l'unité*. Namur: Éditions Grande Lacs.

Sommerfeldt, John. 1982. *Abba: Guides to Wholeness and Holiness, East and West: Papers presented at a Symposium on Spiritual Fatherhood/Motherhood at the Abbey of New Clairvaux, Vina, California, 12–16 June, 1978*. Kalamazoo: Cistercian Publications.

Swindells, John. 1997. *A Human Search: Bede Griffiths Reflects on his Life: An Oral History*. London: Burns & Oates.

Tombeur, James. 1990. *Led by God's Hand*. India: Thirumalai Ashram.

Verdeyen, Paul, and Raffaele Fassetta. 1996. 'Introduction' to *Sermons sur le Cantique*. 5 vols. Sources chrétiennes, no. 414, 431, 452, 472, 511. Paris: Cerf.

Victor, Fr. [Sanmiguel]. 1962. *Kurisumala: A Socio-economic Survey*. Ernakulam, India: I.S. Press.

Vuillaume, Christophe. 1996. 'Un ancient qui soit apte a juger les âmes (RB. 58, 3)—Quelques réflexions à propos du service de Maître des novices,' *Collectanea Cisterciensia* 58 (1996), 262–71.

PERIODICALS

Bangkok—Rencontre monastique (Bruges, Belgium).

Bulletin de l'AIM (Aide inter-monastères, 7 rue d'Issy, 92170 Vanves, France).

Cistercian Studies Quarterly (Abbey of Our Lady of New Clairvaux, Vina, California).
  Vol. 29.4 (1994): Francis Acharya, 'Forty years at Kurisumala ashram, A Quest of Monastic Inculturation in India'.

The Clergy Monthly (Vidyajyoti Theological Faculty, Delhi, India).
  Vol. 36.4 (1972): 'India monastic samaj'.

Collectanea Cisterciansia (Monastic spirituality quarterly published by the Cistercians of the Strict Observance [OCSO], Abbey N-D. de Soleilmont, 6220 Fleurus, Belgium).

Echos de la Compagnie de Jésus (Rue Fauchille 6, 1150 Brussels, Belgium).
  Number 6.48 (December 1990): 'Notice sur le P. Edouard Hambye'.

Église vivante (1949–1971) (Louvain).

Études (Monthly founded in 1856 by the Fathers of the Company of Jesus. Rue d'Assas 14, Paris, France).

Hallel. A Review of Monastic Spirituality and Liturgy (Roscrea Abbey, Ireland)
  Vol. 24.2 (1999): Dom Colmcille O'Toole, 'Kurisumala ashram'.

Indian Theological Studies
  1984: F. Acharya, 'Kurisumala ashram after twenty–five years'.

Monastic Studies (Mount Saviour Monastery, Pine City, New York).
  1966: Bede Griffiths, 'Monastic life in India today'.

L'Orient Syrien (Study and research quarterly on the syriac language churches.. Avenue Paul-Doumer 93 Paris 75016).
  1962: E. Hambye, 'L'ashram syro–malankar de Kurisumala'.

Reunion Record (1960–1961) (Periodical of the diocese of Tiruvalla [Kerala]).

Revue du Cercle Saint Jean-Baptiste (1955–1967) (Paris).

'Revue Sainte-Marie' (1958–59) (Institut Sainte-Marie, chaussée de Haecht, 1030 Brussels, Belgium).
  1988: Memorial of the Institut Sainte-Marie, collection of articles and souvenirs published on the occasion of its 100th anniversary.

Rhythmes du Monde (43rd year—1969–).

Vidya Jyoti (indian Jesuits' periodical).

PRIVATELY PRINTED DOCUMENTS CITED IN THE TEXT
(LISTED CHRONOLOGICALLY)

Dom Anselme Le Bail and Father Colomban Bock. 1950. *Abbaye N-D. de Scourmont, un siècle de vie monastique.* [Booklet published by the abbey on the occasion of its hundredth anniversary.]

Acharya, Francis. 1966. *Five years of cattle breeding and dairy farming on the wastelands of Kerala (1961–1966).* Kurisumala Ashram.

———. 1972. *Chronique des douze années: 1958–1970.* Vanves, France: Alliance Inter Monastères.

———. *Saints and Sages of Asia.*

———. *Odes of Solomon.*

———. 1978. *Yoga/Meditation für Christen.* Mölding.

Rencontre Monastique d'Asie—Kandi, Sri Lanka—August 18–24, 1980. Vanves, France: Alliance Inter Monastères.

Bharatiya Puja. 1987. *A Plea for the Approval of an India–rite Eucharist.* Kurisumala Ashram.

Acts of the General Chapter of Rocca di Papa (OCSO). 1996.

Acts of the General Chapter of Lourdes (OCSO). 1999.

UNPUBLISHED

Chronicles and archives of Our Lady of Scourmont Abbey

(for example, letters from Father Francis to his superiors and brothers, from 1934 to 2001, and journal kept by Father Francis during the occupation from 1942 to 1944)

Letters from Father Francis to his family (1955–2001)

Letters from Father Francis to Father Le Saux (1952–55)

Letters from Father Francis to Mrs Toni Sussman (1955–60)

Letters from Father Francis to his community of Kurisumala (1978–99)

Liber lectionum in cella novitiorum (1945–50)

Kurisumala's Christmas Chronicles (1957–62)

Father Francis' Diaries from 1955 to 2001

Archives of Kurisumala Ashram

Charles de Landtsheer's travel journal about his trip to India (1971–72)

INDEX OF PROPER NAMES

Achamma 319, 326, 332, 352, 370, 373

Ajit 252, 274

Alapatt, Dom Bénédict 89, 92, 116, 137, 146

Alberic 347, 351

Amaland 370

Amaldas 274, 306, 309, 210

Amandus, Dom 345

Anthony (Saint) 80, 81, 134, 192, 369

Anugrah 253, 256, 274, 286, 313, 319

Ashoka 132

Athanasios (Mar Zacharias) 141, 142, 146, 152, 156, 157, 160, 161, 162, 165, 167, 173, 179, 181, 184, 186, 189, 202, 215, 228, 230, 233, 307, 316, 317, 372, 380

Athanasius (Saint) 80

Baden-Powell 13

Baker, Laurie 204, 205, 206, 251

Baldwin of Ford 53

Baranger, Pierre 222, 288, 291

Bargellini, Dom Emmanuele 368

Baselios, Cyril Mar 374

Basil (Saint) 81, 82

Baudet, Dom Guerric ix, 50, 52, 55, 83, 84, 87, 88, 89, 90, 92, 93, 96, 97, 99, 100, 101, 103, 104, 106, 107, 109, 110, 111, 112, 113, 115, 116, 119, 120, 122, 123, 129, 132, 135, 148, 149, 150, 151, 152, 156, 157, 160, 167, 171, 178, 183, 184, 199, 203, 208, 214, 226, 290, 292, 316, 320, 328

Baumer, Bettina 250, 294

Beatrice of Nazareth 357

Beauduin, Canon Edouard 222

Belorgey, Dom Godefroid 36, 37, 91, 106, 107, 112, 113, 116, 184

Benedict (Saint) 39, 47, 48, 51, 78, 81, 82, 92, 98, 152 n6, 160, 162, 163, 180, 220, 347, 363

Benni (Msgr) 194, 195, 214

Bernard (Saint) 37, 38, 40, 41, 42, 43, 48, 51, 53, 71, 78, 95, 101, 180, 219, 220, 258, 275, 297, 341, 347

Blanpain, Father Jacques ix, 82, 110, 119, 292
Bock, Father Colomban 62, 67, 68, 86, 148, 229
Bossuet 38
Boylan, Dom Eugene 113
Brock, Sebastian 209, 210, 250, 312, 328

Carlyle, Dom Aelred 74,
Casey, Father Michael 285, 347, 349, 350, 351–52
Cassian 81, 98
Cattani, Alina 206, 275, 369
Cherian, Father 275, 279, 331
Christudas 274, 306, 309, 327, 340, 367, 368370, 375
Claudel, Paul 45
Coff, Sr Pascaline 296
Cornille, Catherine 308, 332
Courcoux, Françoise 28
Coussa, Msgr 183
Cuttat, Jacques-Albert 179, 195, 208, 221, 238

Dadisho Katraya 194
Daly, Father Anthony 52
Daniélou, Cardinal Jean 96, 101, 102, 103, 141, 223
Darmananda, Swami 281
David, Dr George 361, 364, 365, 371
De Haene, Father Théodore 66, 67, 290, 291
Delférière, Father Vincent 44, 45, 67
De Mello, Father Anthony 243, 244, 252, 261, 284

Derzelle, Dom Albert 37, 38, 43, 44, 45, 48, 54, 60, 67, 69, 70, 76, 77, 79, 80, 83, 85, 93, 94, 96, 97, 99, 101, 102, 103, 104, 105, 106, 107, 108, 109, 112, 113, 149, 150, 160, 291, 318, 319, 334, 369
De Saegher, Father Chrysostome 28
De Smet, Father 275
De Vinck, Father 67
Dharma, Father 145
Dharmananda 263, 264, 265, 292
Dominic (Saint) 51
Doom-Vandemaele, Marthe 9, 16, 19, 26, 27, 28, 31, 44, 123
Dumont, Father Charles ix, xv, 68, 81, 109, 123, 299
Duperray, Father Edouard 145, 222, 291

Eliade, Mircea 146
Ephrem of Edessa 82, 146, 154, 155, 210, 211, 212, 219, 250 n11, 312, 328, 328 n3, 329, 346
Evagrius 40, 40 n1, 90, 91, 154, 347
Evely, Louis 11, 159, 293

Fernandez, Msgr 281
Ferrière, Dr André 88, 89, 90, 288, 292, 293
Ferrière, Cinette 89, 292
Feuga, Msgr 138, 257
Filliozat, Jean 97, 101, 103, 120
Filomeno, Father 347, 356
Finn Collar, Frank 281

Floris (De), Dom Marie 198, 269, 270, 286, 291
Francis of Assisi (Saint) 20, 24, 55, 99, 290, 296, 314
Francis Xavier (Saint) 140

Galdos, Father 52
Gandhi xii, 22, 73, 83, 85, 92, 100, 118, 130, 156, 174–76, 207, 208, 238, 246, 280, 296, 342, 346
Ghislain, Father Gabriel ix, 342
Give (De), Father Bernard 292
Gregorios (Mar) 145, 146, 186,
Griffiths, Dom Bede xiii, 116, 117, 137, 146, 151, 158, 159, 159 n8, 160, 181, 186, 222, 224, 246, 267, 268, 272, 273 n29, 281, 299, 304, 304 n38, 306 n40, 309, 312, 315, 340, 346, 368, 380

Haas, Father Odo 268
Hadewijch of Antwerp 136, 143
Halflants, Father Corneille 37, 42, 48, 53, 55, 65, 72, 83, 103, 110, 291, 298
Halleux (De), Father André 314, 314 n49, 315, 340
Hambye, Father Edouard 154, 186–89, 193, 202, 216, 217, 221, 221 n14, 222, 224, 275, 281, 283, 292, 380
Harding (Saint Stephen) 61, 347, 351
Hemeleers, Father Etienne 13, 15, 18, 20, 21, 27, 55
Hemerijkx, Dr 134

Henn, Amy 21, 55, 113, 272, 281, 293, 320
Heras, Father 137
Herman, Father 67
Hürth, Father 53

Ignathios, Joshua Mar 372
Ignatius of Antioch 81, 243
Ingle, Arthur 159, 164, 202, 215, 221, 222
Isaac of Nineveh 154, 168, 171
Isaac of Stella 53
Isabel, Sister 336
Ishananda 271, 273, 275, 319, 323, 324, 326, 327, 333, 334, 340, 359, 360, 367
Ivanios (Mar) 140, 160

Jacob, Dr George 326, 332, 335, 353, 356, 359, 360, 361, 362, 364, 365 n32
Jean-Marie, Dom 354
John XXIII 190, 240
Joseph 182, 183, 242, 370

Kartha, Mr 175, 177, 178, 199
Khouri–Sarkis, Msgr 154, 217
Kochayankanal, Pandit Thomas 144
Kurilos, Thomas Mar 371

Lacombe, Olivier 97, 101, 120, 291
Lakshmi Pandit, Mrs Vijaya 118, 119
Lanza del Vasto 73, 85, 100
Le Bail, Dom Anselme xii, xv, 36– 38, 45, 48–50, 54–56, 58, 59,

61–63, 65–68, 71, 72, 74–78, 80, 83–87, 90, 92, 93, 99, 101, 105, 106, 112, 123, 147, 151, 183, 291, 292, 319, 334, 343, 348

Lebbe, Vincent 11, 77, 80, 93, 102, 113, 196, 256

Leclercq, Dom Jean 222, 268, 271, 281, 285 nn34–35

Lemarié, Joseph 237, 238 n1

Leo XIII 185, 190

Le Saux, Henri (Abhishiktananda) xii, xiii, 92–94, 97, 101, 104, 107, 110–112, 114, 116, 118, 123, 124, 127–30, 134, 136– 38, 142, 145, 180, 197, 230, 237–41, 238 n1, 239, 241, 245, 250–54, 255 n18, 257, 261, 261 n22, 265, 285, 304, 305, 308, 310, 346, 380

Leveugle, Father Godefroid ix, 82, 148, 291

Lialine, Dom Clément 81

Liégeois, Simone 200, 221

Litt, Father Thomas 57, 67, 68, 69, 70, 81, 99, 148, 151

Lobo, Father 275, 331

Lopez, Mother Marie-Isabelle 358

Louf, Dom André 269, 296

Maharshi, Ramana 107

Mahieu, Albert 8, 9, 10

Mahieu, André ix, 3, 6, 9, 12, 20, 27, 44, 55

Mahieu, Charles ix, 3, 4, 9, 12, 26, 27, 292, 293, 300

Mahieu De Praetere, Marthe xiv, 300, 371

Mahieu-Doom, Euphrasie 5, 8, 9, 11, 26

Mahieu-Eeckman, Marie-Thérèse (Rithé) ix, 3, 8, 12, 16, 17, 47, 55, 70, 91, 159, 223, 292, 293, 299

Mahieu, Paul 3, 9, 12, 28, 31

Mahieu, René 3, 5–11, 14, 15, 30, 31, 39, 55, 72, 104

Mahieu-Torrecuso, Antoinette 3, 6, 8, 10, 16, 17, 26, 27, 29, 44, 291, 297

Makhlouf, Sharbel 191

Marcel, Gabriel 81,

Marcq, Father Marc 60, 113, 170

Marcuse, Herbert 269

Mariabhakta ix, 294, 325, 331, 336, 361, 364, 365

Mariadas ix, 245, 275, 279, 280, 318, 332, 333, 335, 361, 370, 380

Mariananda 327, 335, 340, 341, 342, 345, 353, 354, 358, 359, 361, 363, 371, 375

Marie-Paul, Mother 337, 348, 349, 351, 356, 360

Masson-Oursel 101

Mathai 304

Meester, Father Emmanuel De 136, 163, 171

Meeus, Father Baudouin 25, 67, 69, 70, 87, 90

Meiborg, Dr 59, 62, 63, 65

Mendonça, Msgr 92, 120, 134, 253

Merton, Thomas 267, 267 n27, 269, 271

Mitterhöffer, Father Jacob 288

Moeyersoen, Father 189

Molesmes (Saint Robert of) 347
Monchanin, Father Jules xi, xii,
    xiii, 53, 54, 83, 85, 92–94, 97,
    102, 103, 105, 110, 111, 112,
    114, 116, 123, 130, 134, 135,
    138, 142, 143, 145, 146, 147,
    159, 160, 179, 180, 193, 196,
    197, 202, 222, 230, 233, 237,
    238, 240, 241, 253, 254, 255,
    255 n18, 256, 265, 278, 282,
    296, 304, 305, 306 n40, 308,
    338, 346, 380

Narsai 154
Nehru 118, 176, 200
Nirmalananda 336, 366, 370
Nobili (De), Roberto 77, 92, 196,
    243, 256
Nogues, Dom Dominique 81, 87

Olivera (Dom Bernardo) 276, 336,
    337, 338, 340, 343, 347, 348,
    348 n22, 356, 381
O'Neill, Sister Kathleen 351, 352
    n27

Panikkar, Raimundo 137, 238,
    251, 261, 281, 286, 295, 346
Paul VI 197, 256, 259, 343
Paule-Marie, Sister x, 336
Pennington, Father Basil 296
Philipose 182, 183, 273, 274, 275,
    318, 364
Philoxenus of Mabbug 146
Pignedoli, Cardinal 281
Pius XI 54, 198
Pius XII 54, 198

Quirijnen, Father 130, 132

Ricci, Matteo 11, 196
Rogers, Murray 238, 251
Rosadini, Father 53
Rubin, Cardinal 313

Sapor I 194
Scheuer, Father Jacques 261
Schuon, Father Gall 50, 52, 53, 67,
    69, 81
Seraphim of Sarov (Saint) 82
Sevananthen, Msgr
Sina, Dr Hildegarde 206, 272, 275,
    284, 301, 324, 326, 360, 368,
    371, 377 n35
Sivananda, Swami 248
Sortais, Dom Gabriel 155, 156,
    157
Standaert, Father Maur 47, 48, 55,
    56, 68, 71, 73, 83, 86, 91, 103,
    104, 109, 111, 112, 122, 148,
    150, 152, 155, 223, 281, 290
Stuart, Emmeline 281
Suenens, Cardinal Joseph 91, 240
Sussman, Antonietta (Mother Toni)
    117, 123, 137
Sylvester 162, 166, 181, 183, 203,
    215, 228, 231, 244, 271, 273,
    274, 275, 286, 287, 294, 318,
    326, 373

Taft, Robert 314, 315
Tagore, Rabindranath 204, 293
Tamby, Antoine 49, 90, 99
Tappouni, Cardinal 188
Tauler 146
Teilhard de Chardin 141, 196

Thekeparampil, Father Jacob 327
n1, 376 n34
Tholens, Father Cornélius 270,
293
Thomas Aquinas (Saint) 53, 270
n28
Thomas (Saint) xiii, 138, 144, 154,
185, 315
Thomas Pottenkulam, K. V. 141,
157
Timotheos, Mar Geevargheese
326, 333, 334, 340, 342, 345,
347, 349, 351, 355, 359, 371,
374, 381
Tisserant, Cardinal Eugène 152,
155, 156
Tombeur, Father Jacques (James)
93, 145, 221, 245, 277, 278,
278 n31,
Tomlins, Dom David 343, 345,
346, 347, 348, 349, 350, 351,
355, 358, 361, 367, 377, 381
Tromp, Father 52, 53

Upadyay, Brahmabandhab 254,
254 n17, 255

Vadakel, Father James 349, 349
n23
Vaillent, Father 67
Valeri, Sister Pia x, 198, 268, 269,
270, 286, 291
Van Cangh, Father Jean-Marie x
Vandelanoitte-Mahieu, Anna 3, 4,
5, 6, 8, 9, 10, 11, 15, 31, 39,
47, 104
Vandemaele, Pierre 9, 16, 19, 25,
Vanderelst, Canon 68, 69

Van Gheluwe, Dom Gérard 335,
336, 337, 340, 343
Van Rolleghem, Father Dominique
112, 136, 239, 241, 253
Vargheese 162, 165, 166, 182,
215, 227
Varkey, Father 275, 316, 319
Veilleux, Dom Armand x, xv, 285,
285 n35, 356, 359, 360, 377,
Vellut, Dr Claire 113, 114, 116,
134, 171, 221
Voillaume, René 222
Von Gallen, Msgr 68
Vööbus, Arthur 191, 193, 328
Vuillaume, Christophe 78

Weakland, Dom Rembert 266, 267

Yacoub, Mar 191, 192
Yeshudas 275, 279, 280, 324, 325,
326, 333, 367, 377
Youhanon, Mar 316

Zeck 68, 69, 70
Zelle, Hildebrand 68, 69
Zuzek, Father Ivan 290